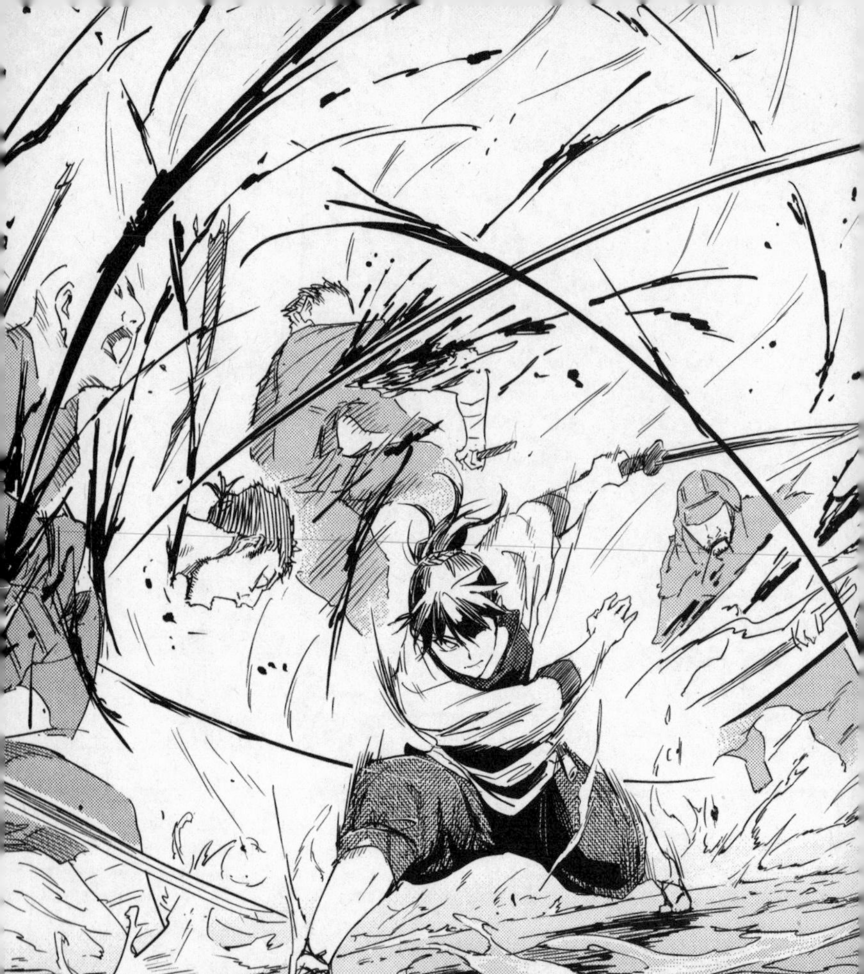
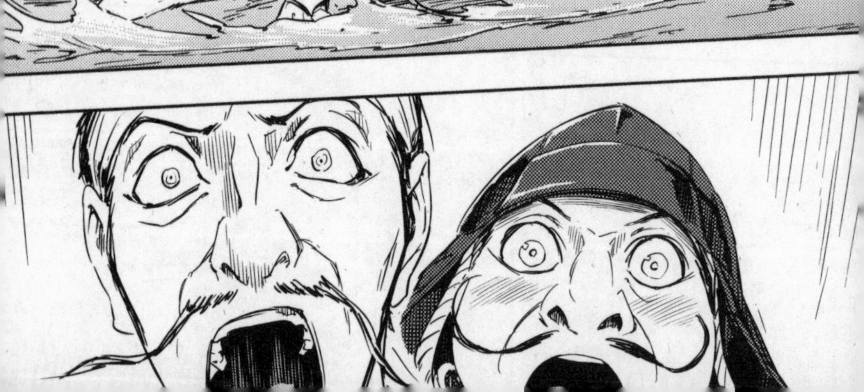

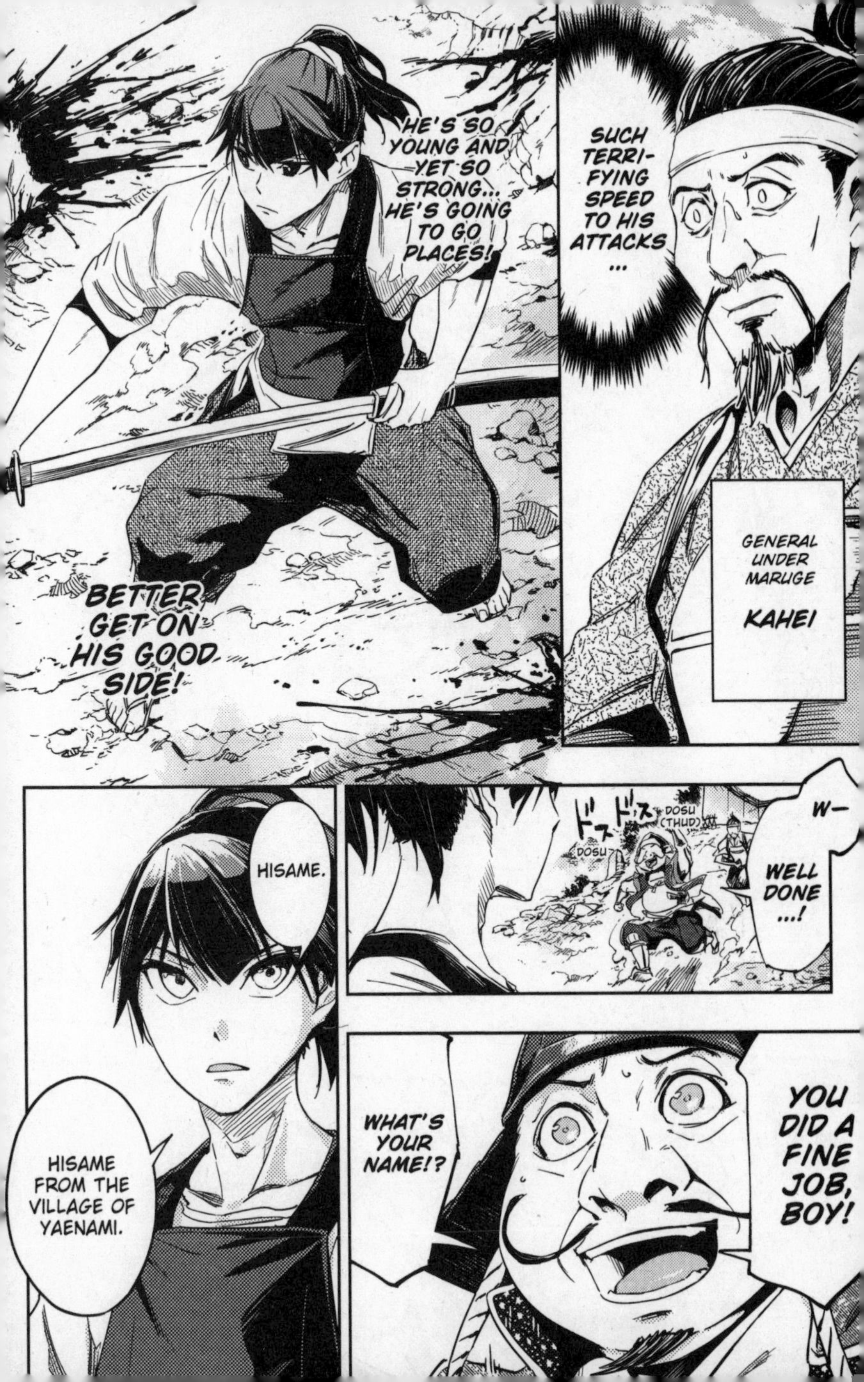
SUCH TERRI-FYING SPEED TO HIS ATTACKS ...
GENERAL UNDER MARUGE
KAHEI
HE'S SO YOUNG AND YET SO STRONG... HE'S GOING TO GO PLACES!
BETTER GET ON HIS GOOD SIDE!
W—
WELL DONE ...!
ドスドス
DOSU (THUD)
DOSU
YOU DID A FINE JOB, BOY!
WHAT'S YOUR NAME!?
HISAME.
HISAME FROM THE VILLAGE OF YAENAMI.

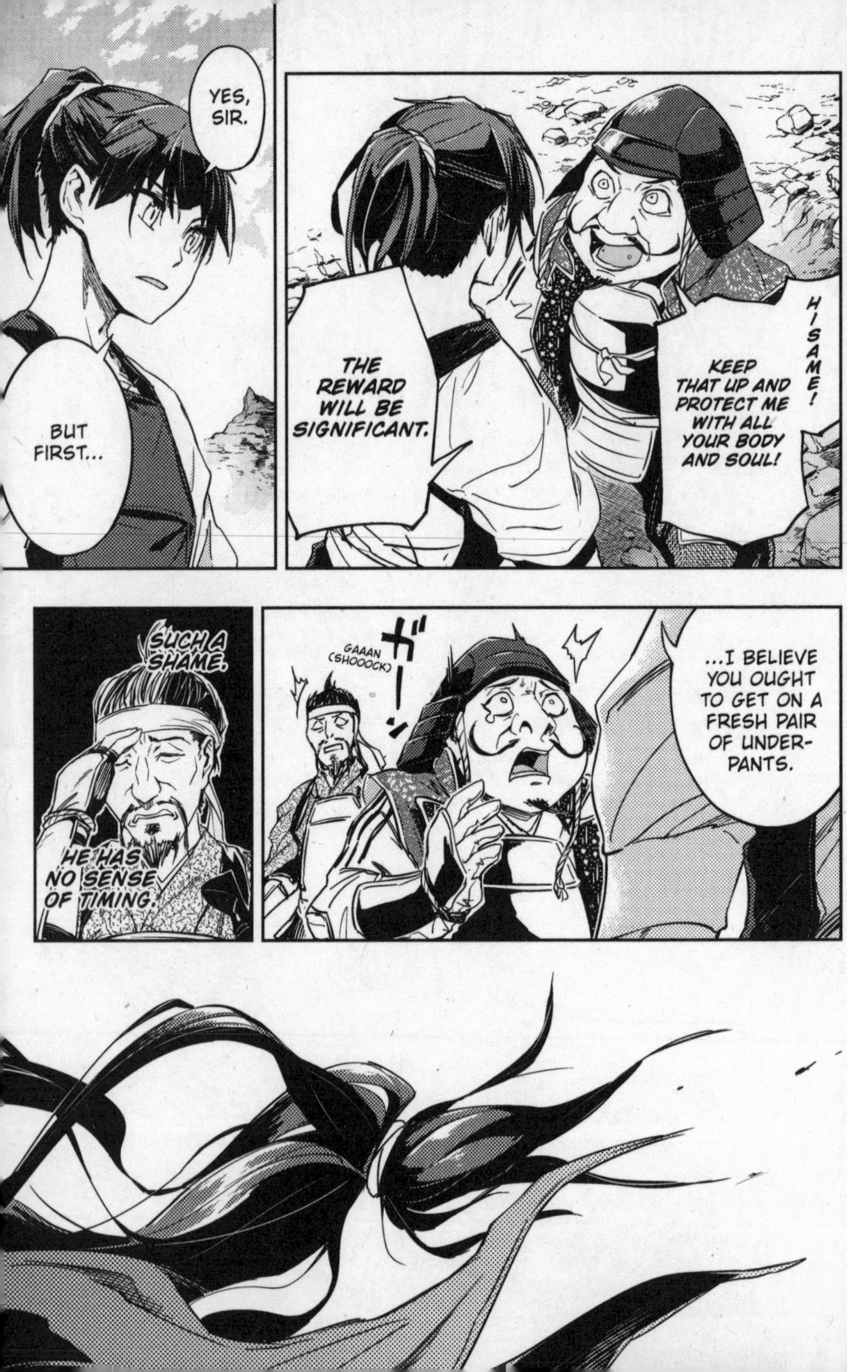
HISAME!
KEEP THAT UP AND PROTECT ME WITH ALL YOUR BODY AND SOUL!
THE REWARD WILL BE SIGNIFICANT.
YES, SIR.
BUT FIRST...
...I BELIEVE YOU OUGHT TO GET ON A FRESH PAIR OF UNDER-PANTS.
GAAAN (SHOOOCK)
SUCH A SHAME.
HE HAS NO SENSE OF TIMING.

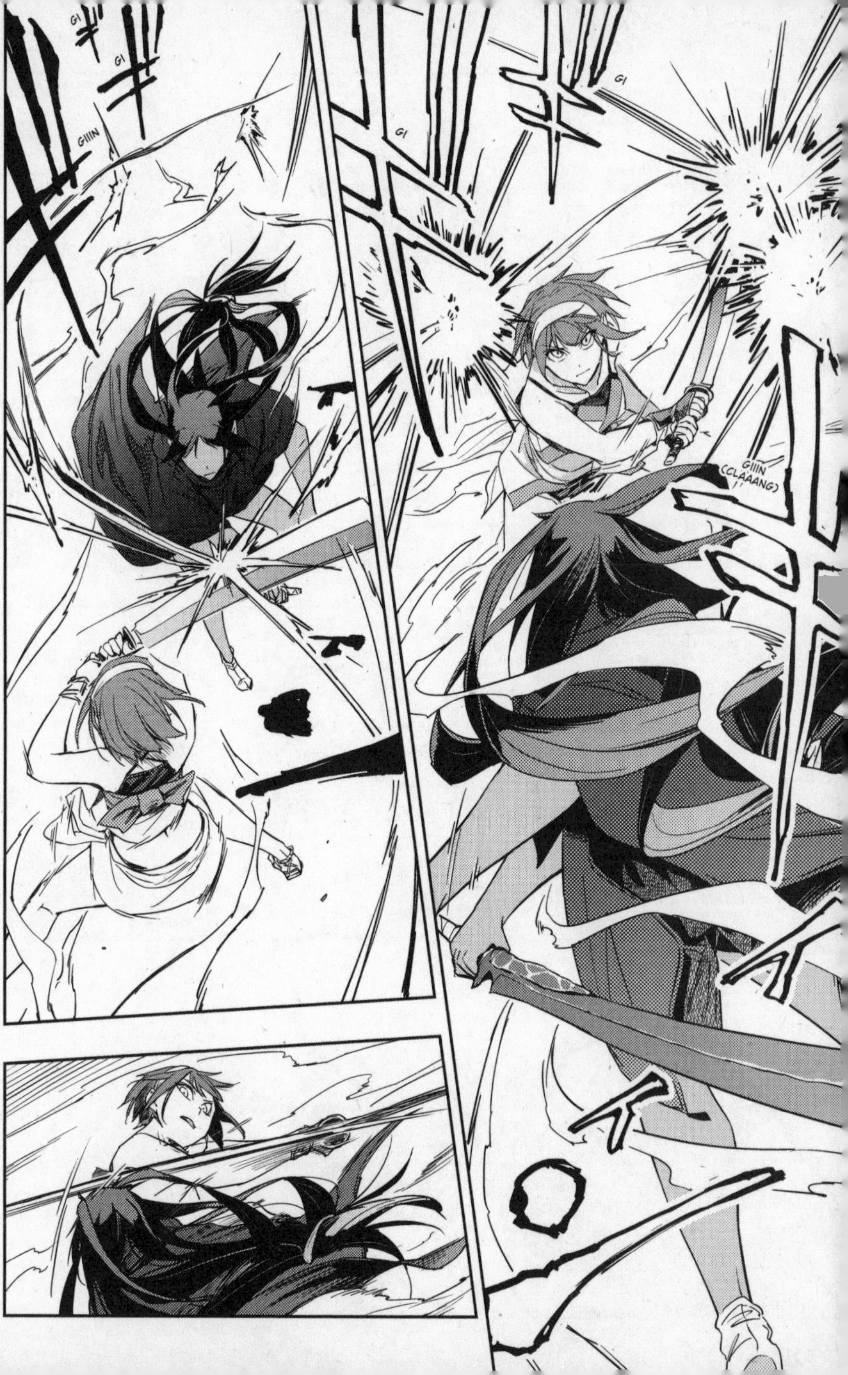
GI
GI
GIIIN
(CLAAANG)
GI
GI
GIIIN

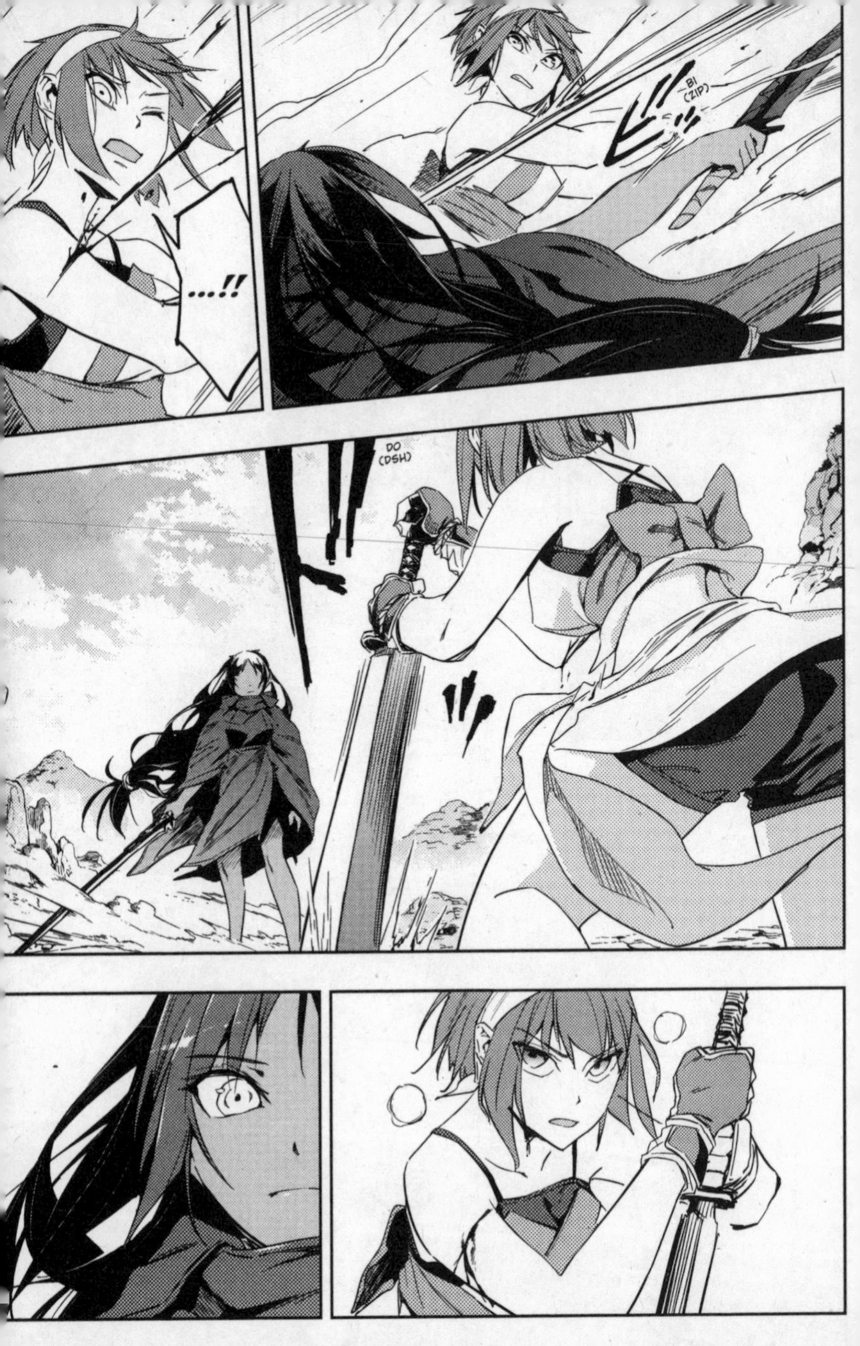
BI
(ZIP)
...!!
DO
(DSH)

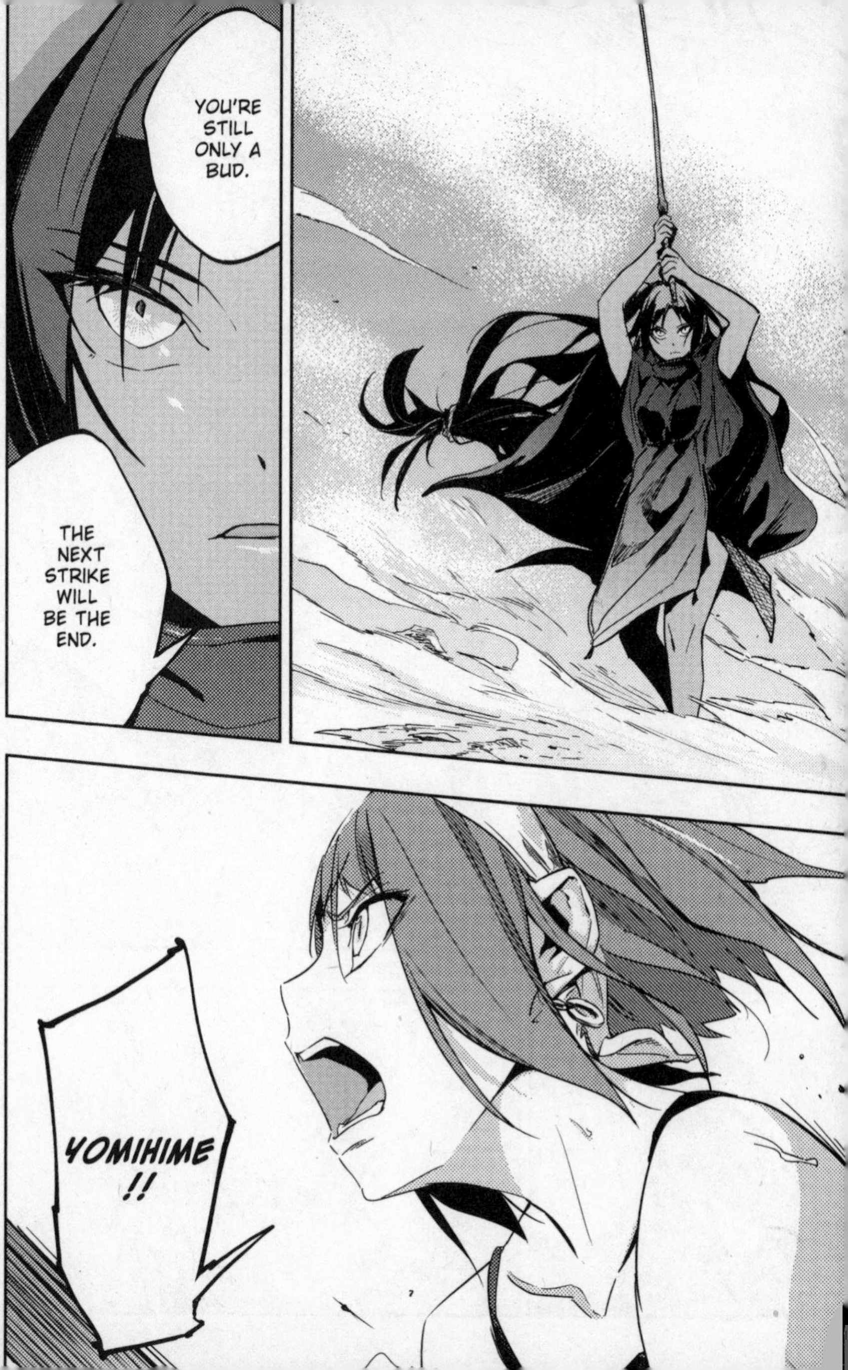
YOU'RE STILL ONLY A BUD.
THE NEXT STRIKE WILL BE THE END.
YOMIHIME !!

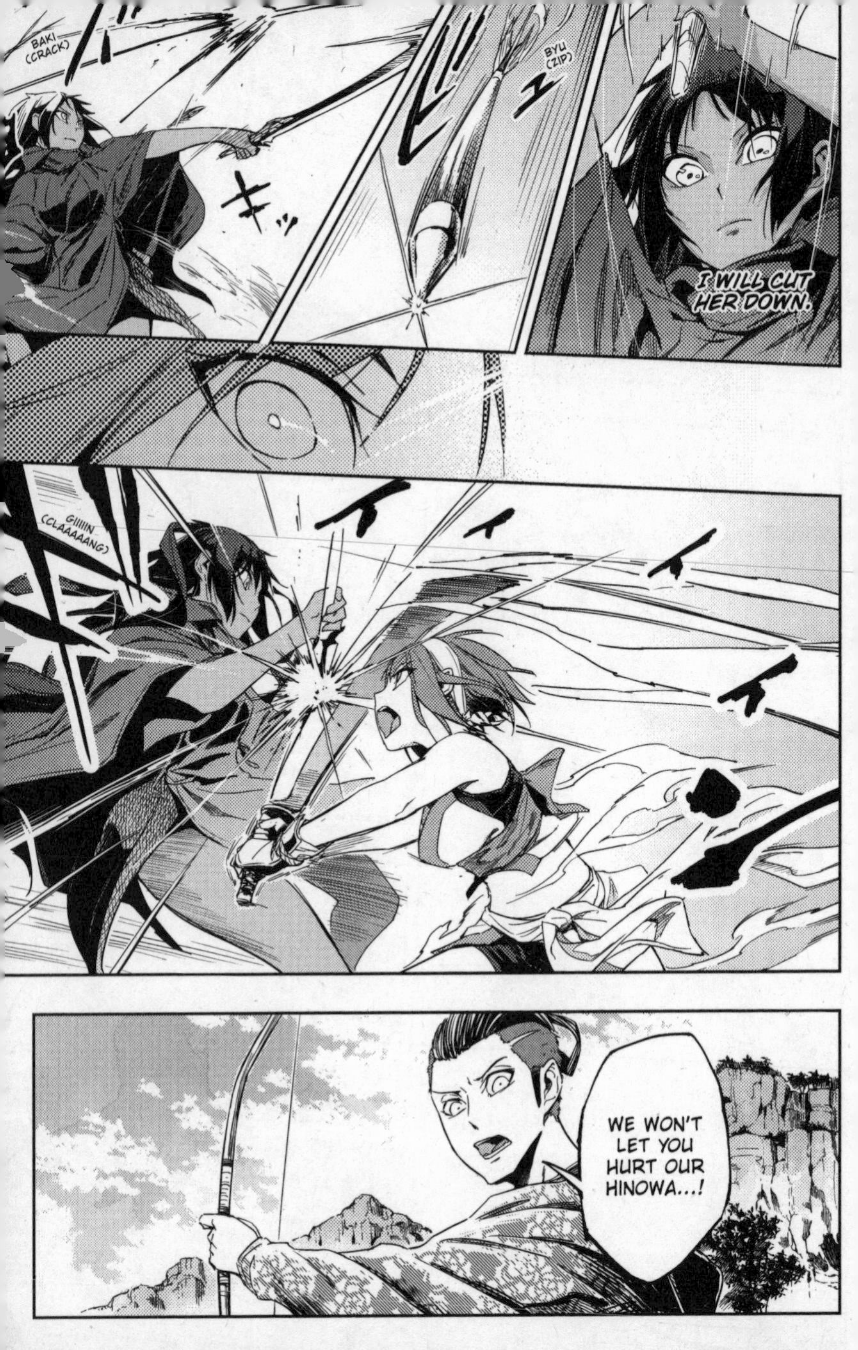
BYU (ZIP)
I WILL CUT HER DOWN.
BAKI (CRACK)
GIIIIN (CLAAAAANG)
WE WON'T LET YOU HURT OUR HINOWA...!

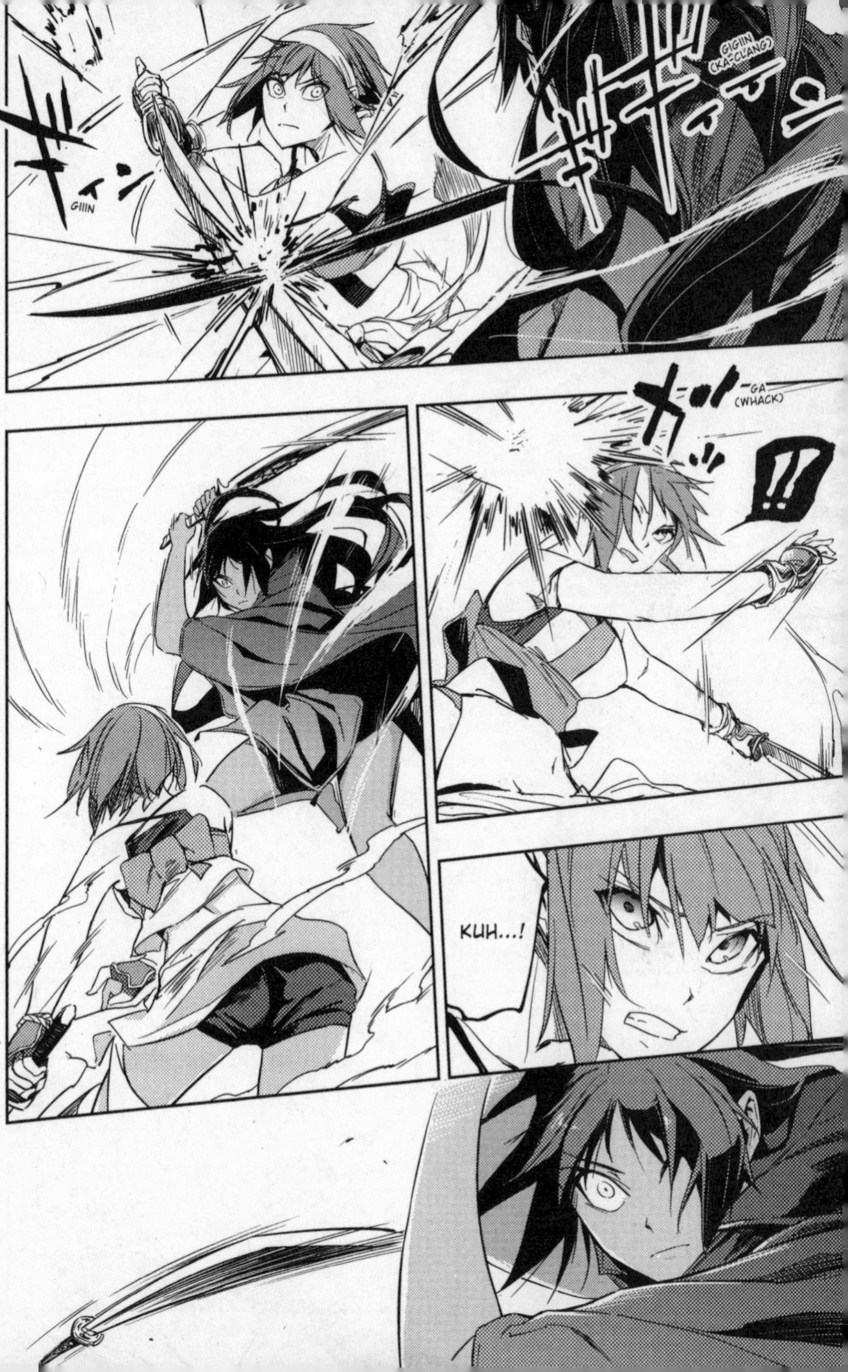
GIGIIN (KA-CLANG)
GIIIN
GA (WHACK)
!!
KUH...!

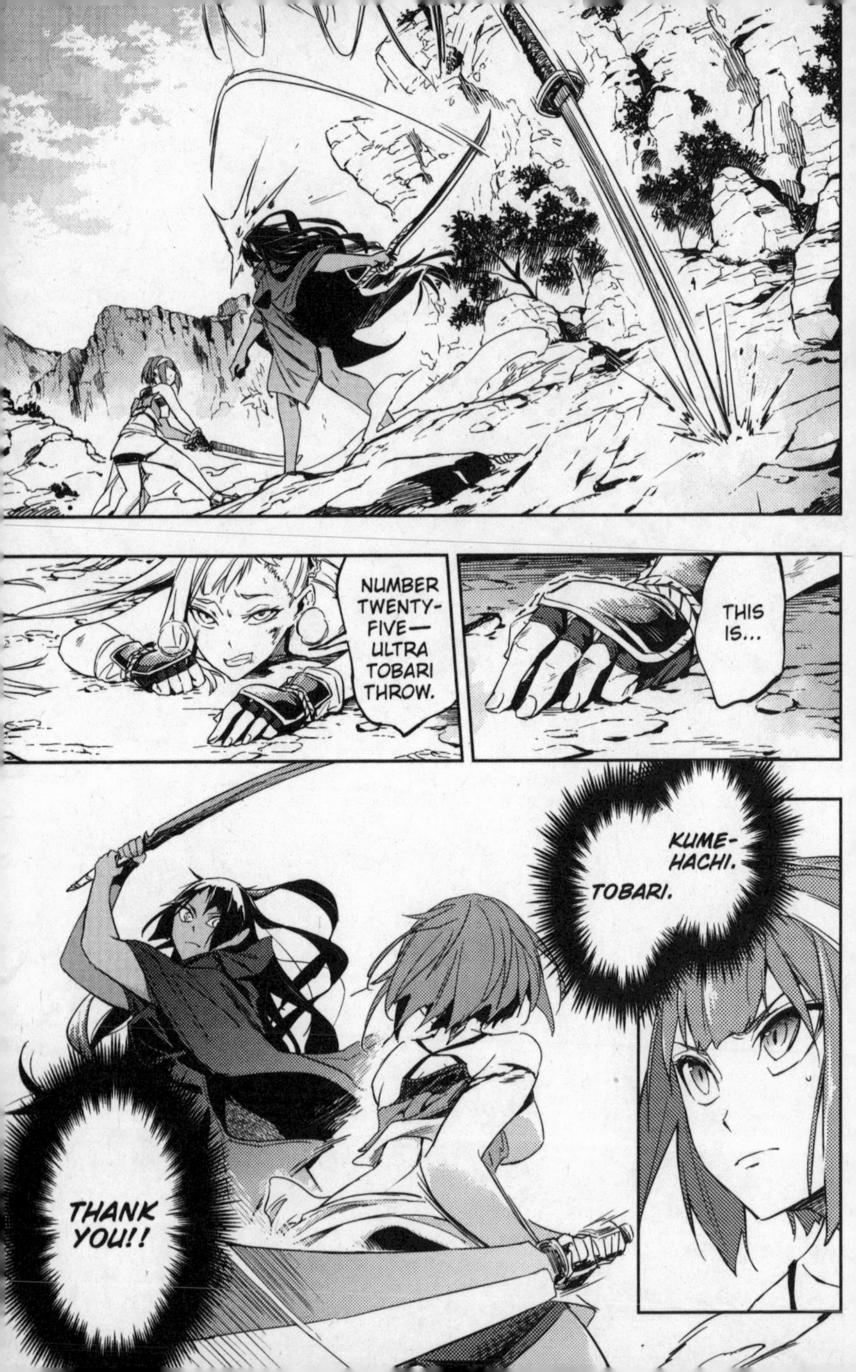
THIS IS...
NUMBER TWENTY-FIVE— ULTRA TOBARI THROW.
KUME-HACHI.
TOBARI.
THANK YOU!!

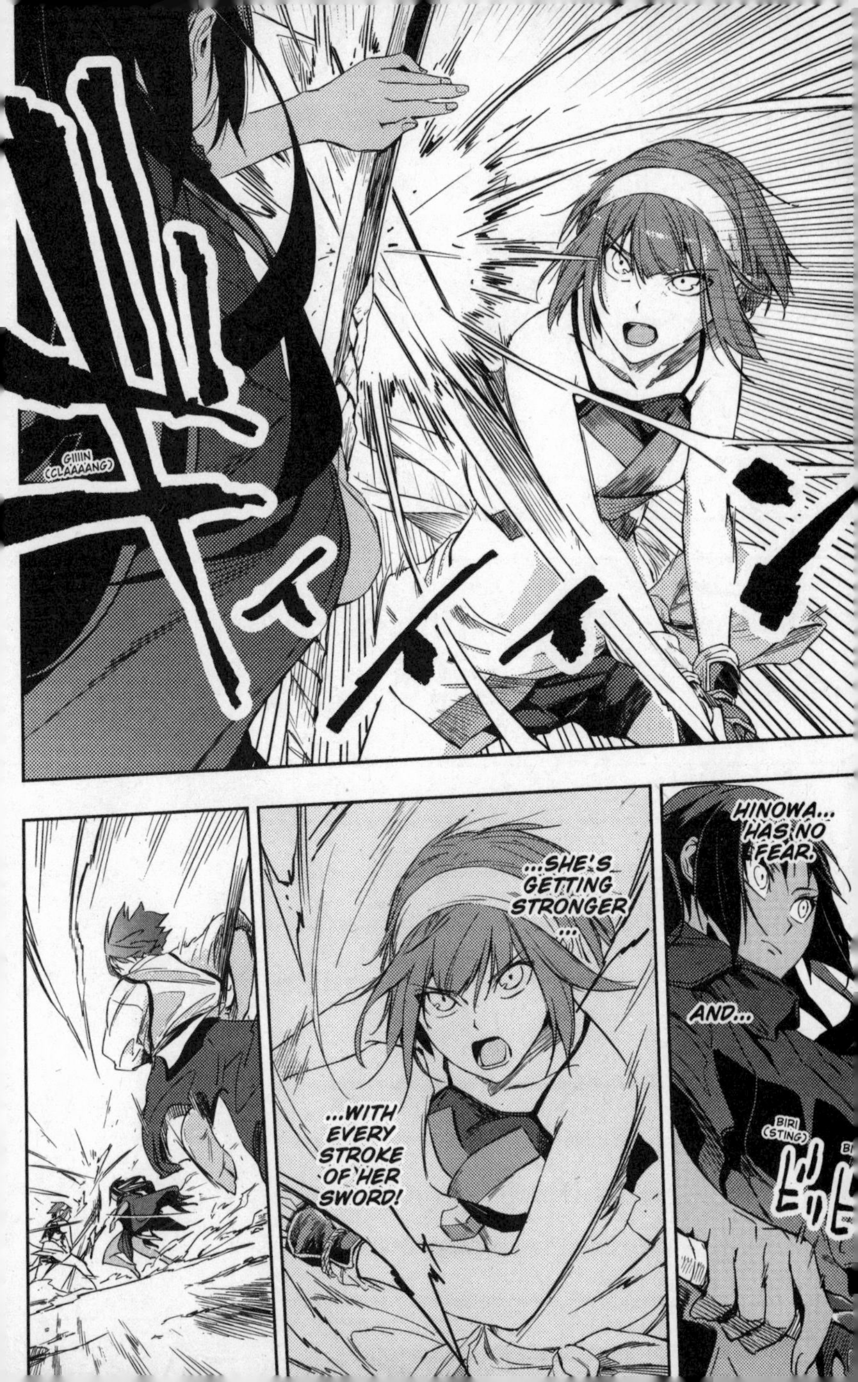
GIIIN (CLAAAANG)
HINOWA... HAS NO FEAR.
AND...
BIRI (STING)
...SHE'S GETTING STRONGER...
...WITH EVERY STROKE OF HER SWORD!

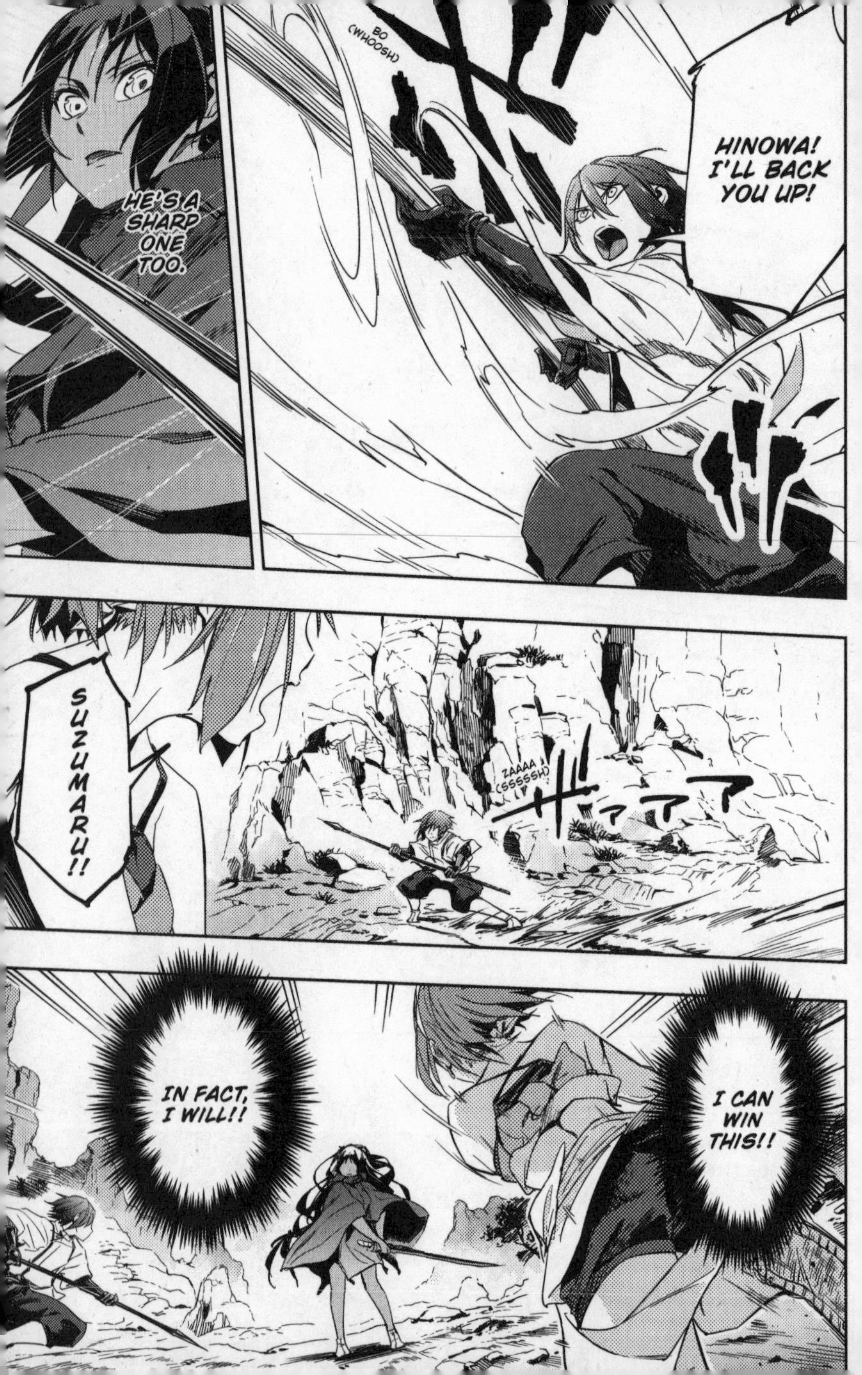
BO (WHOOSH)
HINOWA! I'LL BACK YOU UP!
HE'S A SHARP ONE TOO.
ZAAAA (SSSSSH)
SUZUMARU!!
I CAN WIN THIS!!
IN FACT, I WILL!!

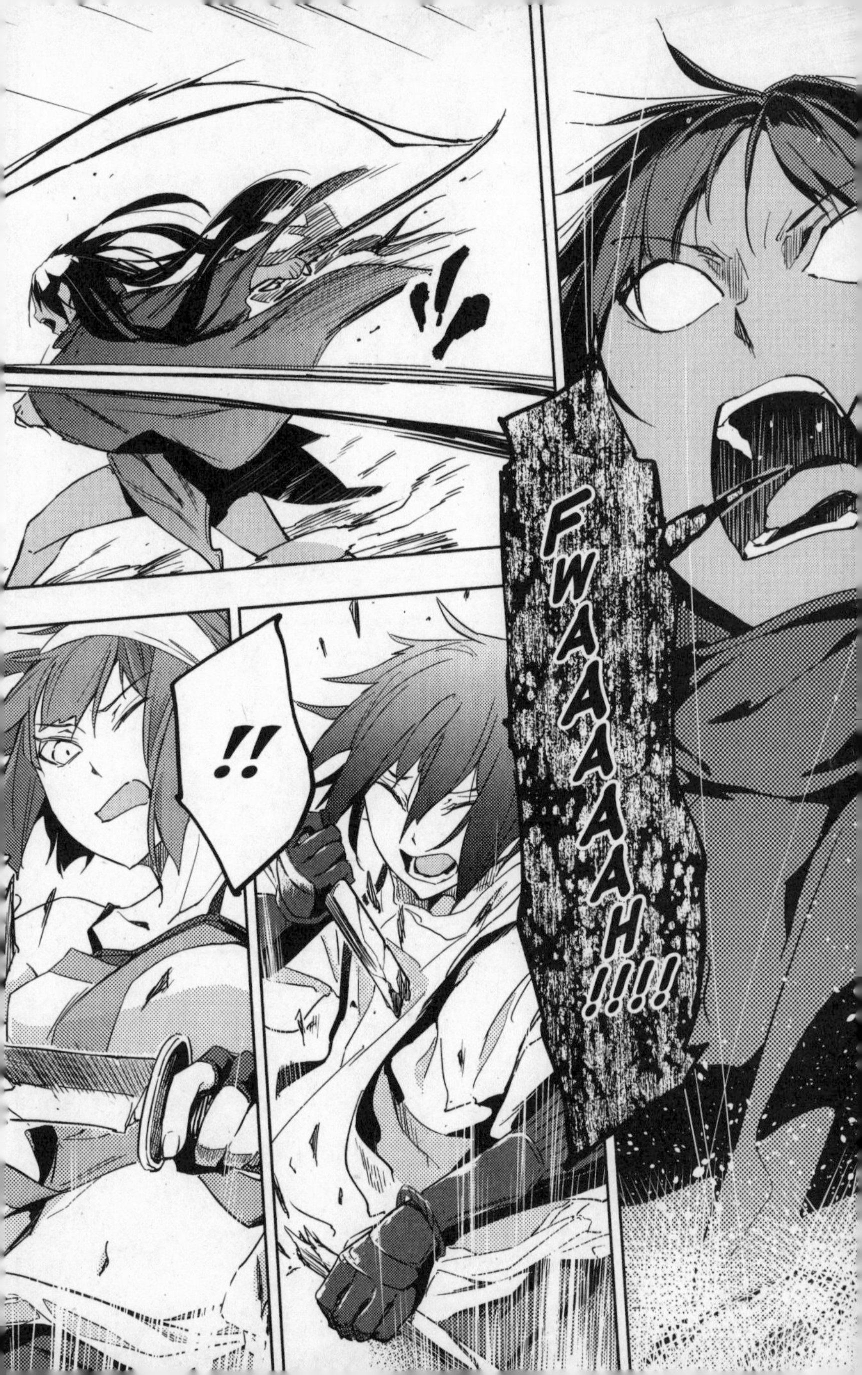
FWAAAAAH!!!!
!!
!!

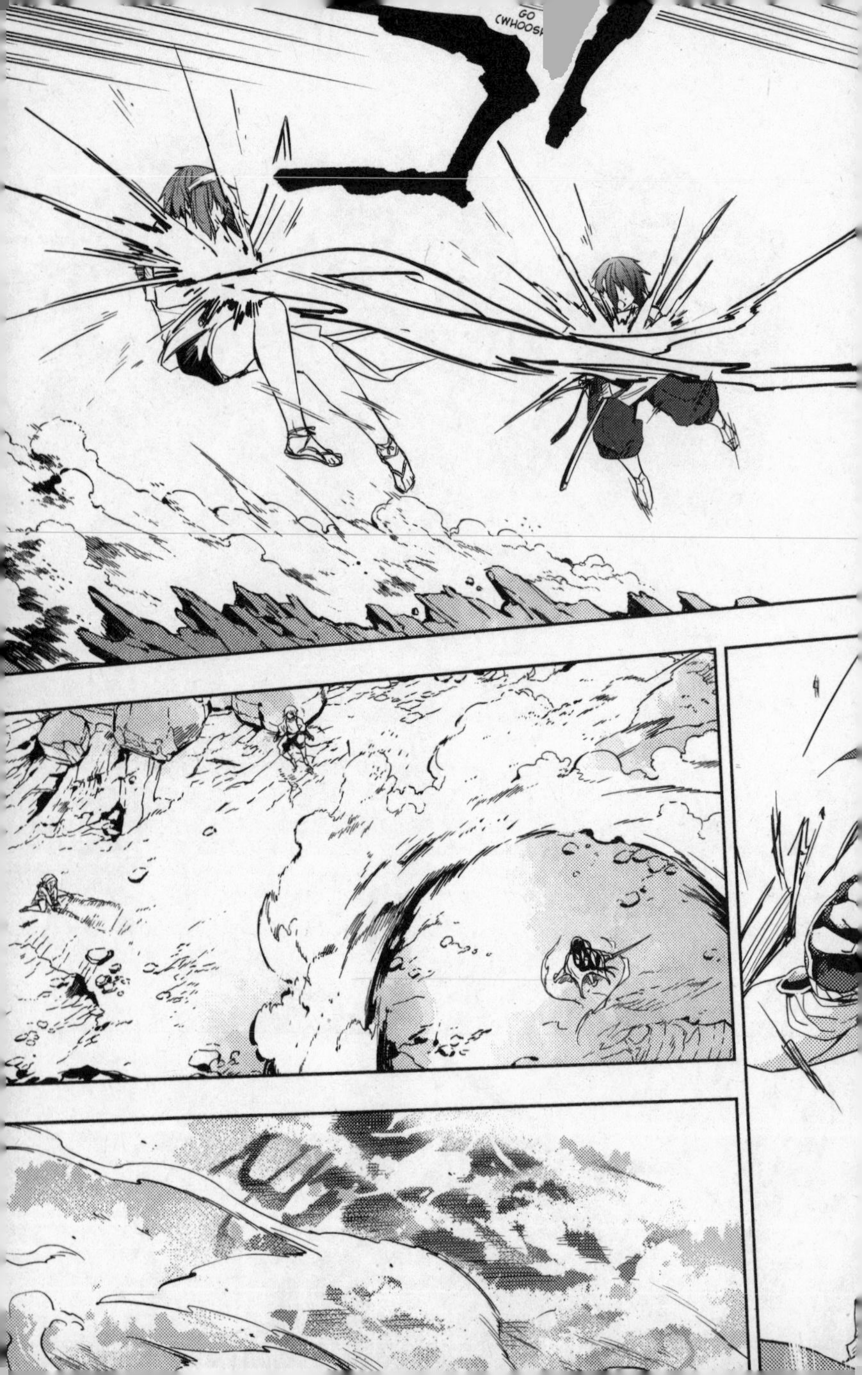
GO
(WHOOS

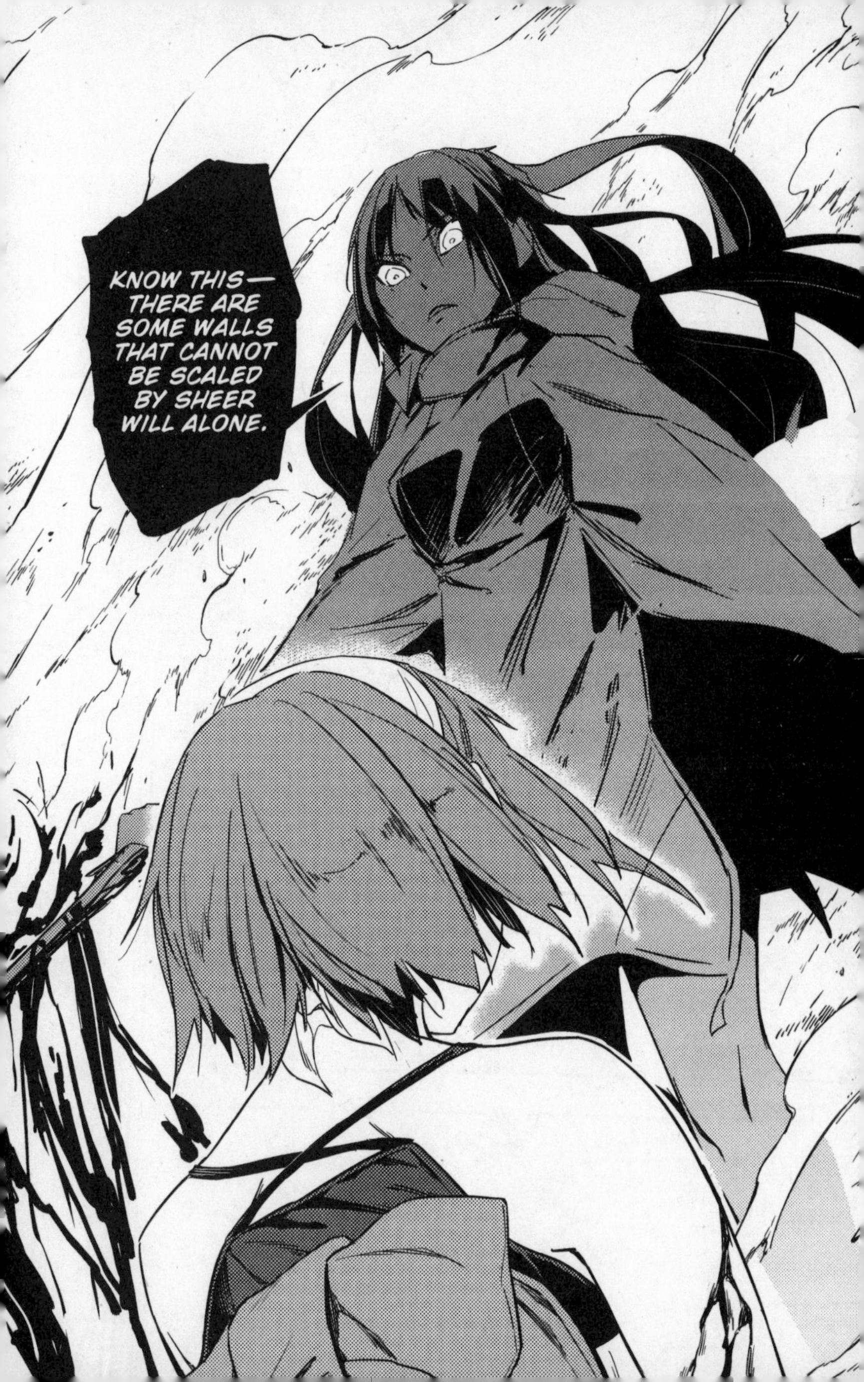
KNOW THIS— THERE ARE SOME WALLS THAT CANNOT BE SCALED BY SHEER WILL ALONE.

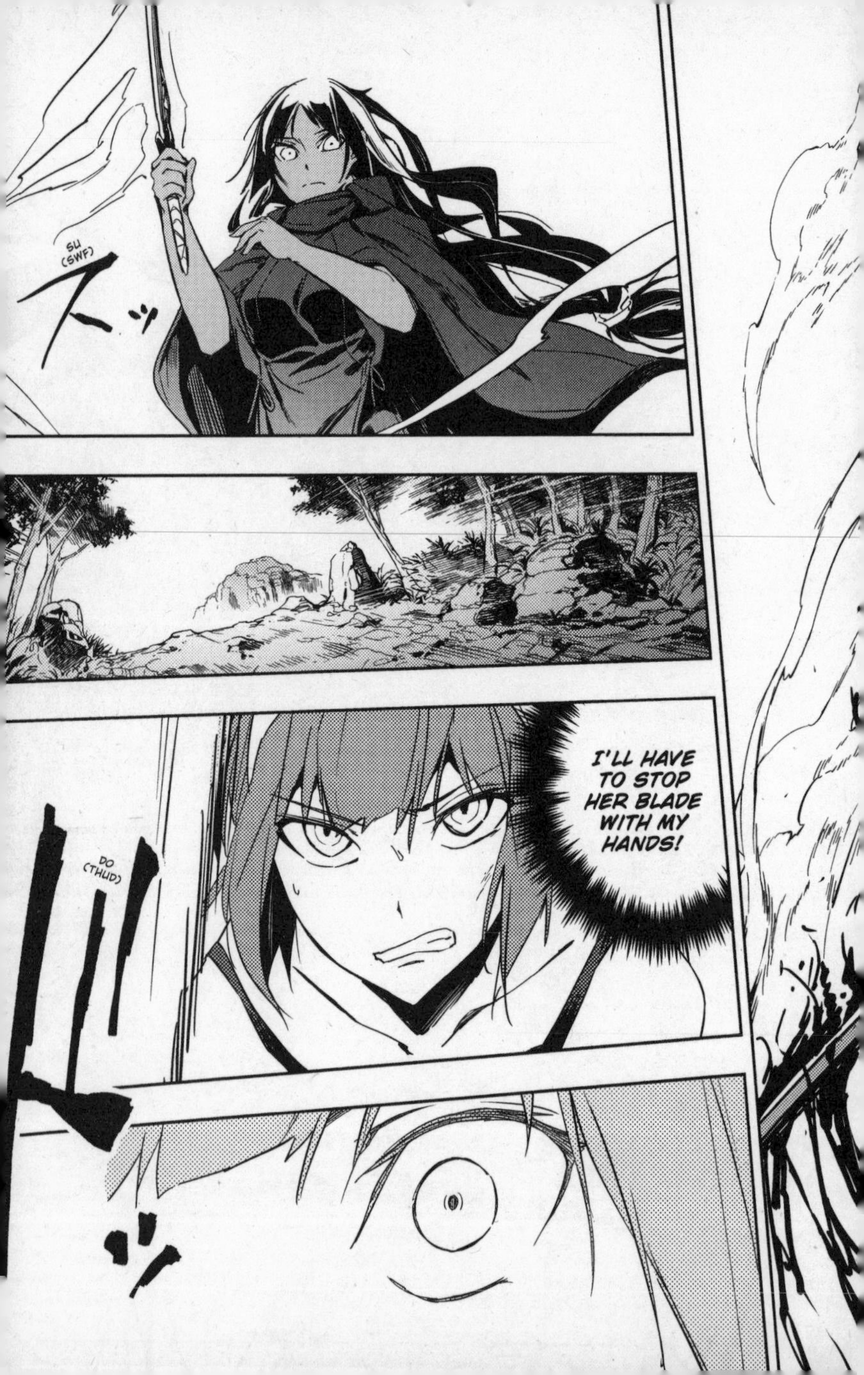
SU
(SWF)
I'LL HAVE TO STOP HER BLADE WITH MY HANDS!
DO
(THUD)

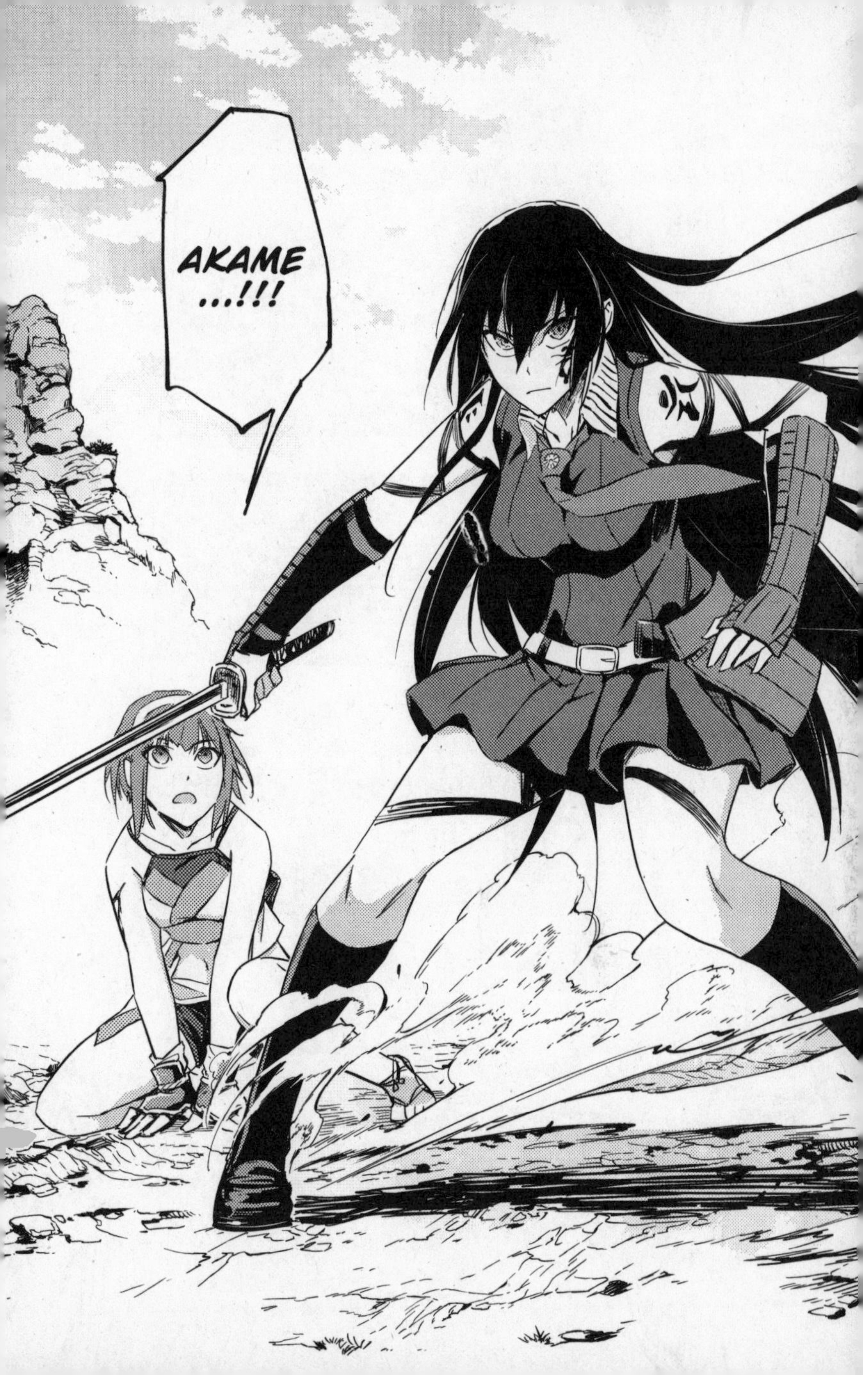
AKAME ...!!!

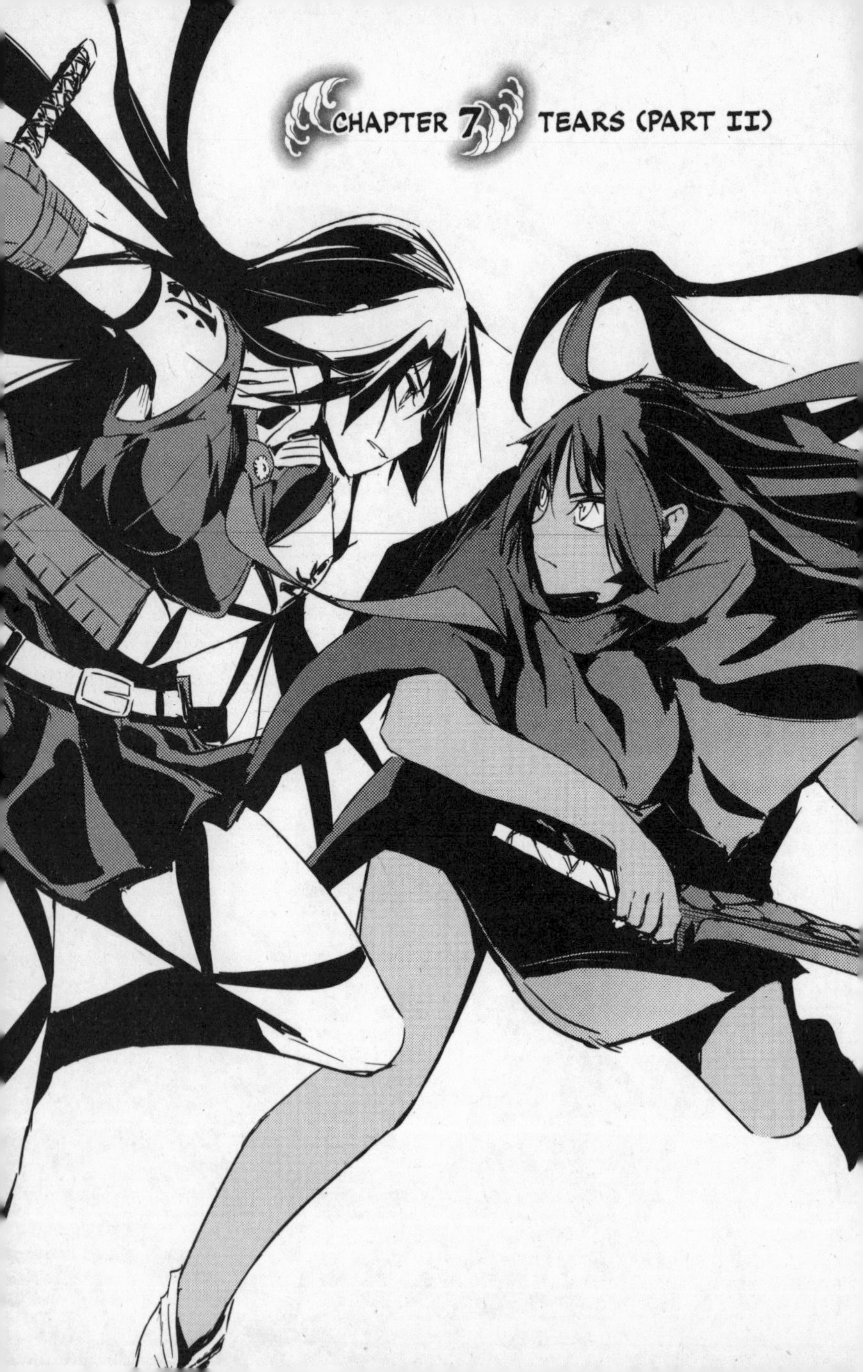
CHAPTER 7 TEARS (PART II)

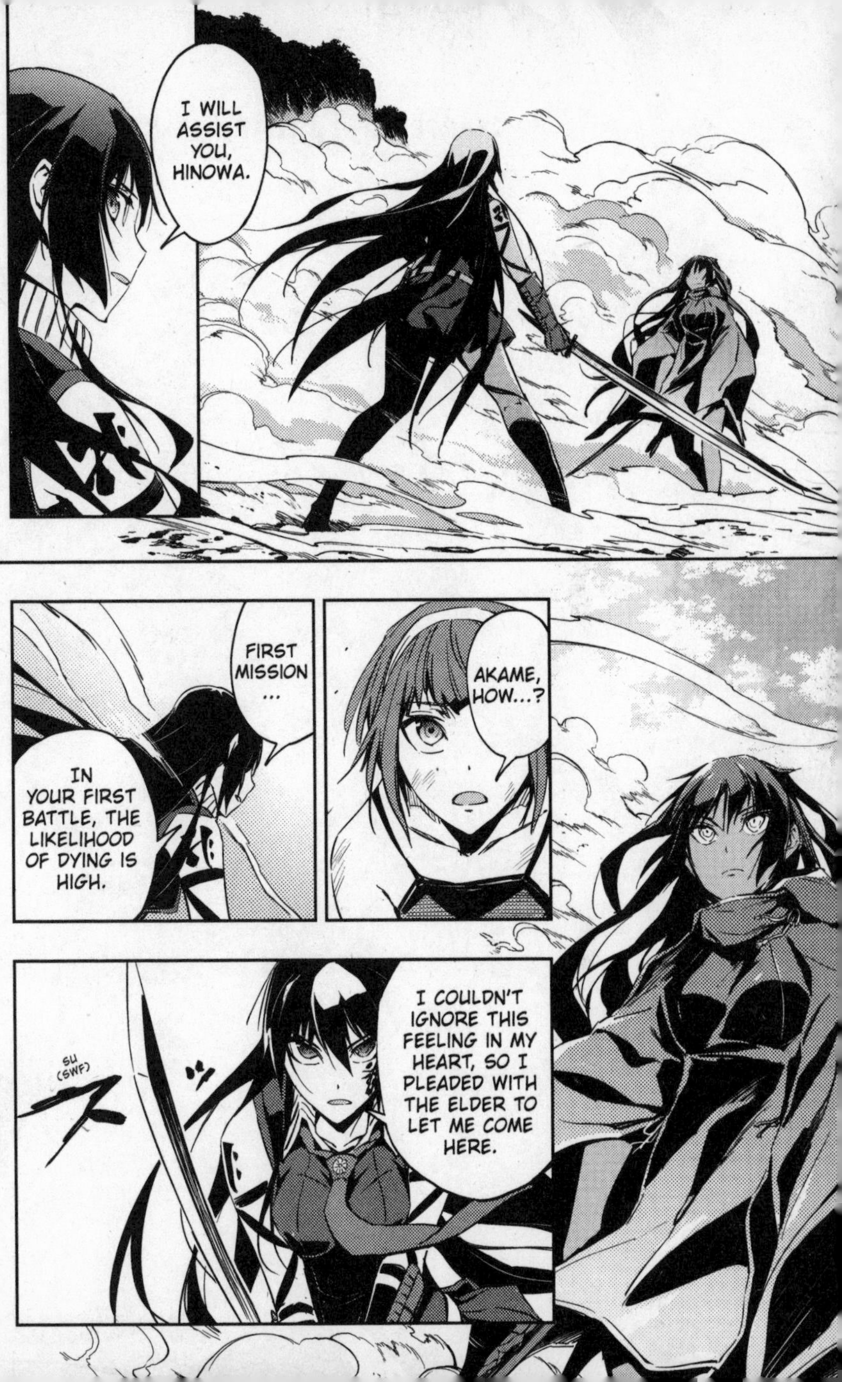
I WILL ASSIST YOU, HINOWA.
AKAME, HOW...?
FIRST MISSION ...
IN YOUR FIRST BATTLE, THE LIKELIHOOD OF DYING IS HIGH.
I COULDN'T IGNORE THIS FEELING IN MY HEART, SO I PLEADED WITH THE ELDER TO LET ME COME HERE.
SU (SWF)

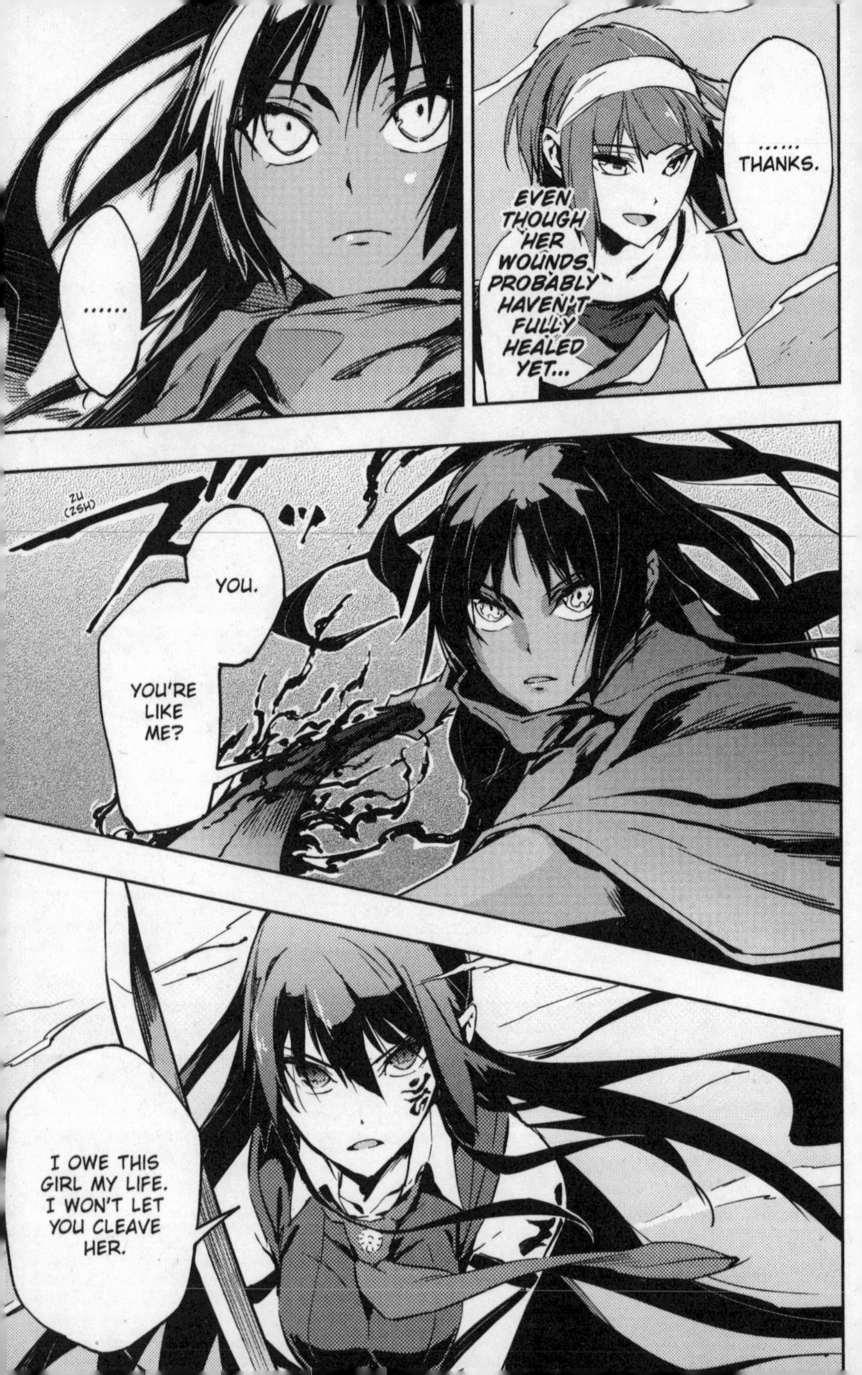
......THANKS.
EVEN THOUGH HER WOUNDS PROBABLY HAVEN'T FULLY HEALED YET...
......
ZU (ZSH)
YOU.
YOU'RE LIKE ME?
I OWE THIS GIRL MY LIFE. I WON'T LET YOU CLEAVE HER.

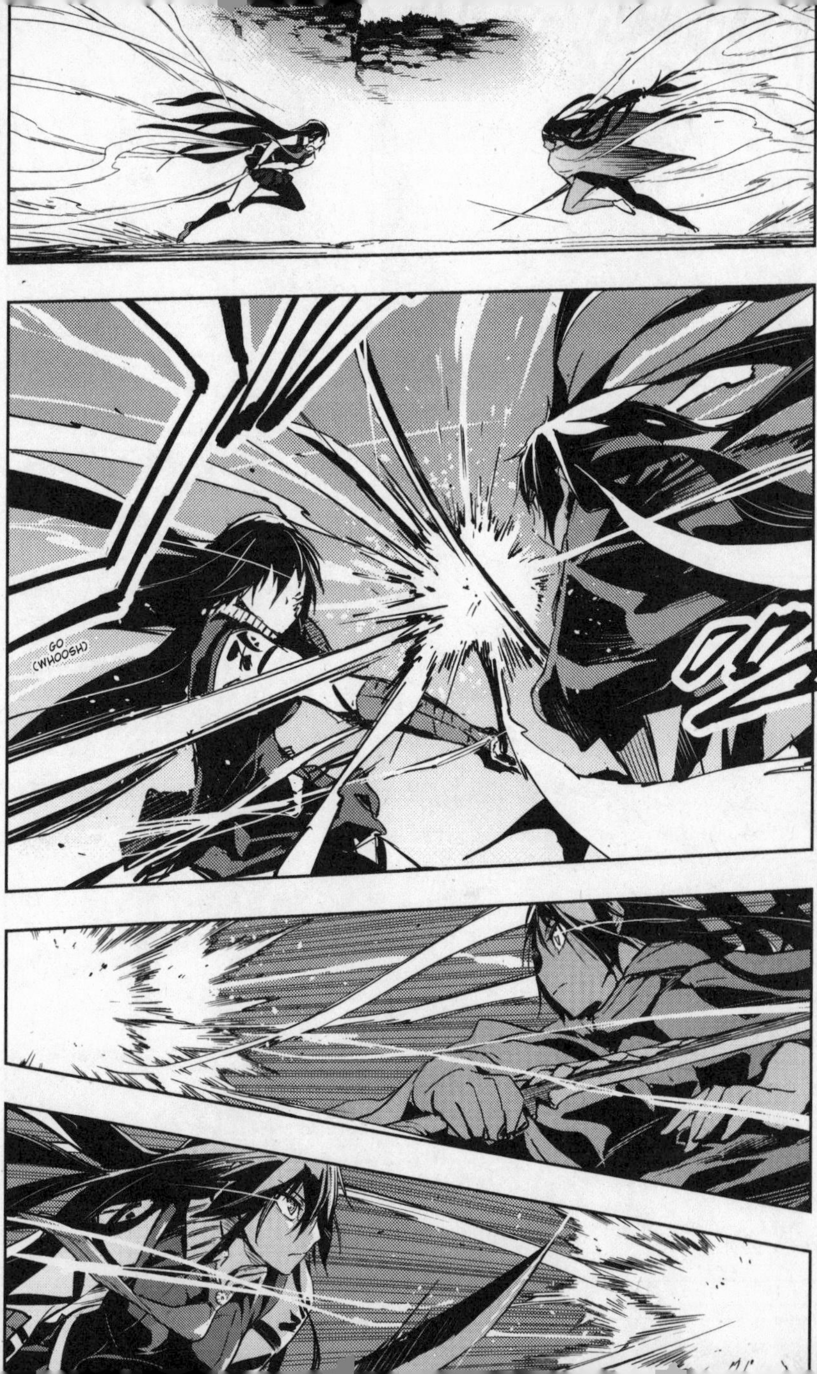
GO
(WHOOSH)

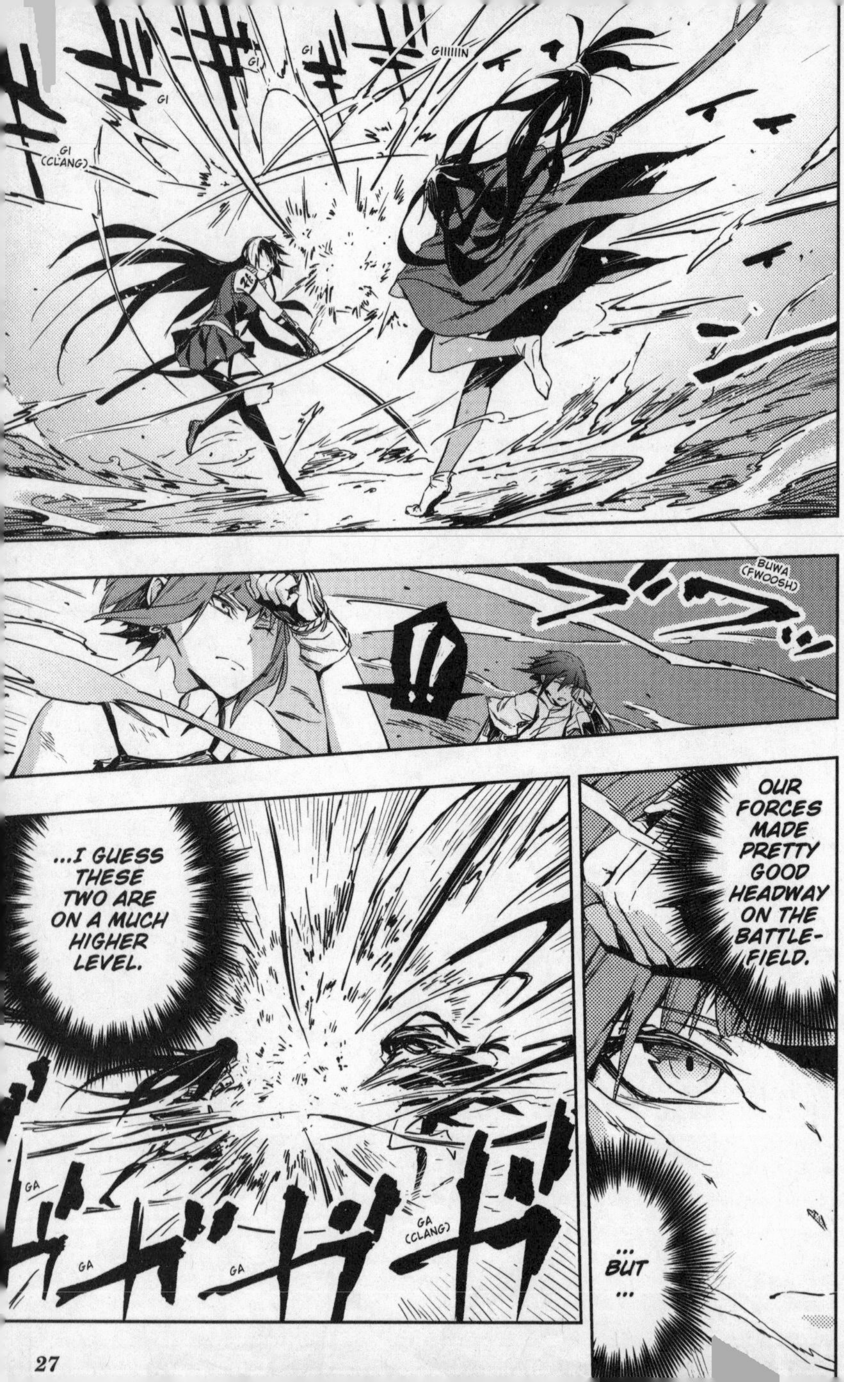
GIIIIIIN
GI
GI
GI
GI (CLANG)
BUWA (FWOOSH)
OUR FORCES MADE PRETTY GOOD HEADWAY ON THE BATTLE-FIELD.
...BUT...
...I GUESS THESE TWO ARE ON A MUCH HIGHER LEVEL.
GA (CLANG)
GA
GA
GA

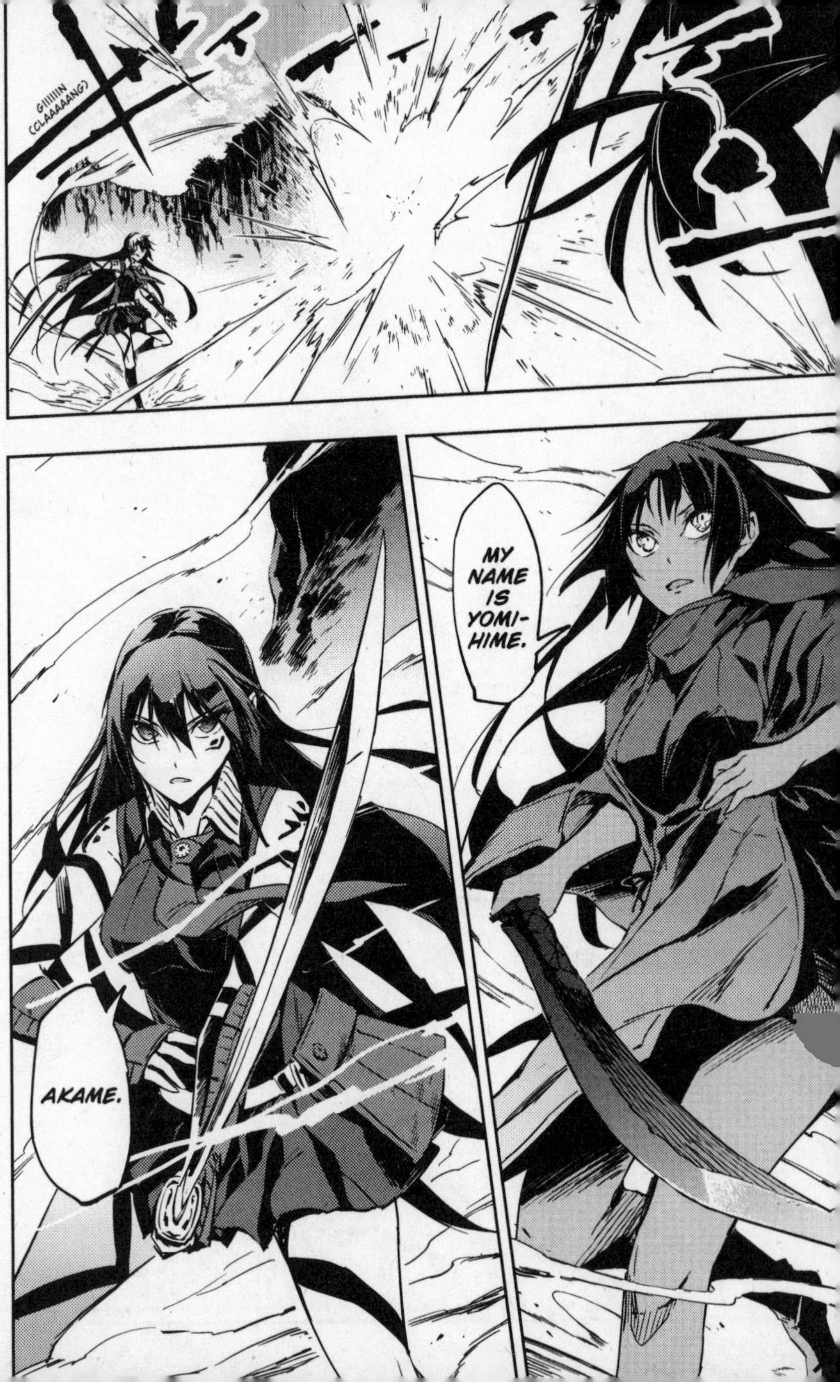
GIIIIIIN
(CLAAAAANG)
MY NAME IS YOMI-HIME.
AKAME.

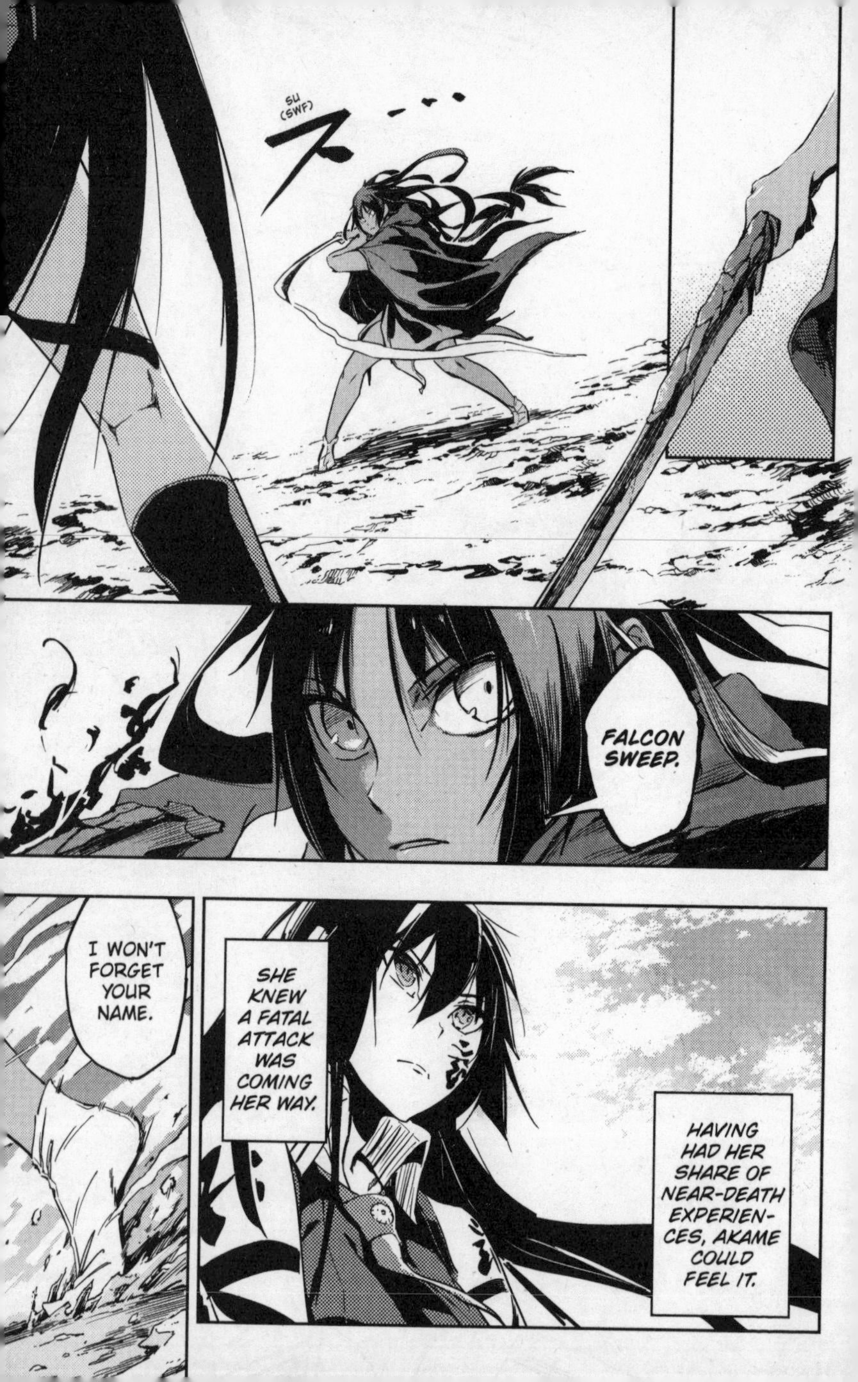
SU (SWF)
FALCON SWEEP.
HAVING HAD HER SHARE OF NEAR-DEATH EXPERIENCES, AKAME COULD FEEL IT.
SHE KNEW A FATAL ATTACK WAS COMING HER WAY.
I WON'T FORGET YOUR NAME.

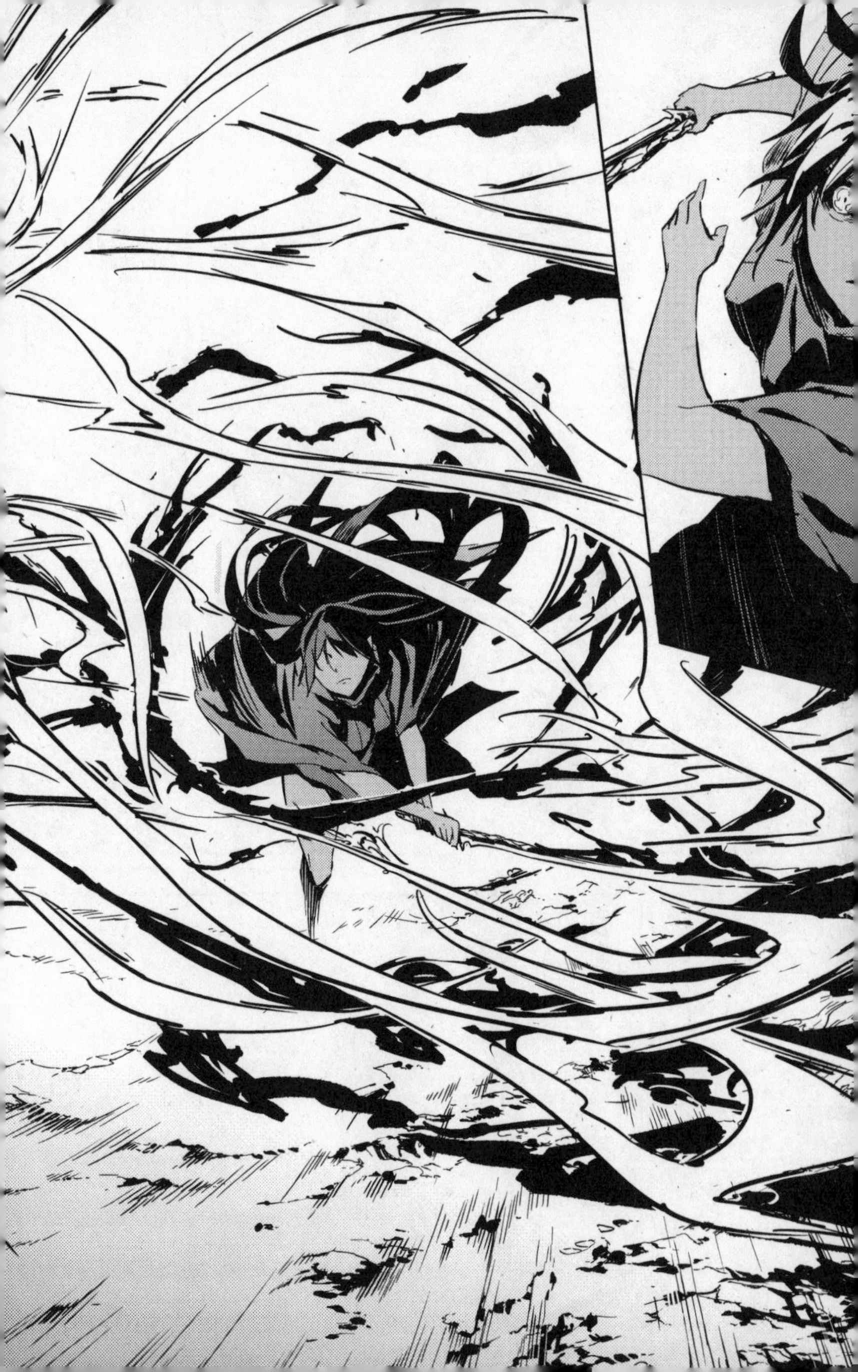

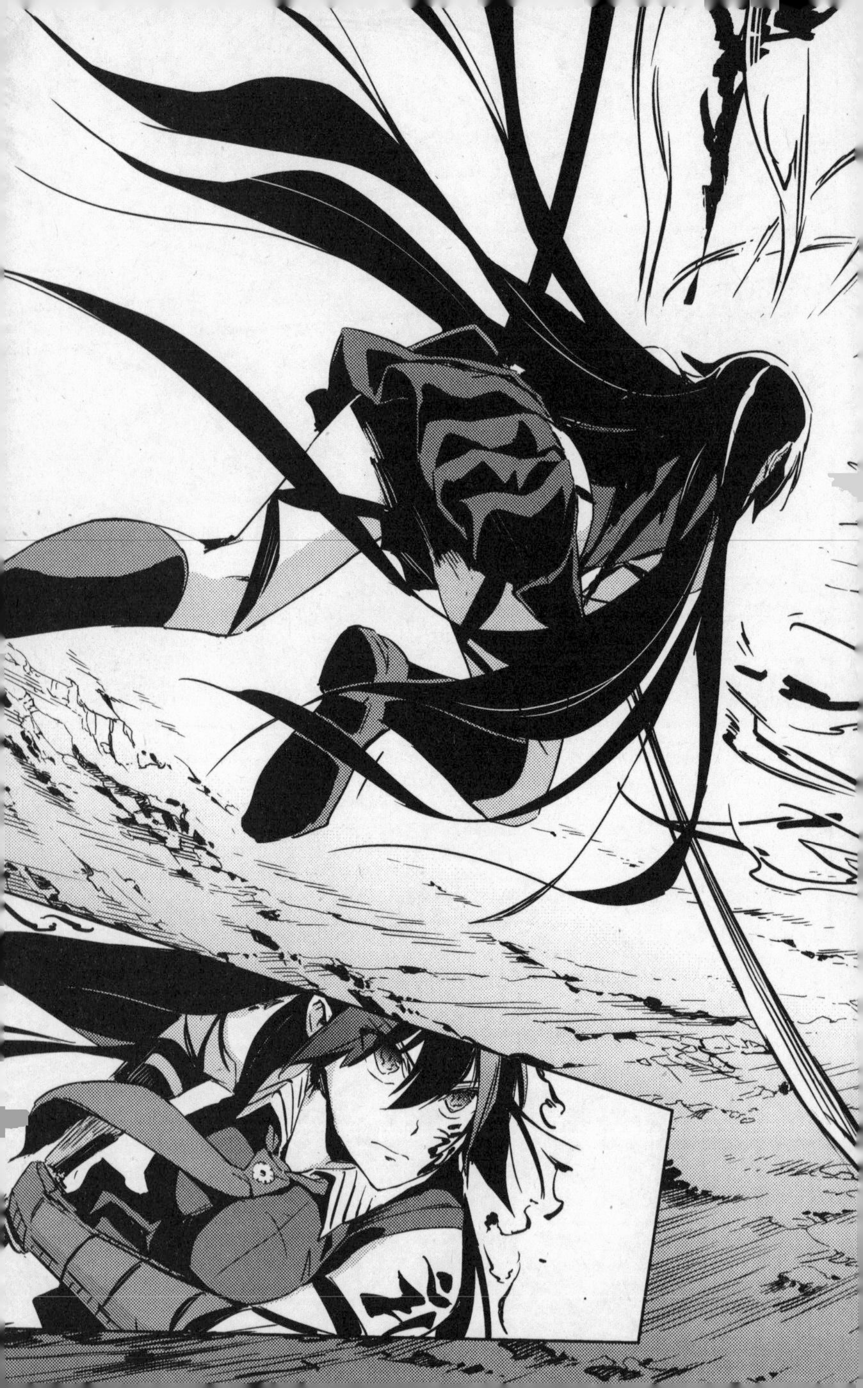

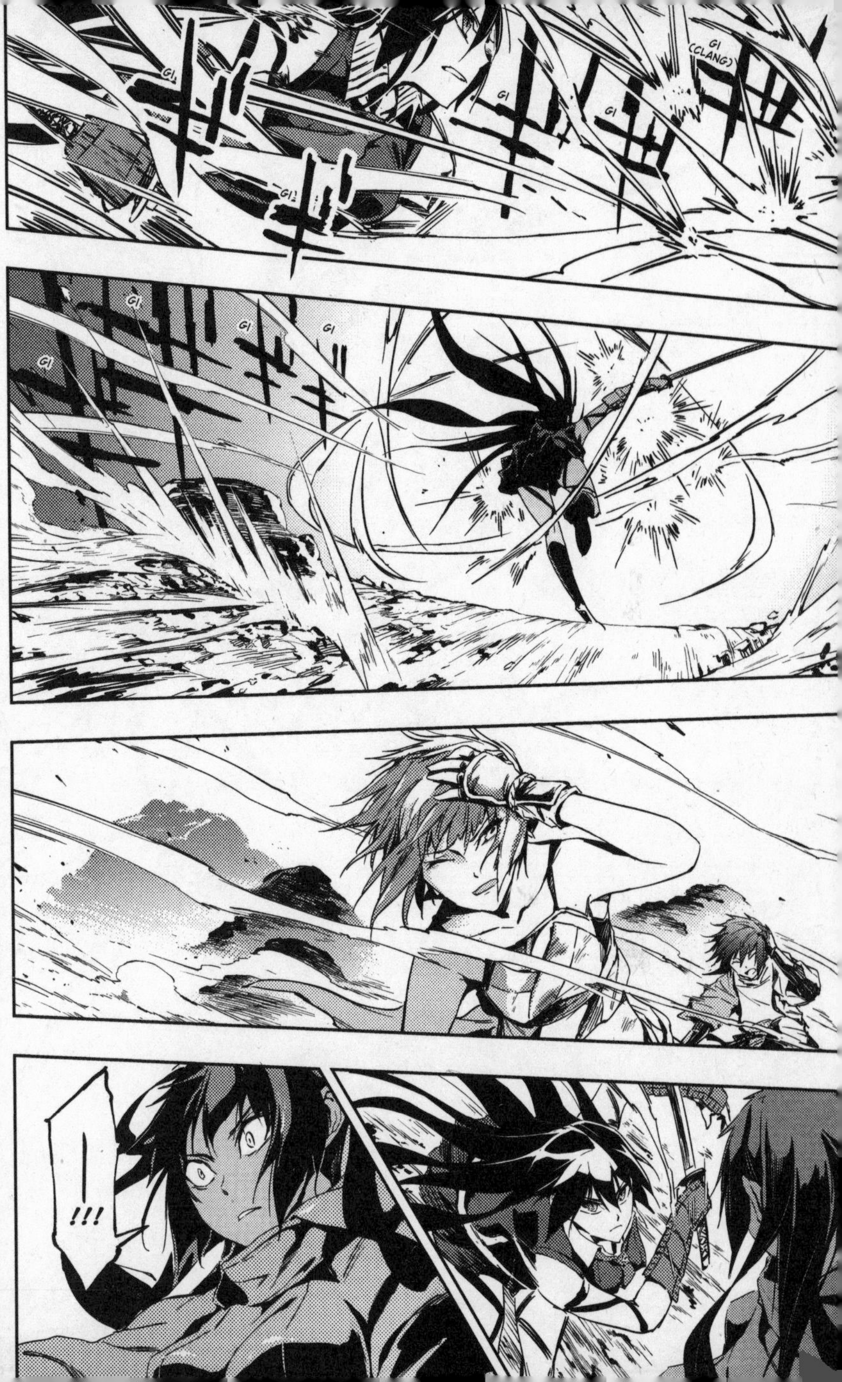
GI
(CLANG)
GI
GI
GI
GI
GI
GI
GI
GI
!!!

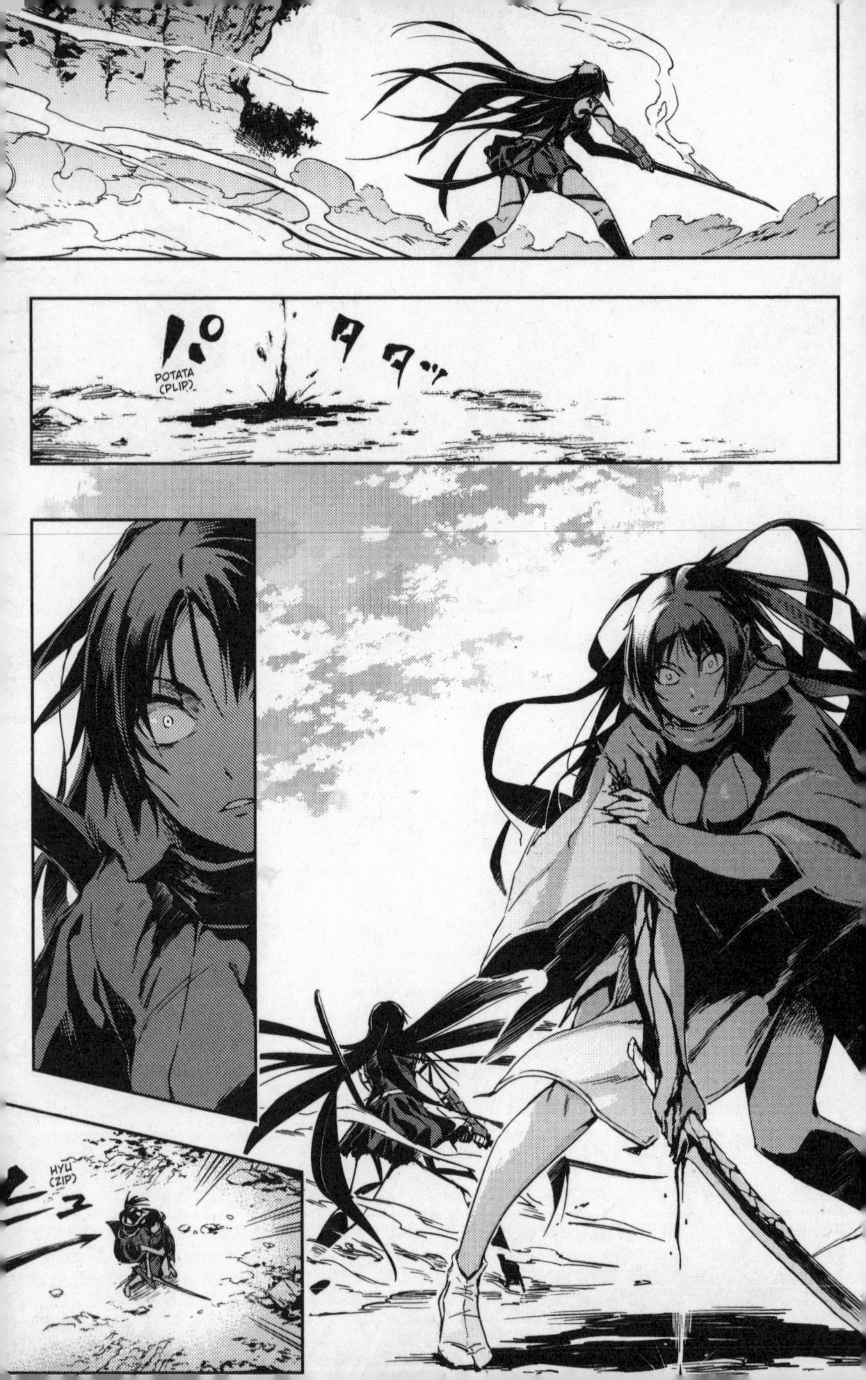
パタタッ
POTATA
(PLIP)
ヒュ
HYU
(ZIP)

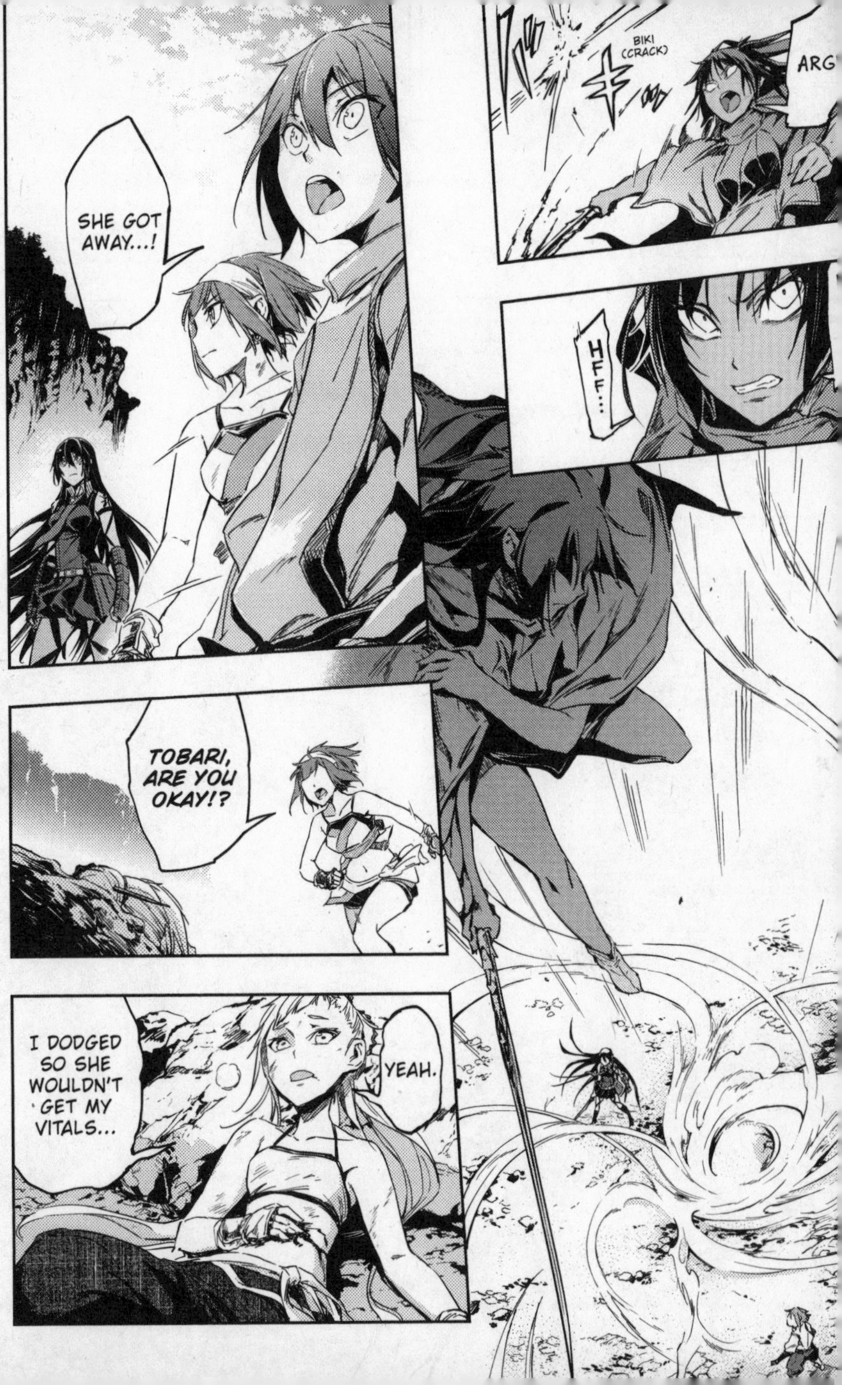
BIKI (CRACK)
ARG
HFF...
SHE GOT AWAY...!
TOBARI, ARE YOU OKAY!?
YEAH.
I DODGED SO SHE WOULDN'T GET MY VITALS...

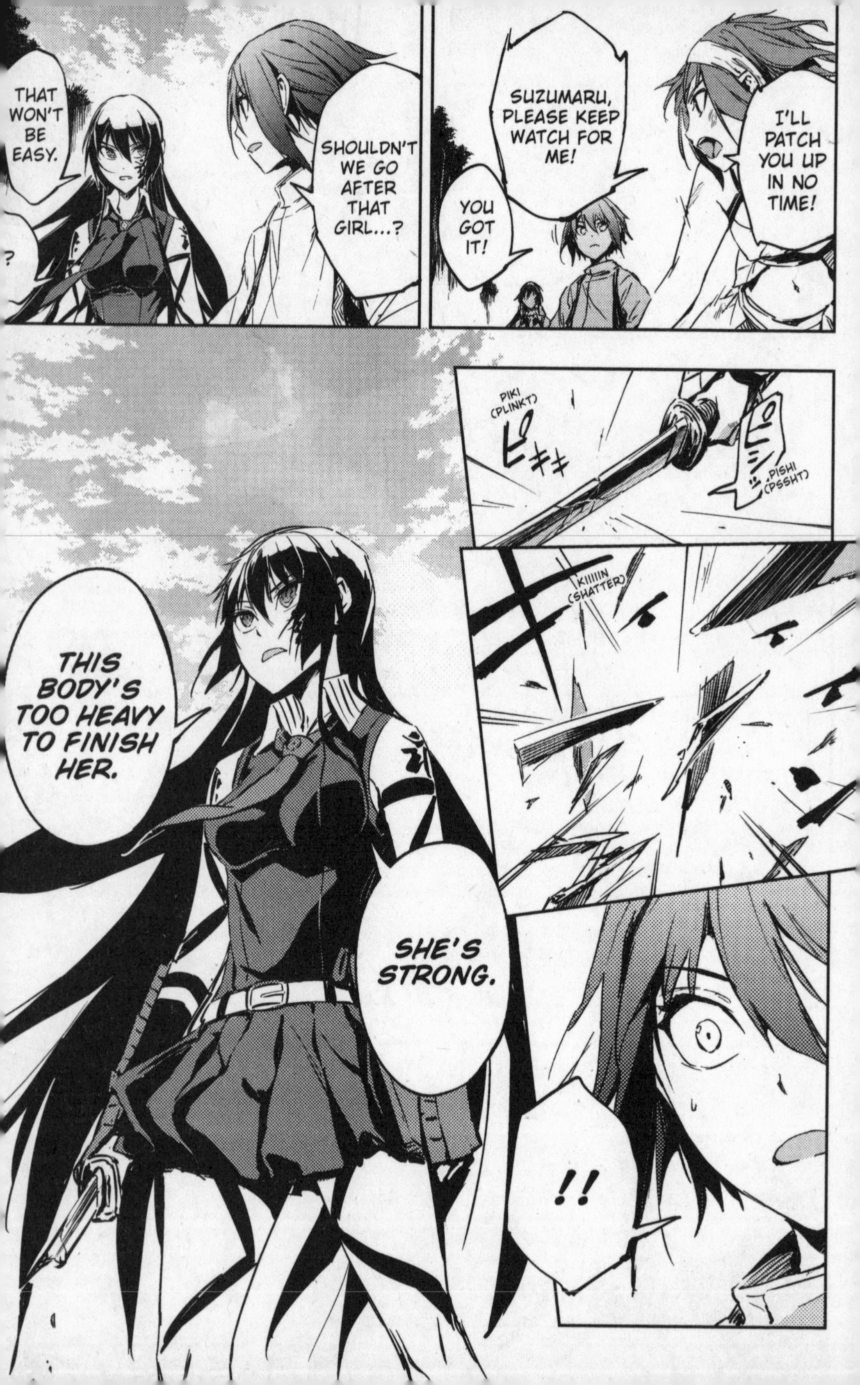
I'LL PATCH YOU UP IN NO TIME!
SUZUMARU, PLEASE KEEP WATCH FOR ME!
YOU GOT IT!
SHOULDN'T WE GO AFTER THAT GIRL...?
THAT WON'T BE EASY.
PIKI (PLINKT)
PISHI (PSSHT)
KIIIIIN (SHATTER)
!!
THIS BODY'S TOO HEAVY TO FINISH HER.
SHE'S STRONG.

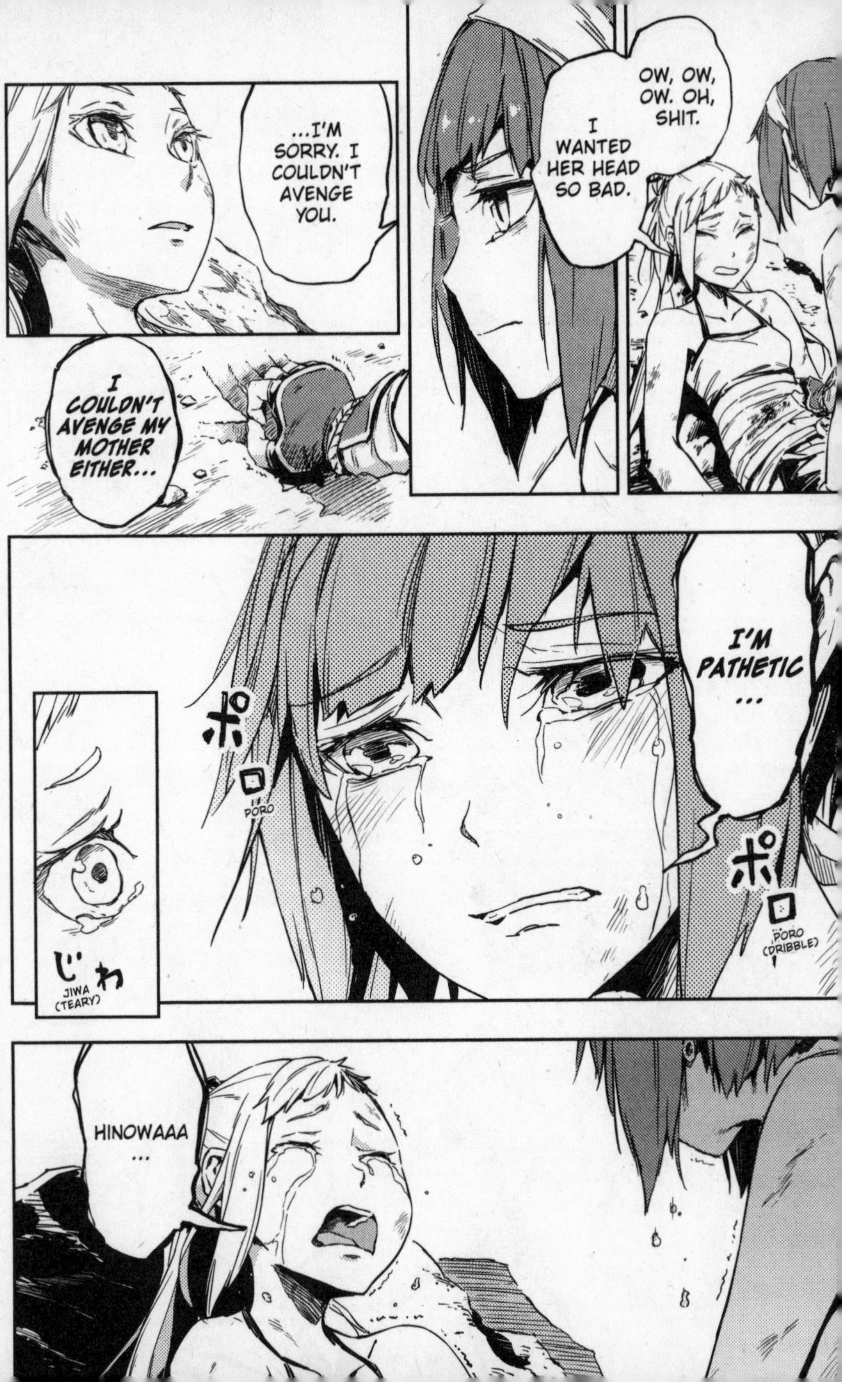
OW, OW, OW. OH, SHIT.
I WANTED HER HEAD SO BAD.
...I'M SORRY. I COULDN'T AVENGE YOU.
I COULDN'T AVENGE MY MOTHER EITHER...
I'M PATHETIC...
ポロ
PORO (DRIBBLE)
ポロ
PORO
じわ
JIWA (TEARY)
HINOWAAA...

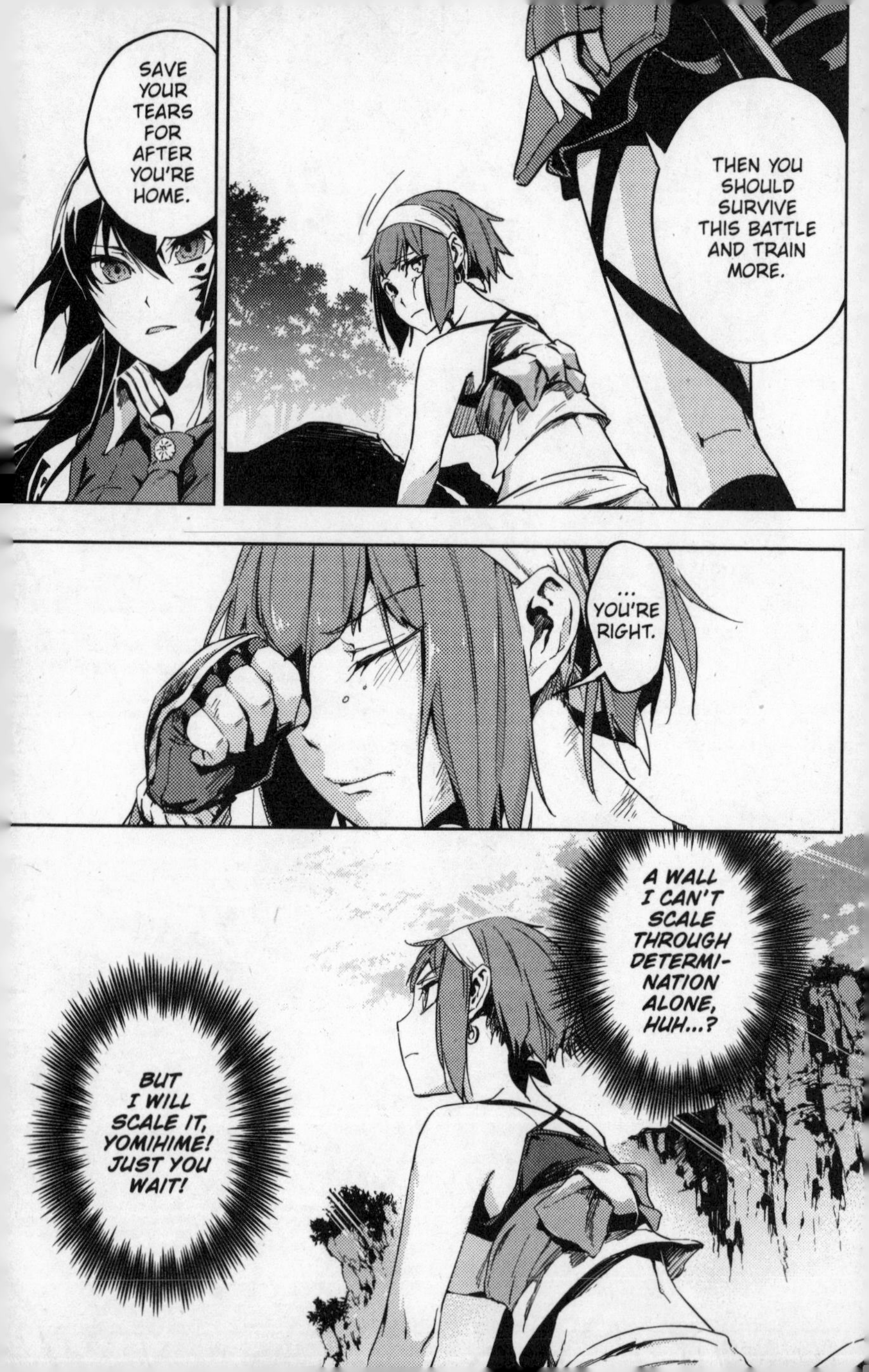
THEN YOU SHOULD SURVIVE THIS BATTLE AND TRAIN MORE.
SAVE YOUR TEARS FOR AFTER YOU'RE HOME.
...YOU'RE RIGHT.
A WALL I CAN'T SCALE THROUGH DETERMINATION ALONE, HUH...?
BUT I WILL SCALE IT, YOMIHIME! JUST YOU WAIT!

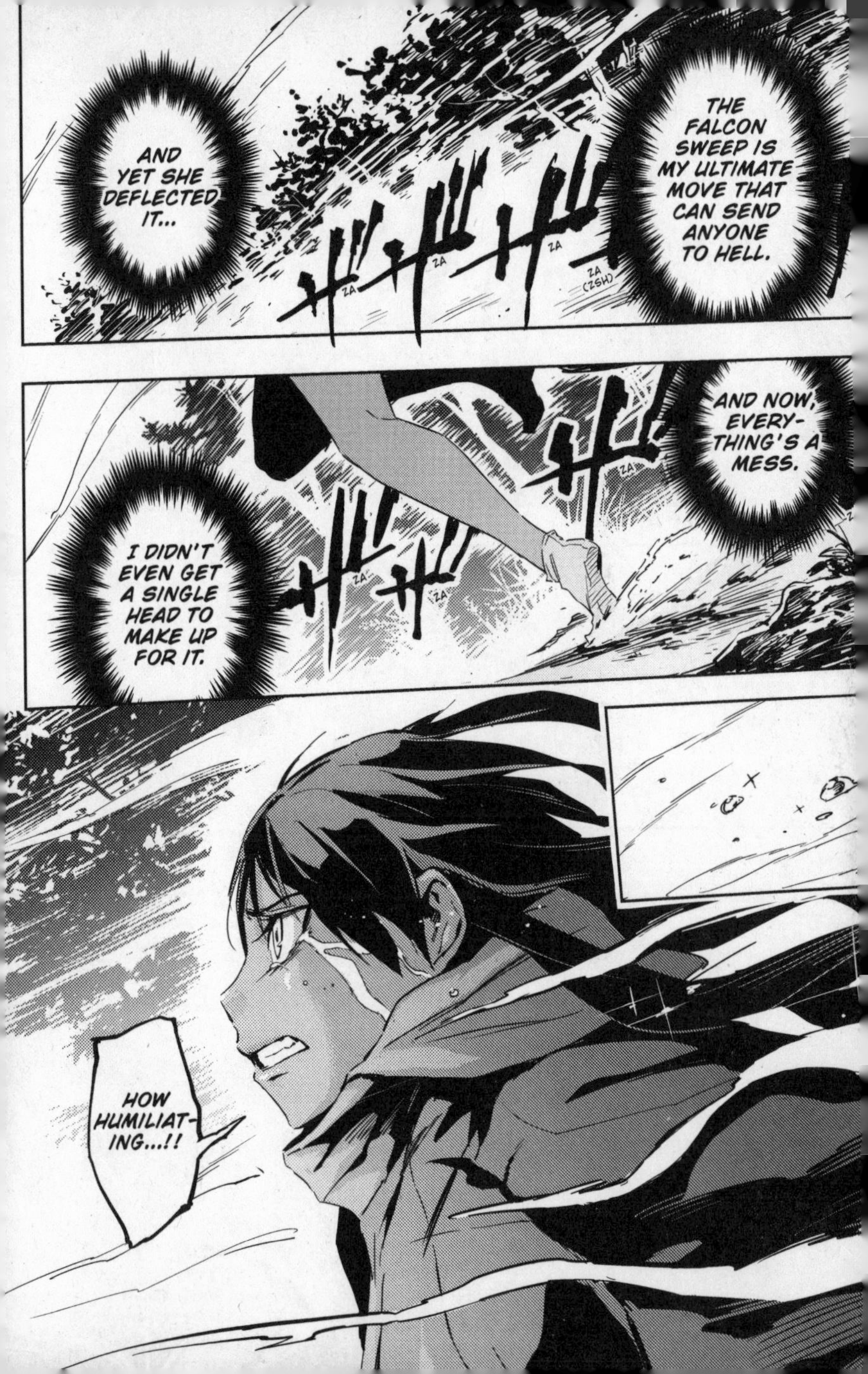
THE FALCON SWEEP IS MY ULTIMATE MOVE THAT CAN SEND ANYONE TO HELL.
ZA (ZSH)
ZA
ZA
ZA
AND YET SHE DEFLECTED IT...
AND NOW, EVERY-THING'S A MESS.
ZA
ZA
ZA
I DIDN'T EVEN GET A SINGLE HEAD TO MAKE UP FOR IT.
HOW HUMILIAT-ING...!!

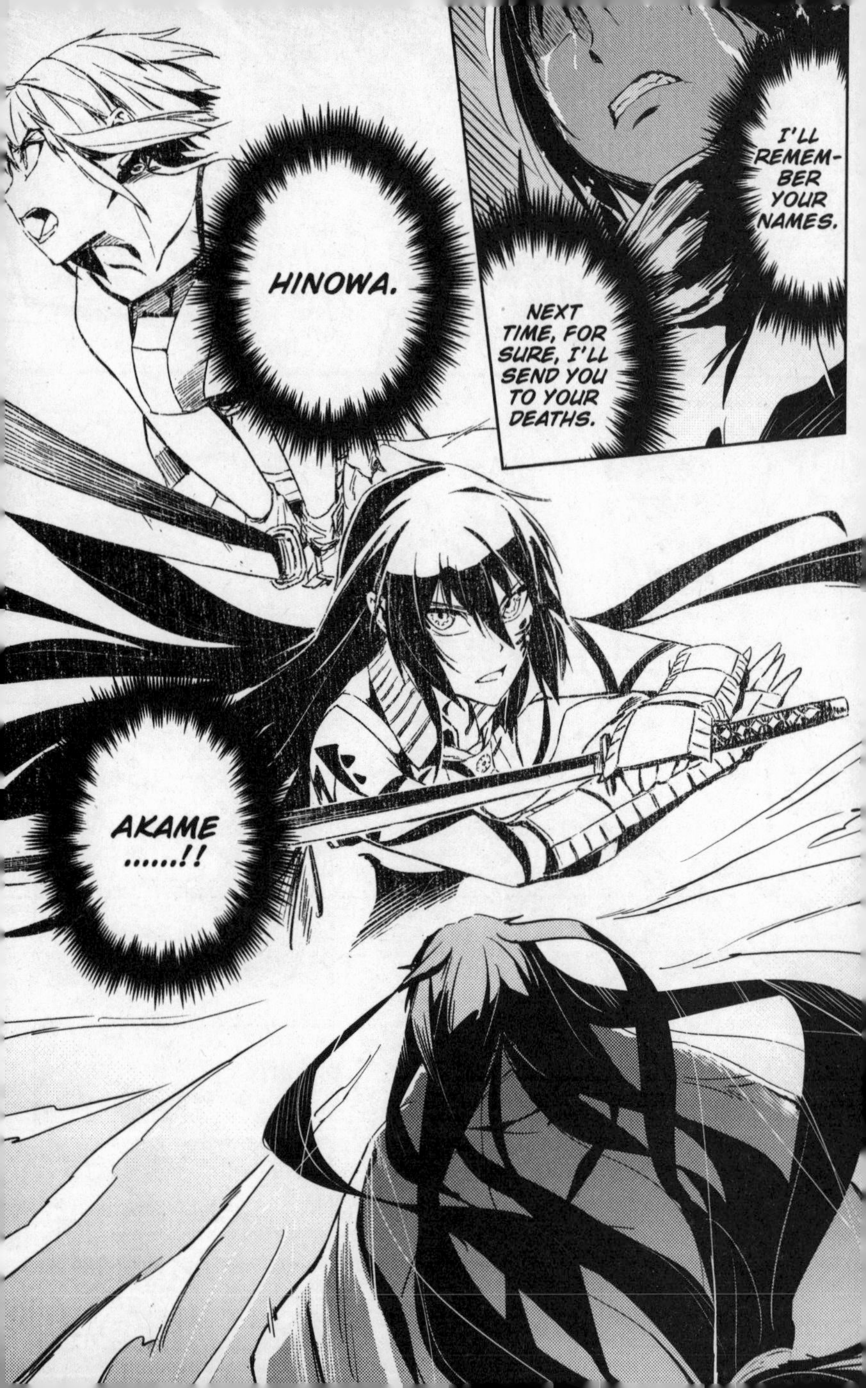
I'LL REMEMBER YOUR NAMES.
NEXT TIME, FOR SURE, I'LL SEND YOU TO YOUR DEATHS.
HINOWA.
AKAME ......!!

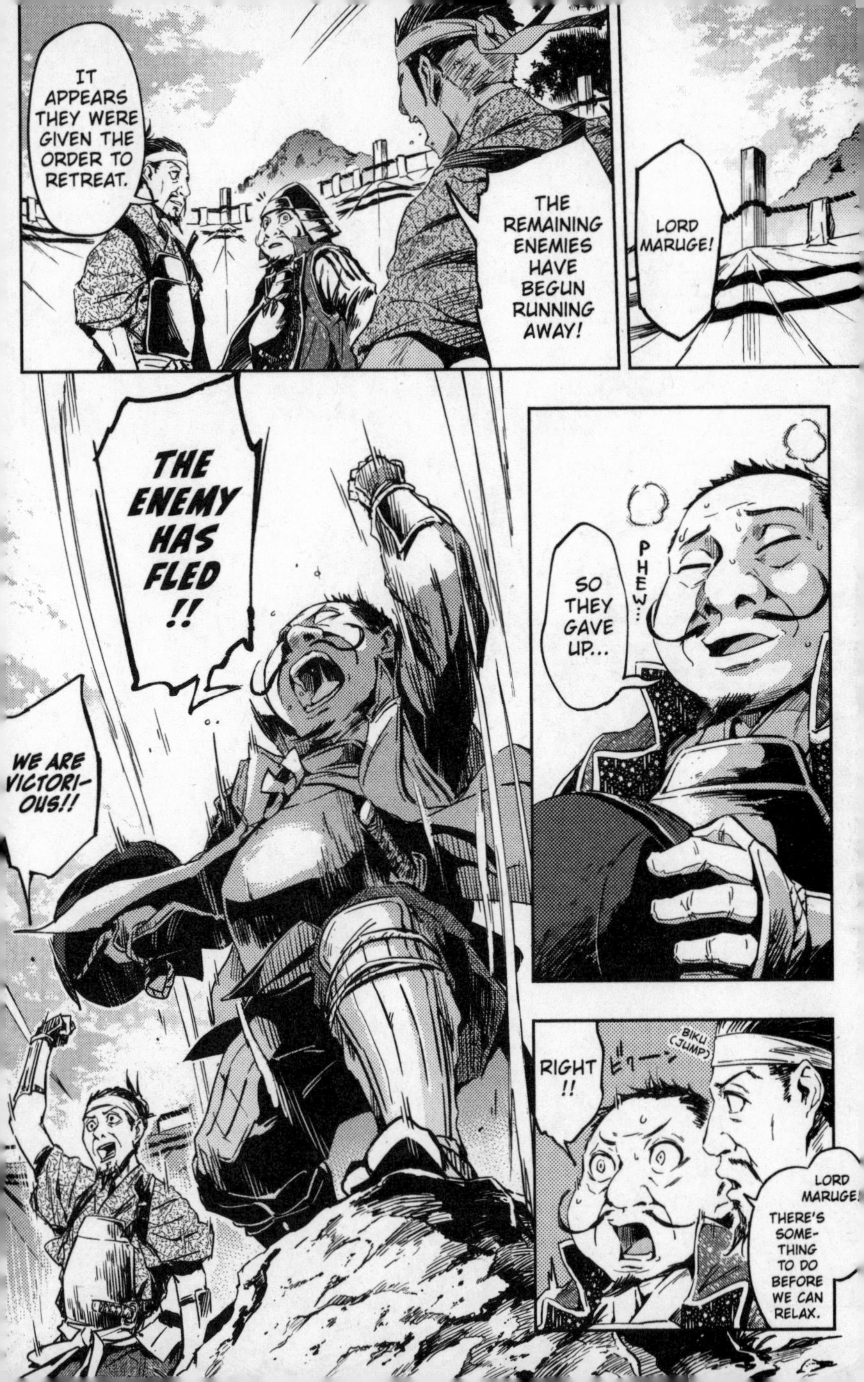
LORD MARUGE!
THE REMAINING ENEMIES HAVE BEGUN RUNNING AWAY!
IT APPEARS THEY WERE GIVEN THE ORDER TO RETREAT.
PHEW...
SO THEY GAVE UP...
LORD MARUGE. THERE'S SOMETHING TO DO BEFORE WE CAN RELAX.
BIKU (JUMP)
RIGHT!!
THE ENEMY HAS FLED!!
WE ARE VICTORIOUS!!

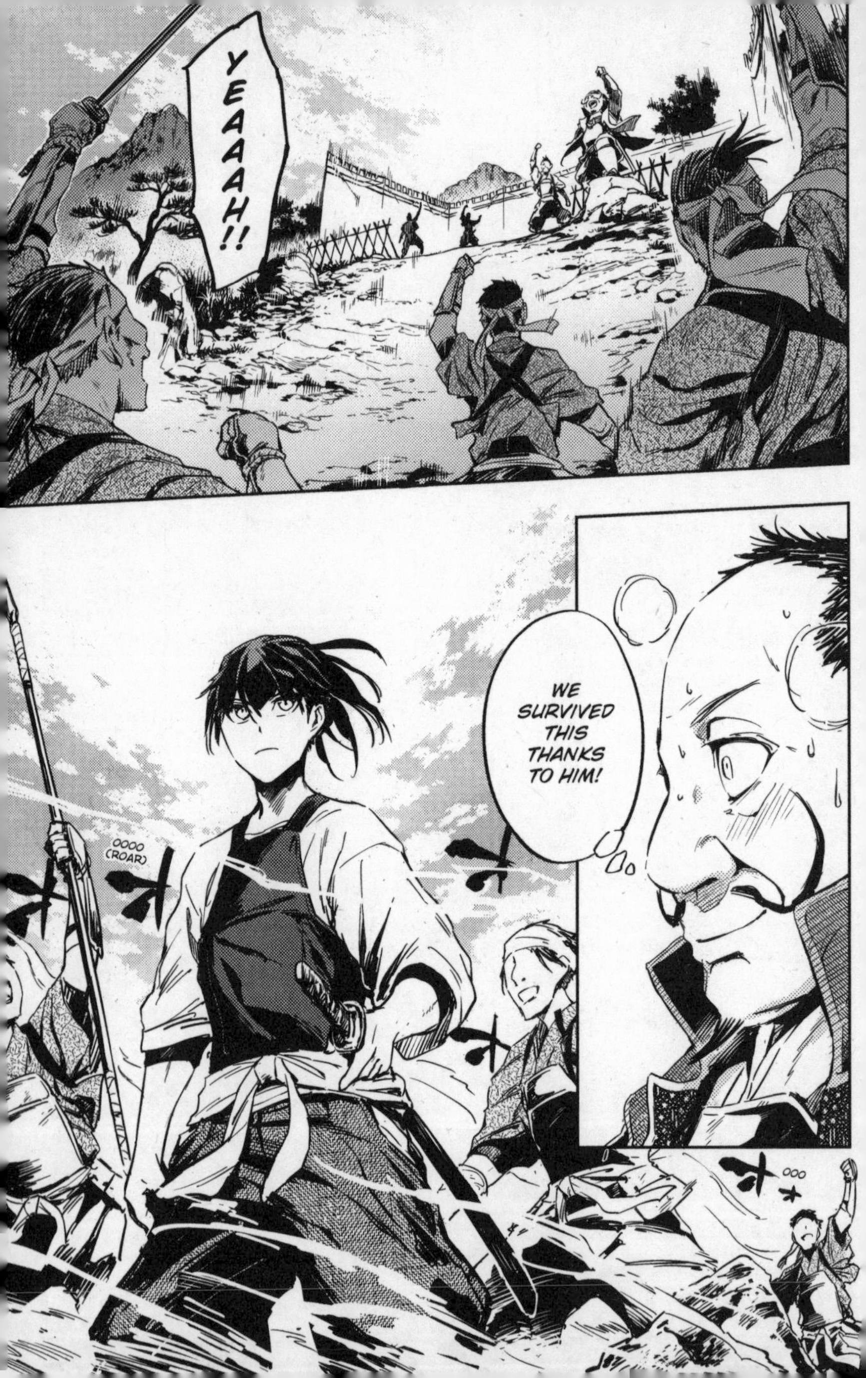
YEAAAAH!!
WE SURVIVED THIS THANKS TO HIM!
OOOO (ROAR)
OOO

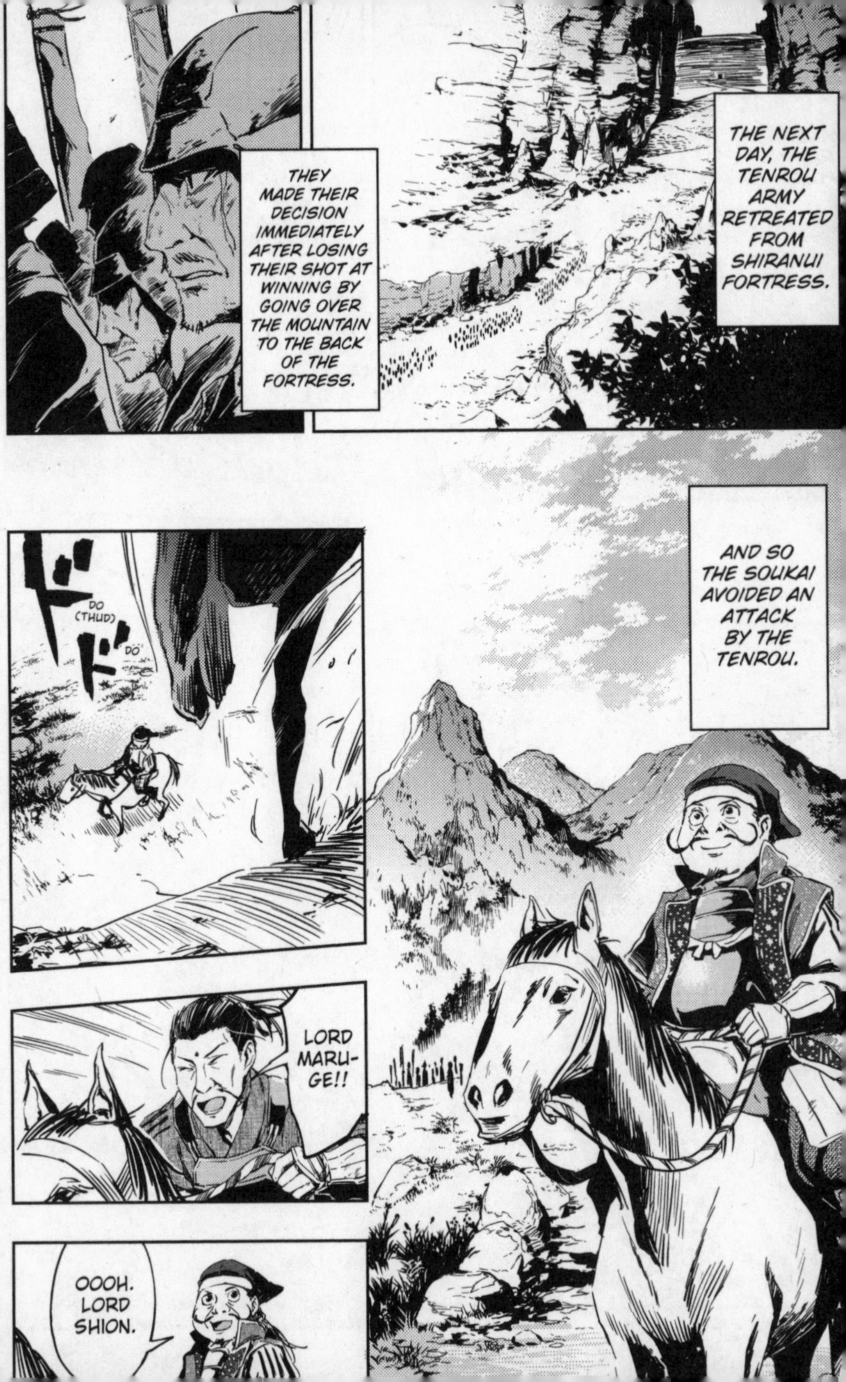
THE NEXT DAY, THE TENROU ARMY RETREATED FROM SHIRANUI FORTRESS.
THEY MADE THEIR DECISION IMMEDIATELY AFTER LOSING THEIR SHOT AT WINNING BY GOING OVER THE MOUNTAIN TO THE BACK OF THE FORTRESS.
AND SO THE SOUKAI AVOIDED AN ATTACK BY THE TENROU.
ド
DO (THUD)
ド
DO
LORD MARUGE!!
OOOH. LORD SHION.

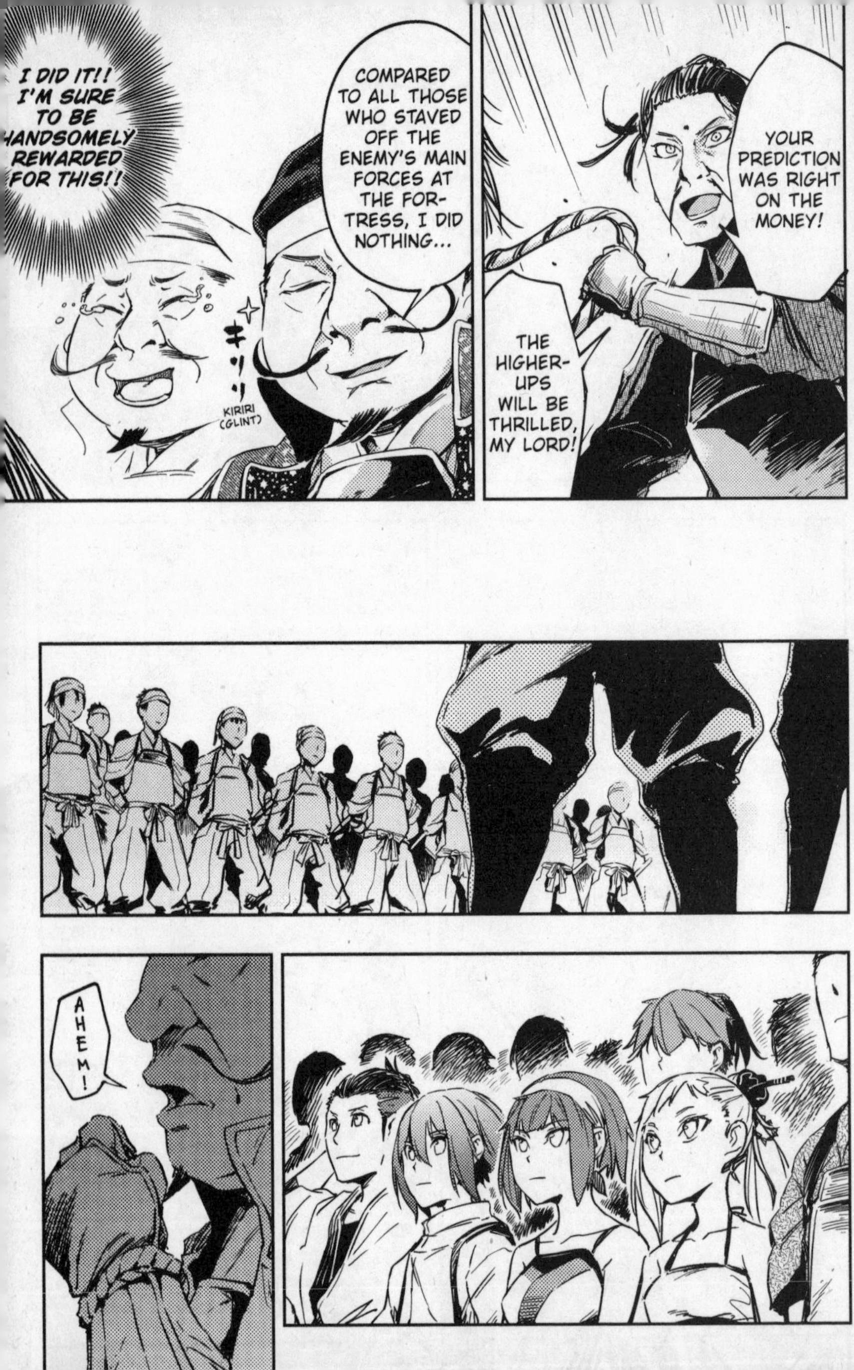
YOUR PREDICTION WAS RIGHT ON THE MONEY!
THE HIGHER-UPS WILL BE THRILLED, MY LORD!
COMPARED TO ALL THOSE WHO STAVED OFF THE ENEMY'S MAIN FORCES AT THE FOR-TRESS, I DID NOTHING...
キリリ
KIRIRI (GLINT)
I DID IT!! I'M SURE TO BE HANDSOMELY REWARDED FOR THIS!!
AHEM!

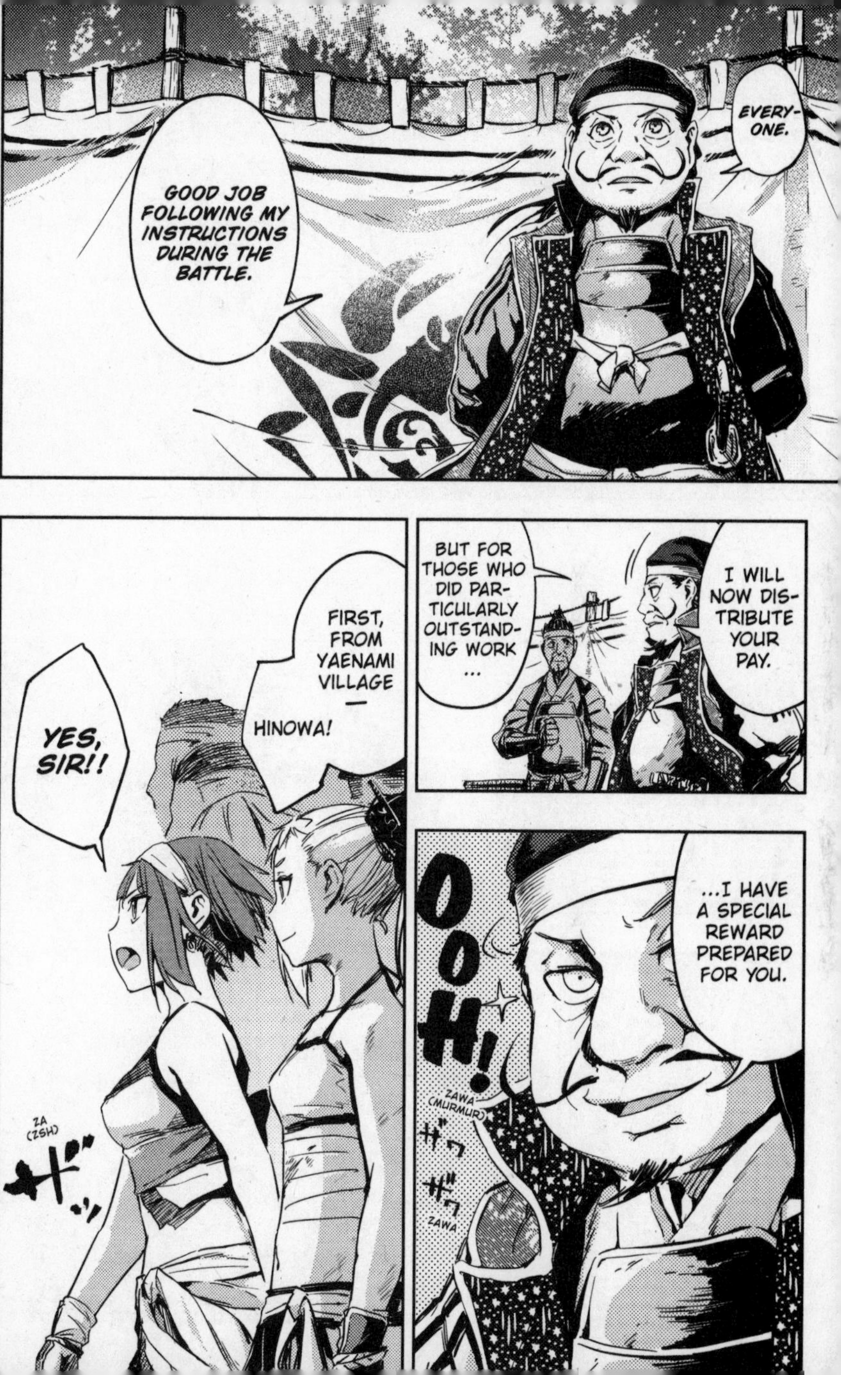
EVERYONE.
GOOD JOB FOLLOWING MY INSTRUCTIONS DURING THE BATTLE.
I WILL NOW DISTRIBUTE YOUR PAY.
BUT FOR THOSE WHO DID PARTICULARLY OUTSTANDING WORK...
...I HAVE A SPECIAL REWARD PREPARED FOR YOU.
OOOH!
ZAWA (MURMUR)
ZAWA
FIRST, FROM YAENAMI VILLAGE — HINOWA!
YES, SIR!!
ZA (ZSH)

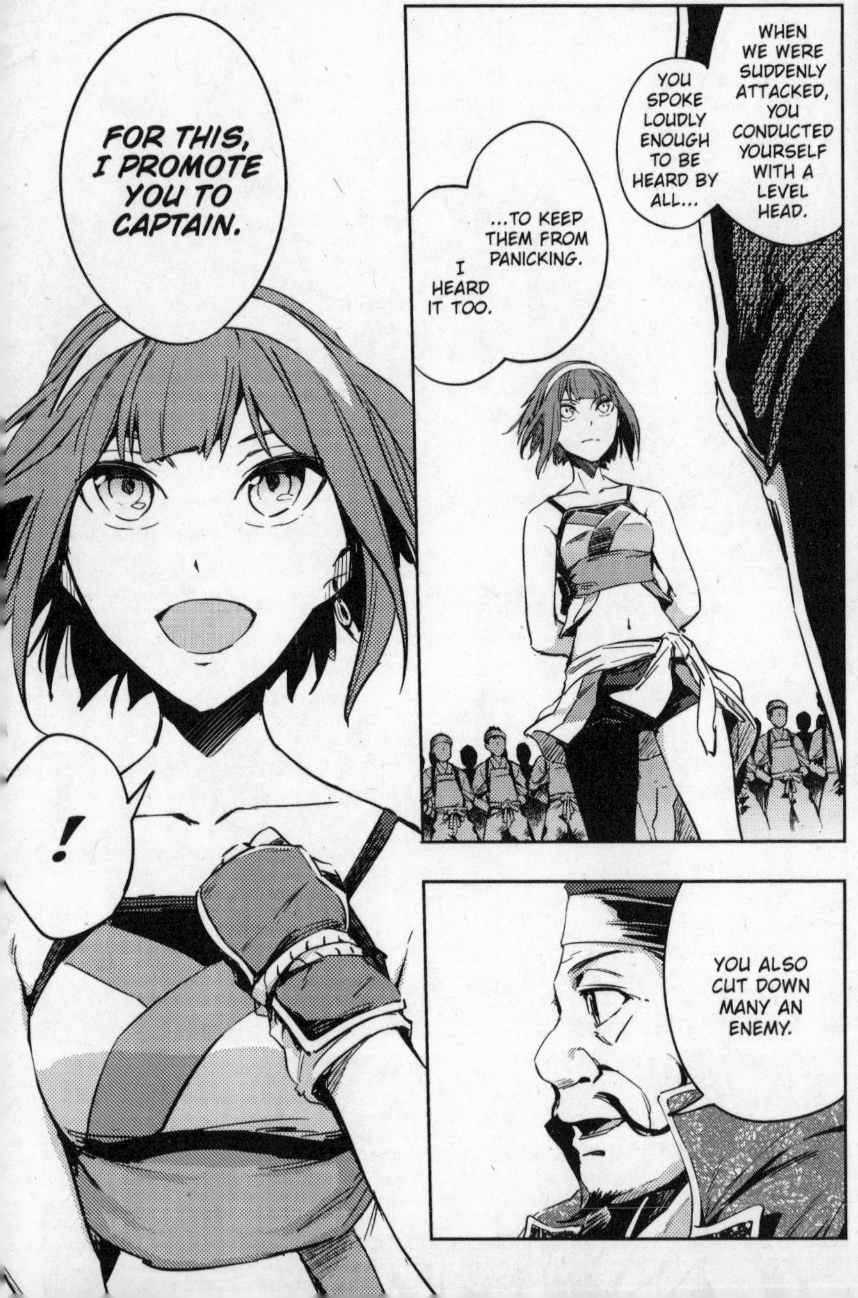
WHEN WE WERE SUDDENLY ATTACKED, YOU CONDUCTED YOURSELF WITH A LEVEL HEAD.
YOU SPOKE LOUDLY ENOUGH TO BE HEARD BY ALL...
...TO KEEP THEM FROM PANICKING.
I HEARD IT TOO.
YOU ALSO CUT DOWN MANY AN ENEMY.
FOR THIS, I PROMOTE YOU TO CAPTAIN.
!

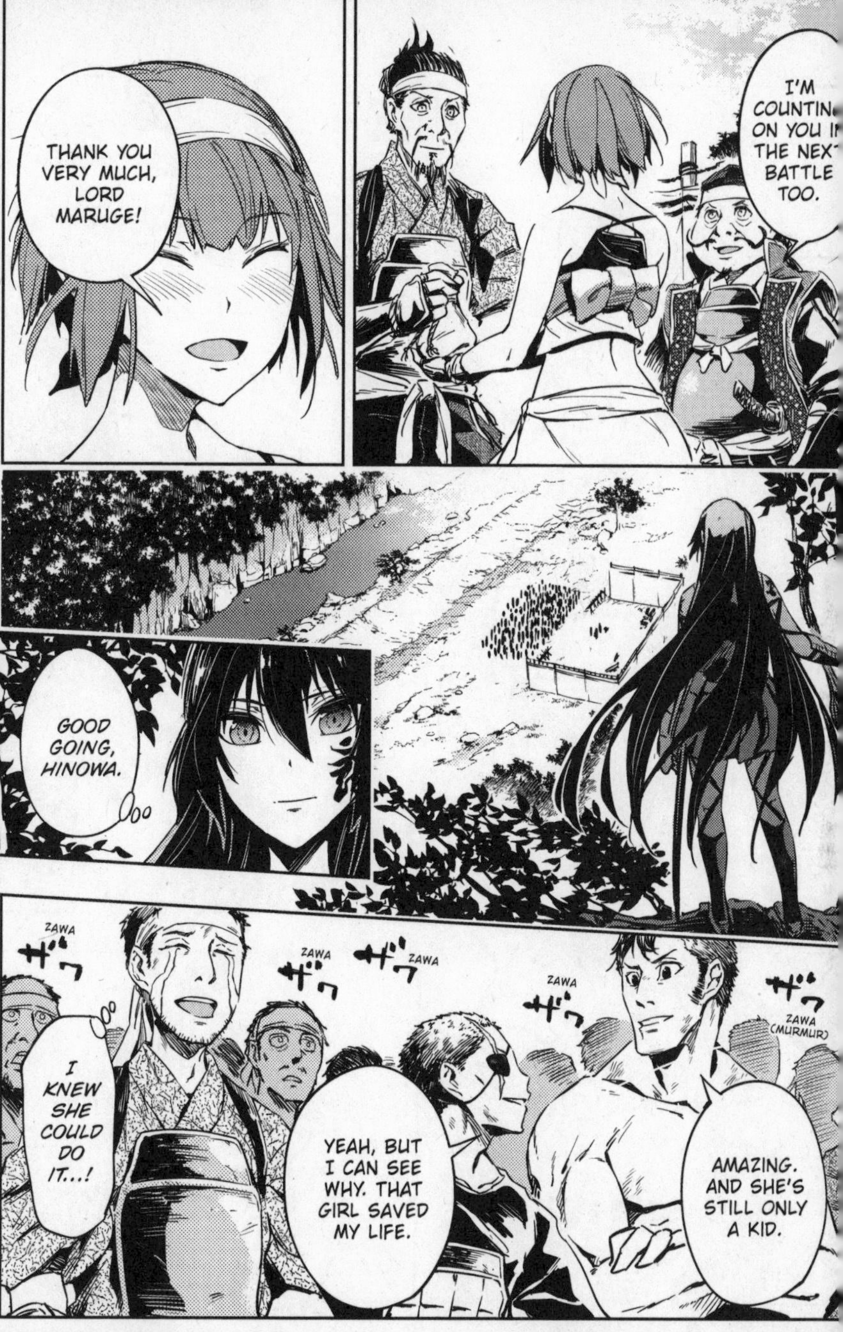
I'M COUNTIN ON YOU I THE NEX BATTLE TOO.
THANK YOU VERY MUCH, LORD MARUGE!
GOOD GOING, HINOWA.
ザワ ZAWA (MURMUR)
ザワ ZAWA
ザワ ZAWA
ザワ ZAWA
ザワ ZAWA
AMAZING. AND SHE'S STILL ONLY A KID.
YEAH, BUT I CAN SEE WHY. THAT GIRL SAVED MY LIFE.
I KNEW SHE COULD DO IT...!

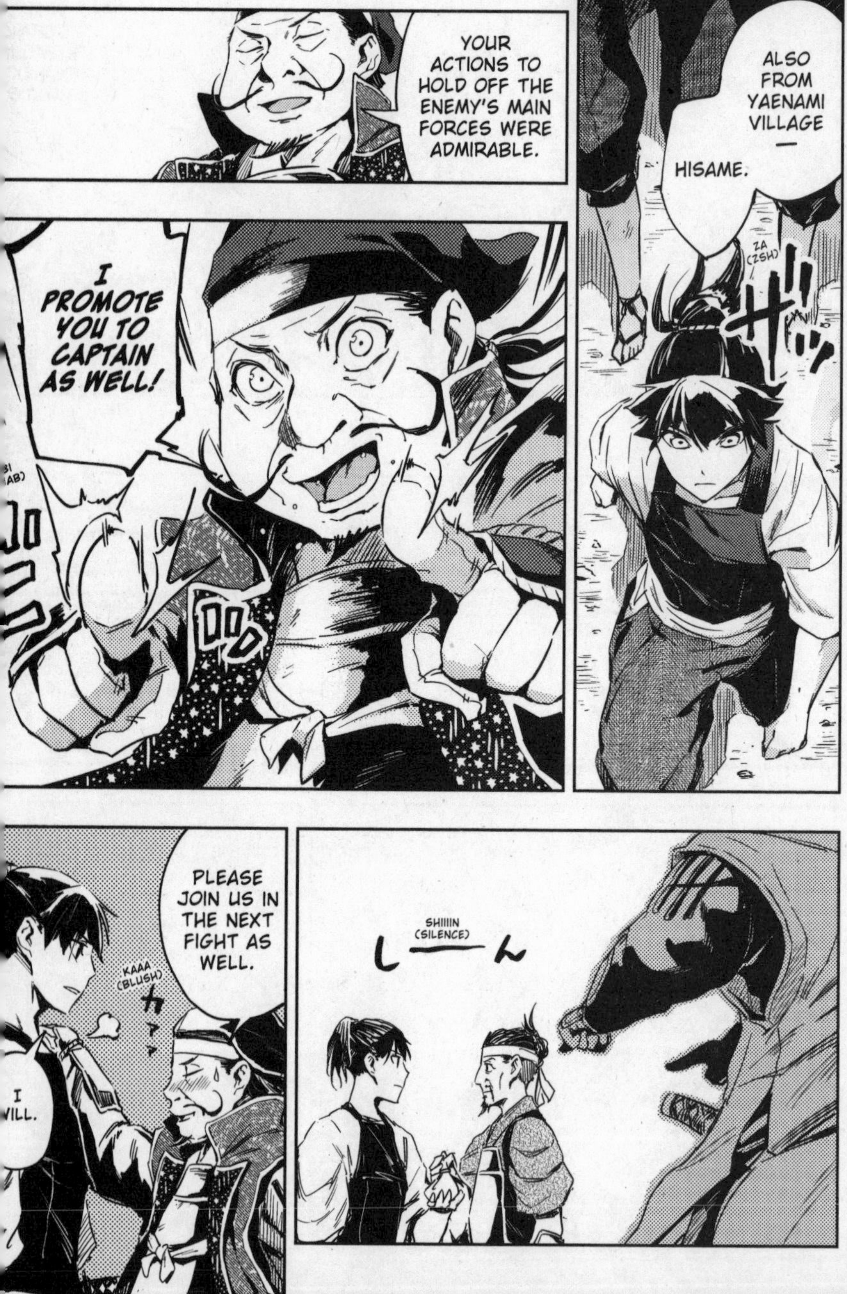
ALSO FROM YAENAMI VILLAGE —
HISAME.
ZA (ZSH)
YOUR ACTIONS TO HOLD OFF THE ENEMY'S MAIN FORCES WERE ADMIRABLE.
I PROMOTE YOU TO CAPTAIN AS WELL!
SHIIIIN (SILENCE)
PLEASE JOIN US IN THE NEXT FIGHT AS WELL.
KAAA (BLUSH)
I WILL.

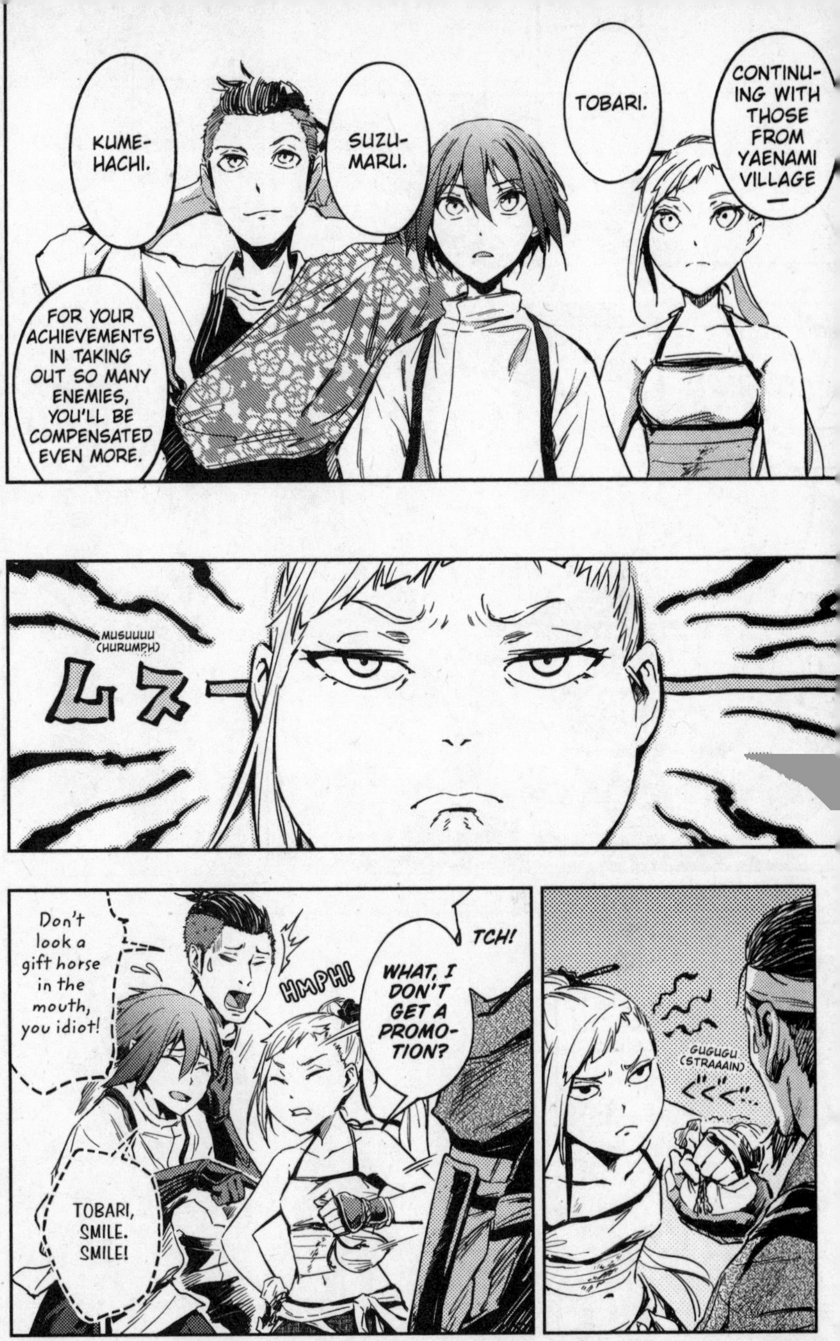
CONTINU-ING WITH THOSE FROM YAENAMI VILLAGE—
TOBARI.
SUZU-MARU.
KUME-HACHI.
FOR YOUR ACHIEVEMENTS IN TAKING OUT SO MANY ENEMIES, YOU'LL BE COMPENSATED EVEN MORE.
MUSUUUU (HURUMPH)
ムスー
GUGUGU (STRAAAIN)
ぐぐぐ…
TCH!
WHAT, I DON'T GET A PROMO-TION?
HMPH!
Don't look a gift horse in the mouth, you idiot!
TOBARI, SMILE. SMILE!

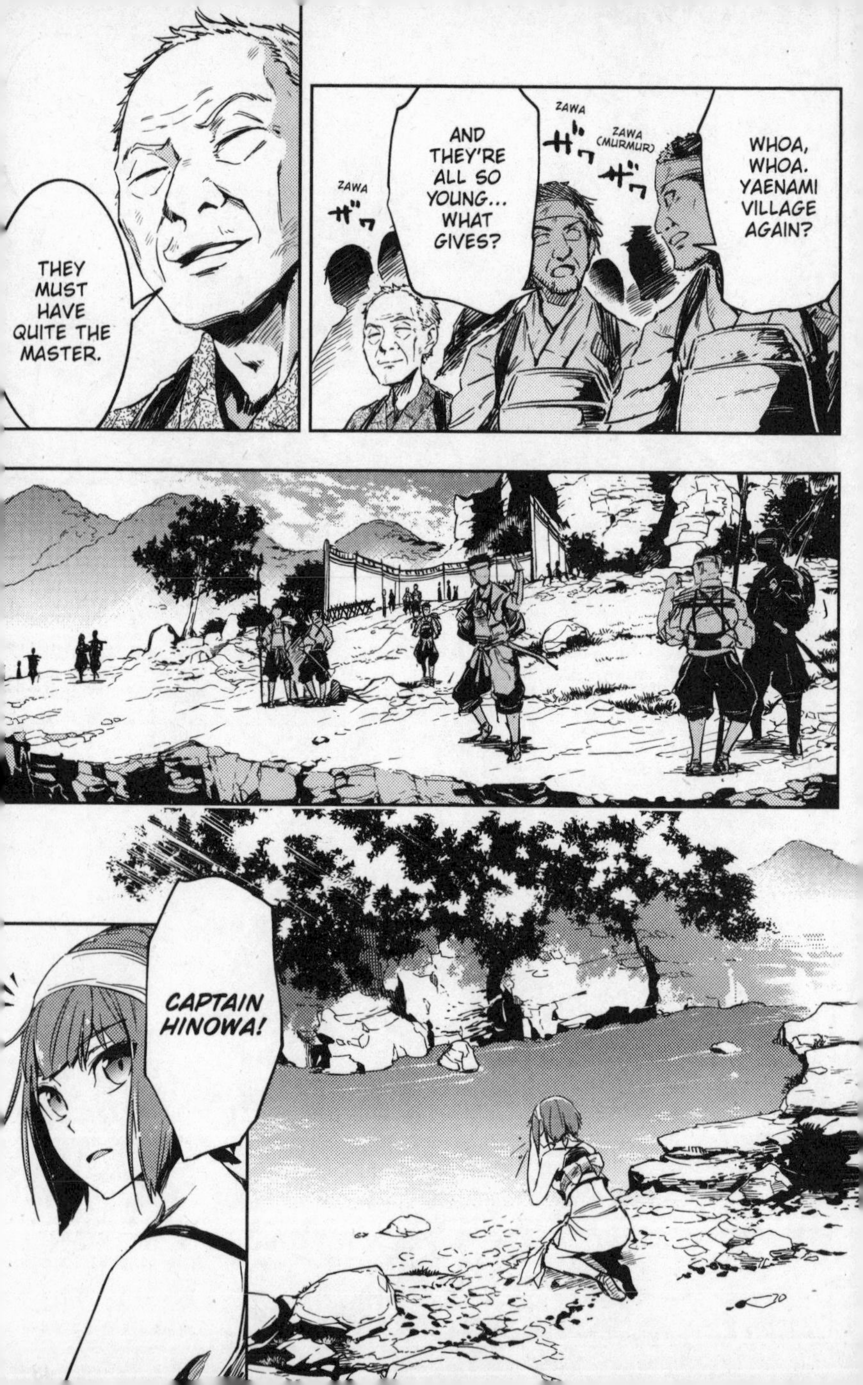
WHOA, WHOA. YAENAMI VILLAGE AGAIN?
ZAWA
ZAWA (MURMUR)
AND THEY'RE ALL SO YOUNG... WHAT GIVES?
ZAWA
THEY MUST HAVE QUITE THE MASTER.
CAPTAIN HINOWA!

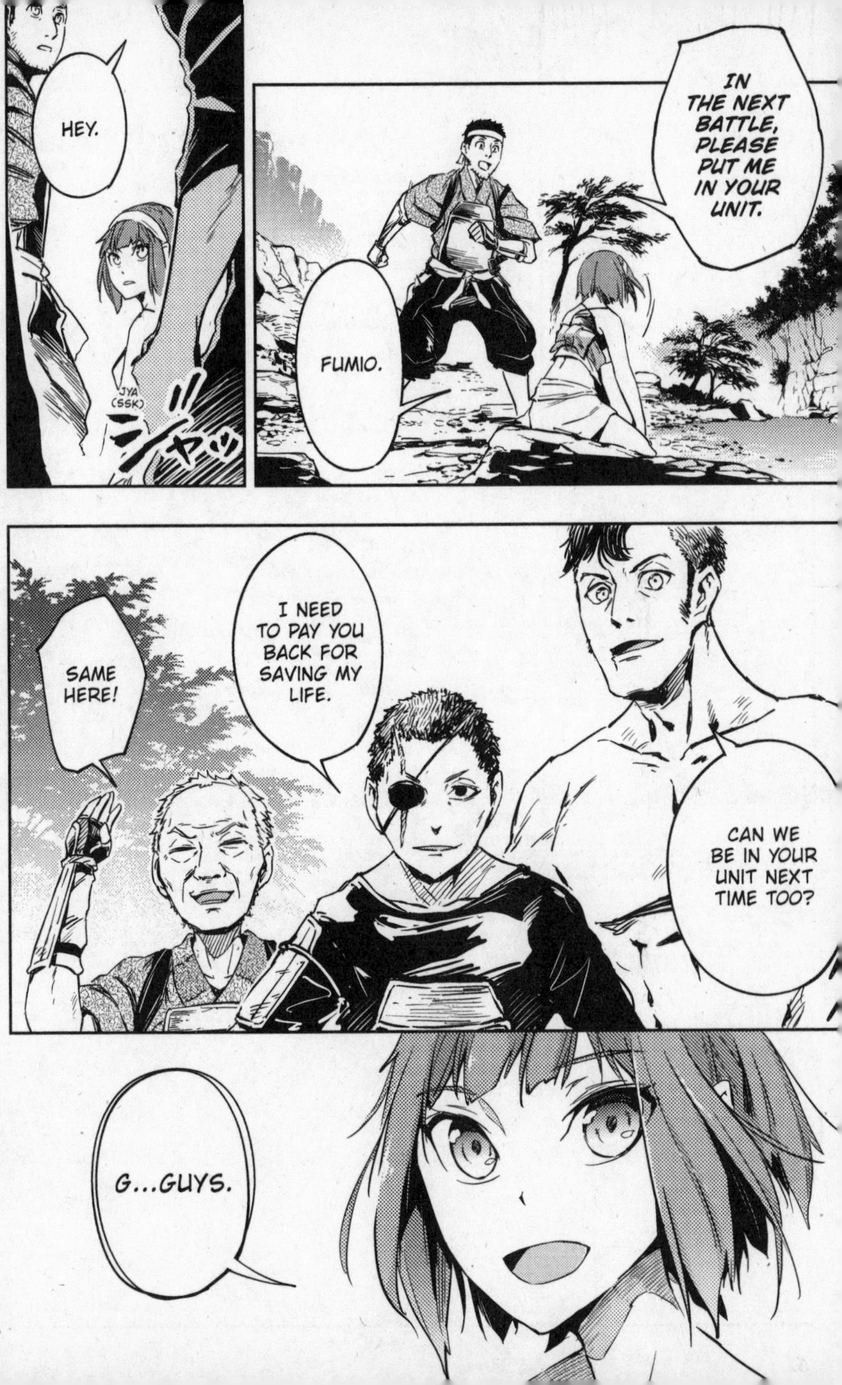
IN THE NEXT BATTLE, PLEASE PUT ME IN YOUR UNIT.
FUMIO.
HEY.
JYA (SSK)
シャッ
CAN WE BE IN YOUR UNIT NEXT TIME TOO?
I NEED TO PAY YOU BACK FOR SAVING MY LIFE.
SAME HERE!
G...GUYS.

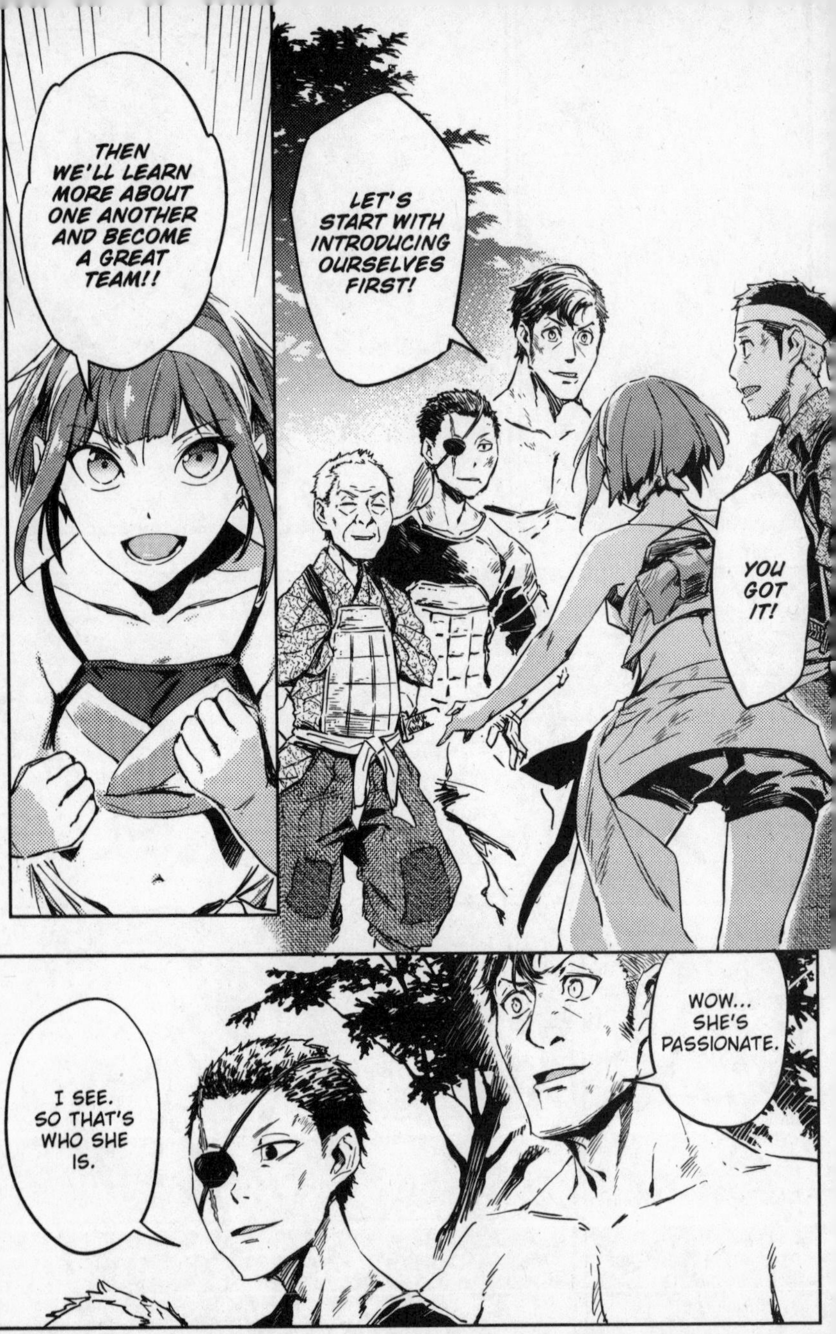
LET'S START WITH INTRODUCING OURSELVES FIRST!
YOU GOT IT!
THEN WE'LL LEARN MORE ABOUT ONE ANOTHER AND BECOME A GREAT TEAM!!
WOW... SHE'S PASSIONATE.
I SEE. SO THAT'S WHO SHE IS.

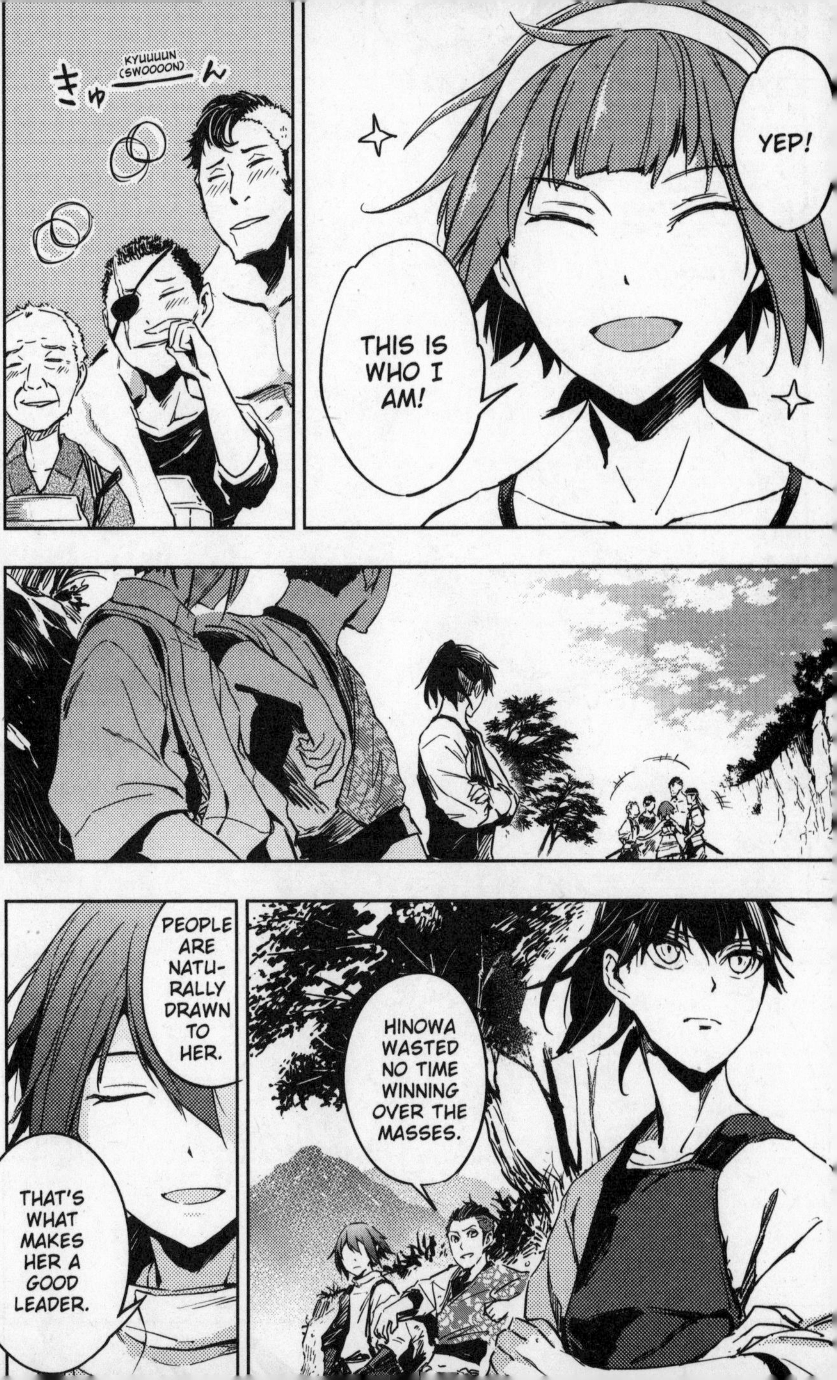
YEP!
THIS IS WHO I AM!
きゅ～ん
KYUUUUN (SWOOOON)
HINOWA WASTED NO TIME WINNING OVER THE MASSES.
PEOPLE ARE NATU-RALLY DRAWN TO HER.
THAT'S WHAT MAKES HER A GOOD LEADER.

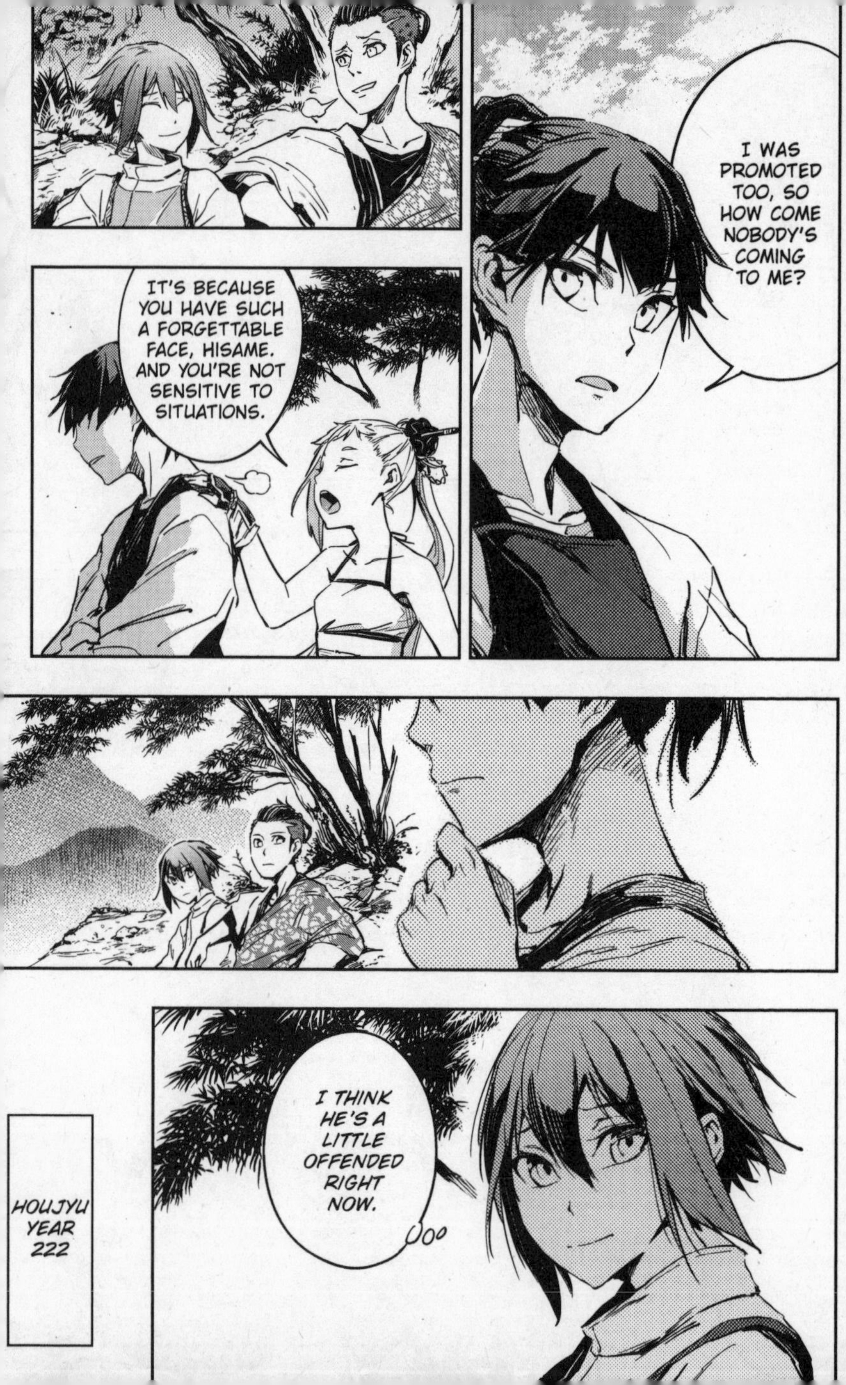
I WAS PROMOTED TOO, SO HOW COME NOBODY'S COMING TO ME?
IT'S BECAUSE YOU HAVE SUCH A FORGETTABLE FACE, HISAME. AND YOU'RE NOT SENSITIVE TO SITUATIONS.
I THINK HE'S A LITTLE OFFENDED RIGHT NOW.
HOUJYU YEAR 222

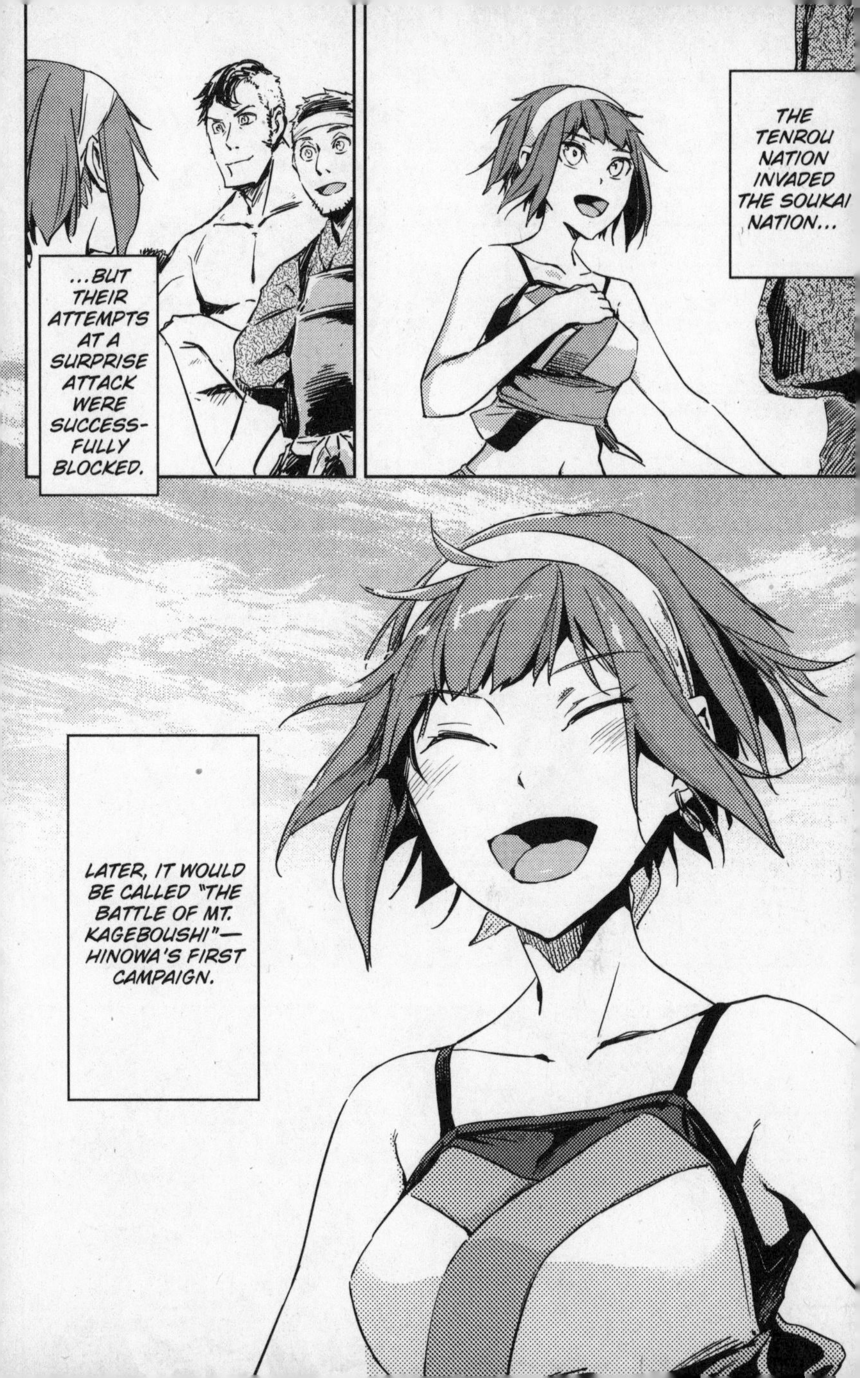
THE TENROU NATION INVADED THE SOUKAI NATION...
...BUT THEIR ATTEMPTS AT A SURPRISE ATTACK WERE SUCCESS-FULLY BLOCKED.
LATER, IT WOULD BE CALLED "THE BATTLE OF MT. KAGEBOUSHI"—HINOWA'S FIRST CAMPAIGN.

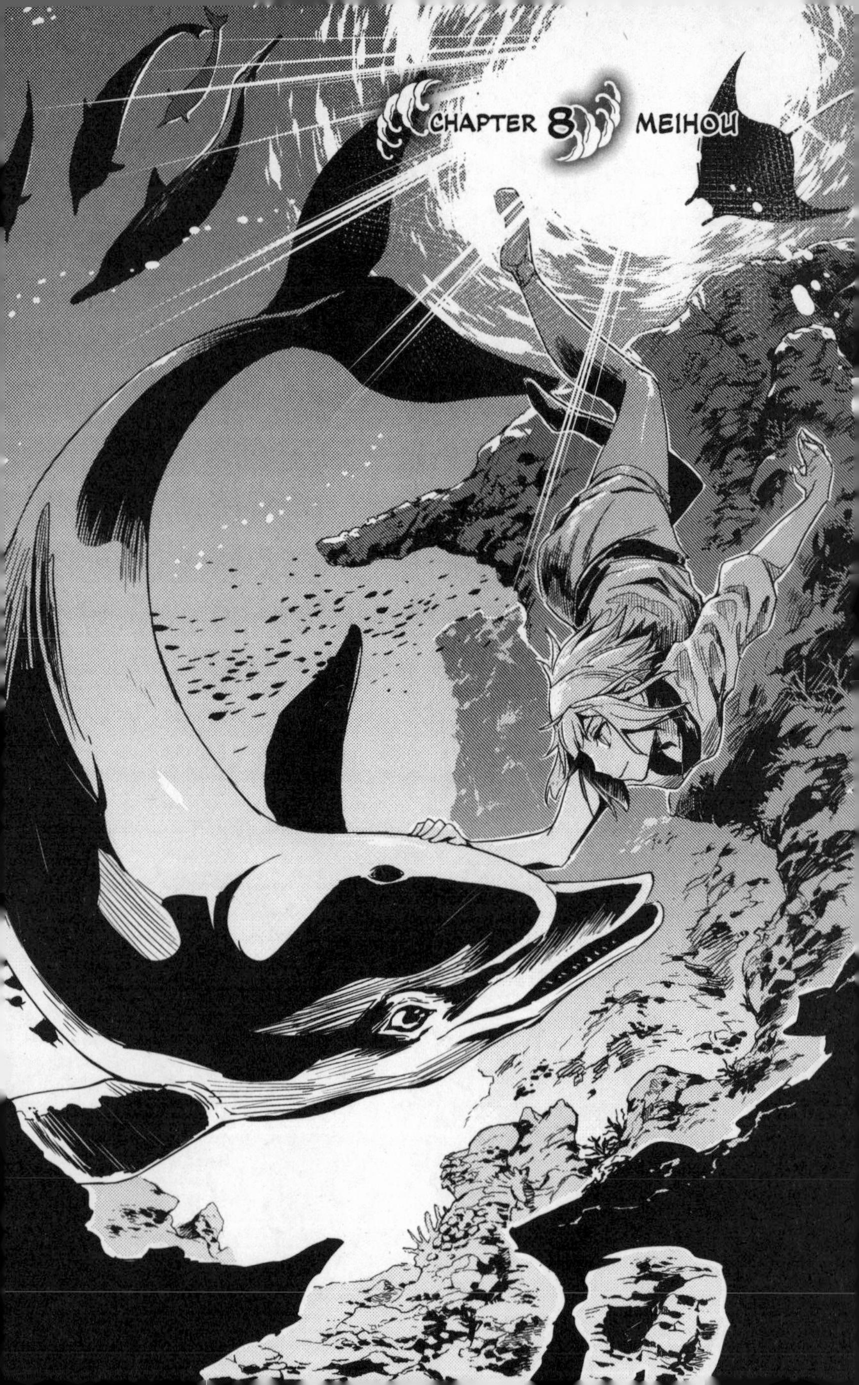
CHAPTER 8 MEIHOU

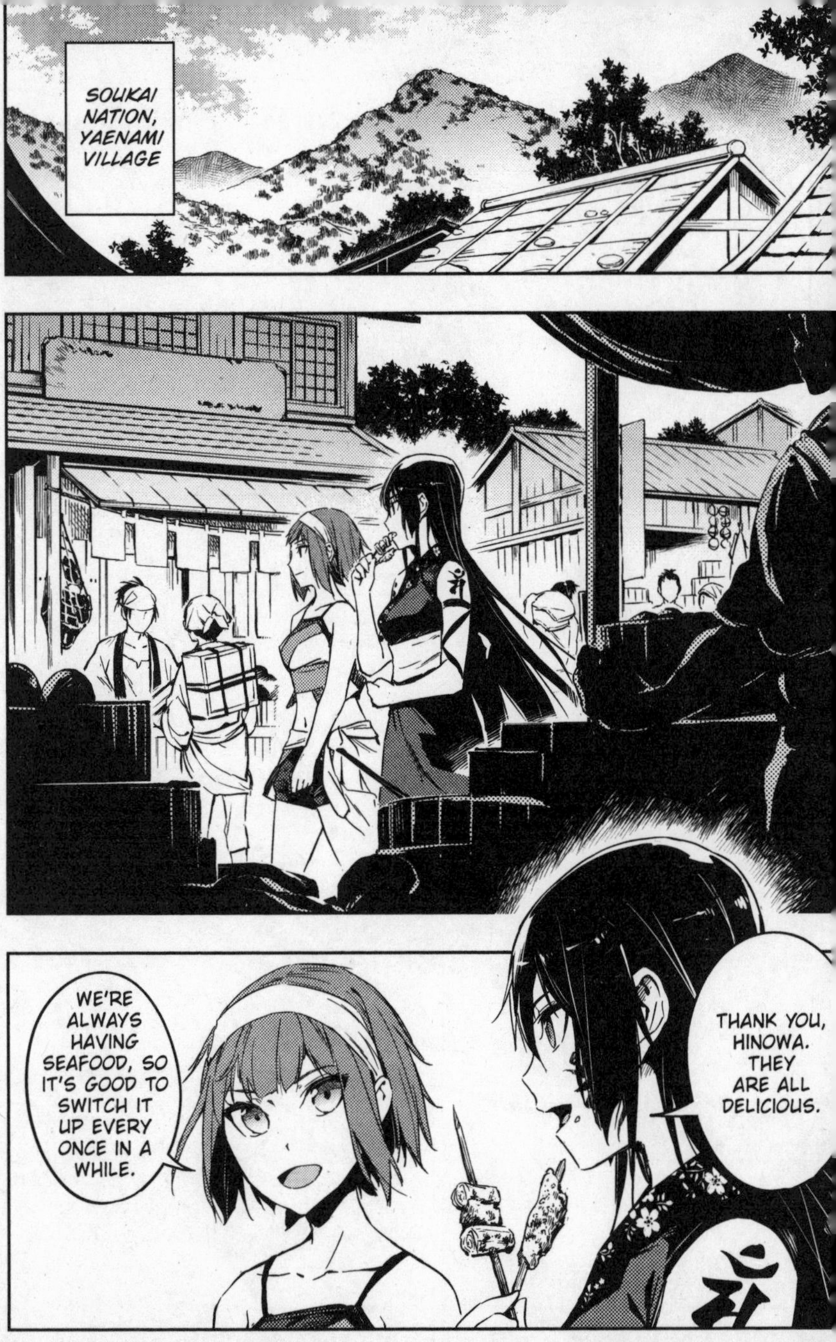
SOUKAI NATION, YAENAMI VILLAGE
THANK YOU, HINOWA. THEY ARE ALL DELICIOUS.
WE'RE ALWAYS HAVING SEAFOOD, SO IT'S GOOD TO SWITCH IT UP EVERY ONCE IN A WHILE.

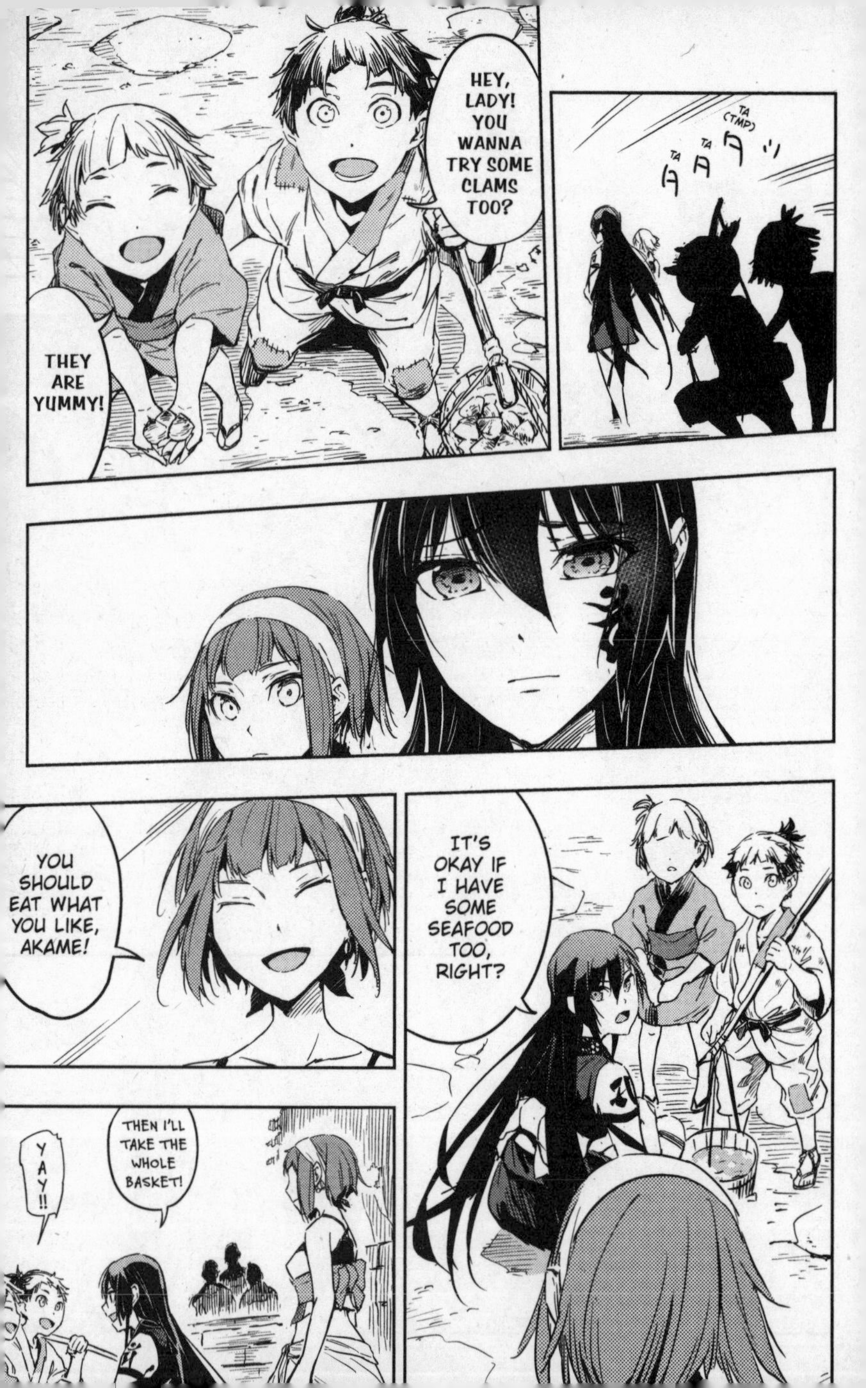

タ TA
タ TA
タッ TA (TMP)
HEY, LADY! YOU WANNA TRY SOME CLAMS TOO?
THEY ARE YUMMY!
IT'S OKAY IF I HAVE SOME SEAFOOD TOO, RIGHT?
YOU SHOULD EAT WHAT YOU LIKE, AKAME!
THEN I'LL TAKE THE WHOLE BASKET!
YAY!!

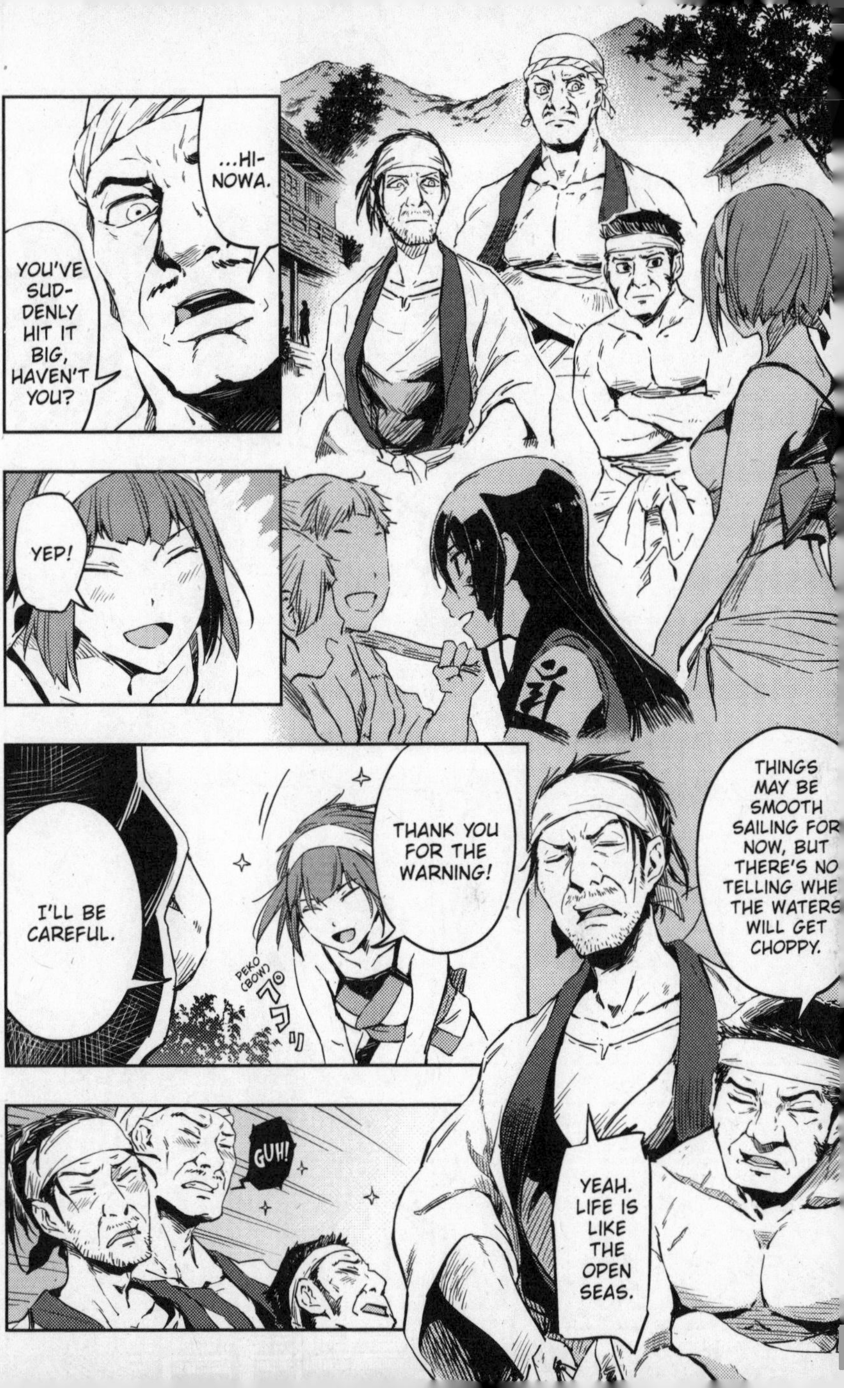
...HI-NOWA.
YOU'VE SUD-DENLY HIT IT BIG, HAVEN'T YOU?
YEP!
THINGS MAY BE SMOOTH SAILING FOR NOW, BUT THERE'S NO TELLING WHE THE WATERS WILL GET CHOPPY.
THANK YOU FOR THE WARNING!
PEKO (BOW)
I'LL BE CAREFUL.
YEAH. LIFE IS LIKE THE OPEN SEAS.
GUH!

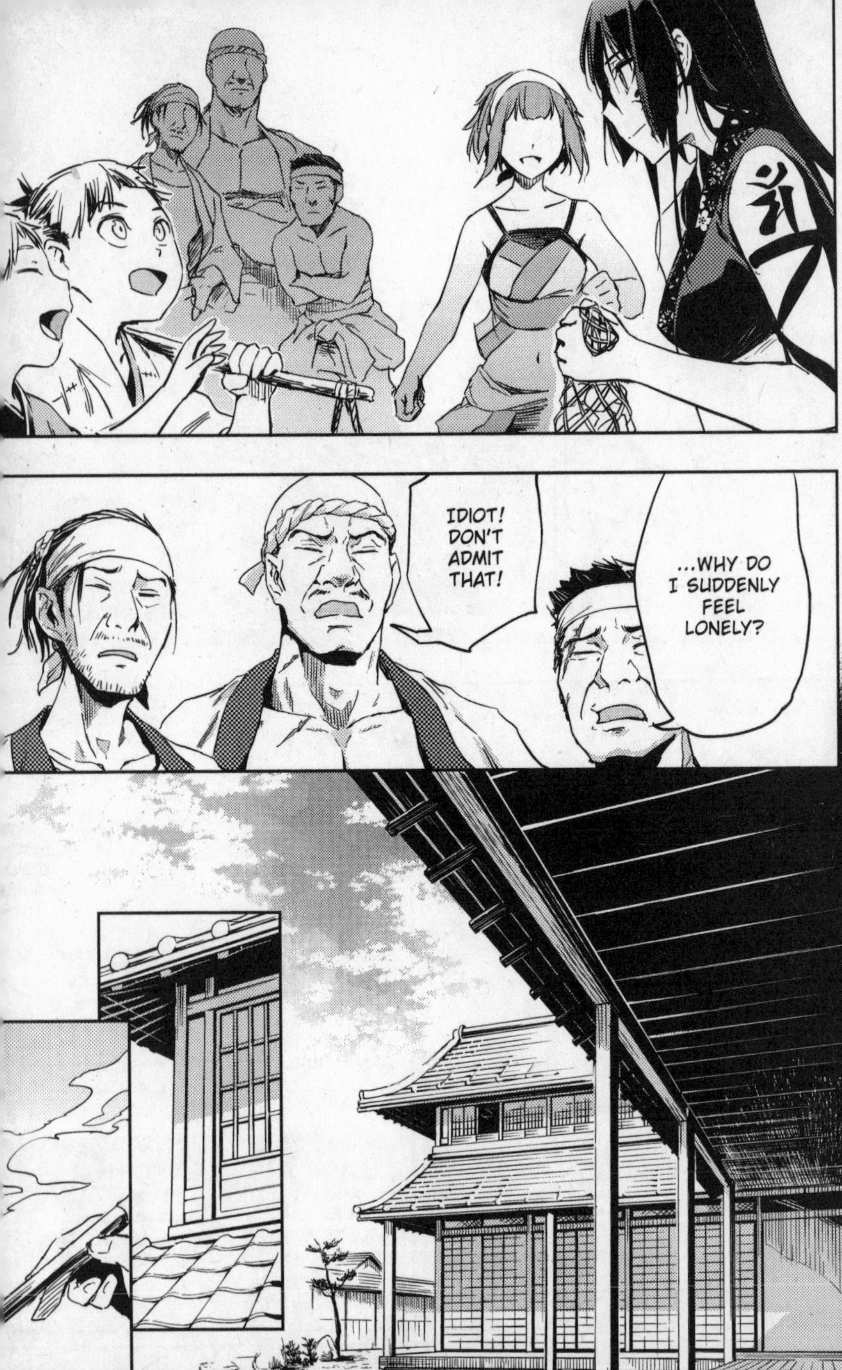
...WHY DO I SUDDENLY FEEL LONELY?
IDIOT! DON'T ADMIT THAT!

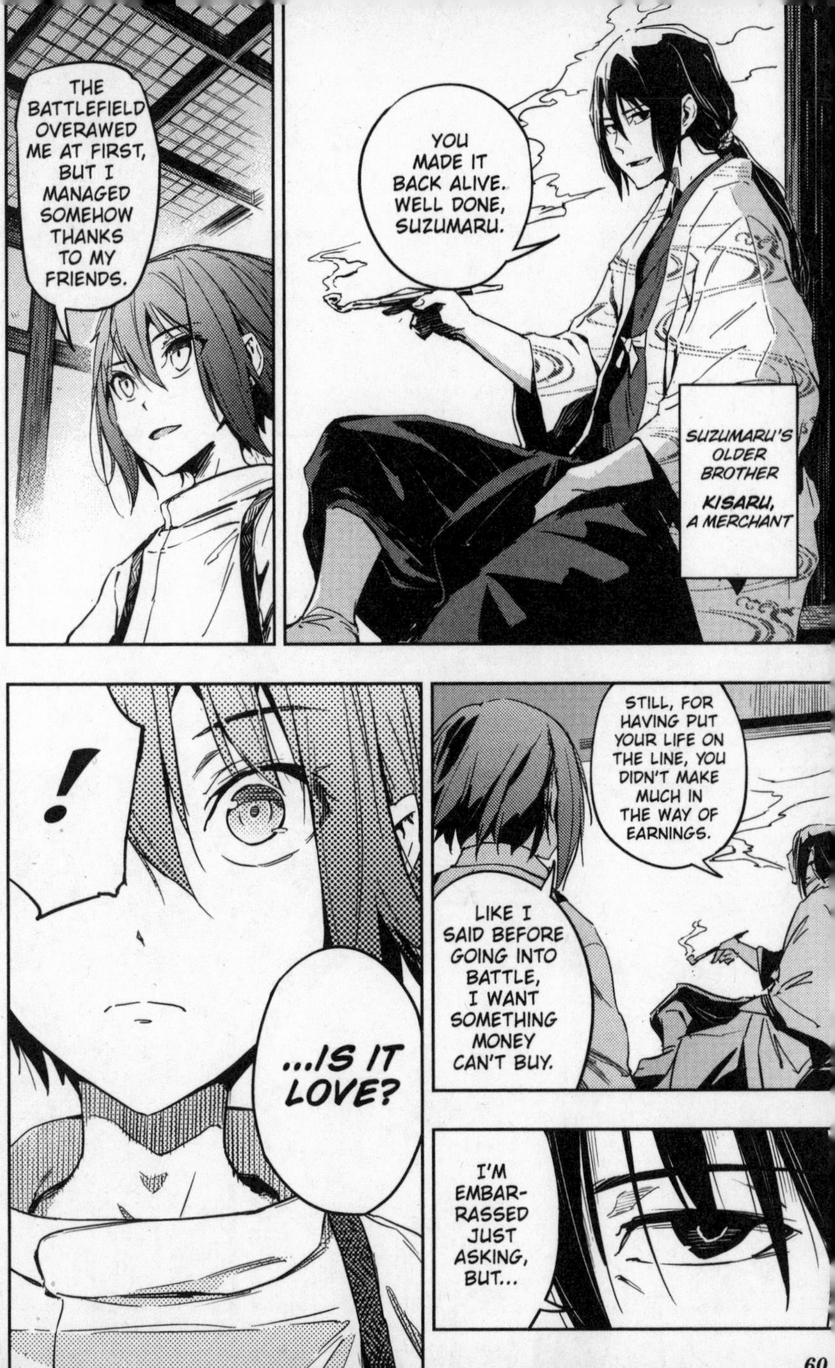
YOU MADE IT BACK ALIVE. WELL DONE, SUZUMARU.
SUZUMARU'S OLDER BROTHER
KISARU, A MERCHANT
THE BATTLEFIELD OVERAWED ME AT FIRST, BUT I MANAGED SOMEHOW THANKS TO MY FRIENDS.
STILL, FOR HAVING PUT YOUR LIFE ON THE LINE, YOU DIDN'T MAKE MUCH IN THE WAY OF EARNINGS.
LIKE I SAID BEFORE GOING INTO BATTLE, I WANT SOMETHING MONEY CAN'T BUY.
I'M EMBAR-RASSED JUST ASKING, BUT...
!
...IS IT LOVE?

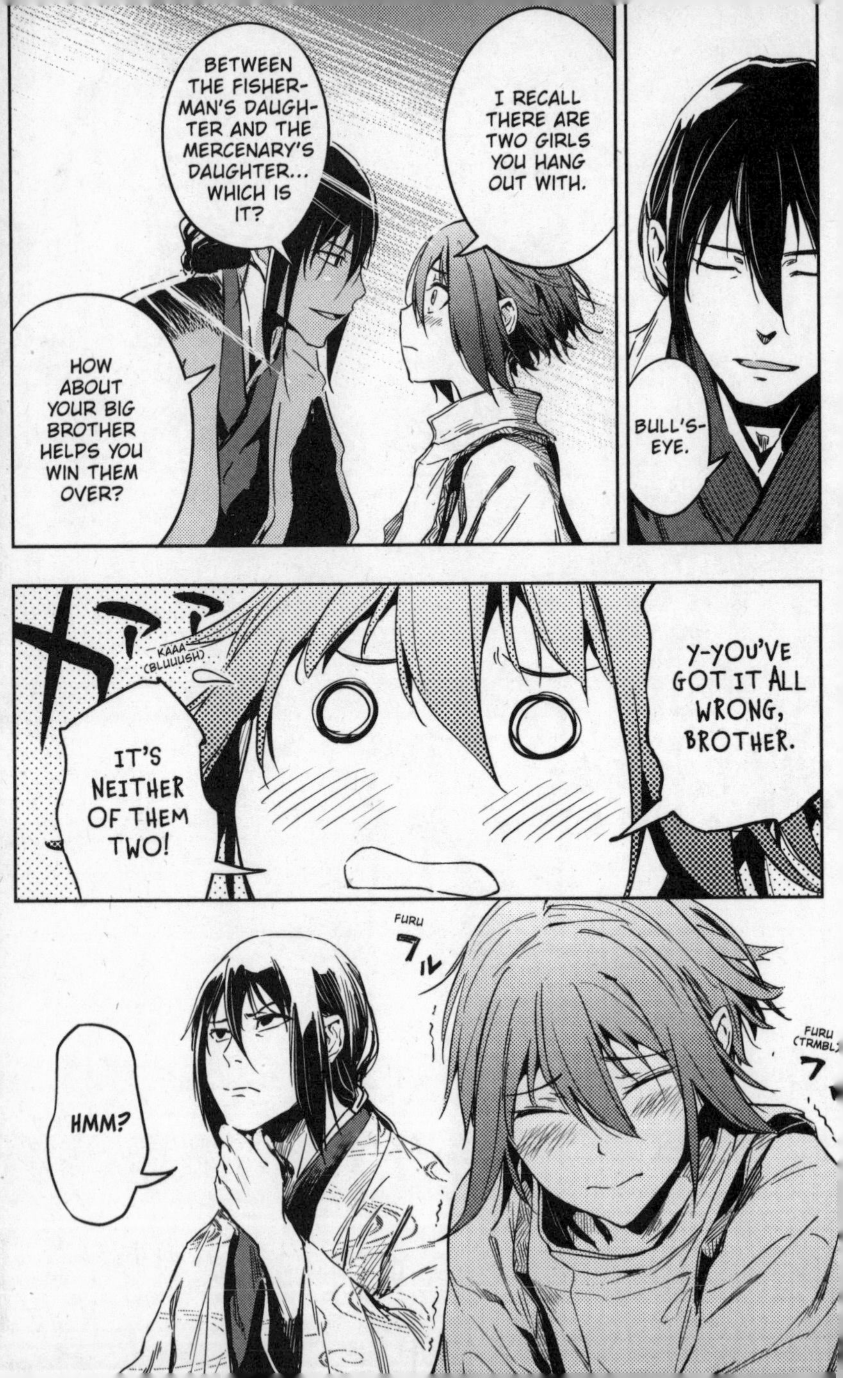
BULL'S-EYE.
I RECALL THERE ARE TWO GIRLS YOU HANG OUT WITH.
BETWEEN THE FISHERMAN'S DAUGHTER AND THE MERCENARY'S DAUGHTER... WHICH IS IT?
HOW ABOUT YOUR BIG BROTHER HELPS YOU WIN THEM OVER?
Y-YOU'VE GOT IT ALL WRONG, BROTHER.
KAAA (BLUUUSH)
IT'S NEITHER OF THEM TWO!
FURU (TRMBL)
FURU
HMM?

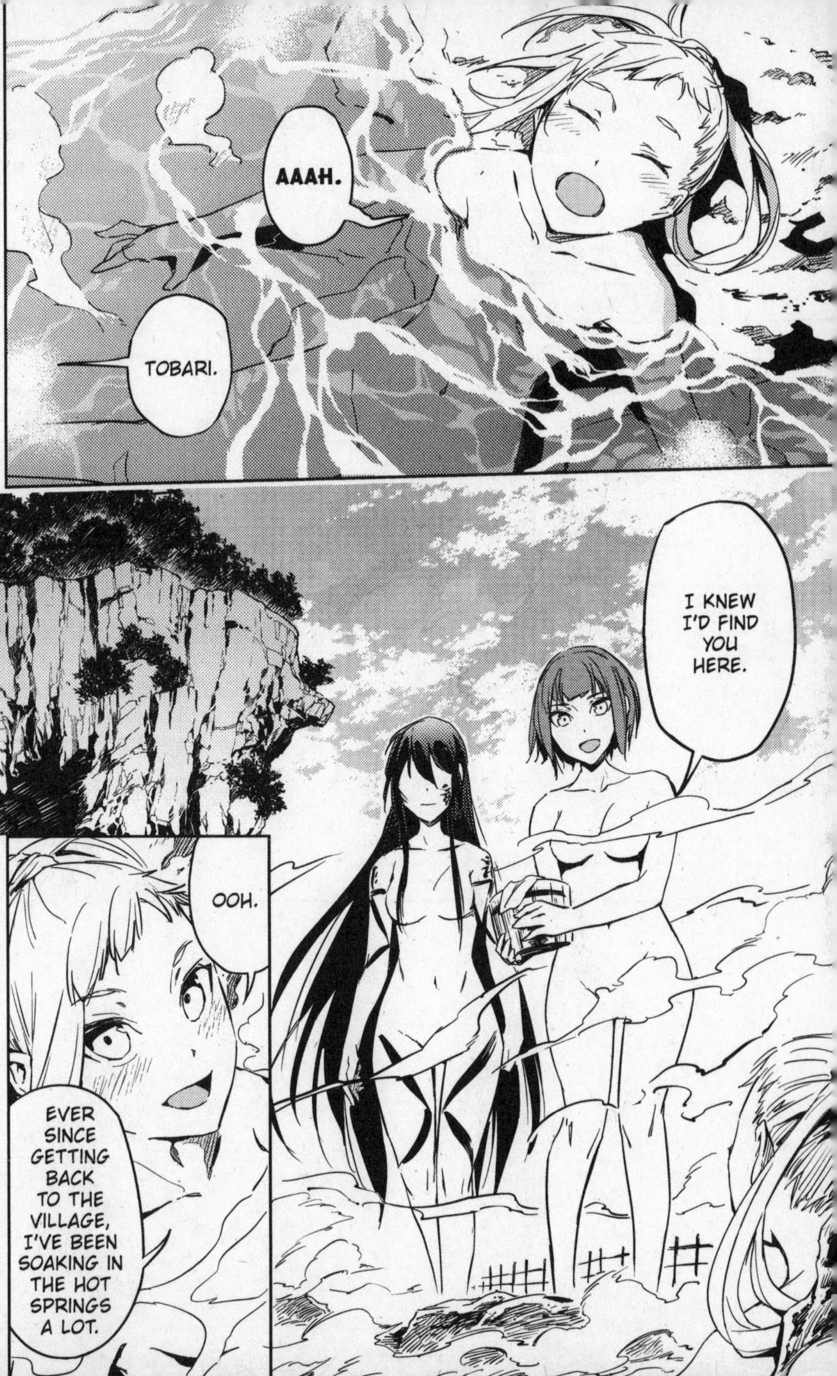
AAAH.
TOBARI.
I KNEW I'D FIND YOU HERE.
OOH.
EVER SINCE GETTING BACK TO THE VILLAGE, I'VE BEEN SOAKING IN THE HOT SPRINGS A LOT.

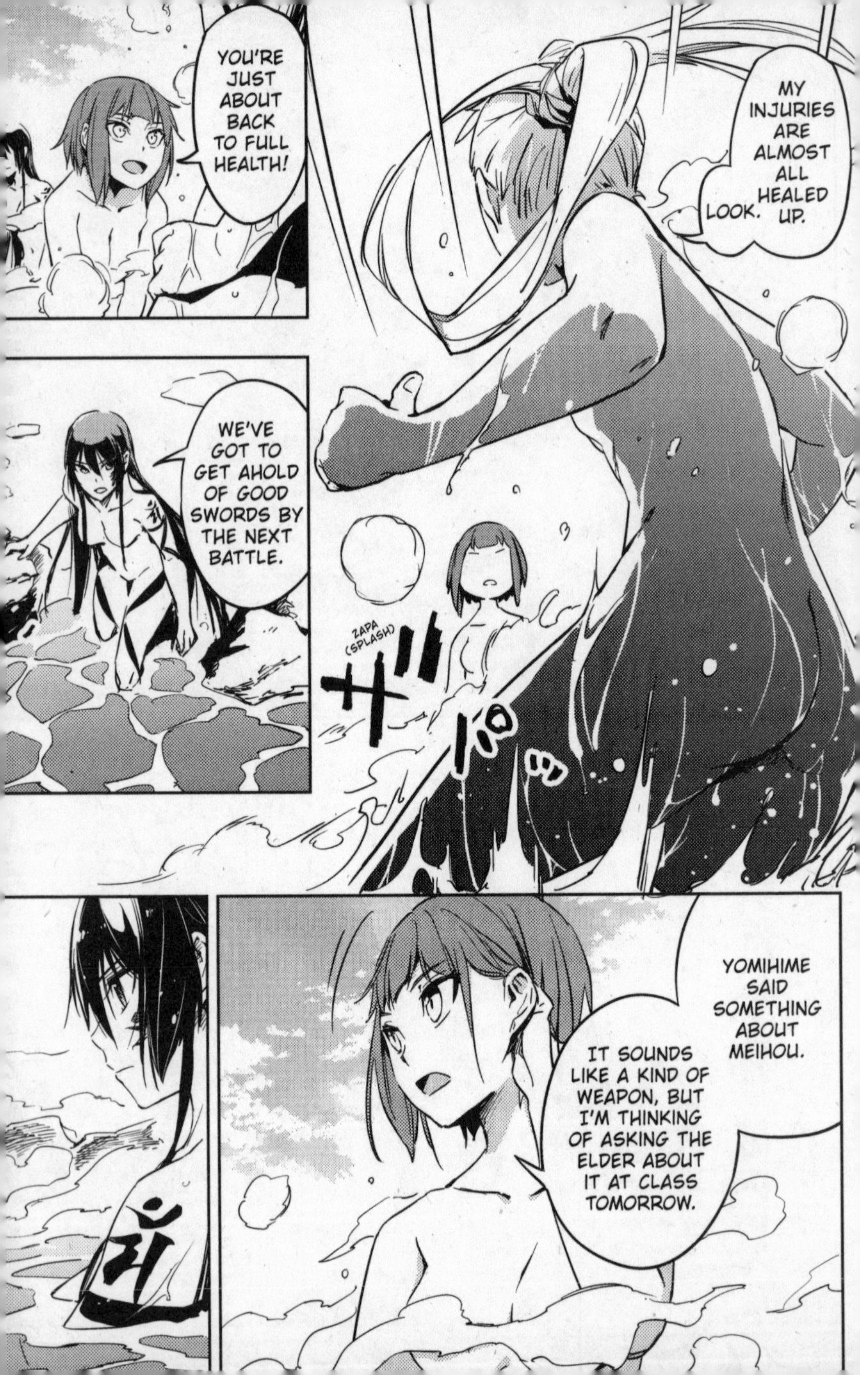
MY INJURIES ARE ALMOST ALL HEALED UP.
LOOK.
ZAPA (SPLASH)
YOU'RE JUST ABOUT BACK TO FULL HEALTH!
WE'VE GOT TO GET AHOLD OF GOOD SWORDS BY THE NEXT BATTLE.
YOMIHIME SAID SOMETHING ABOUT MEIHOU.
IT SOUNDS LIKE A KIND OF WEAPON, BUT I'M THINKING OF ASKING THE ELDER ABOUT IT AT CLASS TOMORROW.

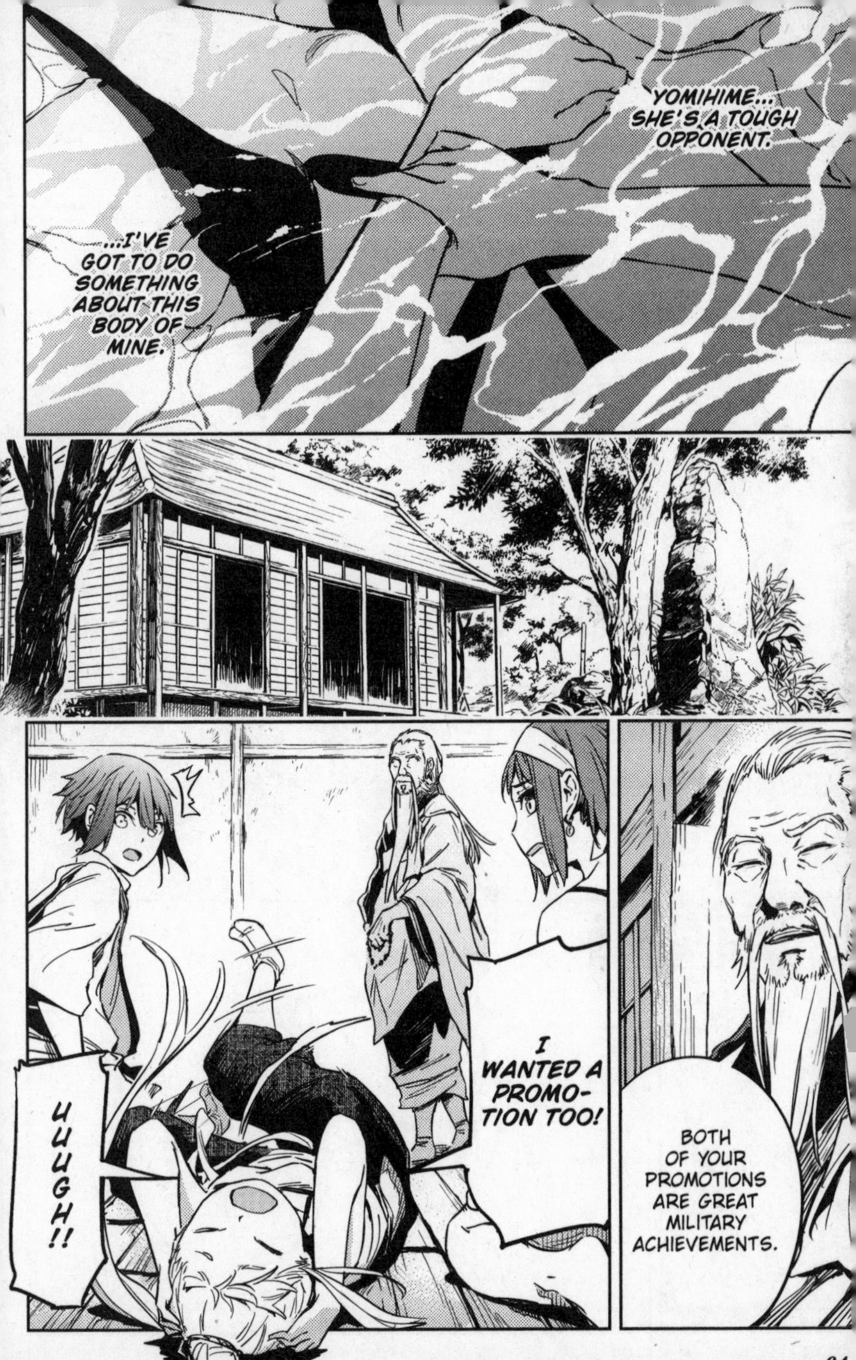
YOMIHIME... SHE'S A TOUGH OPPONENT.
...I'VE GOT TO DO SOMETHING ABOUT THIS BODY OF MINE.
BOTH OF YOUR PROMOTIONS ARE GREAT MILITARY ACHIEVEMENTS.
I WANTED A PROMO-TION TOO!
UUUGH!!

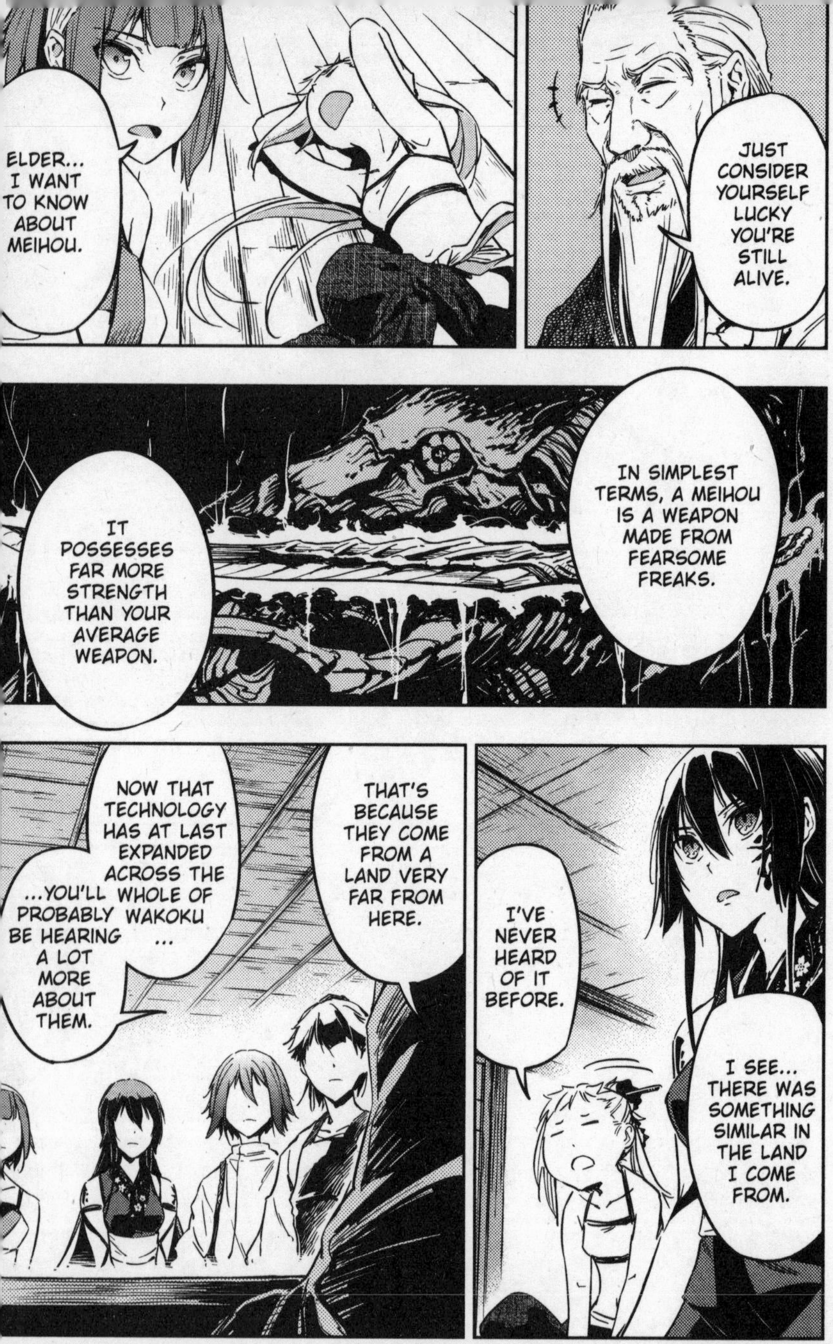
JUST CONSIDER YOURSELF LUCKY YOU'RE STILL ALIVE.
ELDER... I WANT TO KNOW ABOUT MEIHOU.
IN SIMPLEST TERMS, A MEIHOU IS A WEAPON MADE FROM FEARSOME FREAKS.
IT POSSESSES FAR MORE STRENGTH THAN YOUR AVERAGE WEAPON.
I'VE NEVER HEARD OF IT BEFORE.
I SEE... THERE WAS SOMETHING SIMILAR IN THE LAND I COME FROM.
THAT'S BECAUSE THEY COME FROM A LAND VERY FAR FROM HERE.
NOW THAT TECHNOLOGY HAS AT LAST EXPANDED ACROSS THE WHOLE OF WAKOKU ...
...YOU'LL PROBABLY BE HEARING A LOT MORE ABOUT THEM.

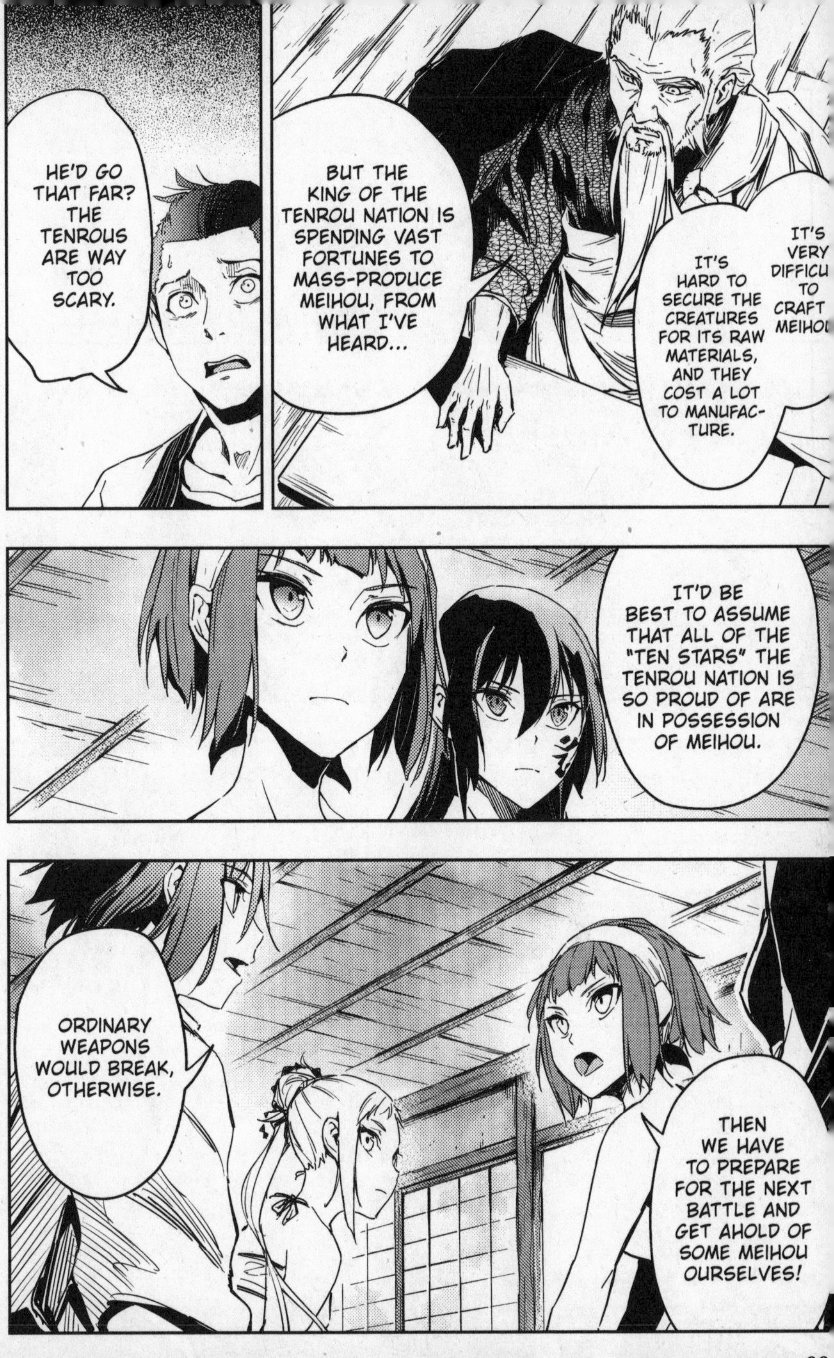
IT'S VERY DIFFICU TO CRAFT MEIHOU
IT'S HARD TO SECURE THE CREATURES FOR ITS RAW MATERIALS, AND THEY COST A LOT TO MANUFAC-TURE.
BUT THE KING OF THE TENROU NATION IS SPENDING VAST FORTUNES TO MASS-PRODUCE MEIHOU, FROM WHAT I'VE HEARD...
HE'D GO THAT FAR? THE TENROUS ARE WAY TOO SCARY.
IT'D BE BEST TO ASSUME THAT ALL OF THE "TEN STARS" THE TENROU NATION IS SO PROUD OF ARE IN POSSESSION OF MEIHOU.
THEN WE HAVE TO PREPARE FOR THE NEXT BATTLE AND GET AHOLD OF SOME MEIHOU OURSELVES!
ORDINARY WEAPONS WOULD BREAK, OTHERWISE.

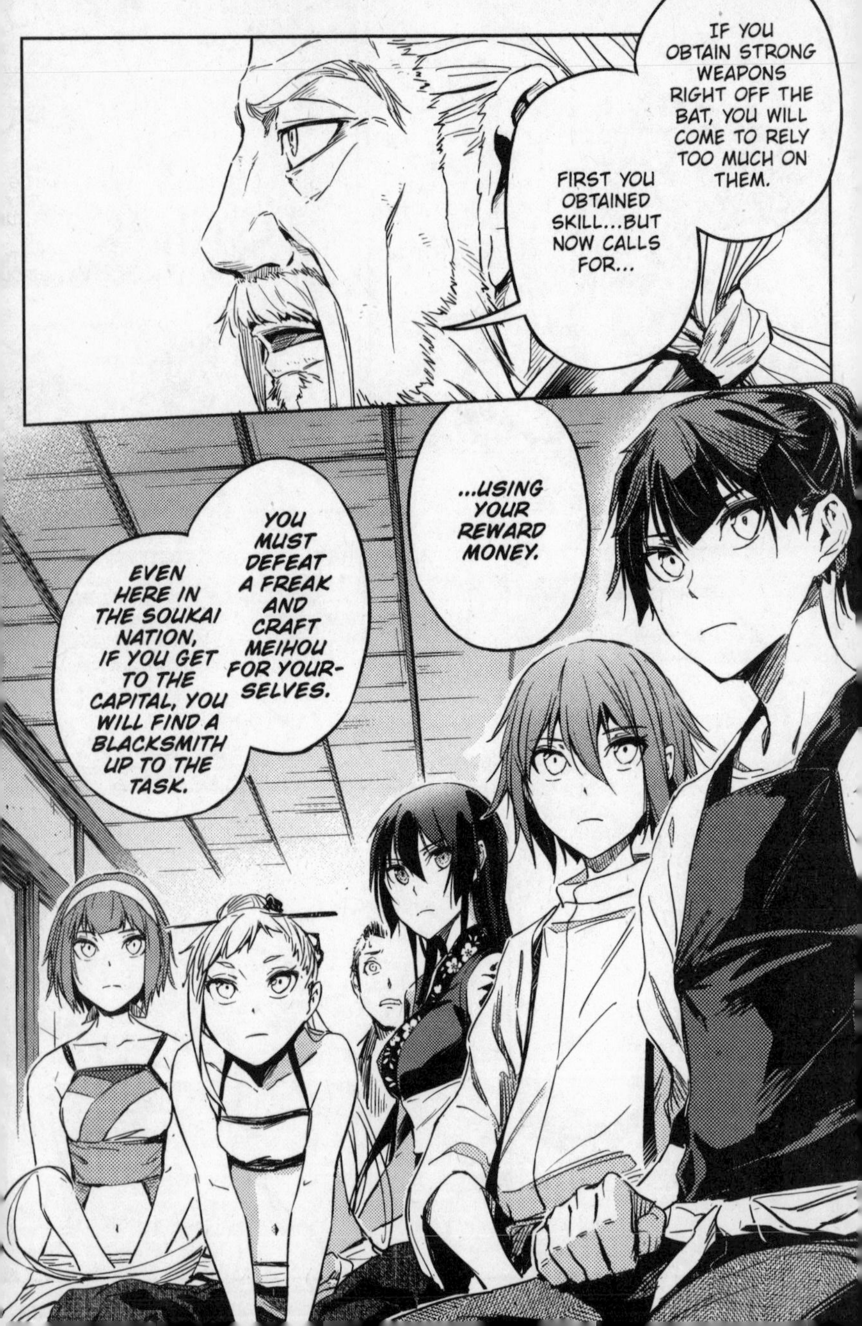
IF YOU OBTAIN STRONG WEAPONS RIGHT OFF THE BAT, YOU WILL COME TO RELY TOO MUCH ON THEM.
FIRST YOU OBTAINED SKILL...BUT NOW CALLS FOR...
...USING YOUR REWARD MONEY.
YOU MUST DEFEAT A FREAK AND CRAFT MEIHOU FOR YOUR-SELVES.
EVEN HERE IN THE SOUKAI NATION, IF YOU GET TO THE CAPITAL, YOU WILL FIND A BLACKSMITH UP TO THE TASK.

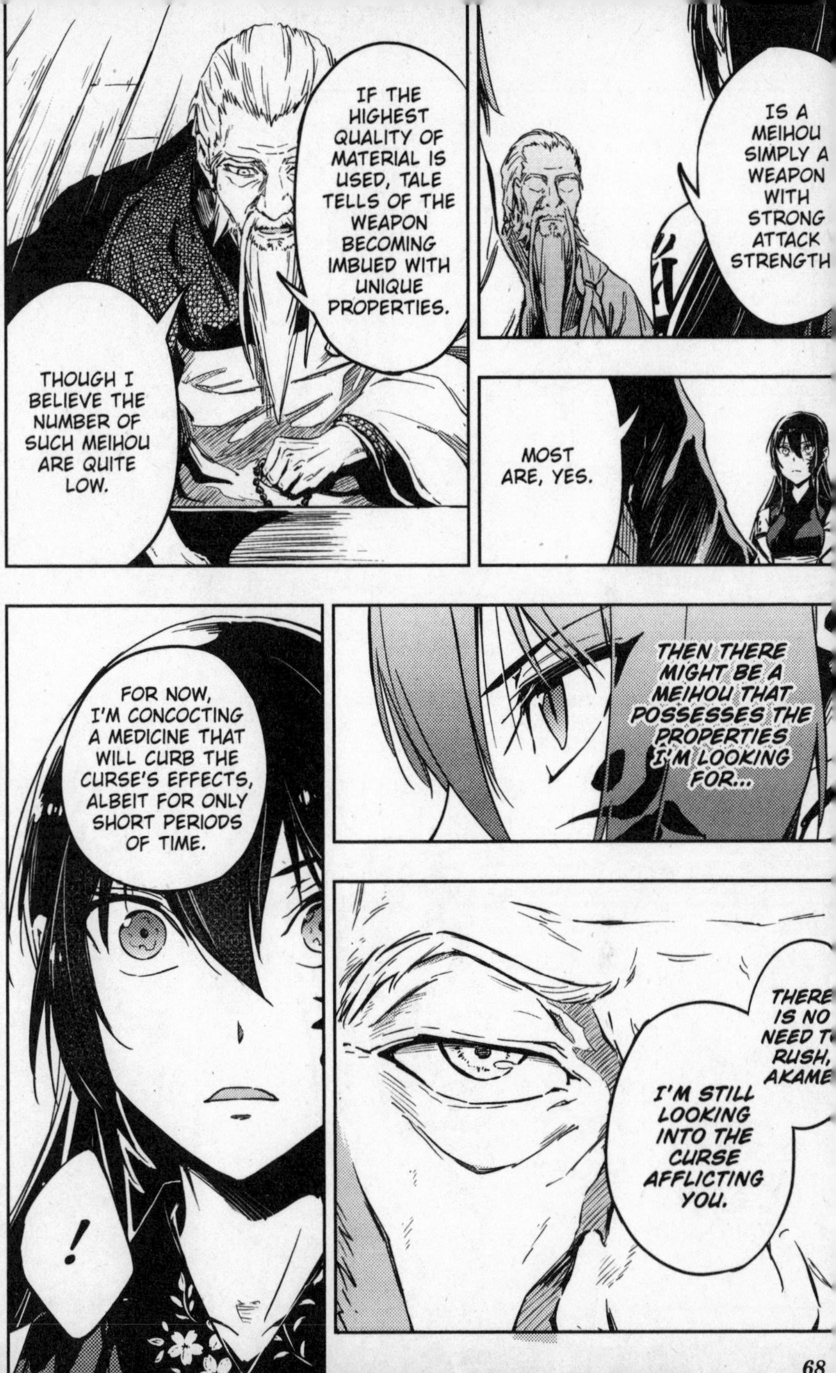
IS A MEIHOU SIMPLY A WEAPON WITH STRONG ATTACK STRENGTH
MOST ARE, YES.
IF THE HIGHEST QUALITY OF MATERIAL IS USED, TALE TELLS OF THE WEAPON BECOMING IMBUED WITH UNIQUE PROPERTIES.
THOUGH I BELIEVE THE NUMBER OF SUCH MEIHOU ARE QUITE LOW.
THEN THERE MIGHT BE A MEIHOU THAT POSSESSES THE PROPERTIES I'M LOOKING FOR...
THERE IS NO NEED T RUSH, AKAME
I'M STILL LOOKING INTO THE CURSE AFFLICTING YOU.
FOR NOW, I'M CONCOCTING A MEDICINE THAT WILL CURB THE CURSE'S EFFECTS, ALBEIT FOR ONLY SHORT PERIODS OF TIME.
!

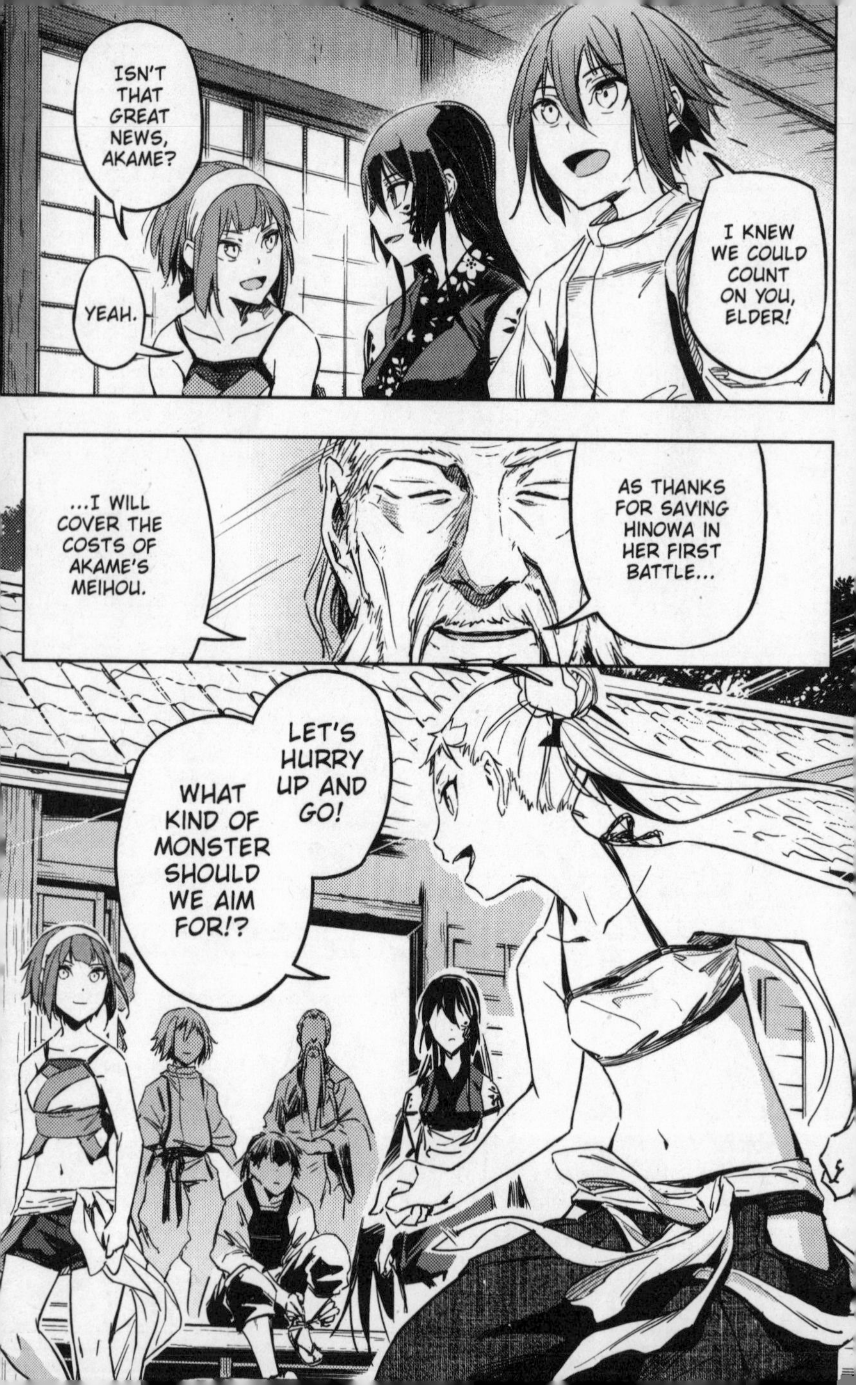
I KNEW WE COULD COUNT ON YOU, ELDER!
ISN'T THAT GREAT NEWS, AKAME?
YEAH.
AS THANKS FOR SAVING HINOWA IN HER FIRST BATTLE...
...I WILL COVER THE COSTS OF AKAME'S MEIHOU.
LET'S HURRY UP AND GO!
WHAT KIND OF MONSTER SHOULD WE AIM FOR!?

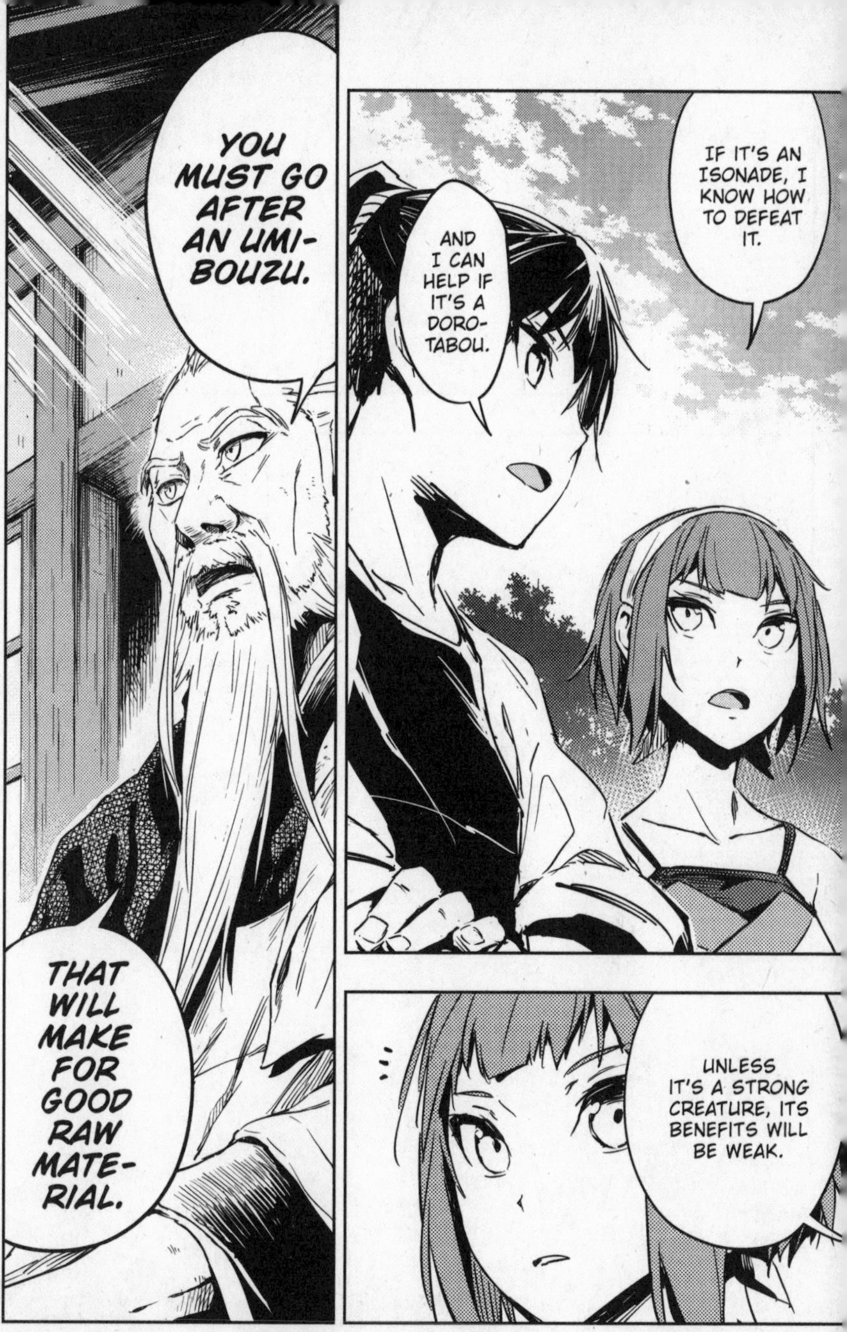
IF IT'S AN ISONADE, I KNOW HOW TO DEFEAT IT.
AND I CAN HELP IF IT'S A DORO-TABOU.
...
UNLESS IT'S A STRONG CREATURE, ITS BENEFITS WILL BE WEAK.
YOU MUST GO AFTER AN UMI-BOUZU.
THAT WILL MAKE FOR GOOD RAW MATE-RIAL.

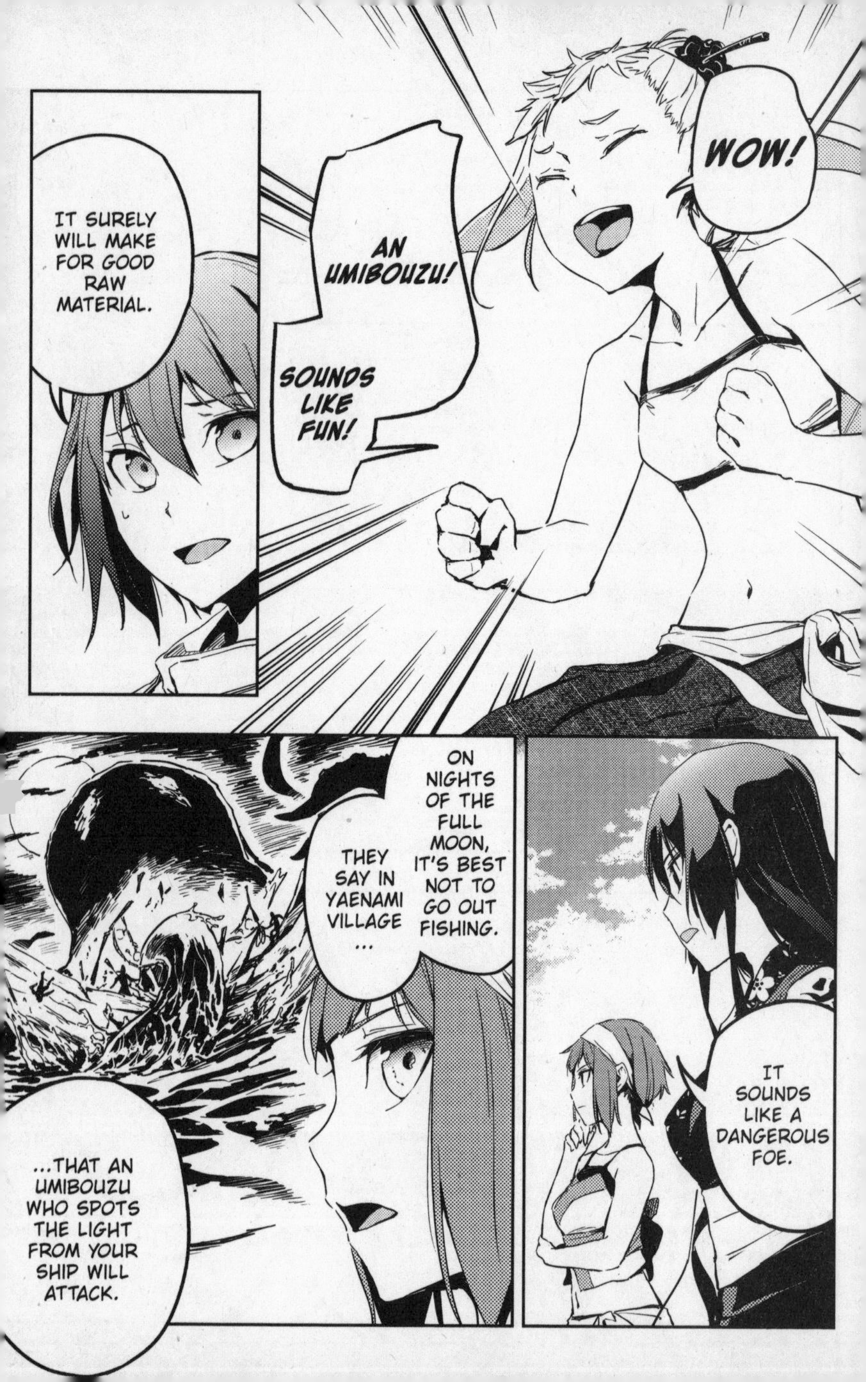
WOW!
AN UMIBOUZU!
SOUNDS LIKE FUN!
IT SURELY WILL MAKE FOR GOOD RAW MATERIAL.
IT SOUNDS LIKE A DANGEROUS FOE.
ON NIGHTS OF THE FULL MOON, IT'S BEST NOT TO GO OUT FISHING.
THEY SAY IN YAENAMI VILLAGE...
...THAT AN UMIBOUZU WHO SPOTS THE LIGHT FROM YOUR SHIP WILL ATTACK.

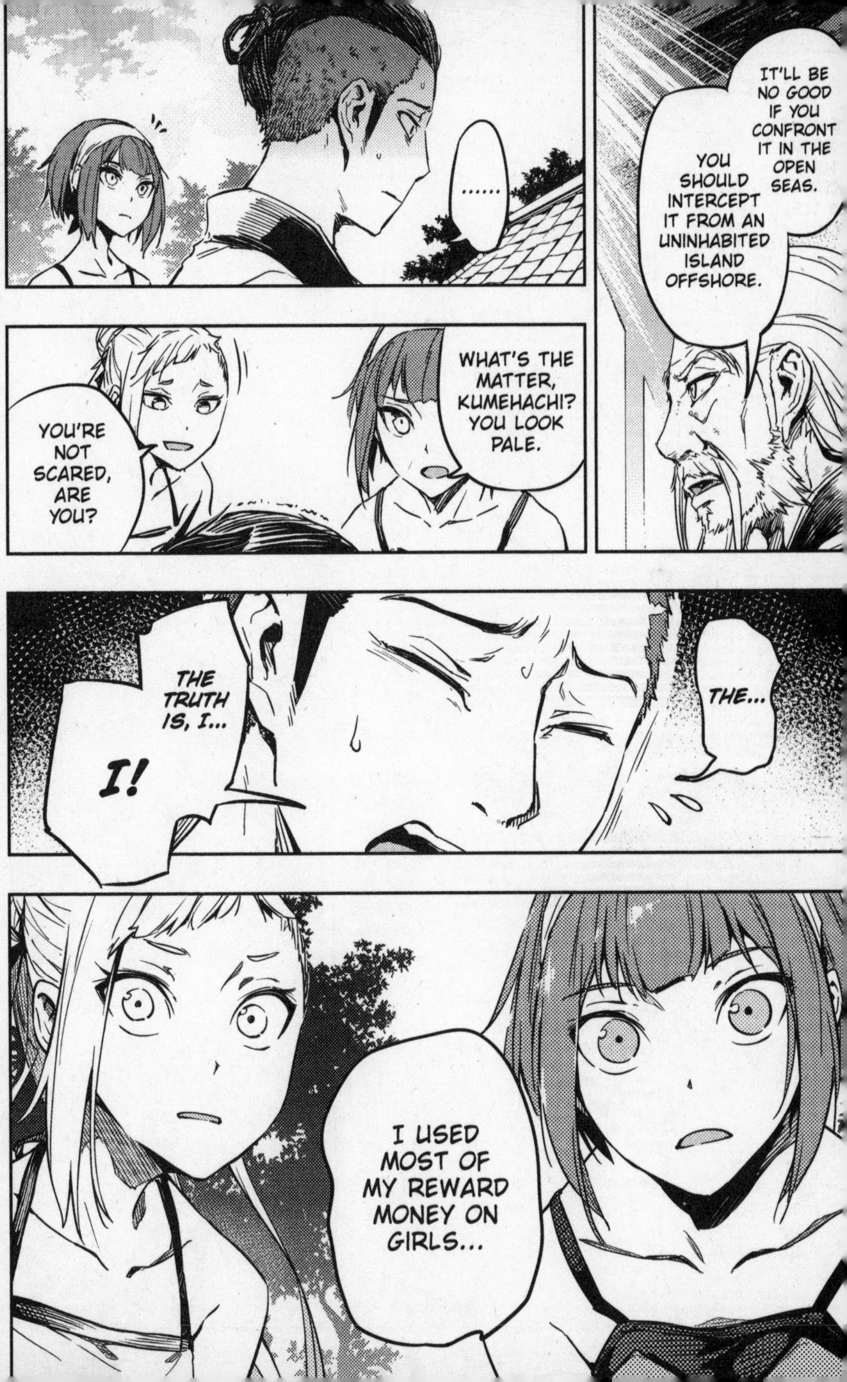
IT'LL BE NO GOOD IF YOU CONFRONT IT IN THE OPEN SEAS.
YOU SHOULD INTERCEPT IT FROM AN UNINHABITED ISLAND OFFSHORE.
......
WHAT'S THE MATTER, KUMEHACHI? YOU LOOK PALE.
YOU'RE NOT SCARED, ARE YOU?
THE...
THE TRUTH IS, I...
I!
I USED MOST OF MY REWARD MONEY ON GIRLS...

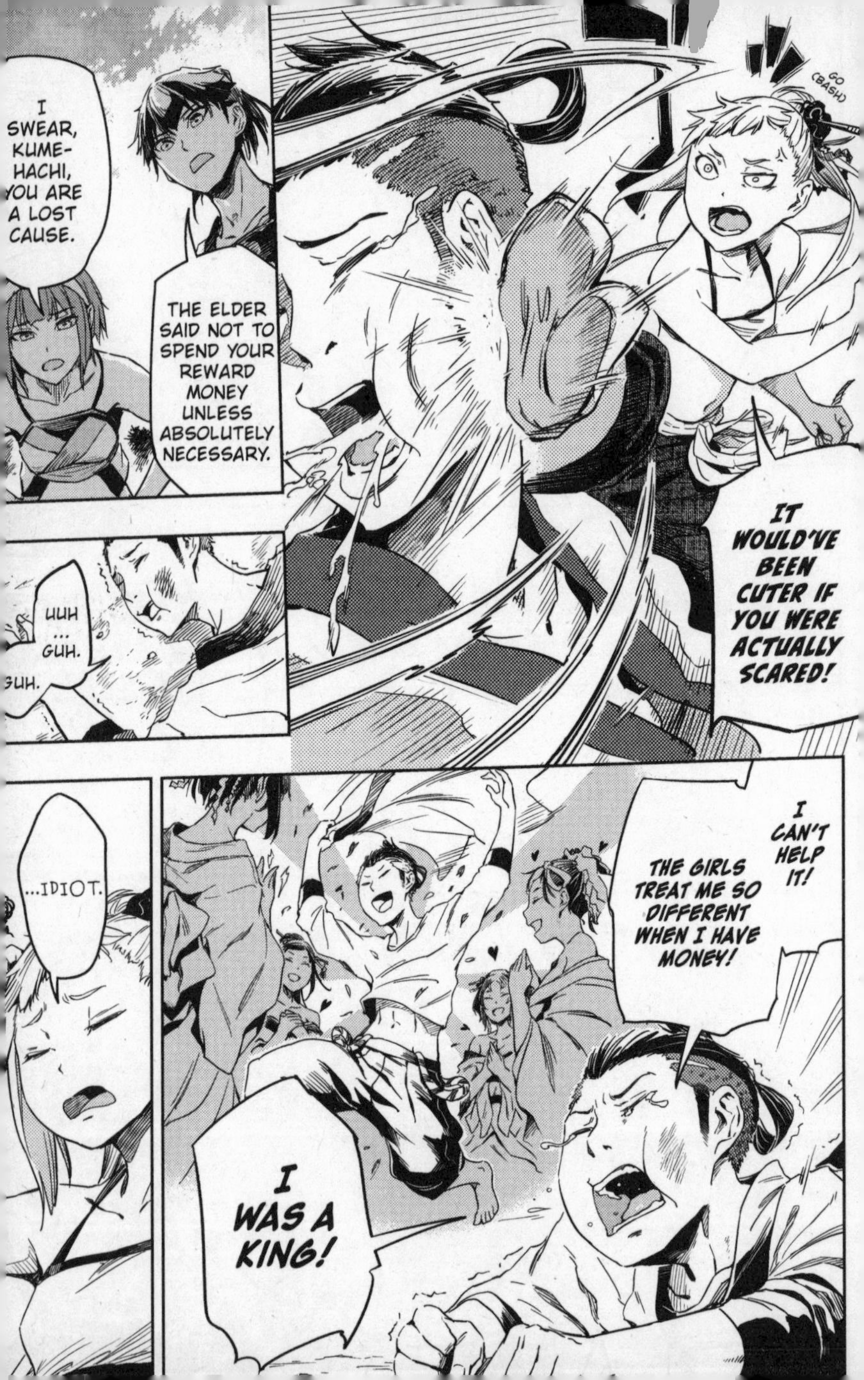
GO (BASH)
IT WOULD'VE BEEN CUTER IF YOU WERE ACTUALLY SCARED!
THE ELDER SAID NOT TO SPEND YOUR REWARD MONEY UNLESS ABSOLUTELY NECESSARY.
I SWEAR, KUME-HACHI, YOU ARE A LOST CAUSE.
UUH ... GUH. GUH.
I CAN'T HELP IT!
THE GIRLS TREAT ME SO DIFFERENT WHEN I HAVE MONEY!
I WAS A KING!
...IDIOT.

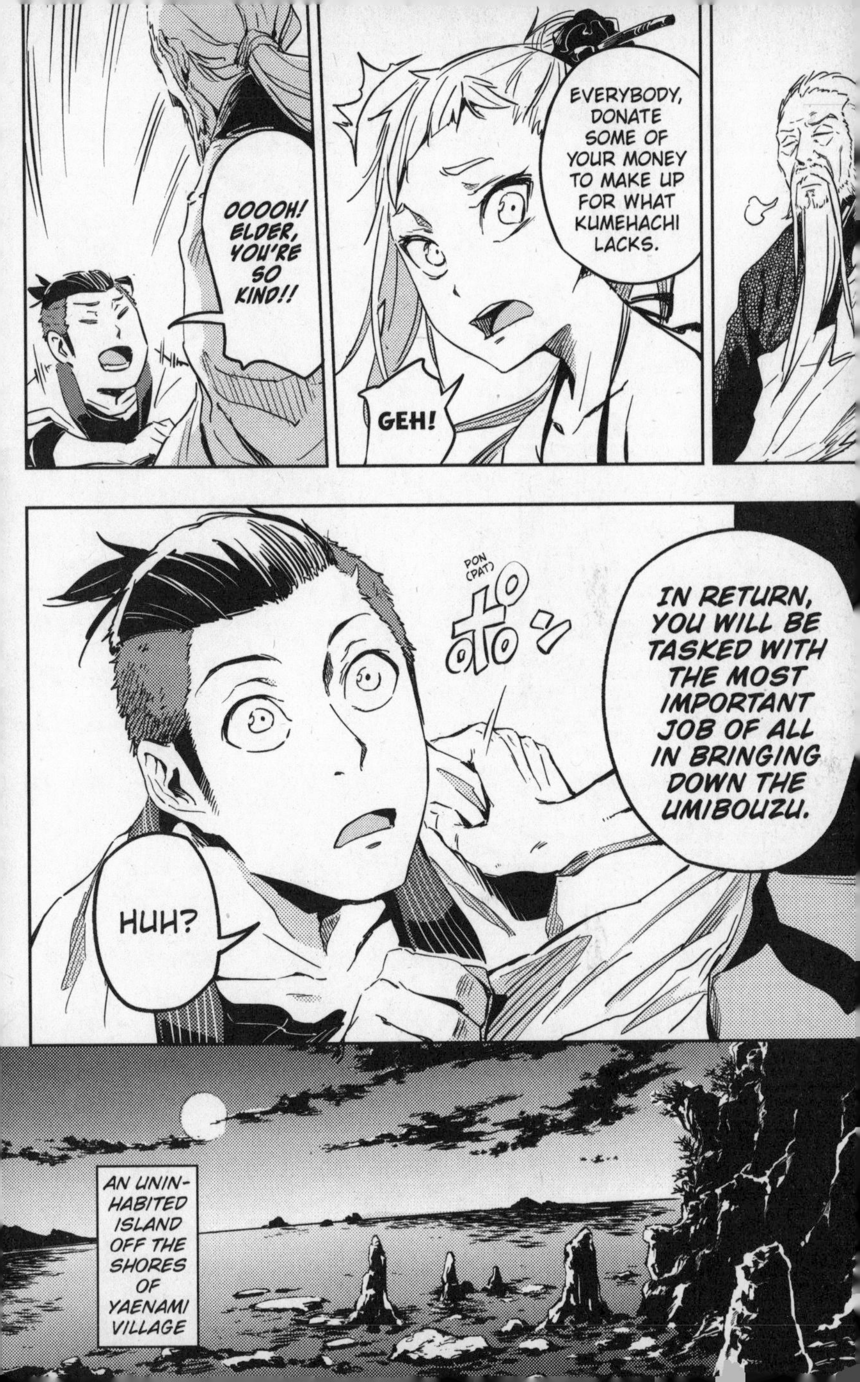
EVERYBODY, DONATE SOME OF YOUR MONEY TO MAKE UP FOR WHAT KUMEHACHI LACKS.
GEH!
OOOOH! ELDER, YOU'RE SO KIND!!
IN RETURN, YOU WILL BE TASKED WITH THE MOST IMPORTANT JOB OF ALL IN BRINGING DOWN THE UMIBOUZU.
PON (PAT)
HUH?
AN UNINHABITED ISLAND OFF THE SHORES OF YAENAMI VILLAGE

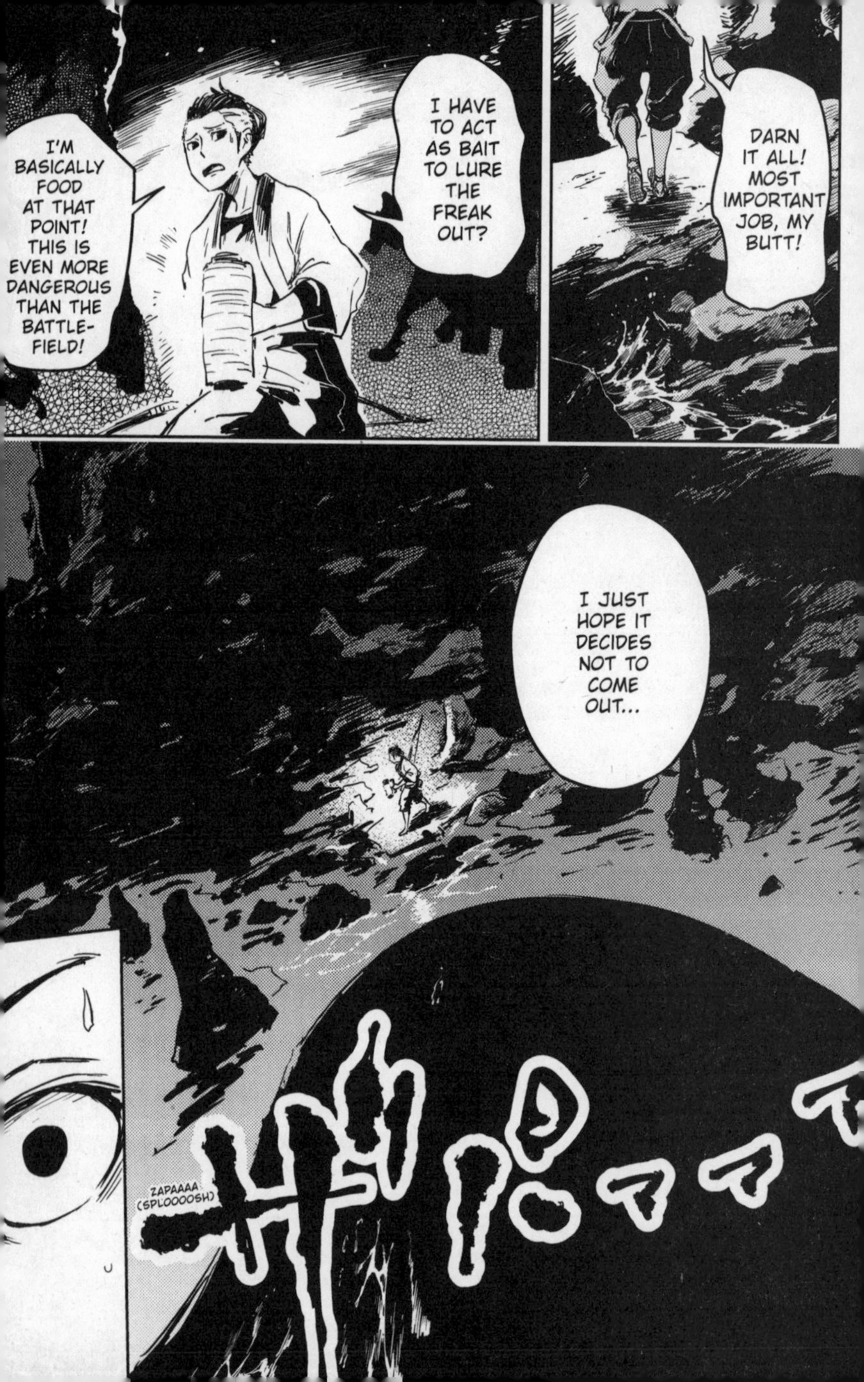
DARN IT ALL! MOST IMPORTANT JOB, MY BUTT!
I HAVE TO ACT AS BAIT TO LURE THE FREAK OUT?
I'M BASICALLY FOOD AT THAT POINT! THIS IS EVEN MORE DANGEROUS THAN THE BATTLEFIELD!
I JUST HOPE IT DECIDES NOT TO COME OUT...
ZAPAAAA (SPLOOOOSH)

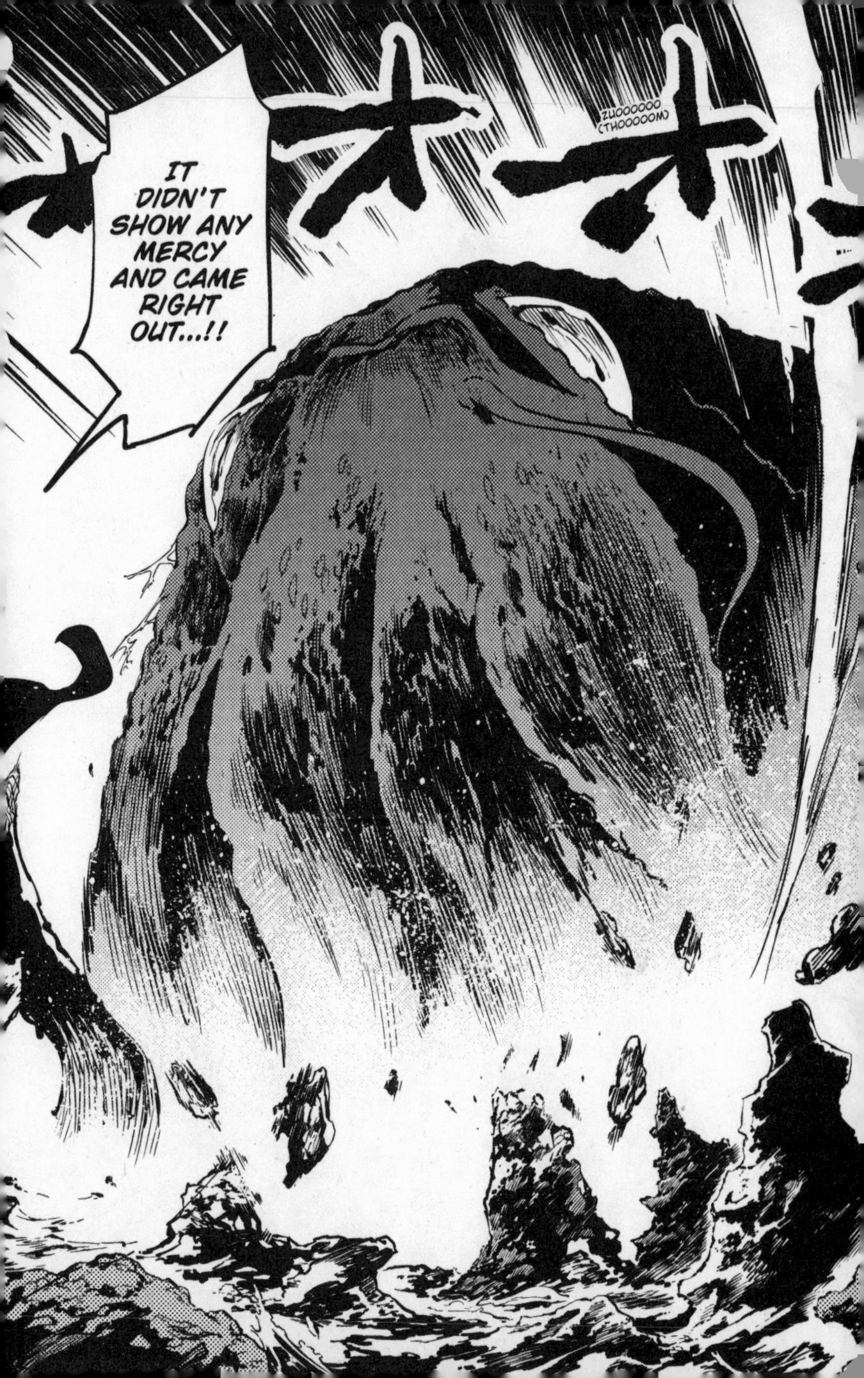
ZUOOOOOO (THOOOOOM)
IT DIDN'T SHOW ANY MERCY AND CAME RIGHT OUT...!!

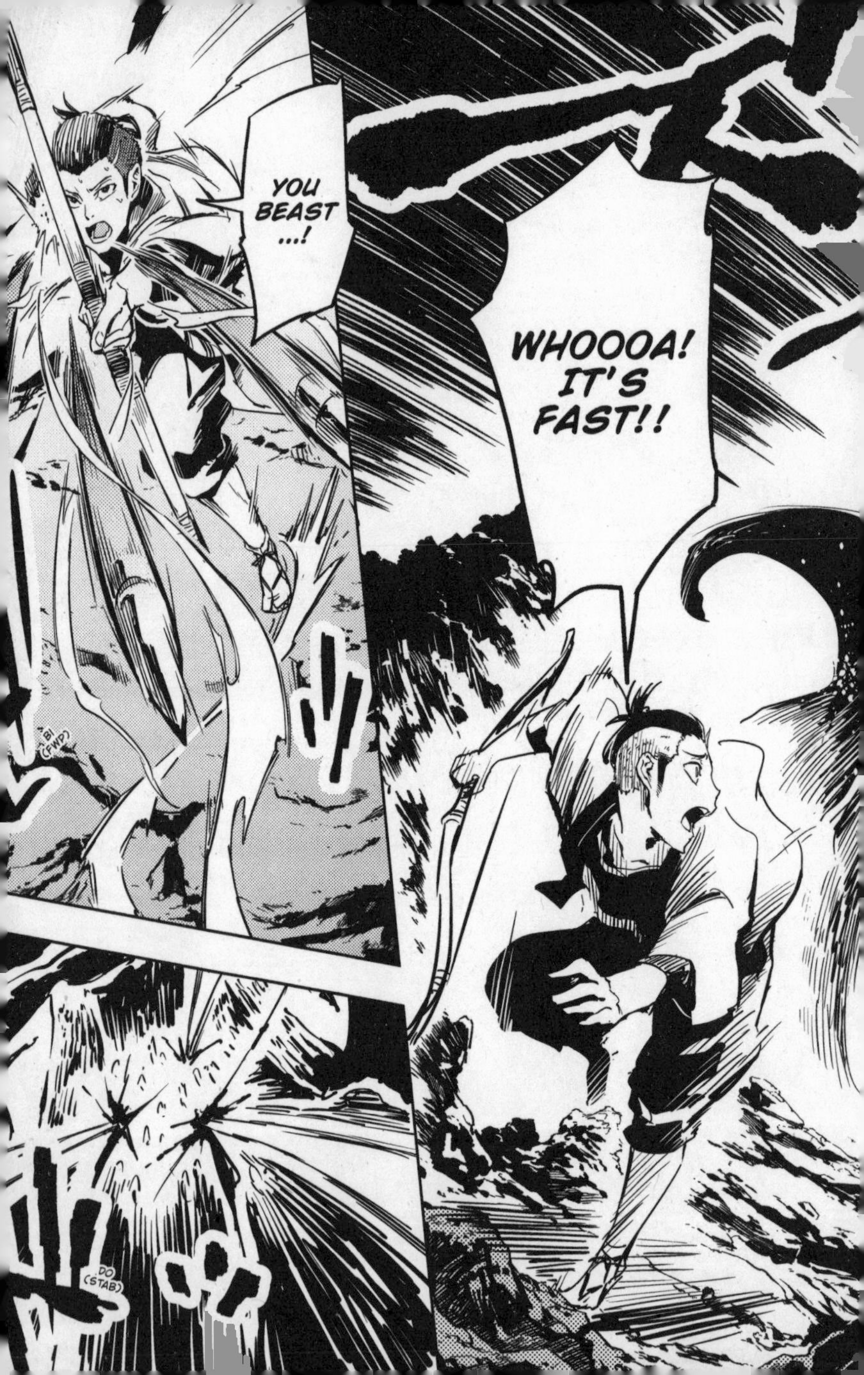
WHOOOA! IT'S FAST!!
YOU BEAST ...!
BI (FWP)
DO (STAB)

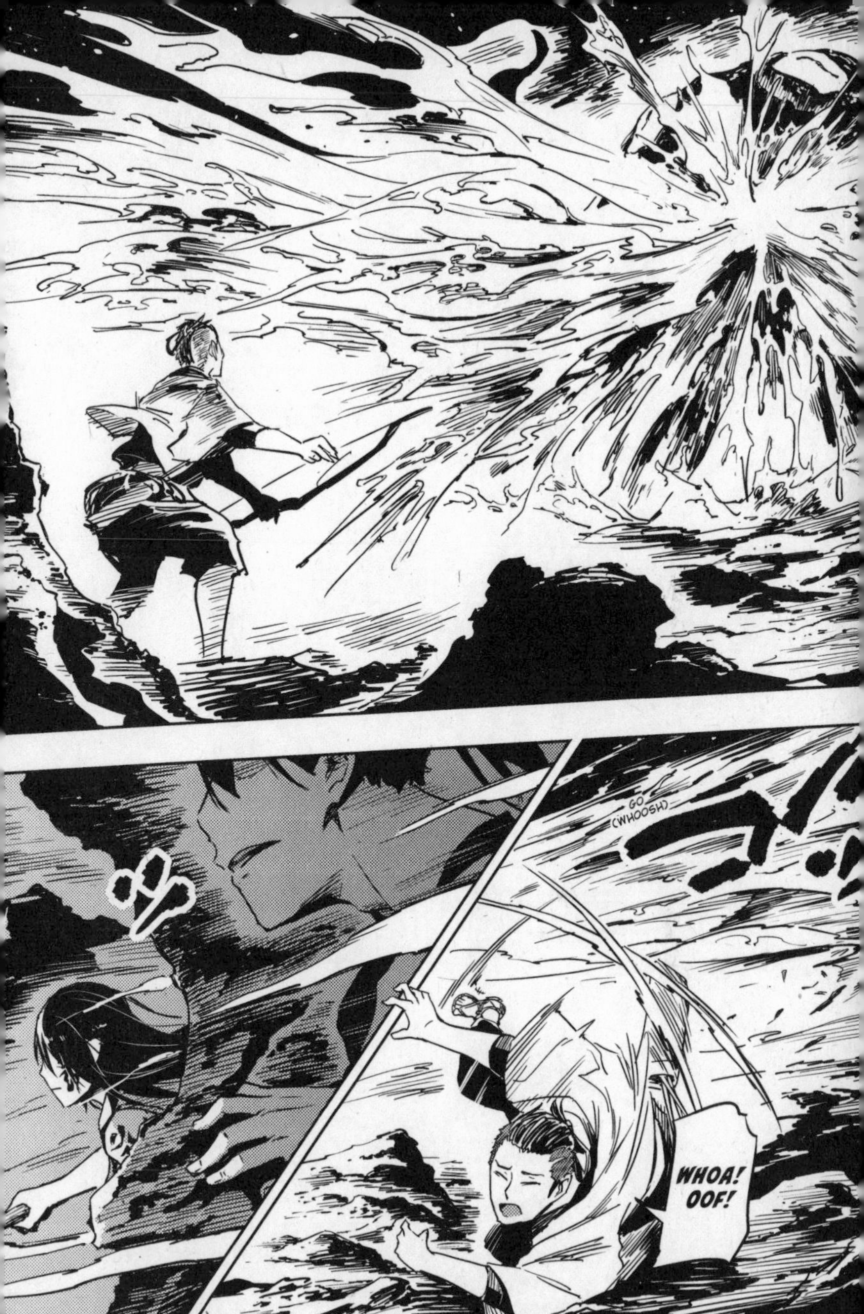
GO (WHOOSH)
WHOA! OOF!

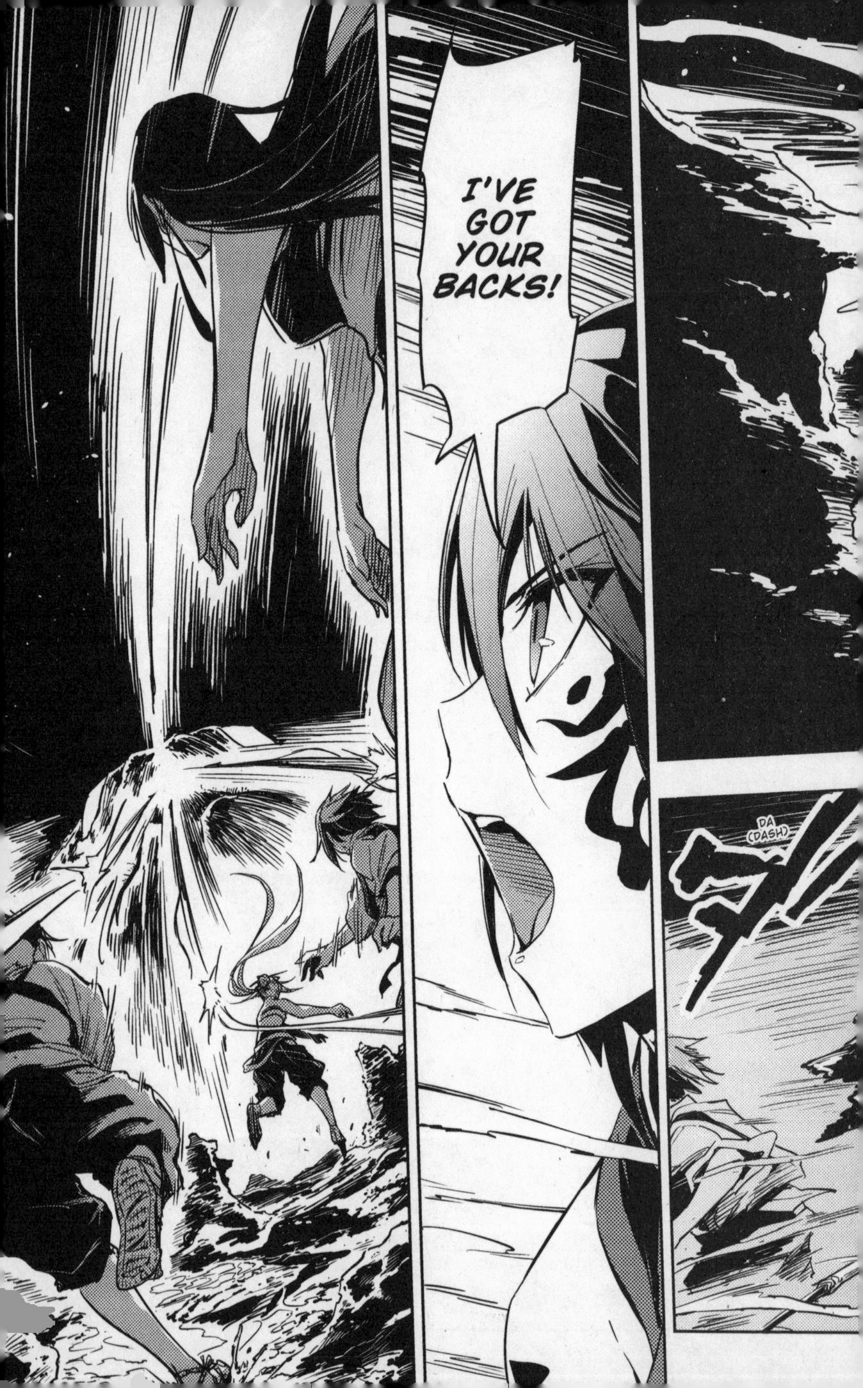
DA (DASH)
I'VE GOT YOUR BACKS!

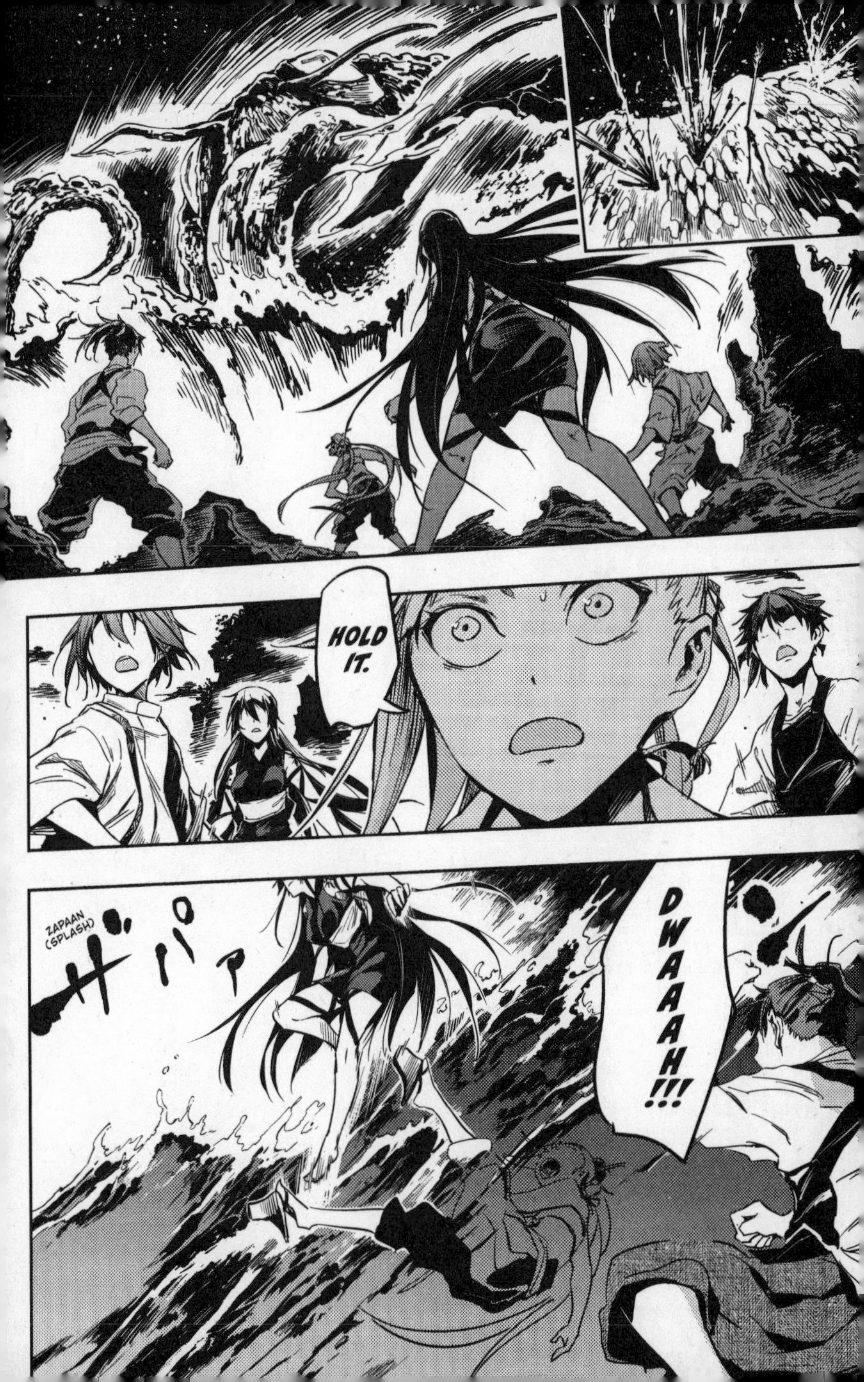
HOLD IT.
DWAAAAH!!!
ザパァ
ZAPAAN (SPLASH)

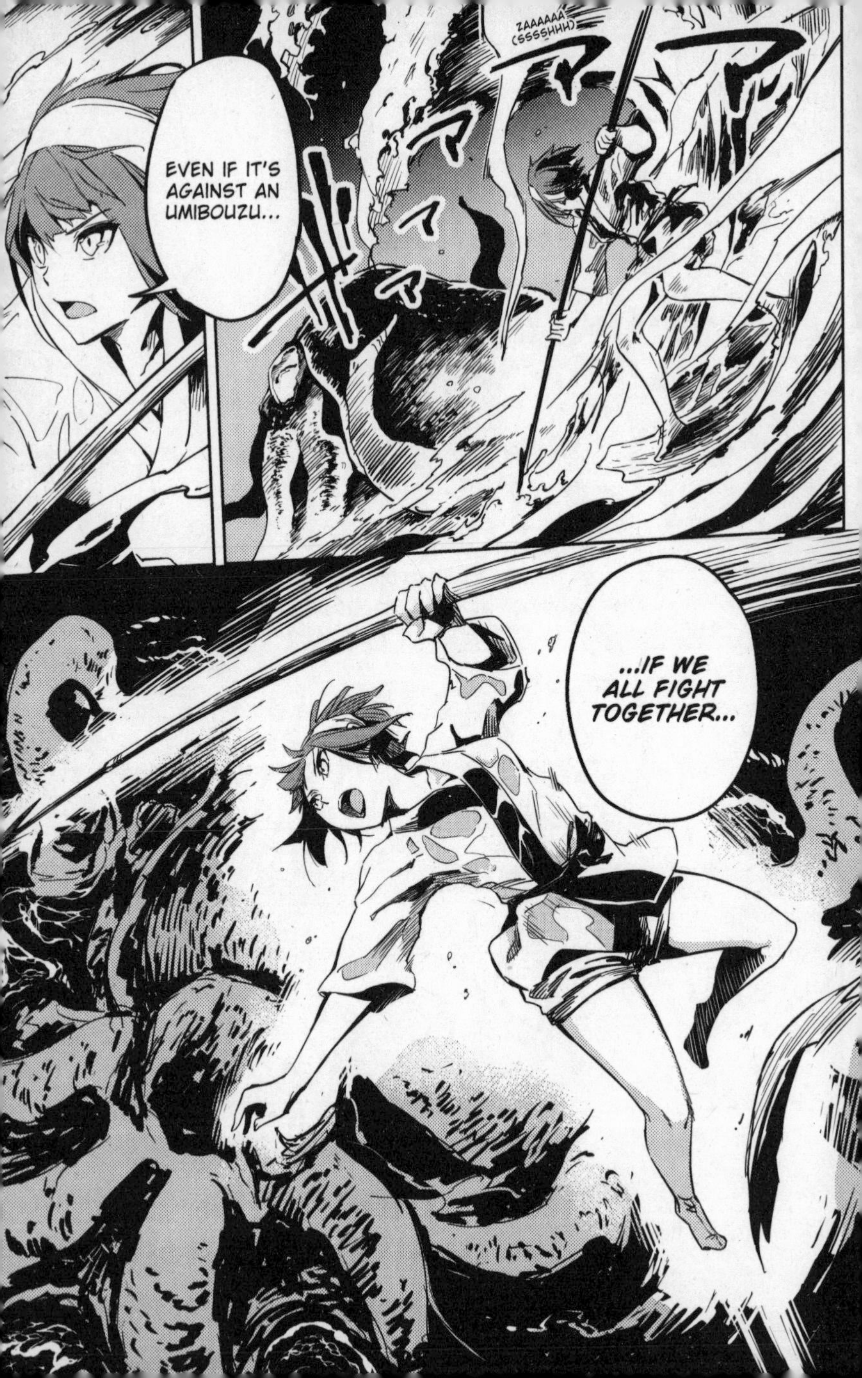
ZAAAAAA (SSSSHHH)
EVEN IF IT'S AGAINST AN UMIBOUZU...
...IF WE ALL FIGHT TOGETHER...

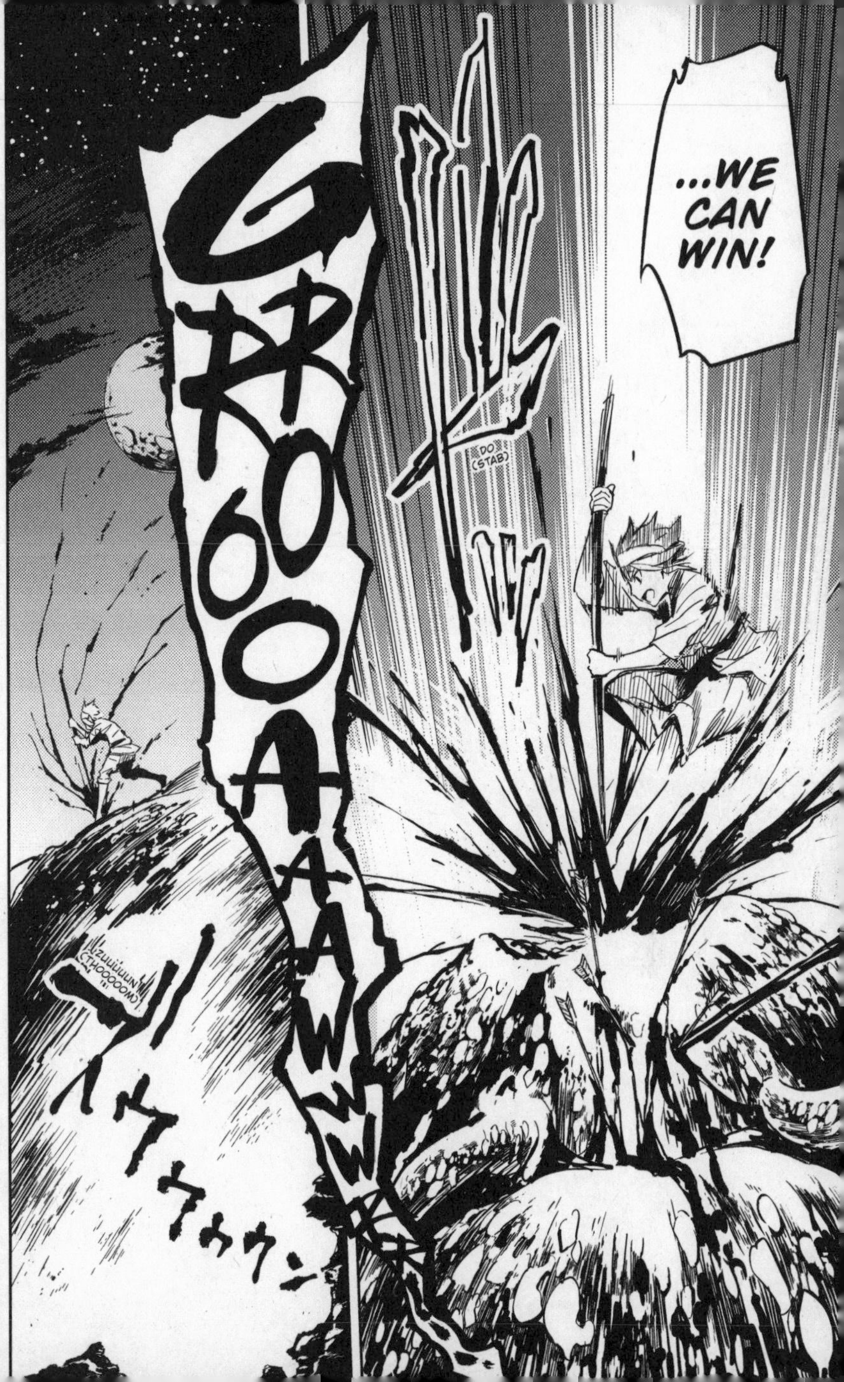
...WE CAN WIN!
DO (STAB)
GROOOAAAWWW
ZUUUUUN (THOOOOOM)!!

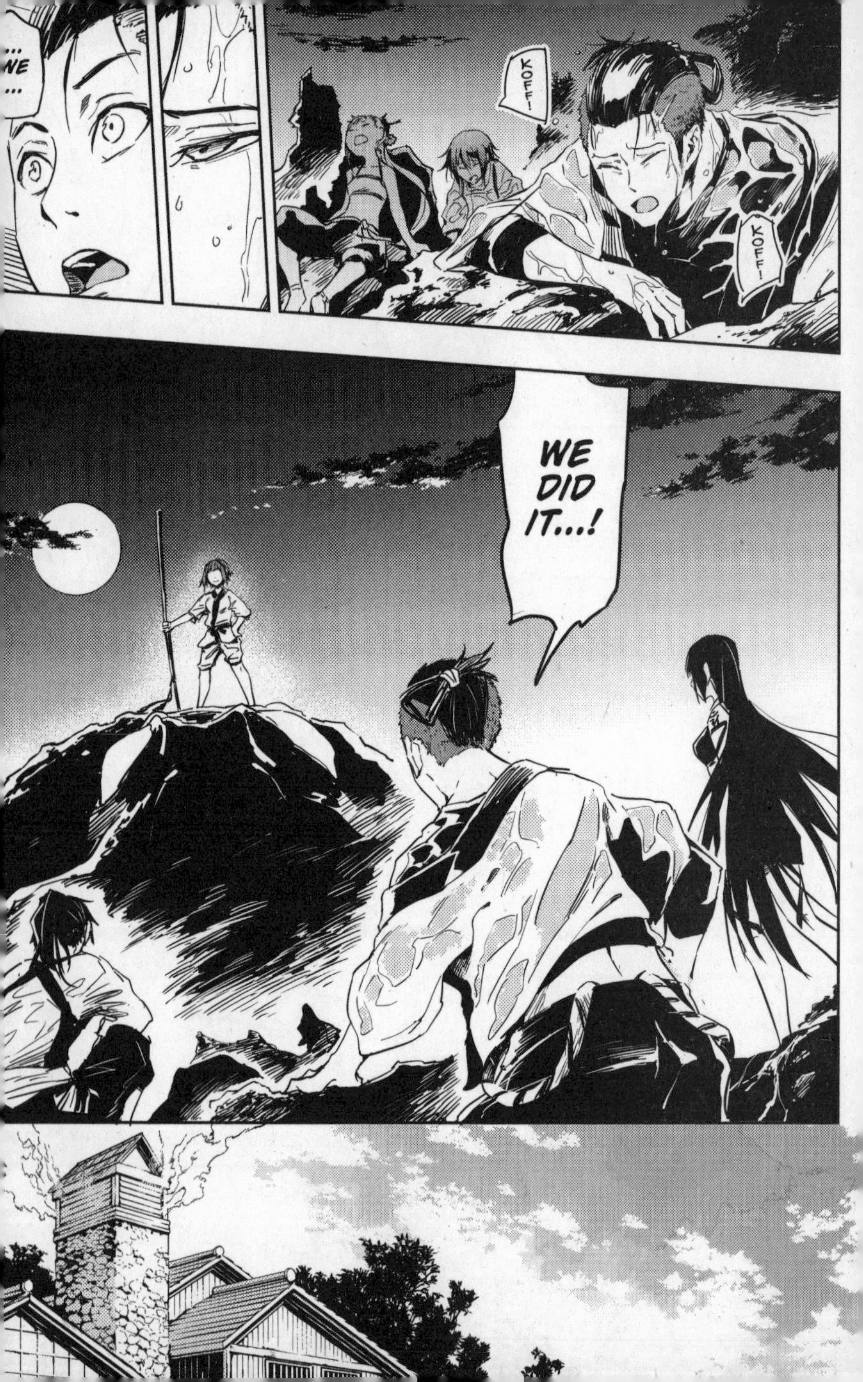
KOFF!
KOFF!
...NE...
WE DID IT...!

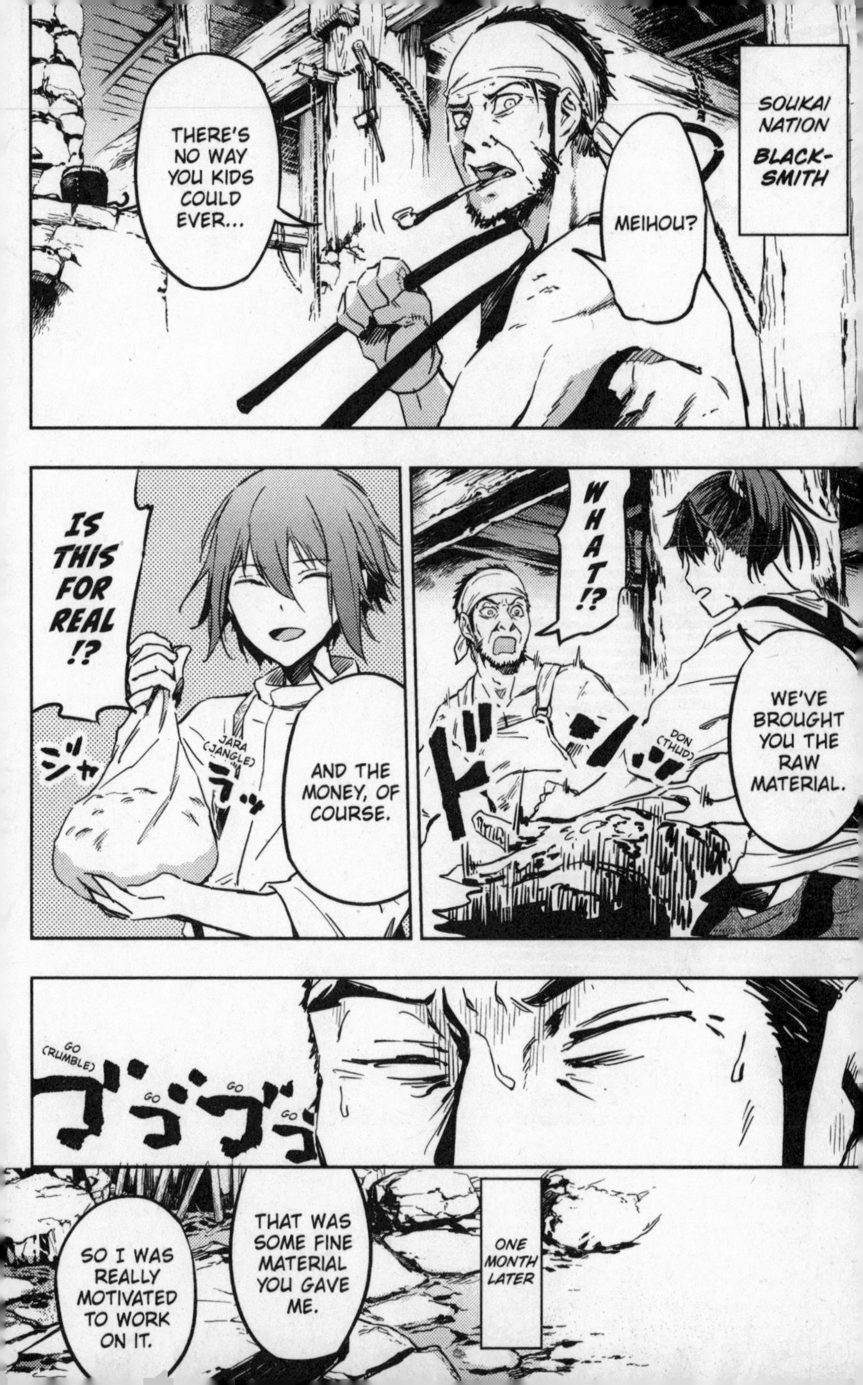
SOUKAI NATION BLACKSMITH
MEIHOU?
THERE'S NO WAY YOU KIDS COULD EVER...
WE'VE BROUGHT YOU THE RAW MATERIAL.
DON (THUD)
WHAT!?
AND THE MONEY, OF COURSE.
JARA (JANGLE)
IS THIS FOR REAL!?
GO (RUMBLE)
GO
GO
GO
ONE MONTH LATER
THAT WAS SOME FINE MATERIAL YOU GAVE ME.
SO I WAS REALLY MOTIVATED TO WORK ON IT.

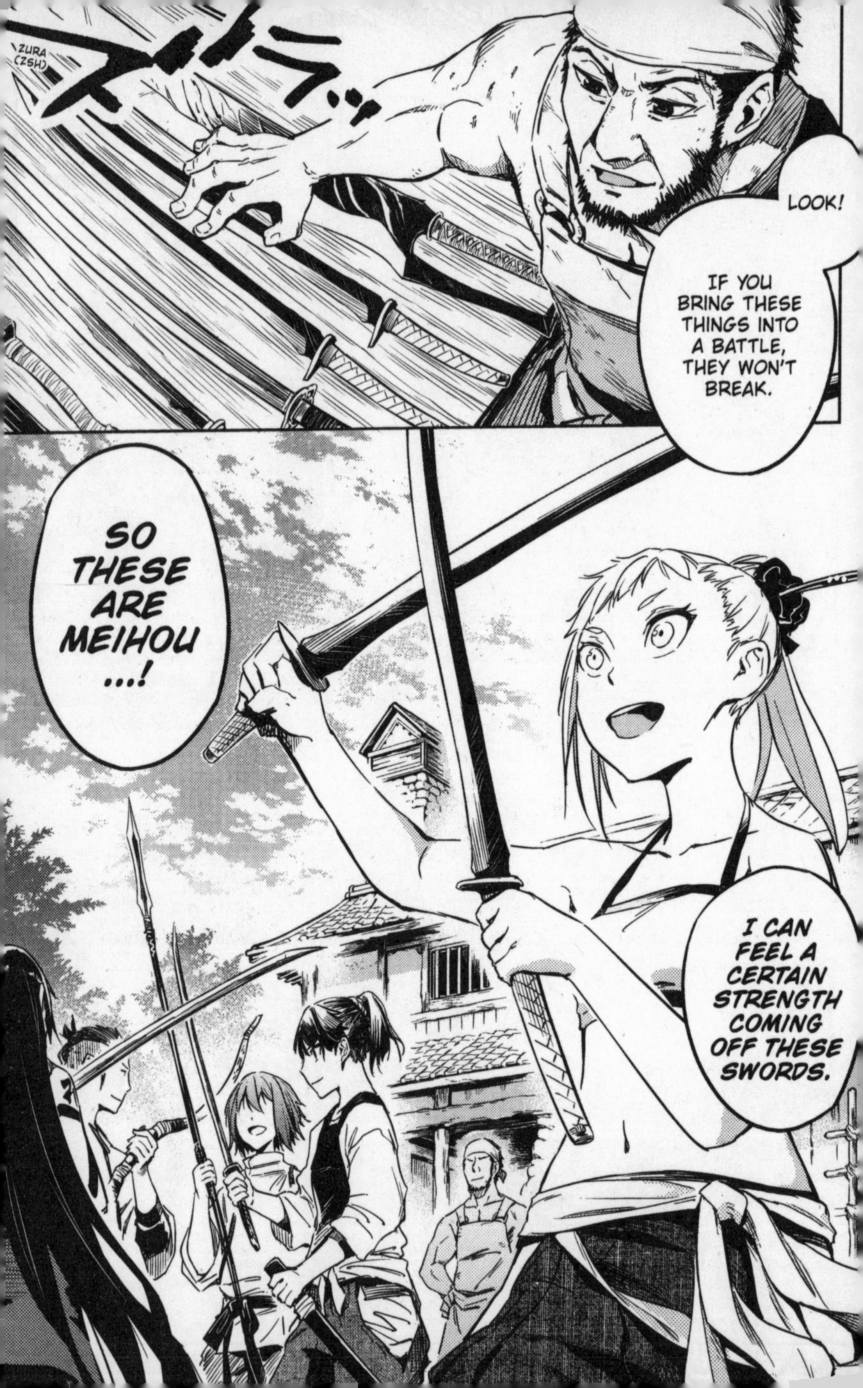
ZURA (ZSH)
LOOK!
IF YOU BRING THESE THINGS INTO A BATTLE, THEY WON'T BREAK.
SO THESE ARE MEIHOU ...!
I CAN FEEL A CERTAIN STRENGTH COMING OFF THESE SWORDS.

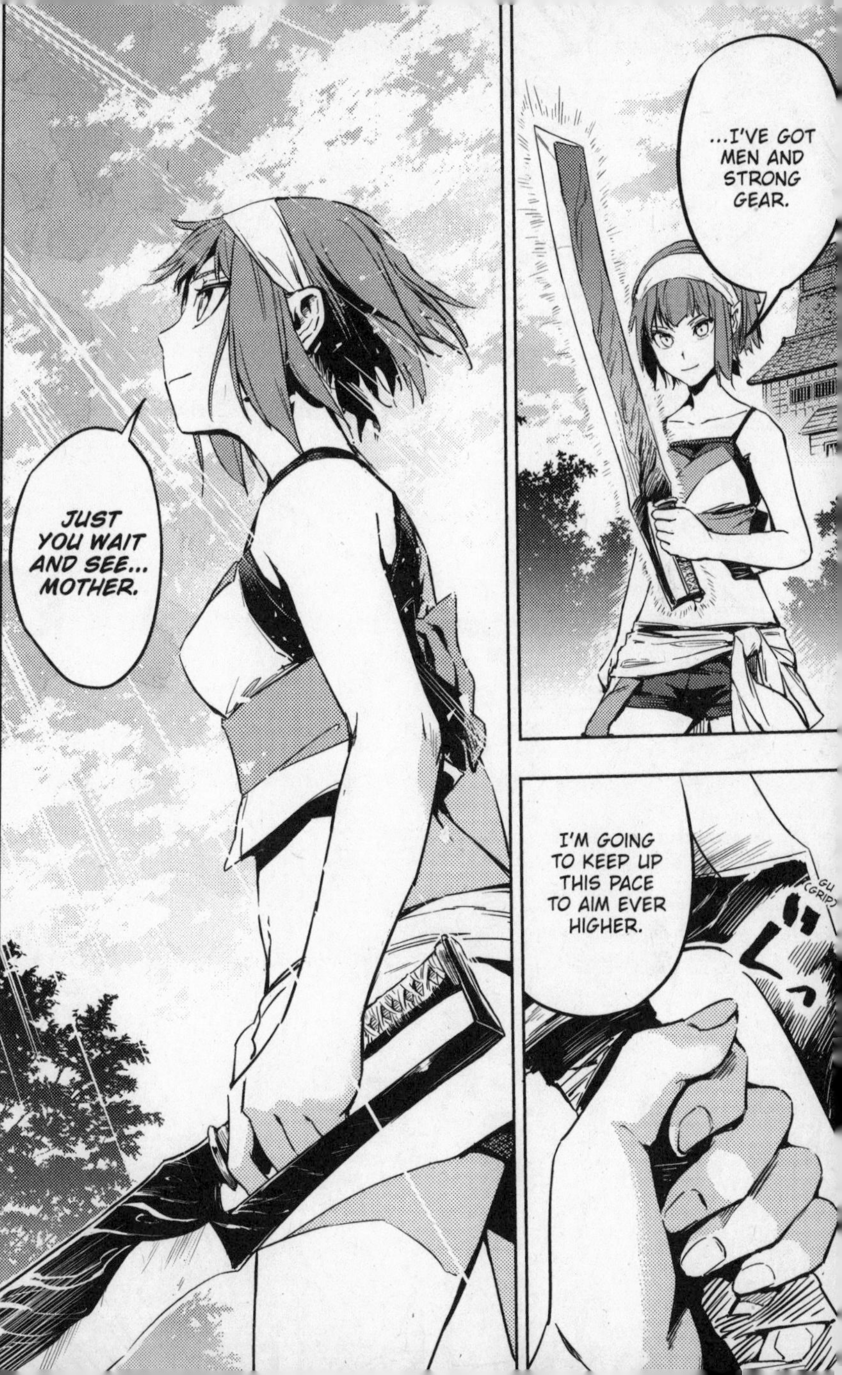
...I'VE GOT MEN AND STRONG GEAR.
I'M GOING TO KEEP UP THIS PACE TO AIM EVER HIGHER.
GU (GRIP)
JUST YOU WAIT AND SEE... MOTHER.

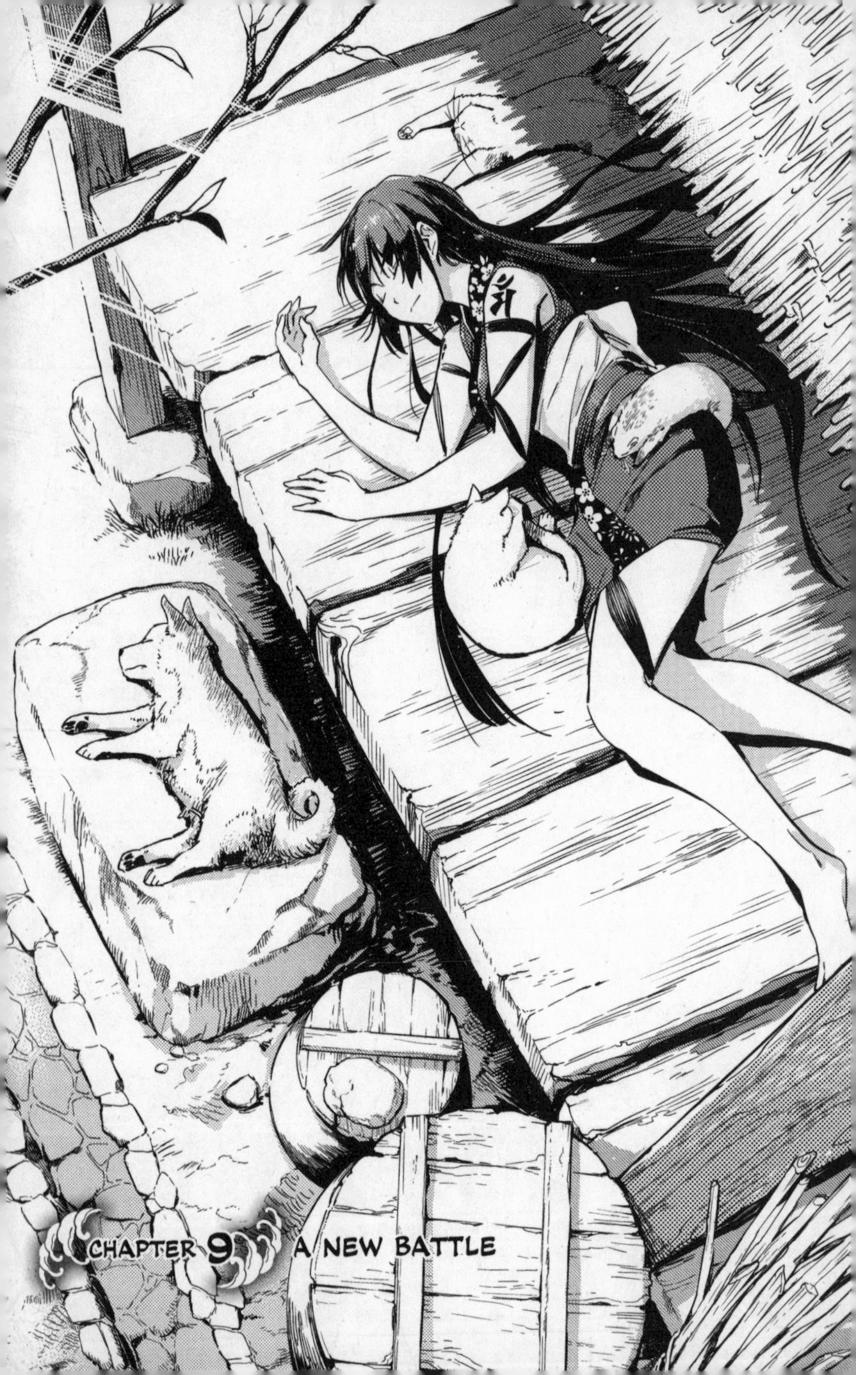
CHAPTER 9 A NEW BATTLE

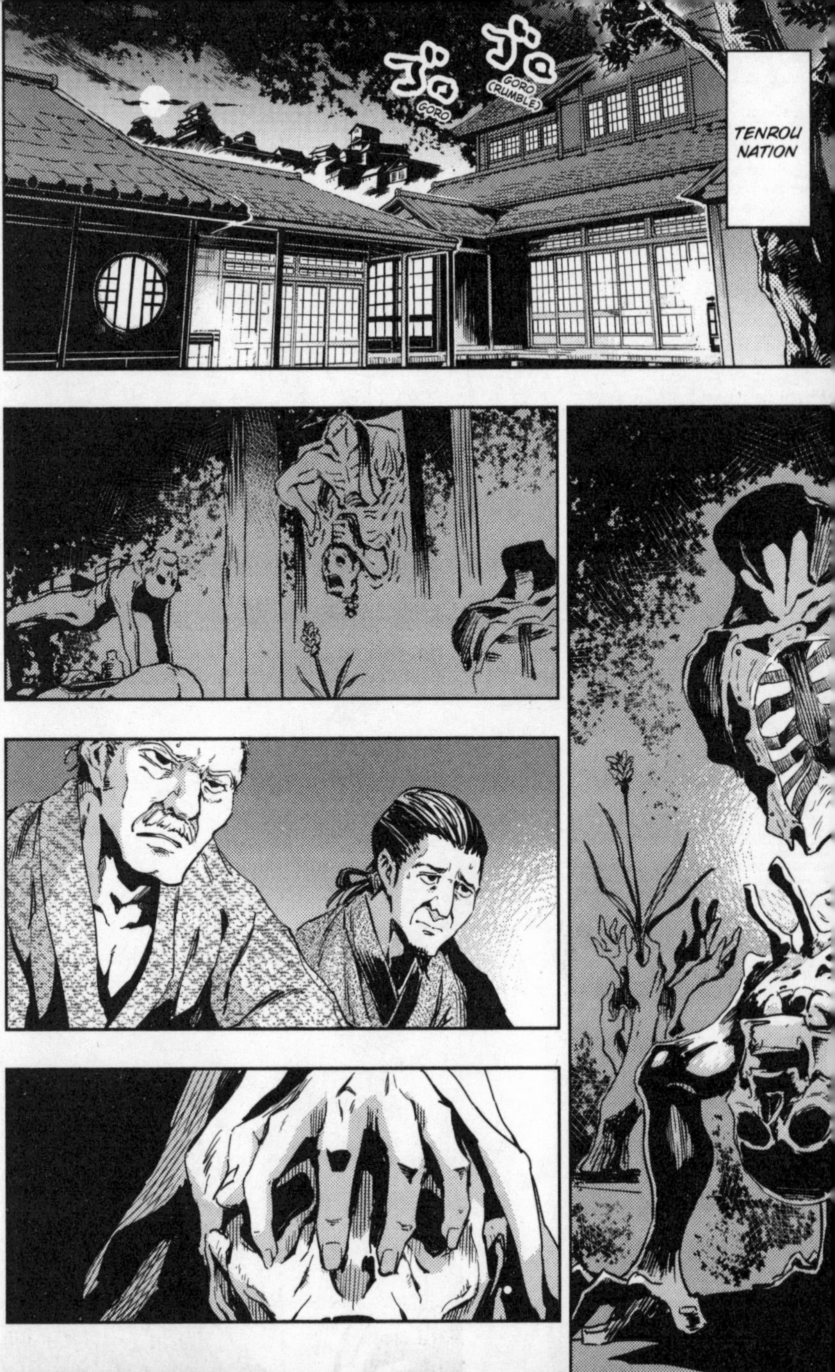
TENROU NATION
ゴロ
GORO (RUMBLE)
ゴロ
GORO

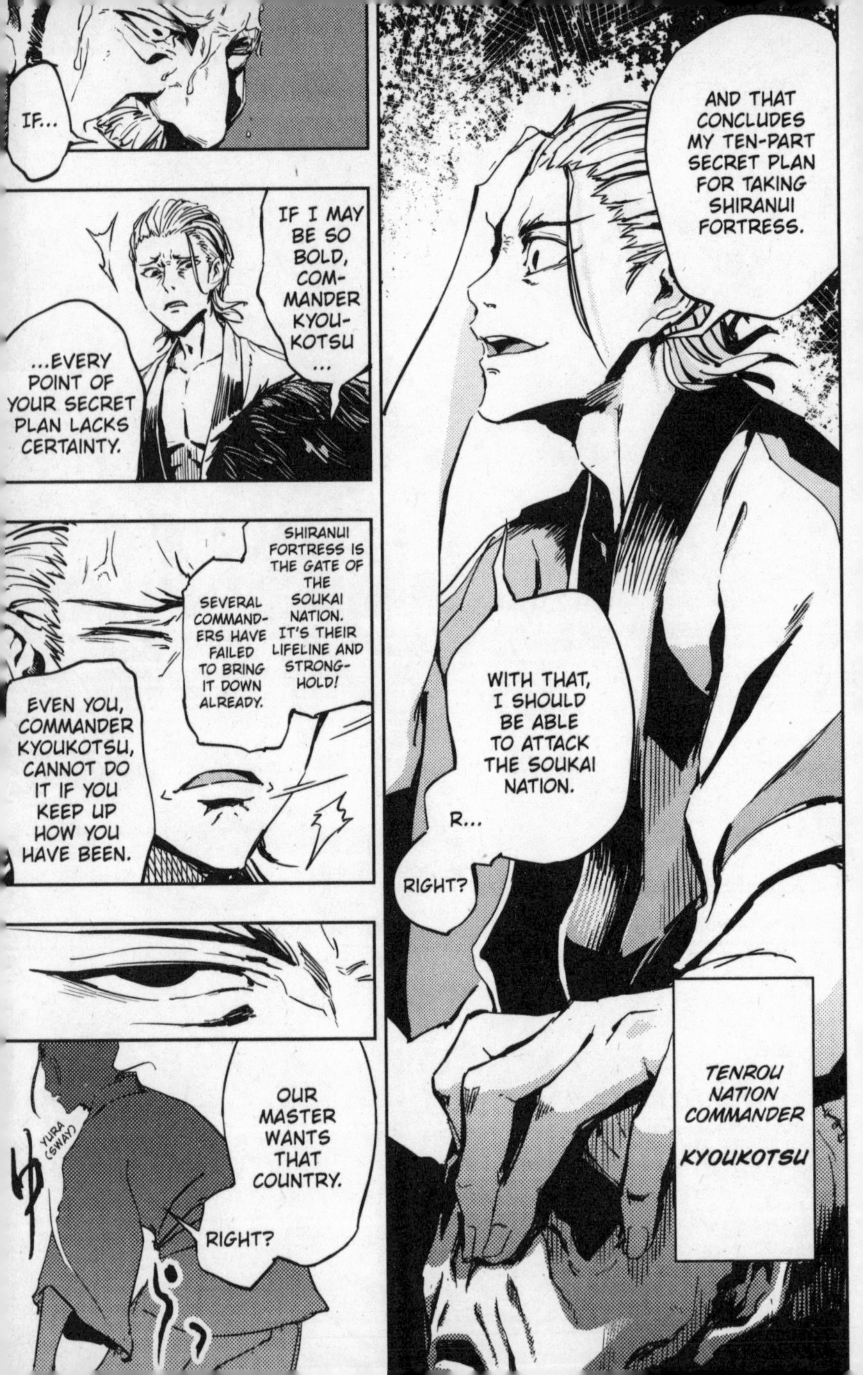
AND THAT CONCLUDES MY TEN-PART SECRET PLAN FOR TAKING SHIRANUI FORTRESS.
WITH THAT, I SHOULD BE ABLE TO ATTACK THE SOUKAI NATION.
R...
RIGHT?
TENROU NATION COMMANDER KYOUKOTSU
IF...
IF I MAY BE SO BOLD, COMMANDER KYOUKOTSU...
...EVERY POINT OF YOUR SECRET PLAN LACKS CERTAINTY.
SHIRANUI FORTRESS IS THE GATE OF THE SOUKAI NATION. IT'S THEIR LIFELINE AND STRONGHOLD!
SEVERAL COMMANDERS HAVE FAILED TO BRING IT DOWN ALREADY.
EVEN YOU, COMMANDER KYOUKOTSU, CANNOT DO IT IF YOU KEEP UP HOW YOU HAVE BEEN.
OUR MASTER WANTS THAT COUNTRY.
YURA (SWAY)
RIGHT?

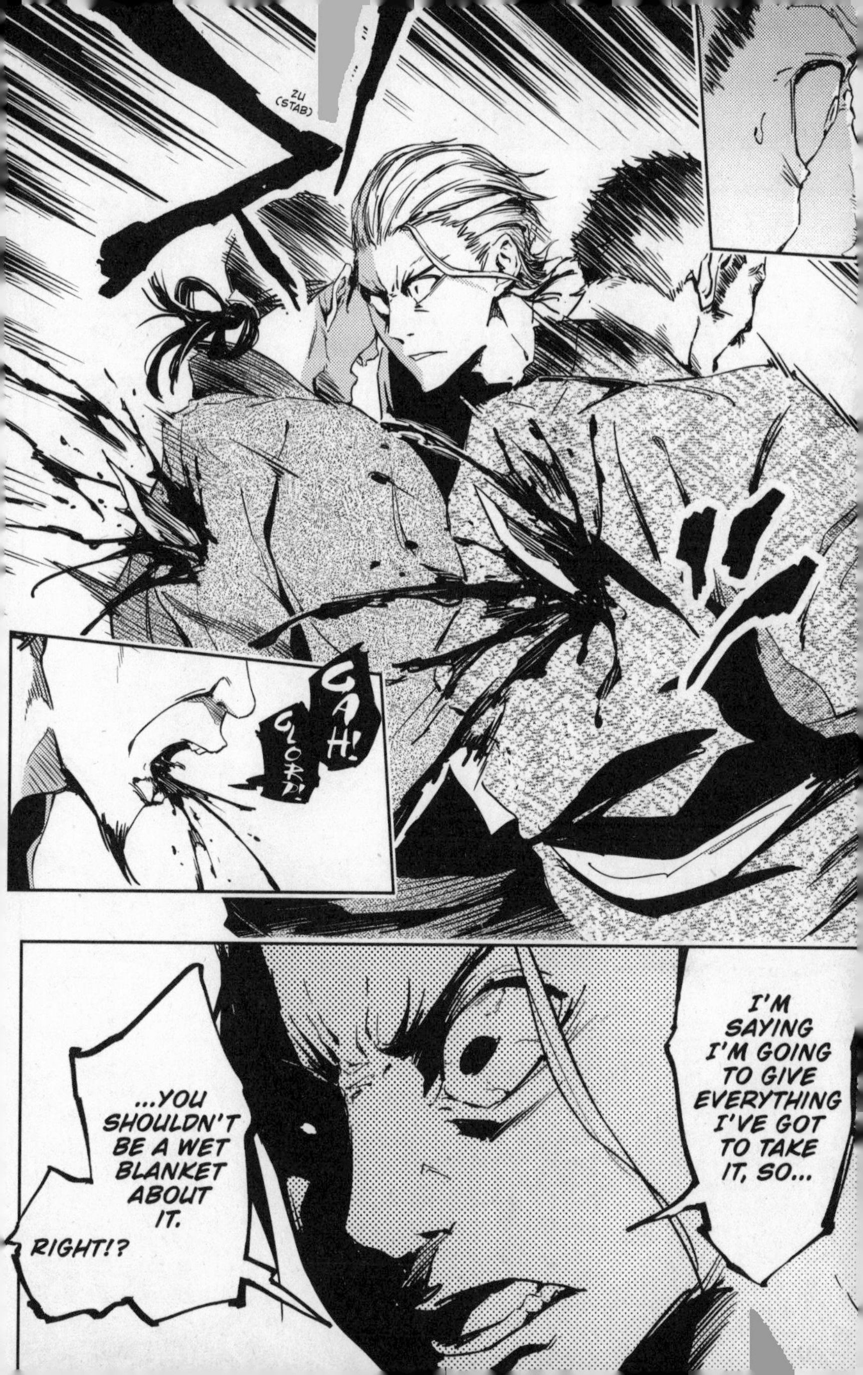
ZU (STAB)
GAH! GLORP!
I'M SAYING I'M GOING TO GIVE EVERYTHING I'VE GOT TO TAKE IT, SO...
...YOU SHOULDN'T BE A WET BLANKET ABOUT IT.
RIGHT!?

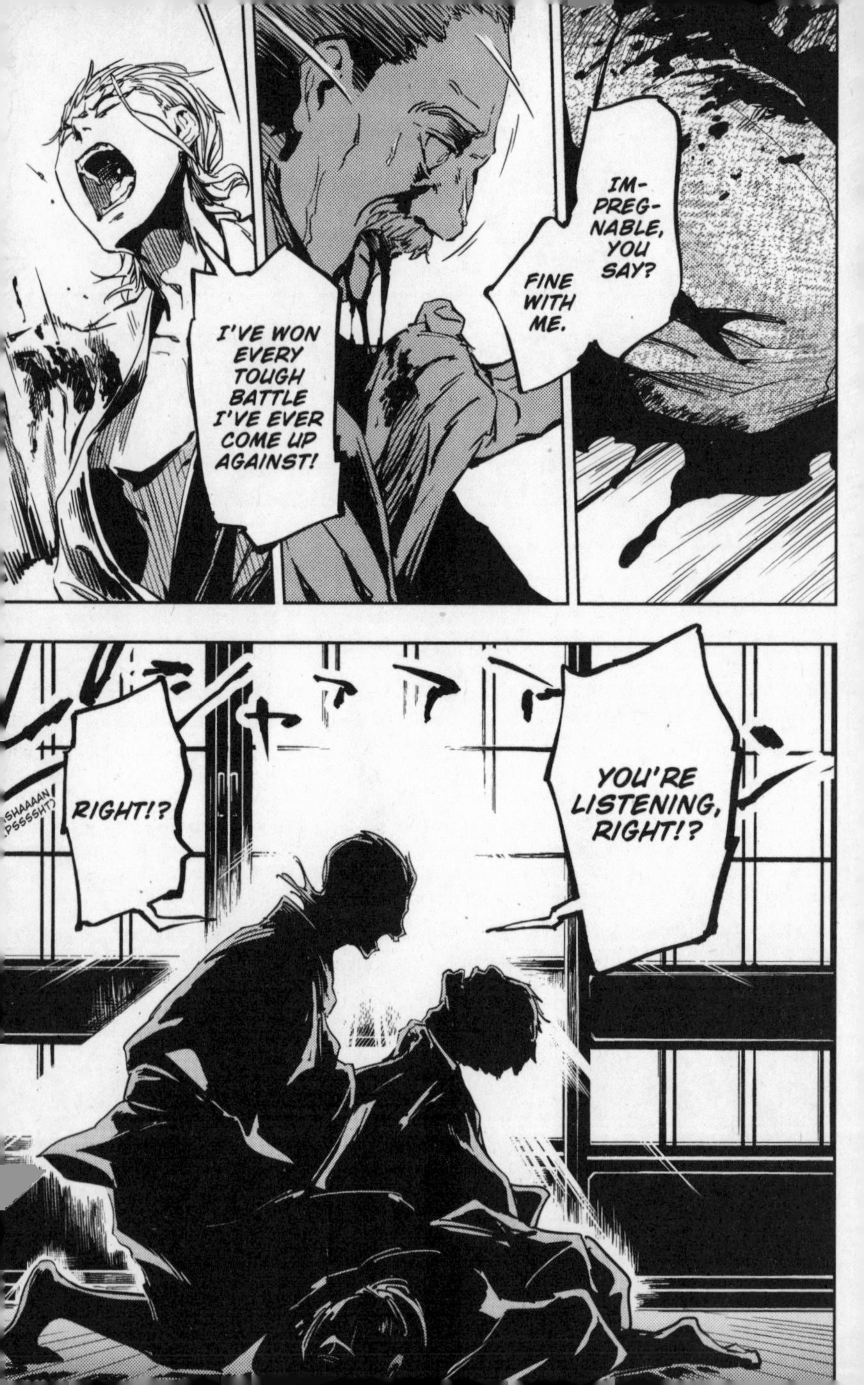
IM-PREG-NABLE, YOU SAY?
FINE WITH ME.
I'VE WON EVERY TOUGH BATTLE I'VE EVER COME UP AGAINST!
YOU'RE LISTENING, RIGHT!?
RIGHT!?
SHAAAAN
PSSSSHT)

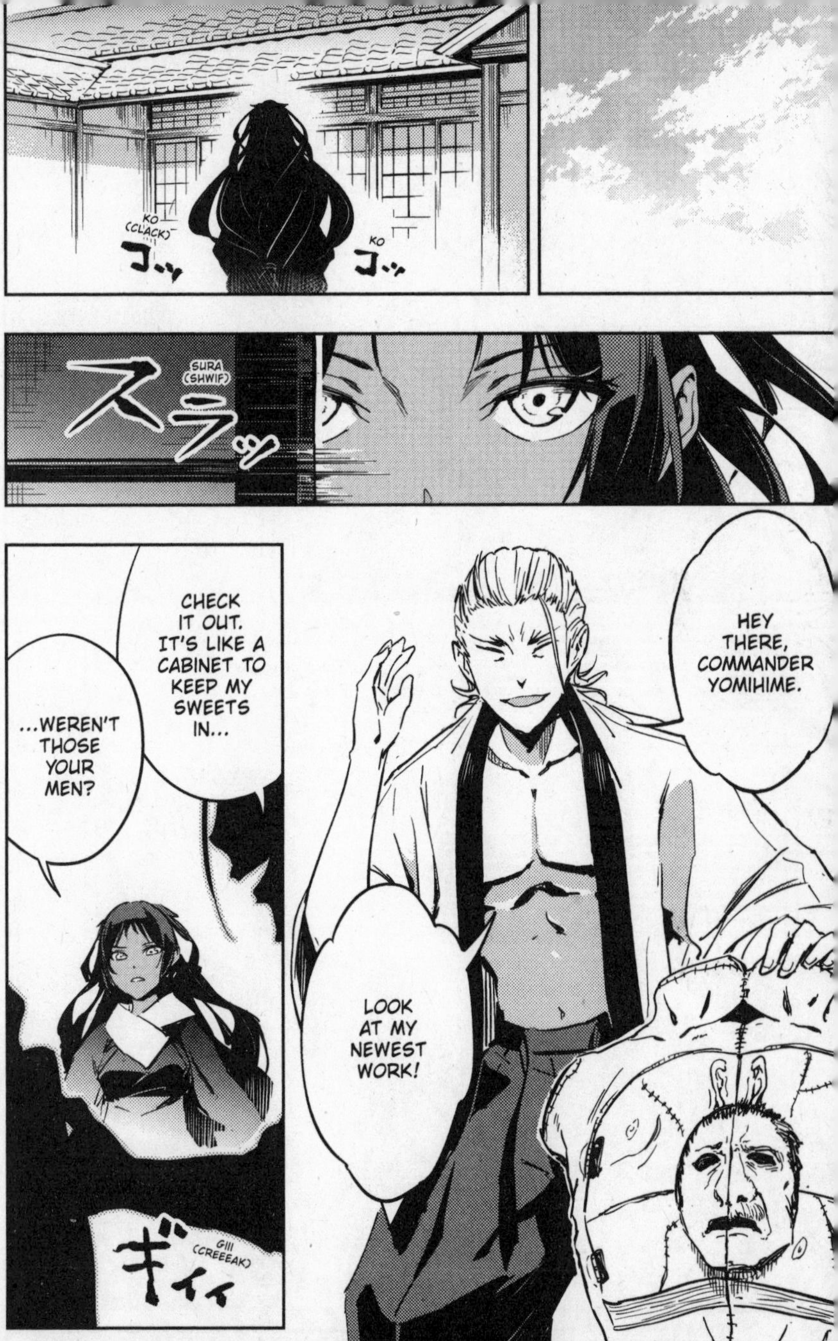

KO
KO (CLACK)
SURA (SHWIF)
HEY THERE, COMMANDER YOMIHIME.
LOOK AT MY NEWEST WORK!
CHECK IT OUT. IT'S LIKE A CABINET TO KEEP MY SWEETS IN...
...WEREN'T THOSE YOUR MEN?
GIII (CREEEAK)

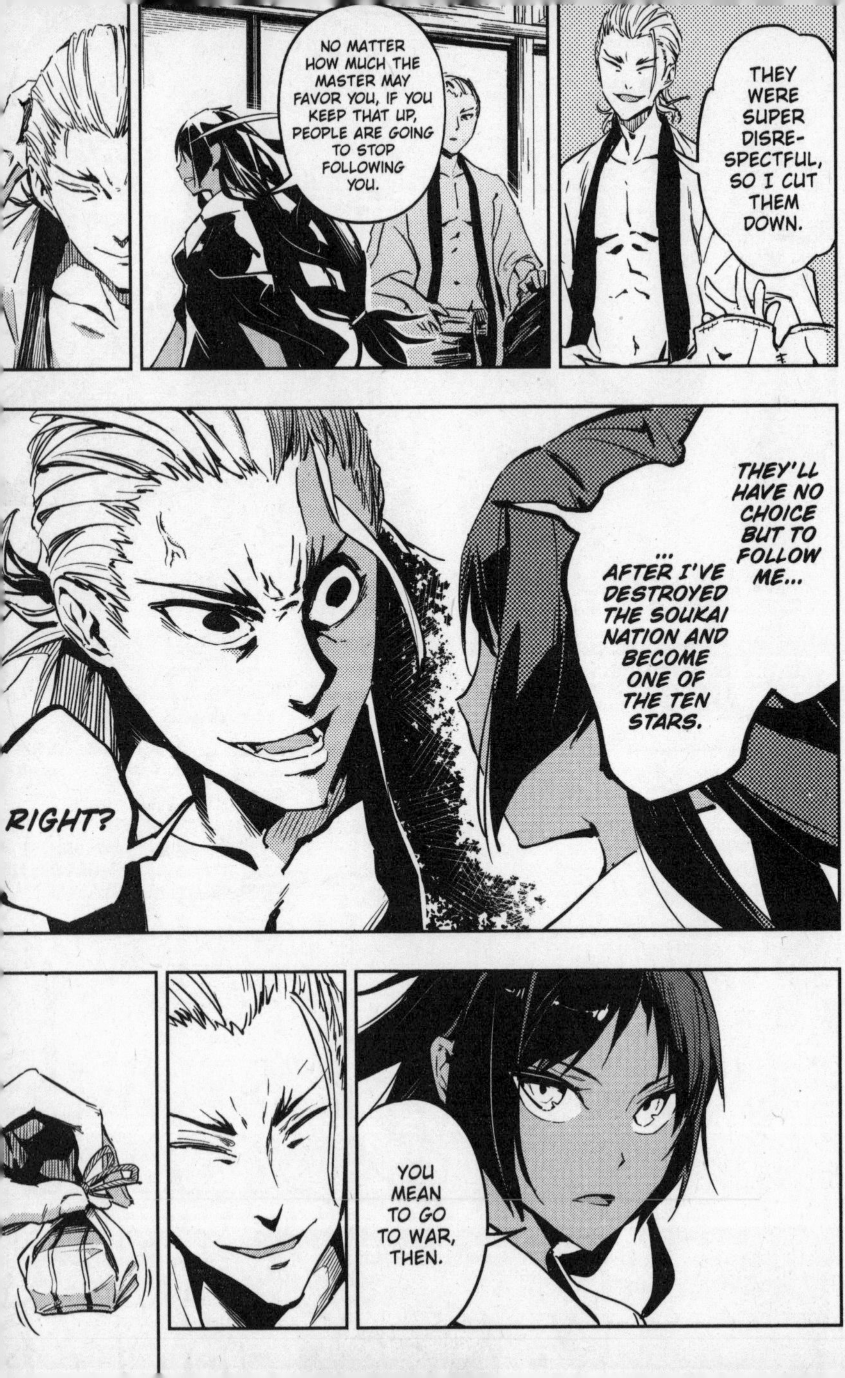
THEY WERE SUPER DISRE-SPECTFUL, SO I CUT THEM DOWN.
NO MATTER HOW MUCH THE MASTER MAY FAVOR YOU, IF YOU KEEP THAT UP, PEOPLE ARE GOING TO STOP FOLLOWING YOU.
THEY'LL HAVE NO CHOICE BUT TO FOLLOW ME...
... AFTER I'VE DESTROYED THE SOUKAI NATION AND BECOME ONE OF THE TEN STARS.
RIGHT?
YOU MEAN TO GO TO WAR, THEN.

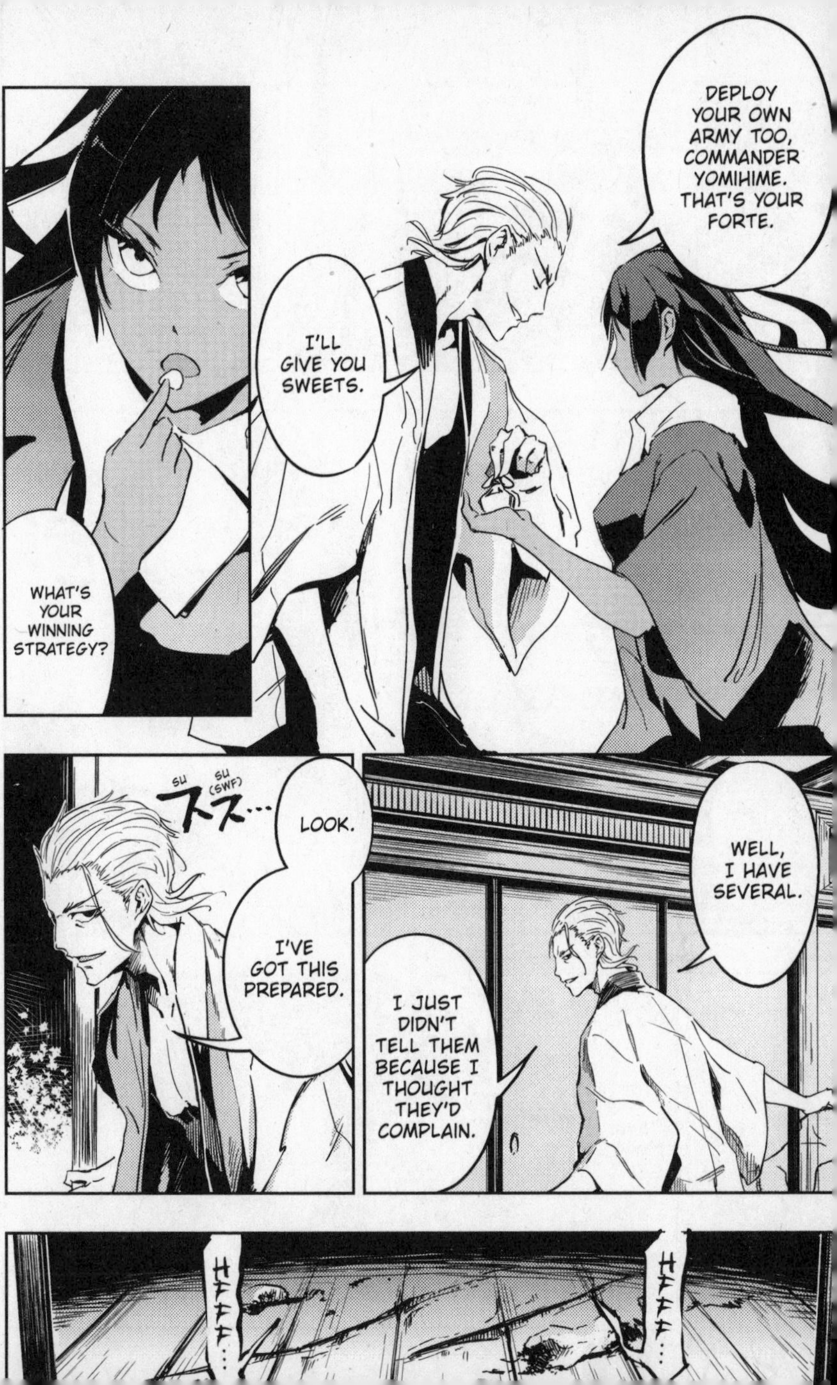
DEPLOY YOUR OWN ARMY TOO, COMMANDER YOMIHIME. THAT'S YOUR FORTE.
I'LL GIVE YOU SWEETS.
WHAT'S YOUR WINNING STRATEGY?
WELL, I HAVE SEVERAL.
I JUST DIDN'T TELL THEM BECAUSE I THOUGHT THEY'D COMPLAIN.
スス…
SU SU (SWF)
LOOK.
I'VE GOT THIS PREPARED.
HFFF...
HFFF...

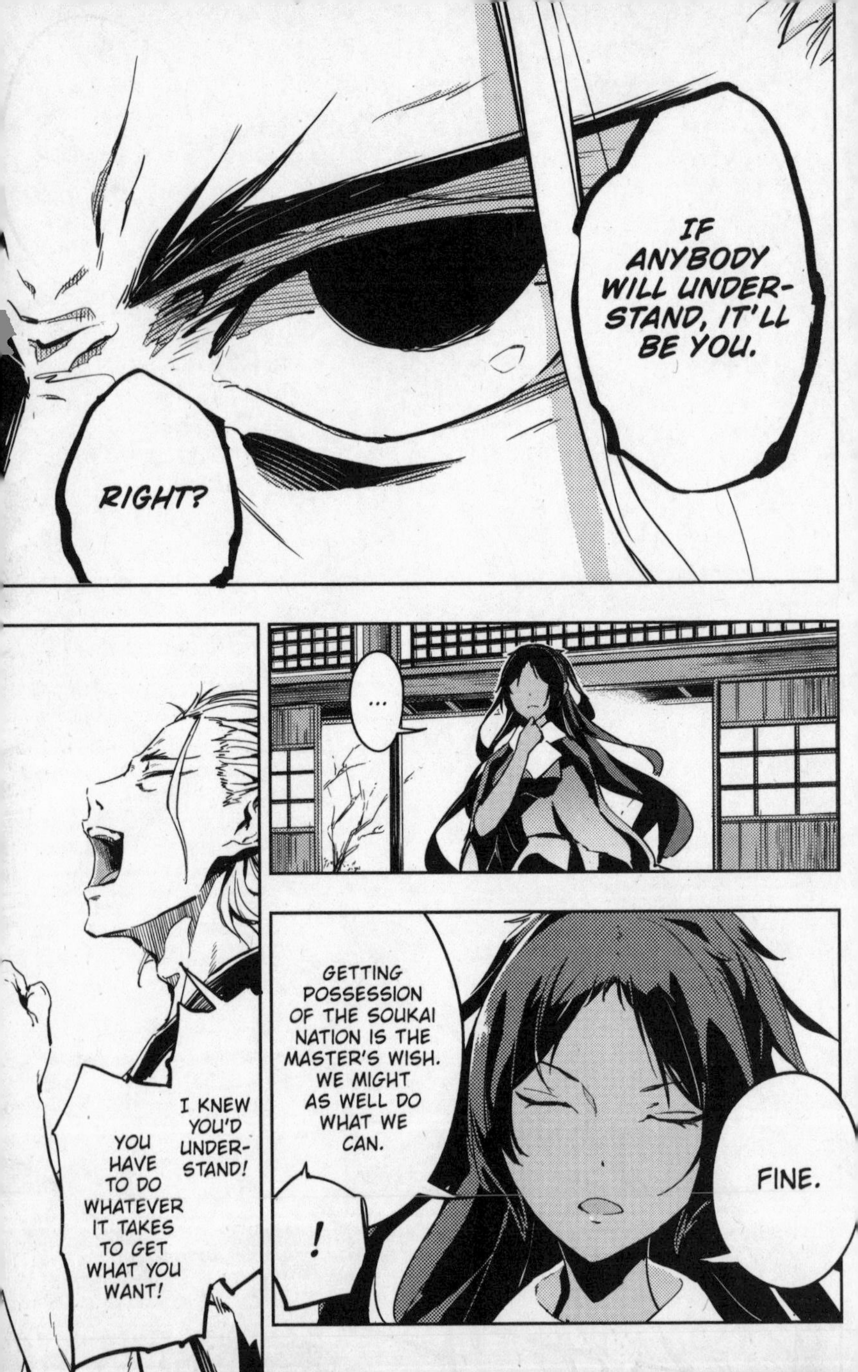
IF ANYBODY WILL UNDERSTAND, IT'LL BE YOU.
RIGHT?
...
FINE.
GETTING POSSESSION OF THE SOUKAI NATION IS THE MASTER'S WISH. WE MIGHT AS WELL DO WHAT WE CAN.
!
I KNEW YOU'D UNDERSTAND!
YOU HAVE TO DO WHATEVER IT TAKES TO GET WHAT YOU WANT!

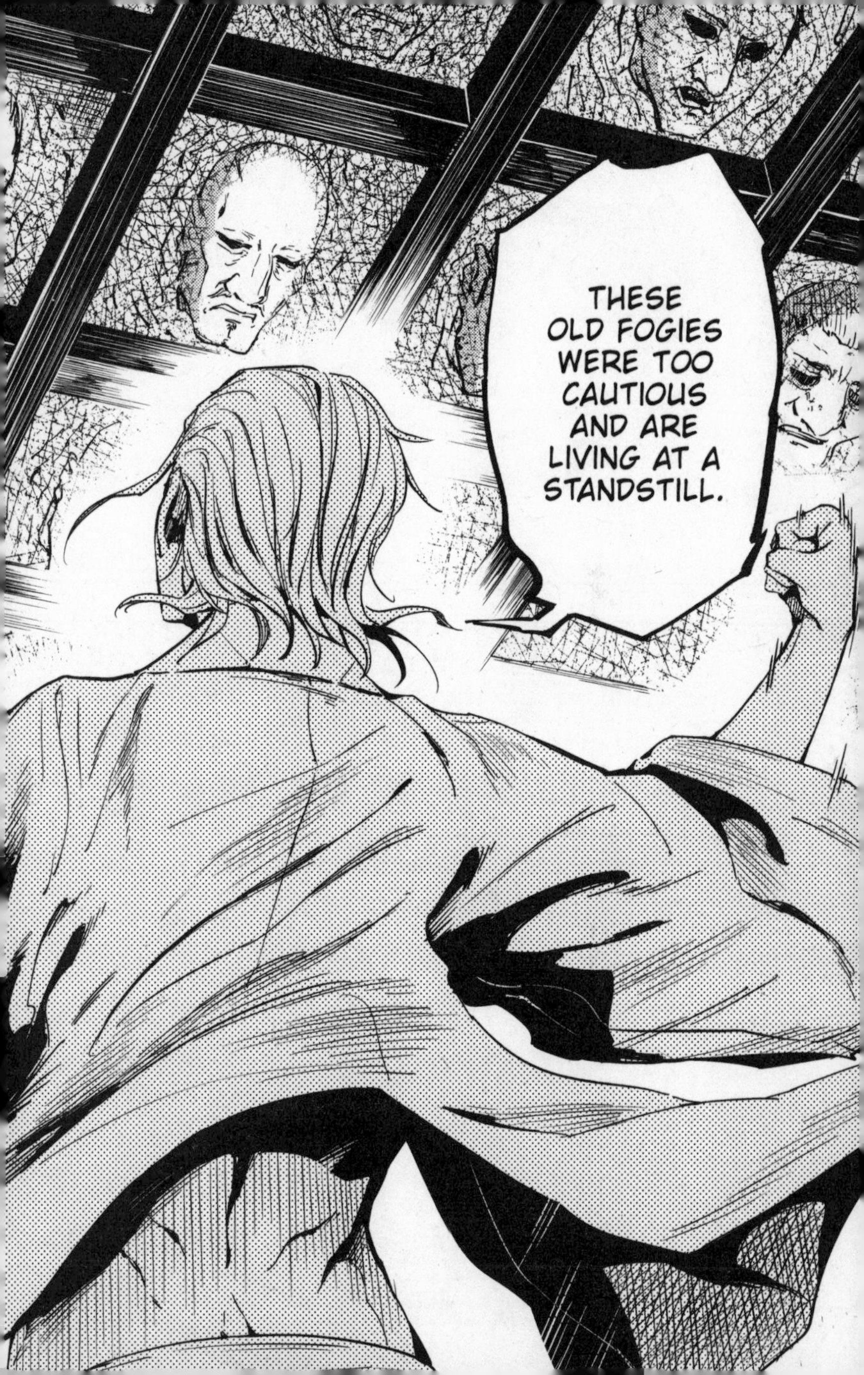
THESE OLD FOGIES WERE TOO CAUTIOUS AND ARE LIVING AT A STANDSTILL.

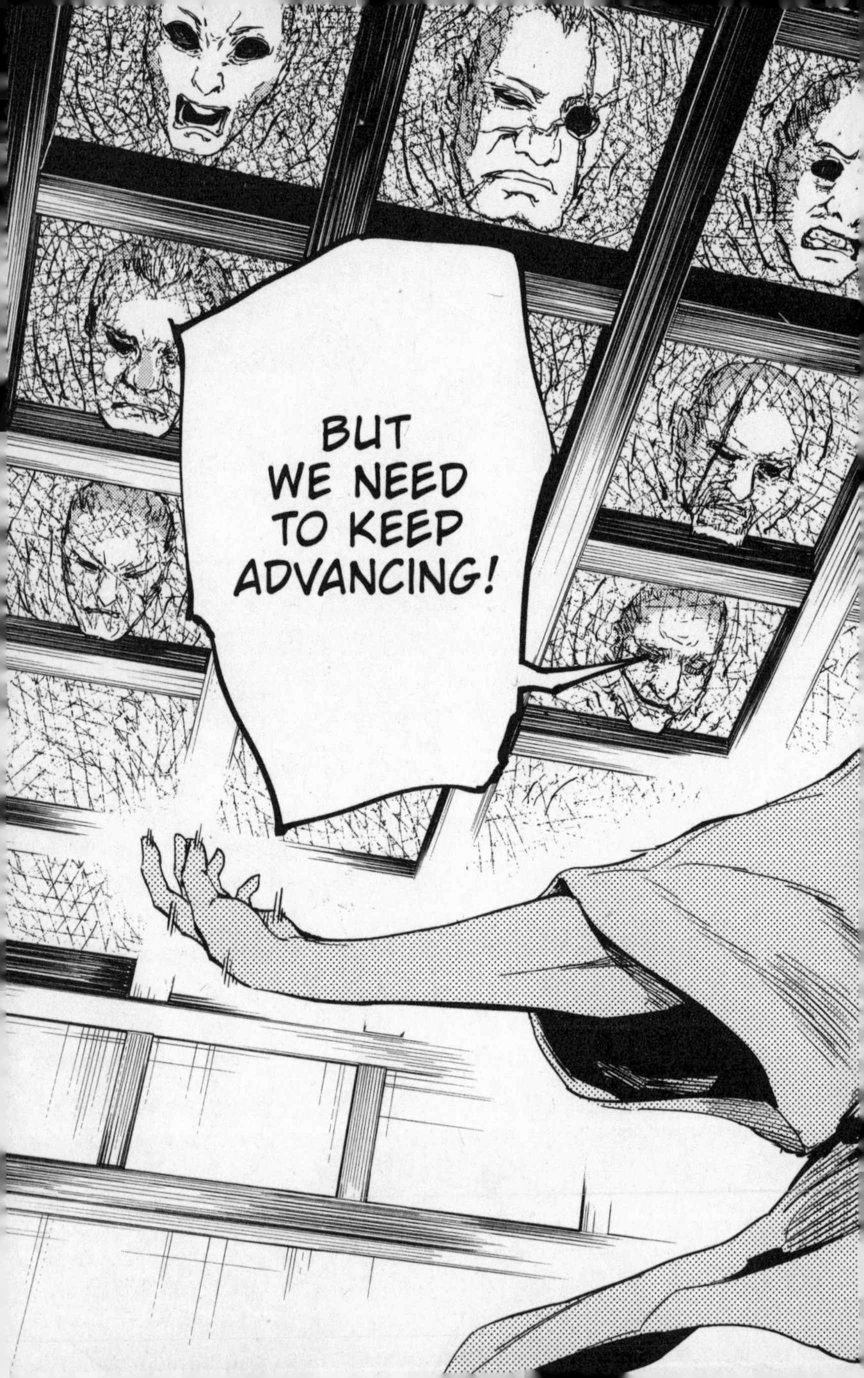
BUT WE NEED TO KEEP ADVANCING!

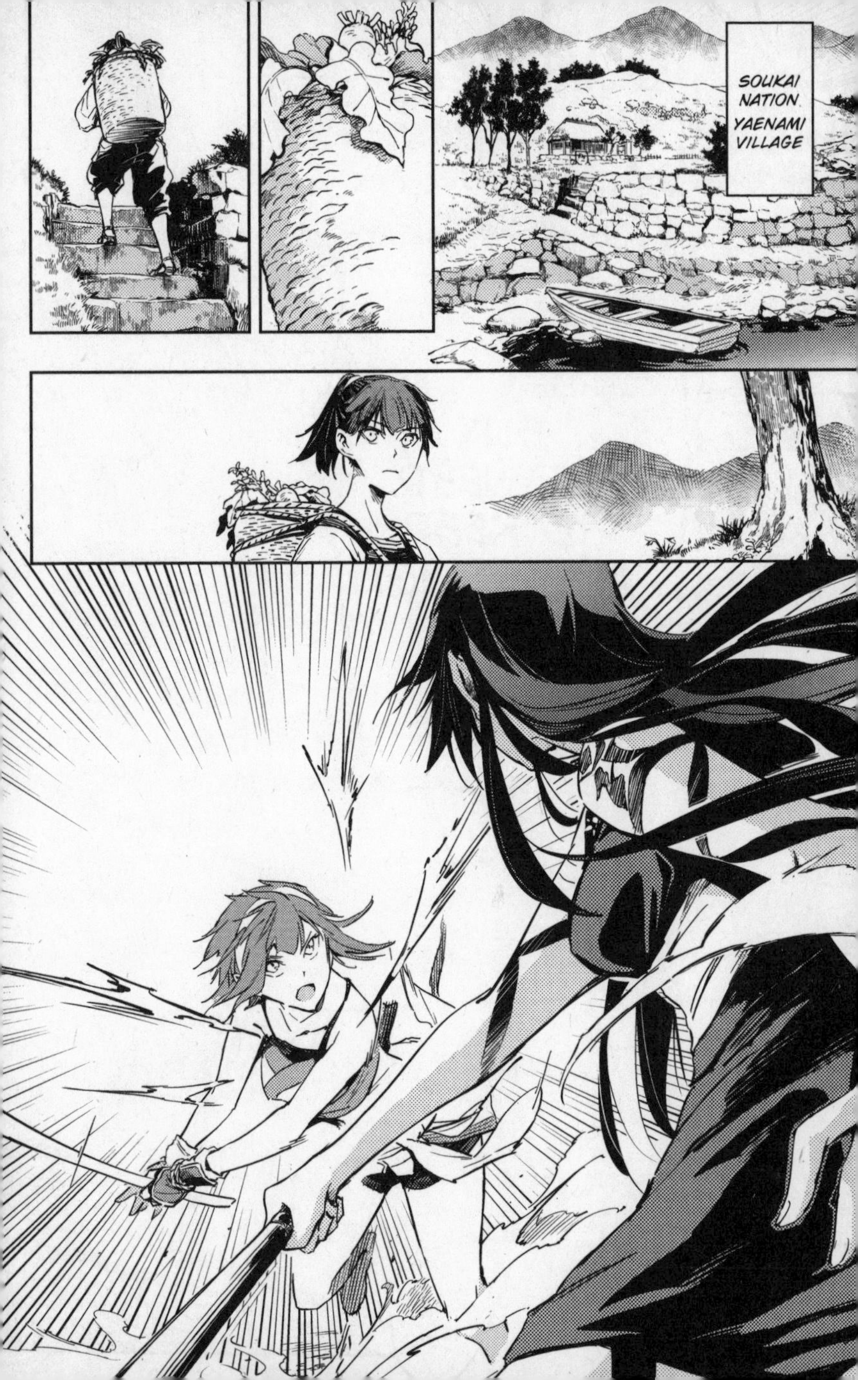
SOUKAI NATION
YAENAMI VILLAGE

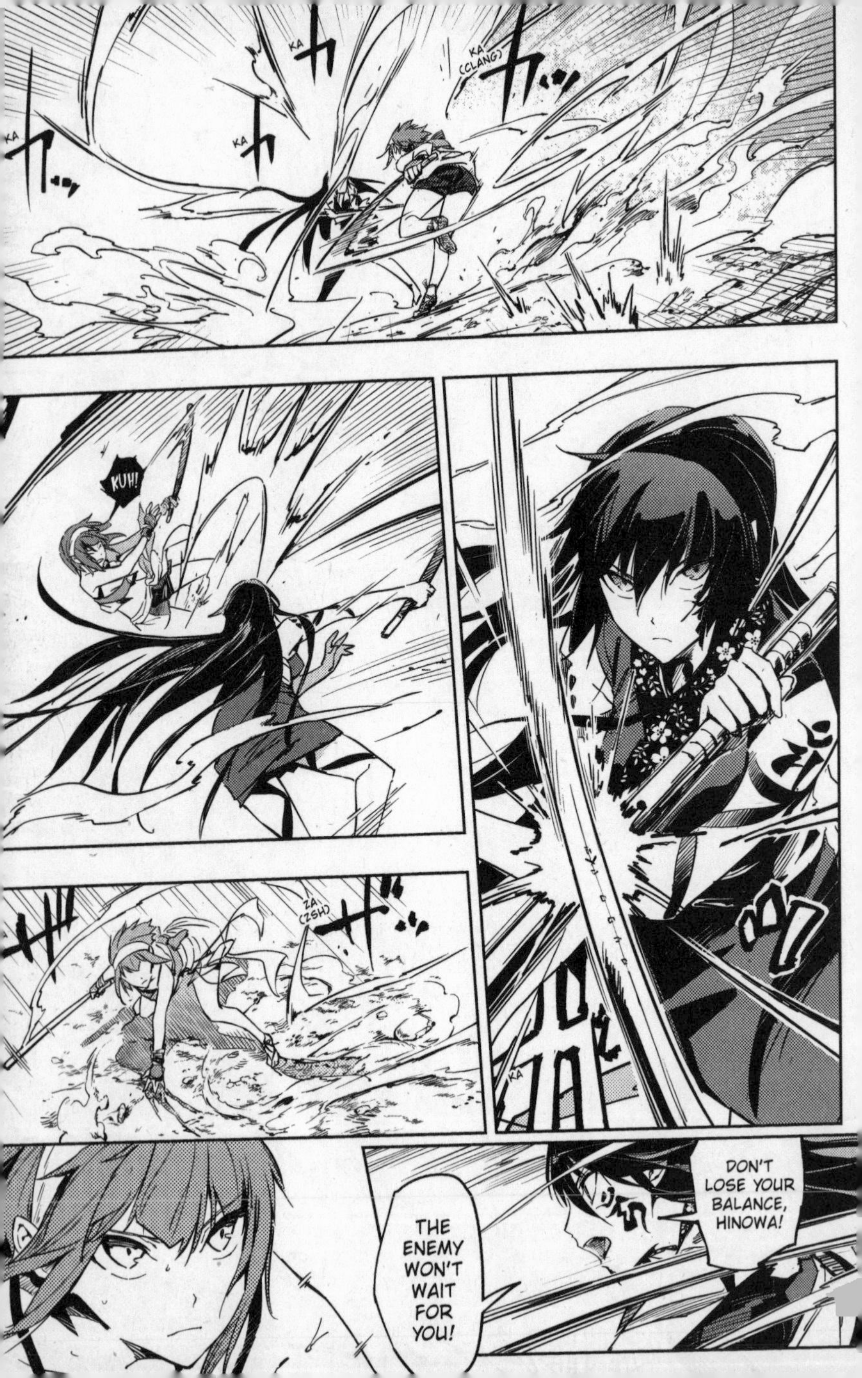
KA
(CLANG)
KA
KA
KA
KA
KUH!
ZA
(ZSH)
DON'T LOSE YOUR BALANCE, HINOWA!
THE ENEMY WON'T WAIT FOR YOU!

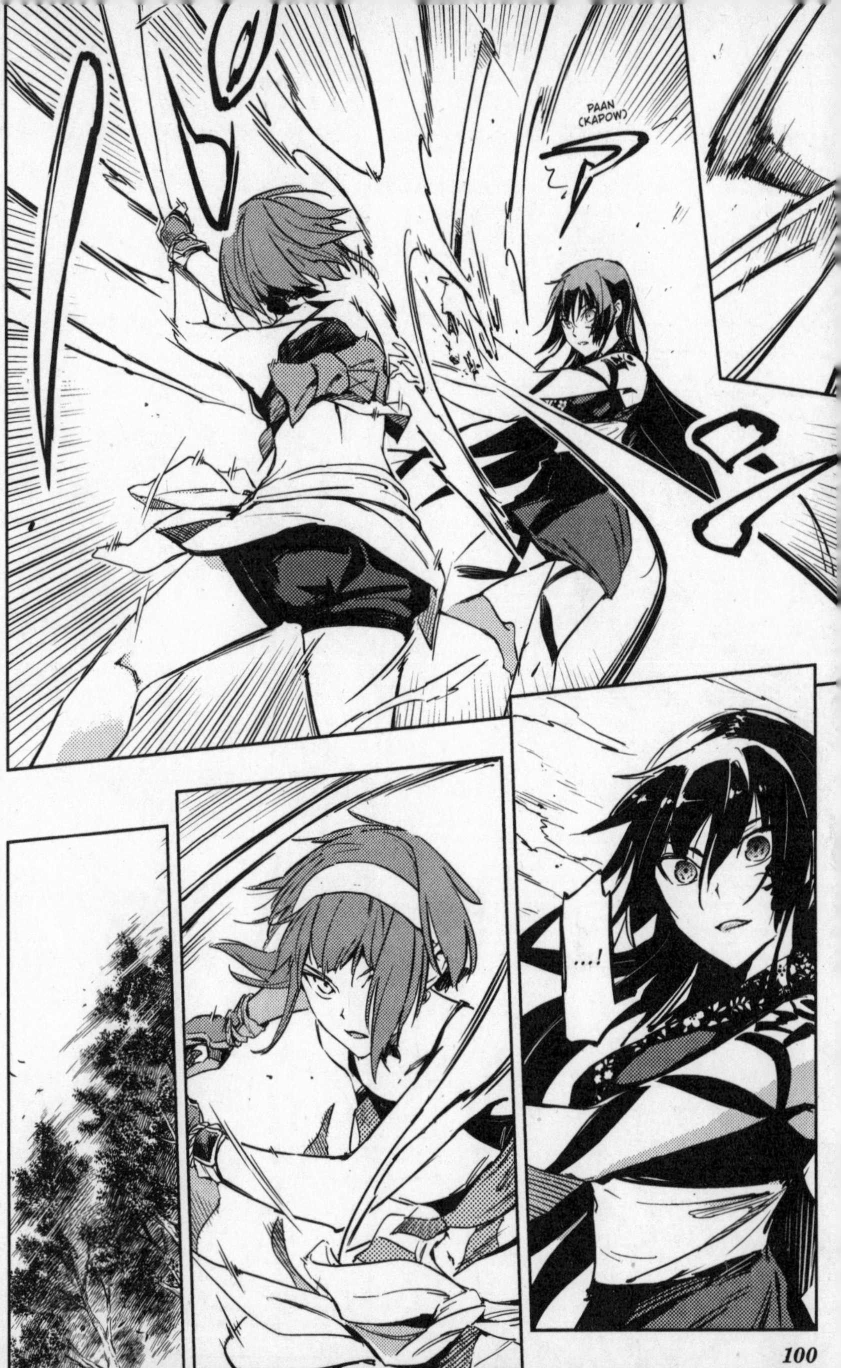
PAAN
(KAPOW)
...!

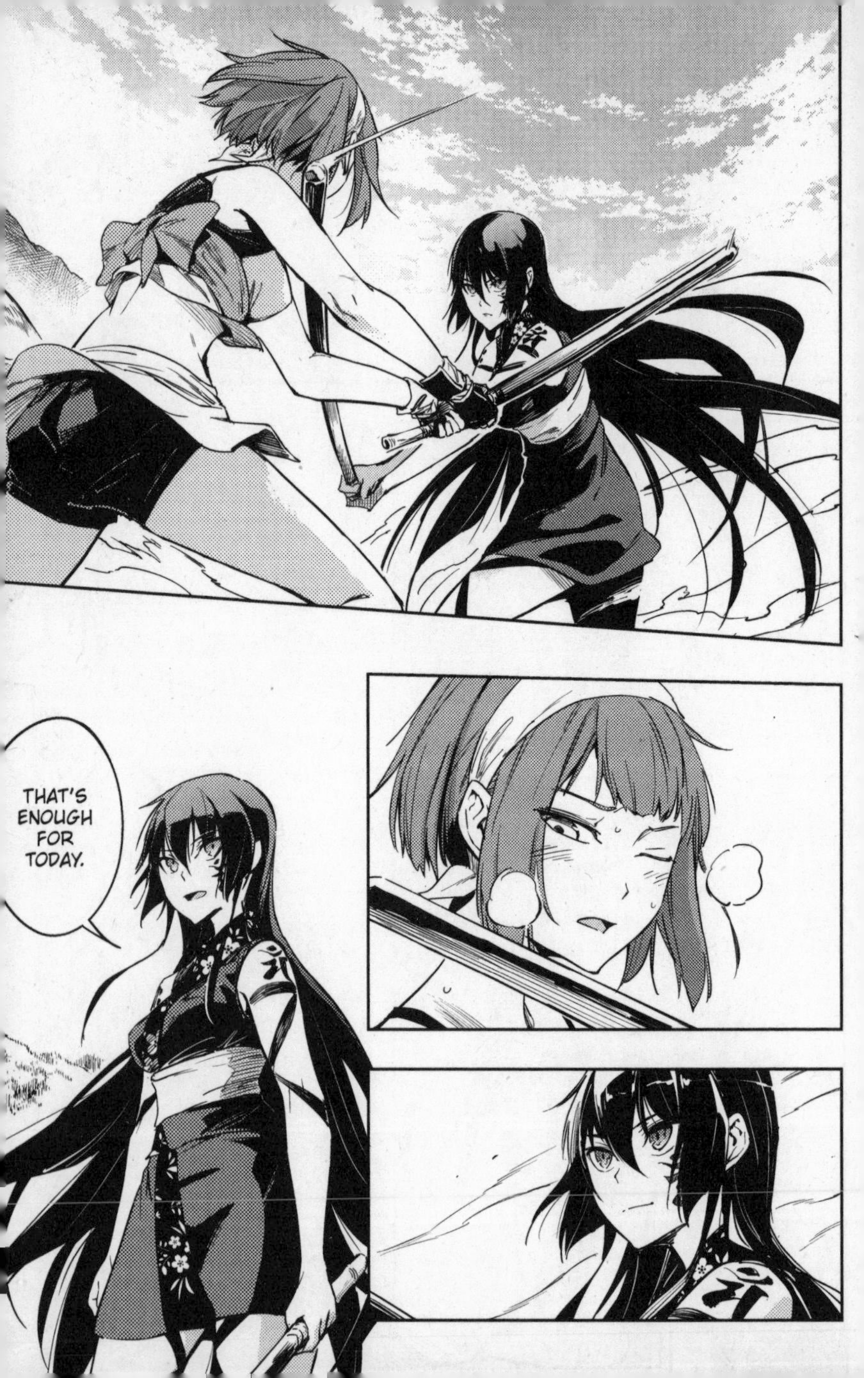
THAT'S ENOUGH FOR TODAY.

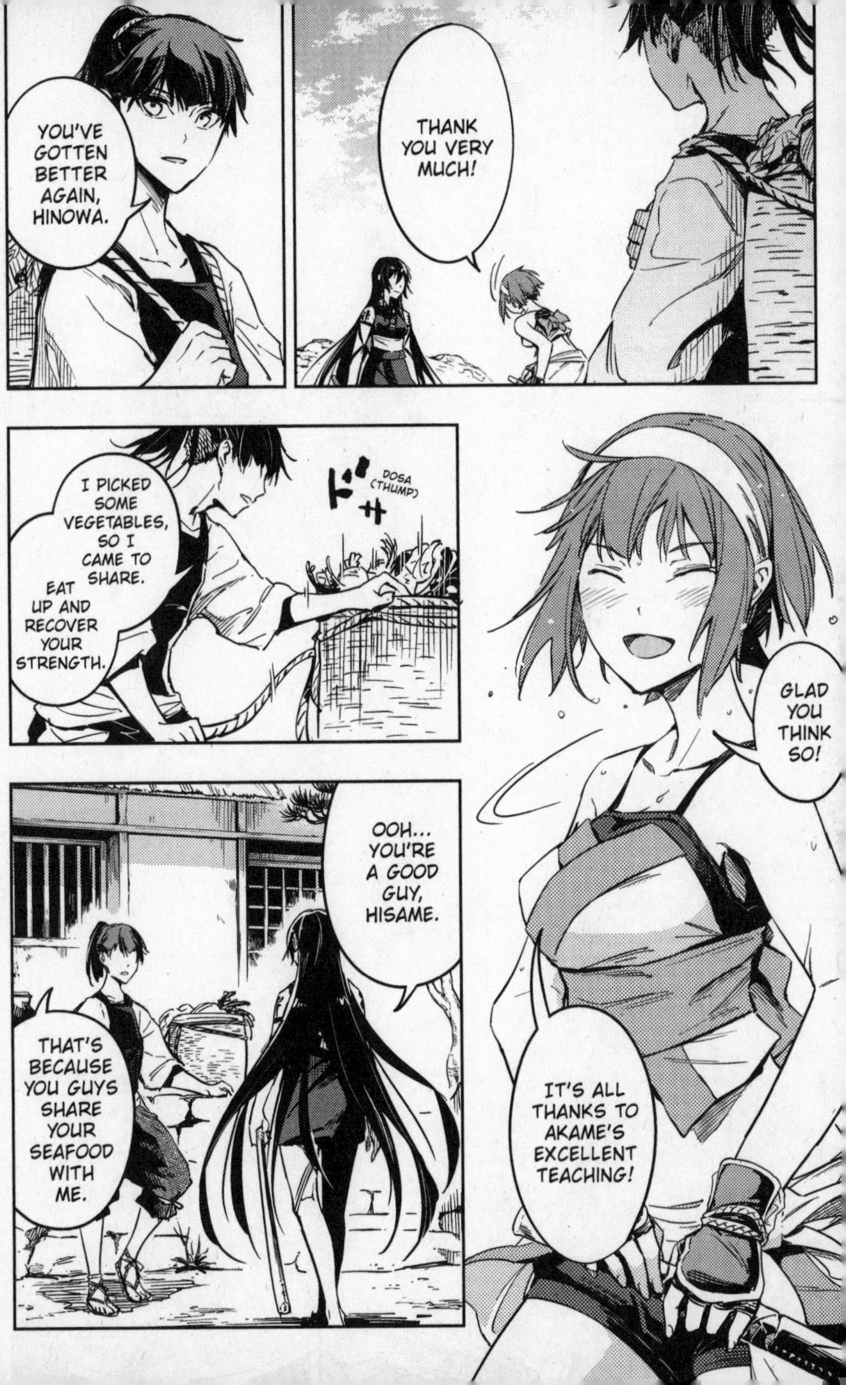
THANK YOU VERY MUCH!
YOU'VE GOTTEN BETTER AGAIN, HINOWA.
GLAD YOU THINK SO!
IT'S ALL THANKS TO AKAME'S EXCELLENT TEACHING!
ドサ
DOSA (THUMP)
I PICKED SOME VEGETABLES, SO I CAME TO SHARE.
EAT UP AND RECOVER YOUR STRENGTH.
OOH... YOU'RE A GOOD GUY, HISAME.
THAT'S BECAUSE YOU GUYS SHARE YOUR SEAFOOD WITH ME.

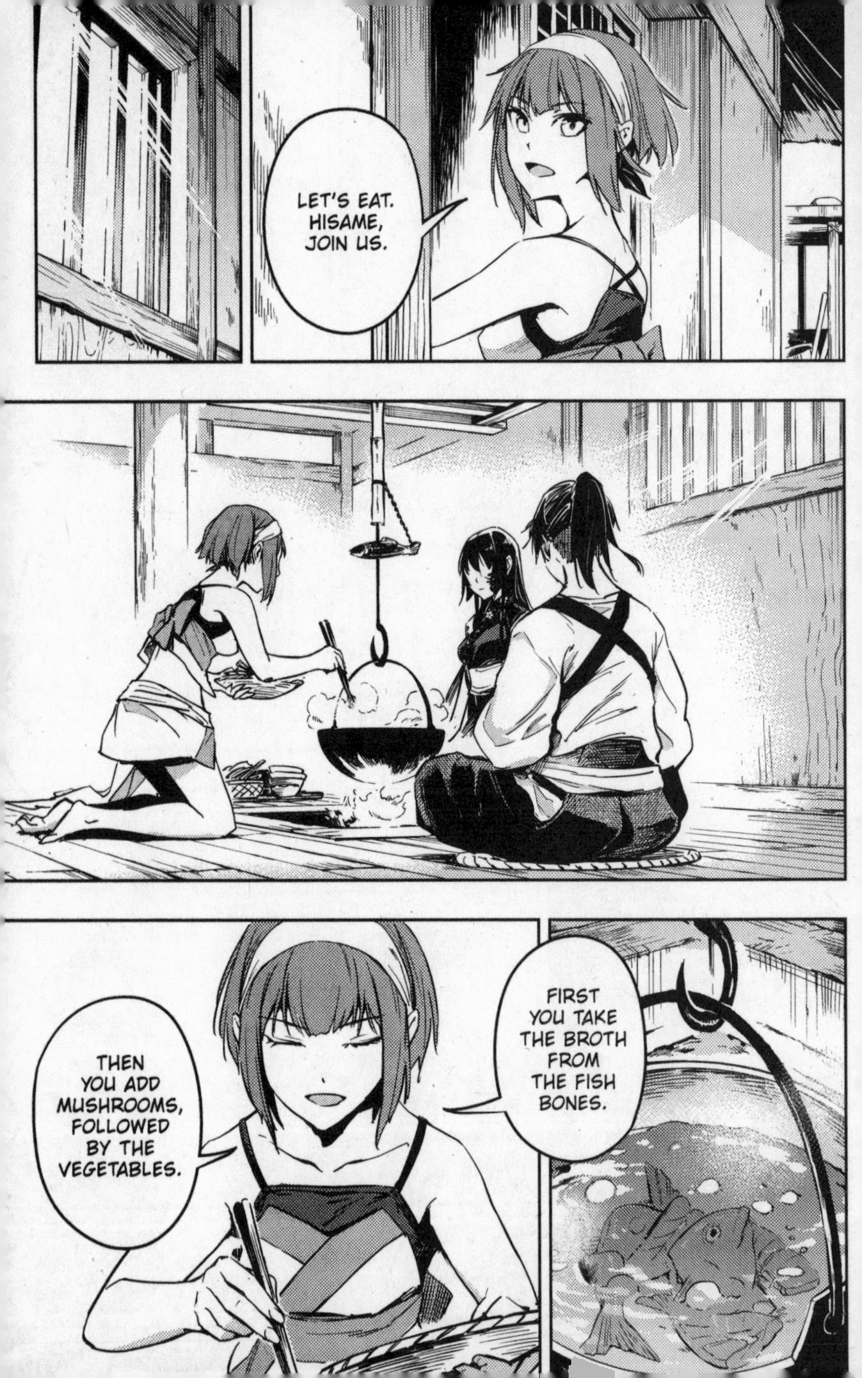
LET'S EAT. HISAME, JOIN US.
FIRST YOU TAKE THE BROTH FROM THE FISH BONES.
THEN YOU ADD MUSHROOMS, FOLLOWED BY THE VEGETABLES.

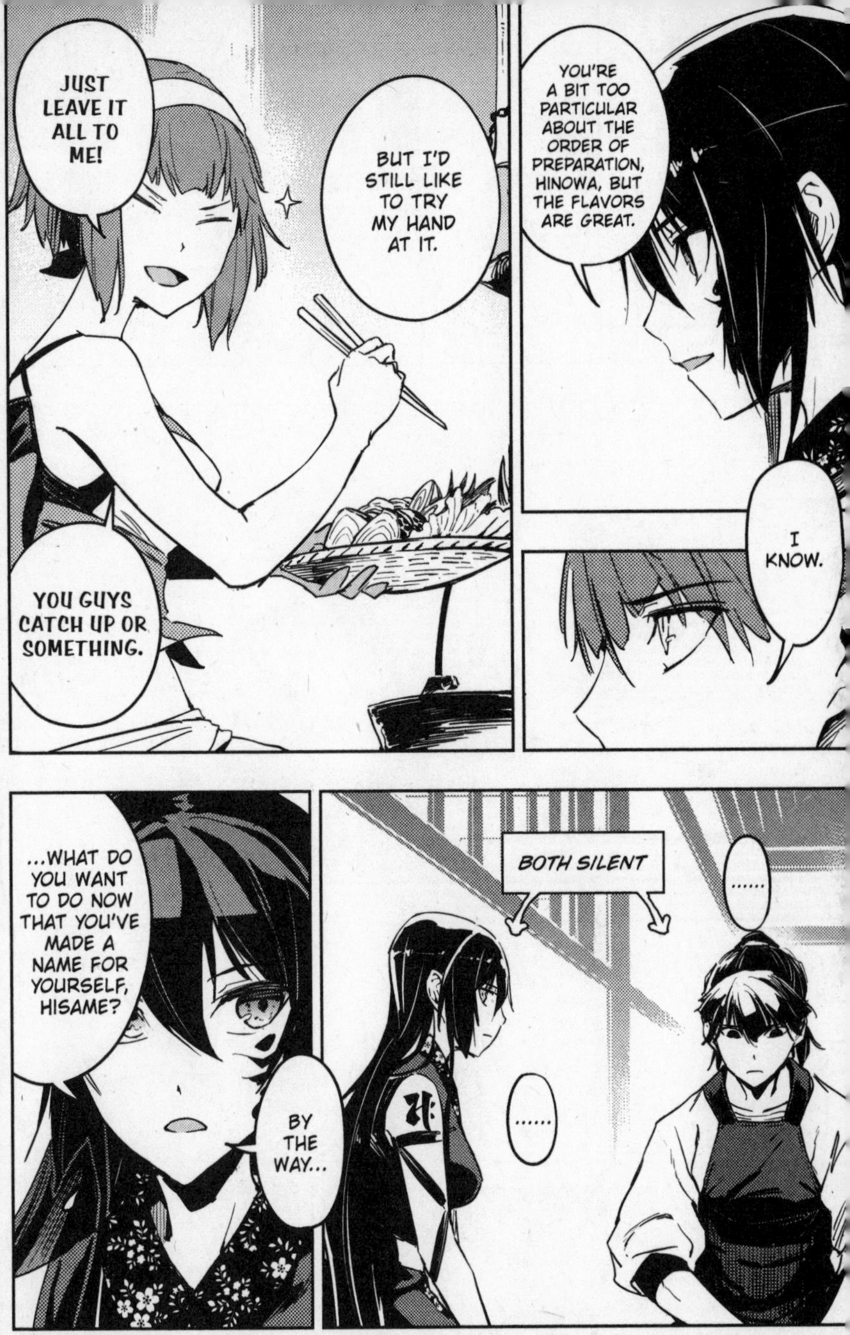
YOU'RE A BIT TOO PARTICULAR ABOUT THE ORDER OF PREPARATION, HINOWA, BUT THE FLAVORS ARE GREAT.
I KNOW.
BUT I'D STILL LIKE TO TRY MY HAND AT IT.
JUST LEAVE IT ALL TO ME!
YOU GUYS CATCH UP OR SOMETHING.
......
BOTH SILENT
......
BY THE WAY...
...WHAT DO YOU WANT TO DO NOW THAT YOU'VE MADE A NAME FOR YOURSELF, HISAME?

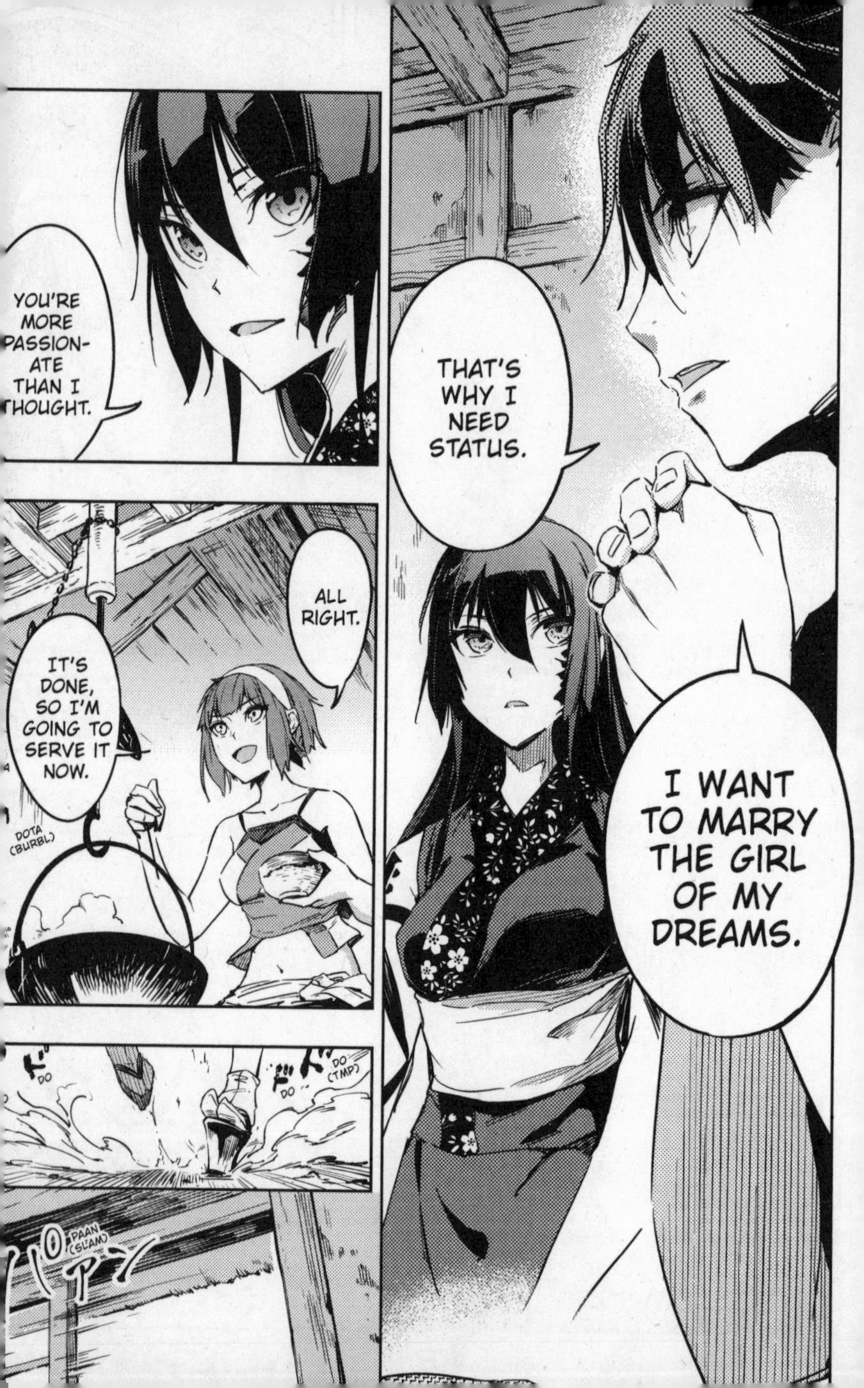
THAT'S WHY I NEED STATUS.
I WANT TO MARRY THE GIRL OF MY DREAMS.
YOU'RE MORE PASSION-ATE THAN I THOUGHT.
ALL RIGHT.
IT'S DONE, SO I'M GOING TO SERVE IT NOW.
DOTA (BURBL)
DO (TMP)
DO
DO
PAAN (SLAM)

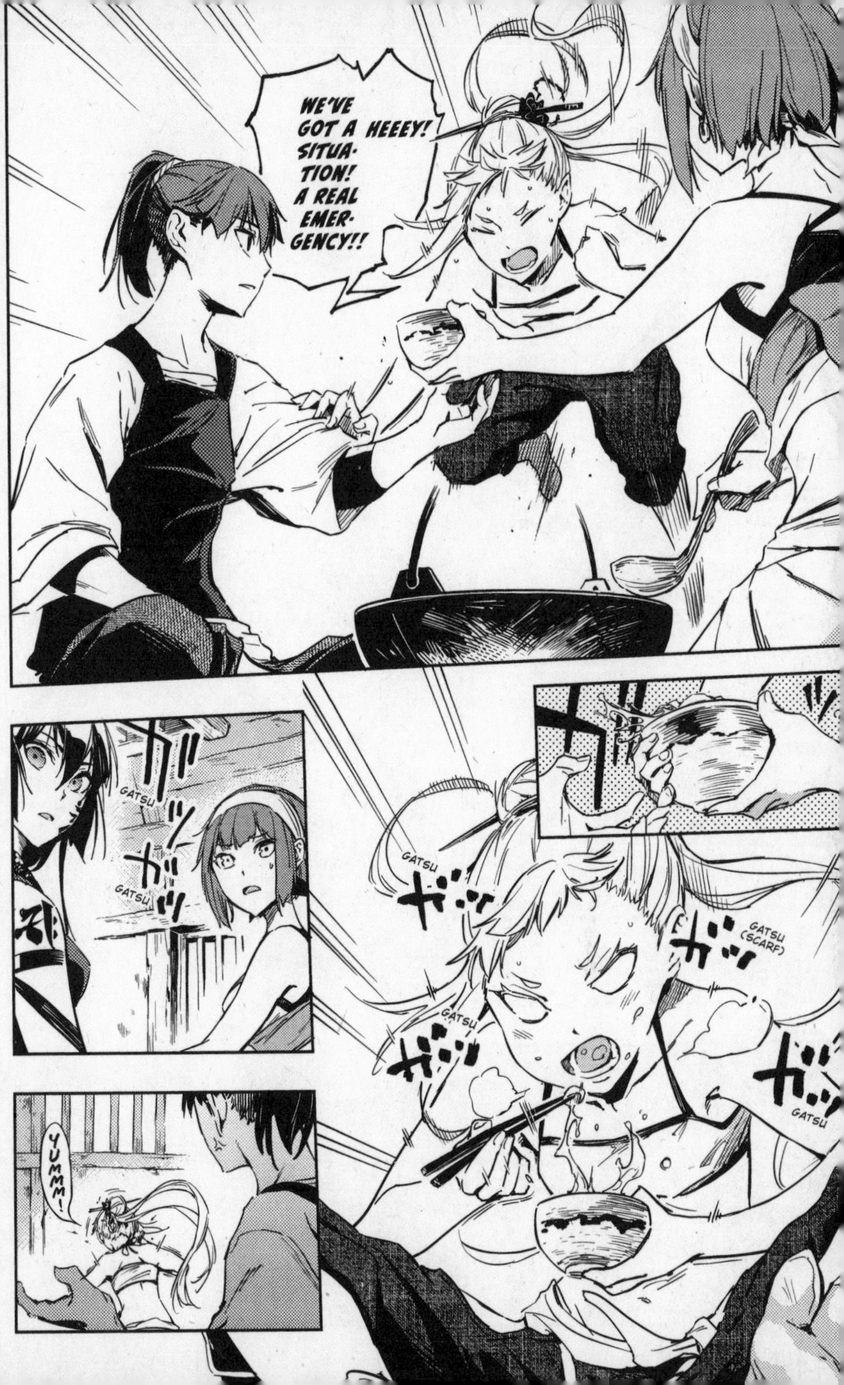
HEEEY!
WE'VE GOT A SITUATION! A REAL EMERGENCY!!
GATSU (SCARF)
GATSU
GATSU
GATSU
GATSU
GATSU
YUMMM!

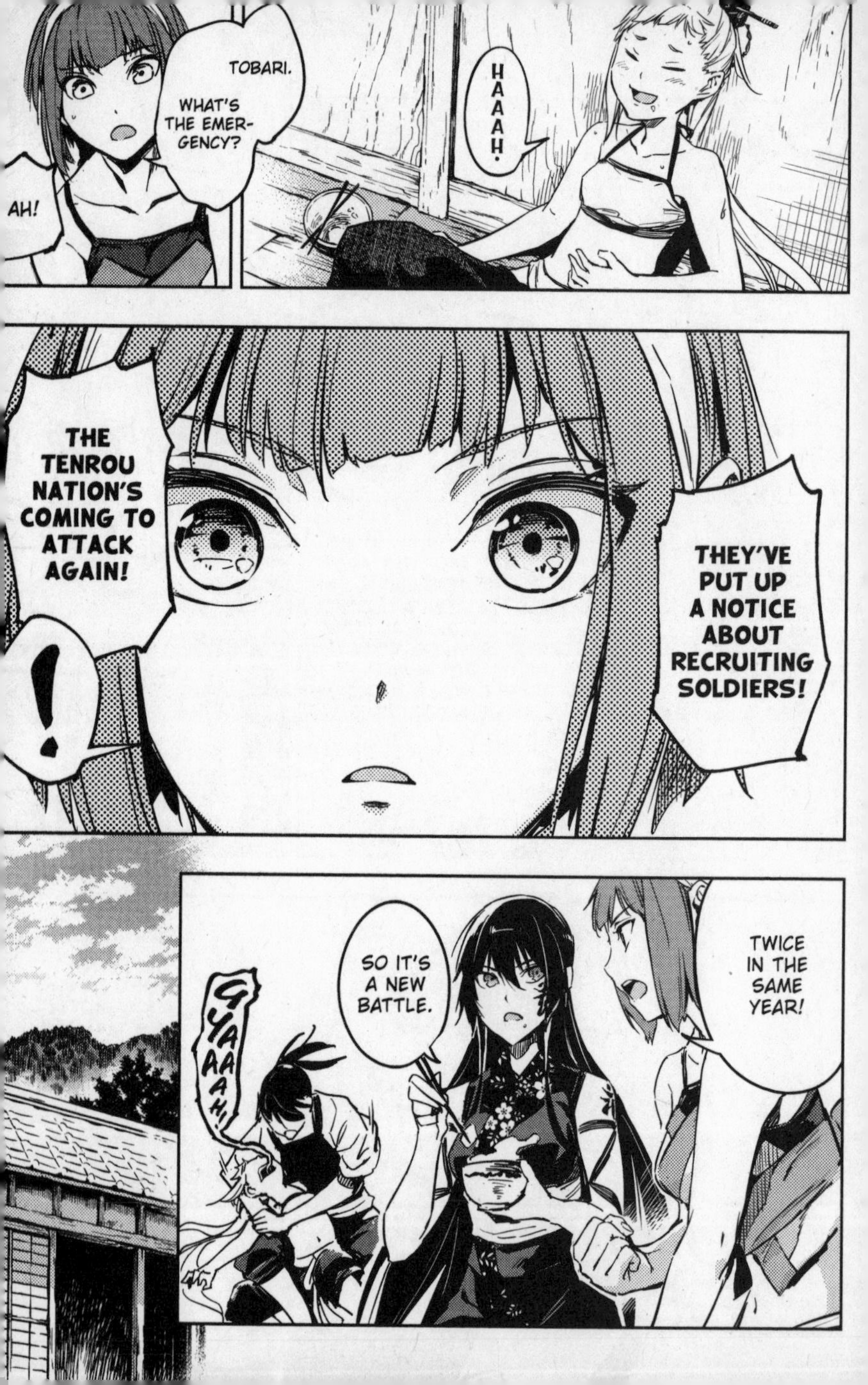
HAAAH.
TOBARI.
WHAT'S THE EMERGENCY?
AH!
THE TENROU NATION'S COMING TO ATTACK AGAIN!
THEY'VE PUT UP A NOTICE ABOUT RECRUITING SOLDIERS!
!
TWICE IN THE SAME YEAR!
SO IT'S A NEW BATTLE.
GYAAAAAH!

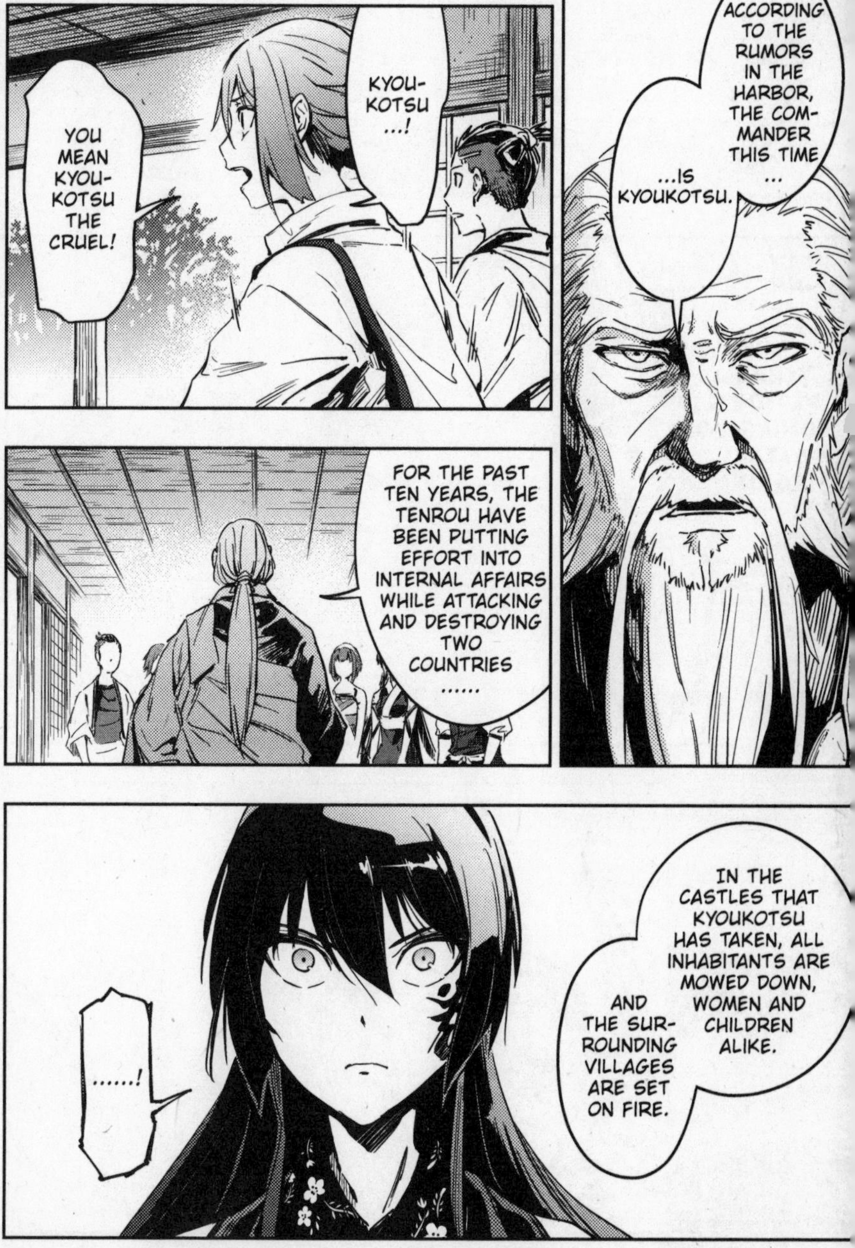
ACCORDING TO THE RUMORS IN THE HARBOR, THE COMMANDER THIS TIME ...
...IS KYOUKOTSU.
KYOUKOTSU ...!
YOU MEAN KYOUKOTSU THE CRUEL!
FOR THE PAST TEN YEARS, THE TENROU HAVE BEEN PUTTING EFFORT INTO INTERNAL AFFAIRS WHILE ATTACKING AND DESTROYING TWO COUNTRIES ......
IN THE CASTLES THAT KYOUKOTSU HAS TAKEN, ALL INHABITANTS ARE MOWED DOWN, WOMEN AND CHILDREN ALIKE.
AND THE SURROUNDING VILLAGES ARE SET ON FIRE.
......!

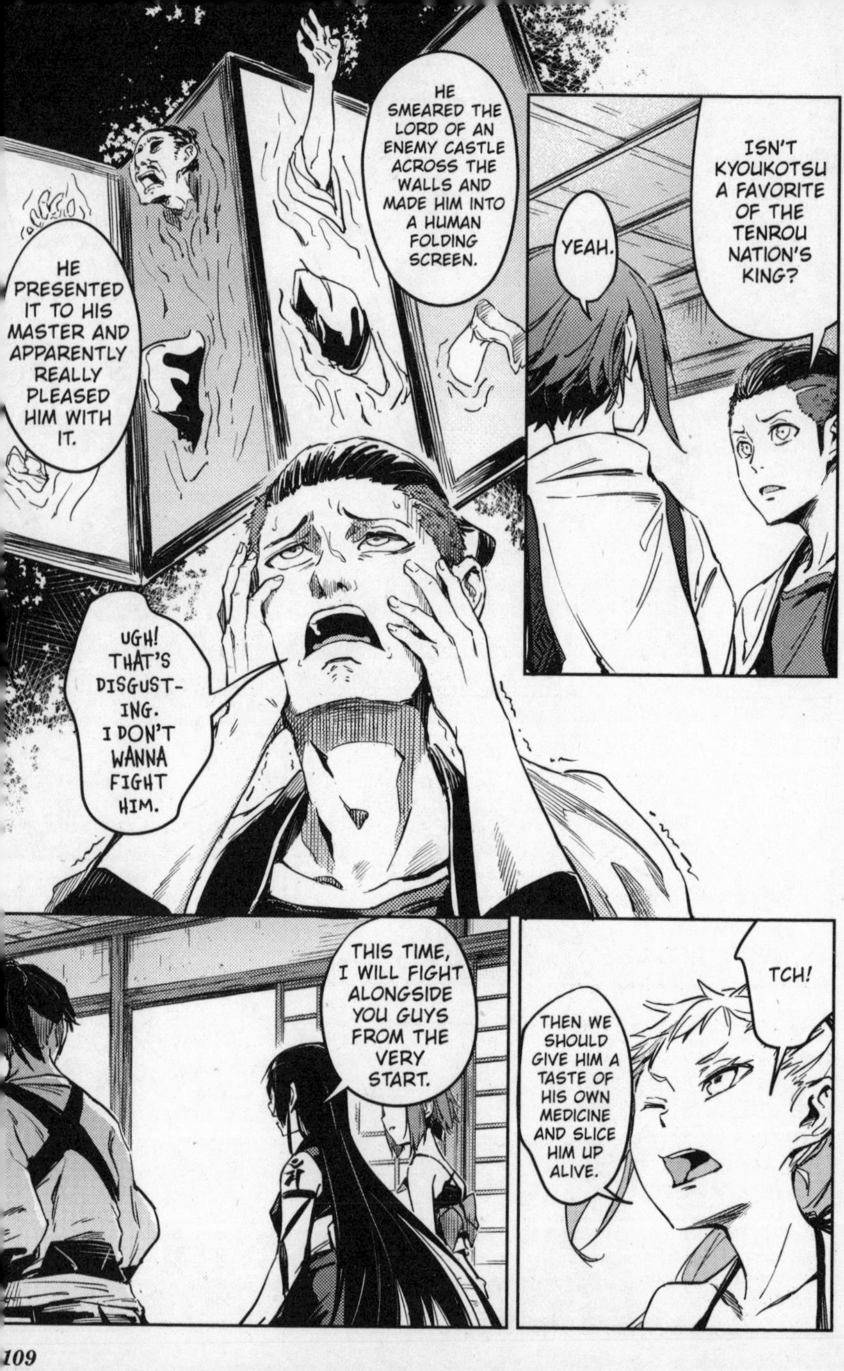

ISN'T KYOUKOTSU A FAVORITE OF THE TENROU NATION'S KING?
YEAH.
HE SMEARED THE LORD OF AN ENEMY CASTLE ACROSS THE WALLS AND MADE HIM INTO A HUMAN FOLDING SCREEN.
HE PRESENTED IT TO HIS MASTER AND APPARENTLY REALLY PLEASED HIM WITH IT.
UGH! THAT'S DISGUST-ING. I DON'T WANNA FIGHT HIM.
TCH!
THEN WE SHOULD GIVE HIM A TASTE OF HIS OWN MEDICINE AND SLICE HIM UP ALIVE.
THIS TIME, I WILL FIGHT ALONGSIDE YOU GUYS FROM THE VERY START.

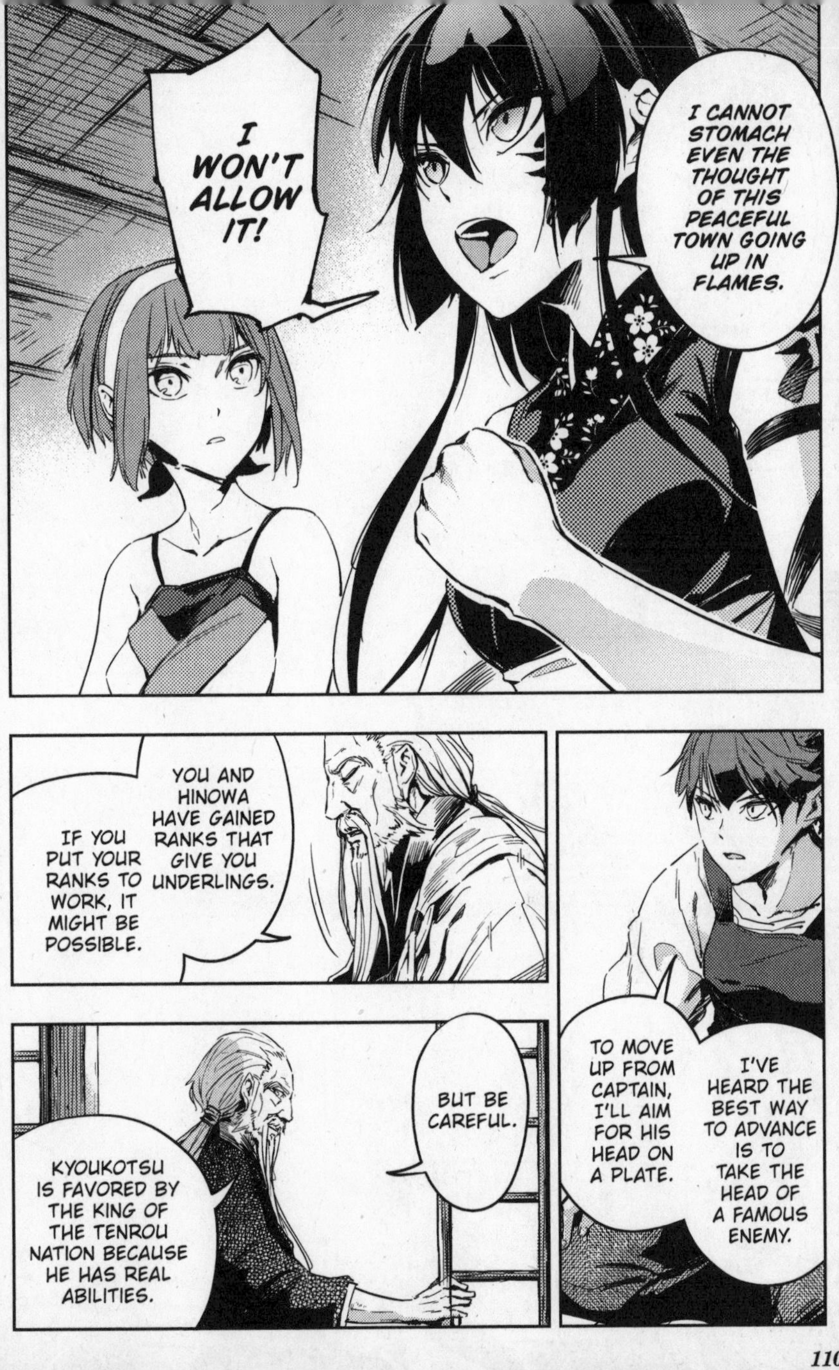
I CANNOT STOMACH EVEN THE THOUGHT OF THIS PEACEFUL TOWN GOING UP IN FLAMES.
I WON'T ALLOW IT!
I'VE HEARD THE BEST WAY TO ADVANCE IS TO TAKE THE HEAD OF A FAMOUS ENEMY.
TO MOVE UP FROM CAPTAIN, I'LL AIM FOR HIS HEAD ON A PLATE.
YOU AND HINOWA HAVE GAINED RANKS THAT GIVE YOU UNDERLINGS.
IF YOU PUT YOUR RANKS TO WORK, IT MIGHT BE POSSIBLE.
BUT BE CAREFUL.
KYOUKOTSU IS FAVORED BY THE KING OF THE TENROU NATION BECAUSE HE HAS REAL ABILITIES.

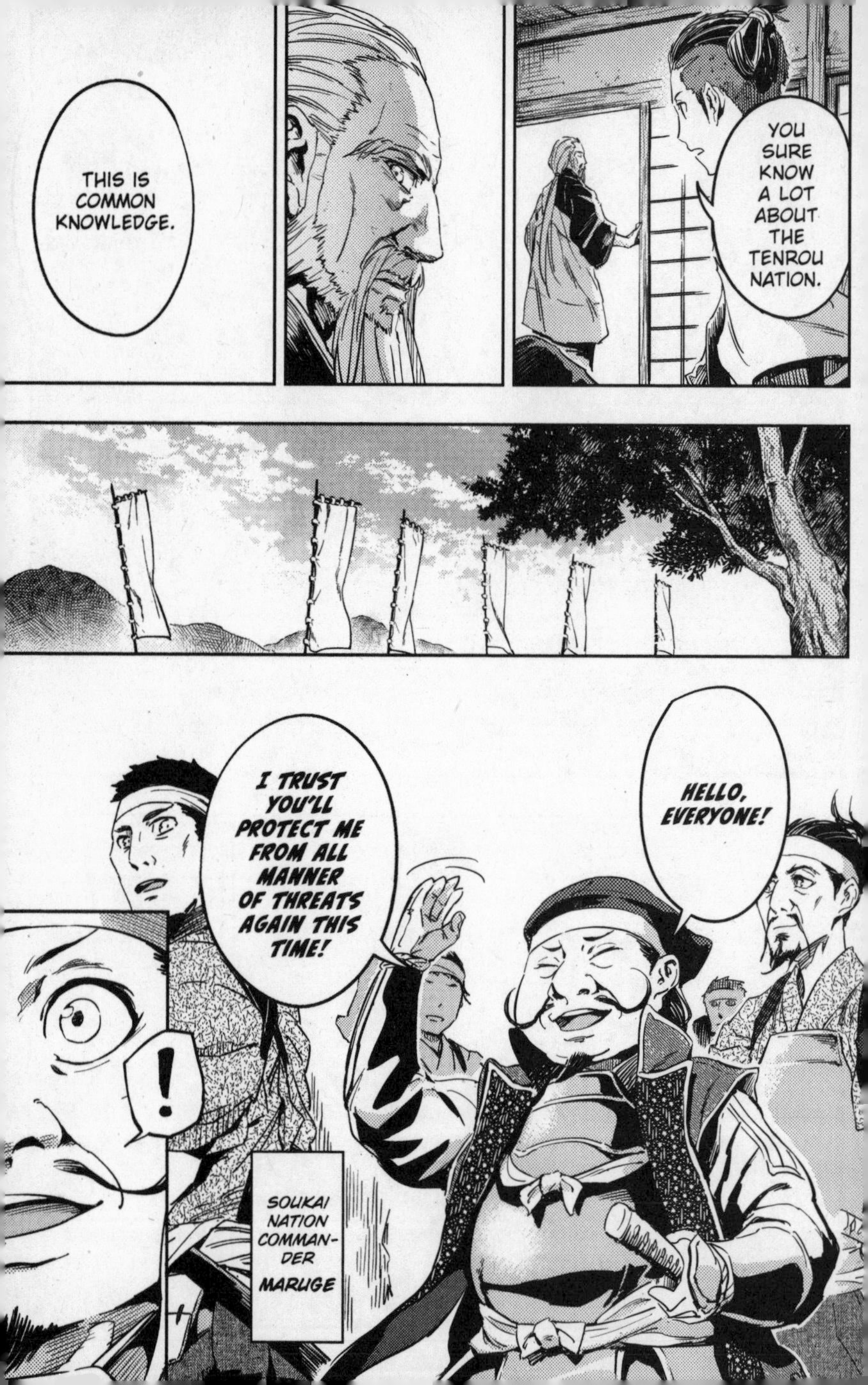
YOU SURE KNOW A LOT ABOUT THE TENROU NATION.
THIS IS COMMON KNOWLEDGE.
HELLO, EVERYONE!
I TRUST YOU'LL PROTECT ME FROM ALL MANNER OF THREATS AGAIN THIS TIME!
SOUKAI NATION COMMAN-DER MARUGE
!

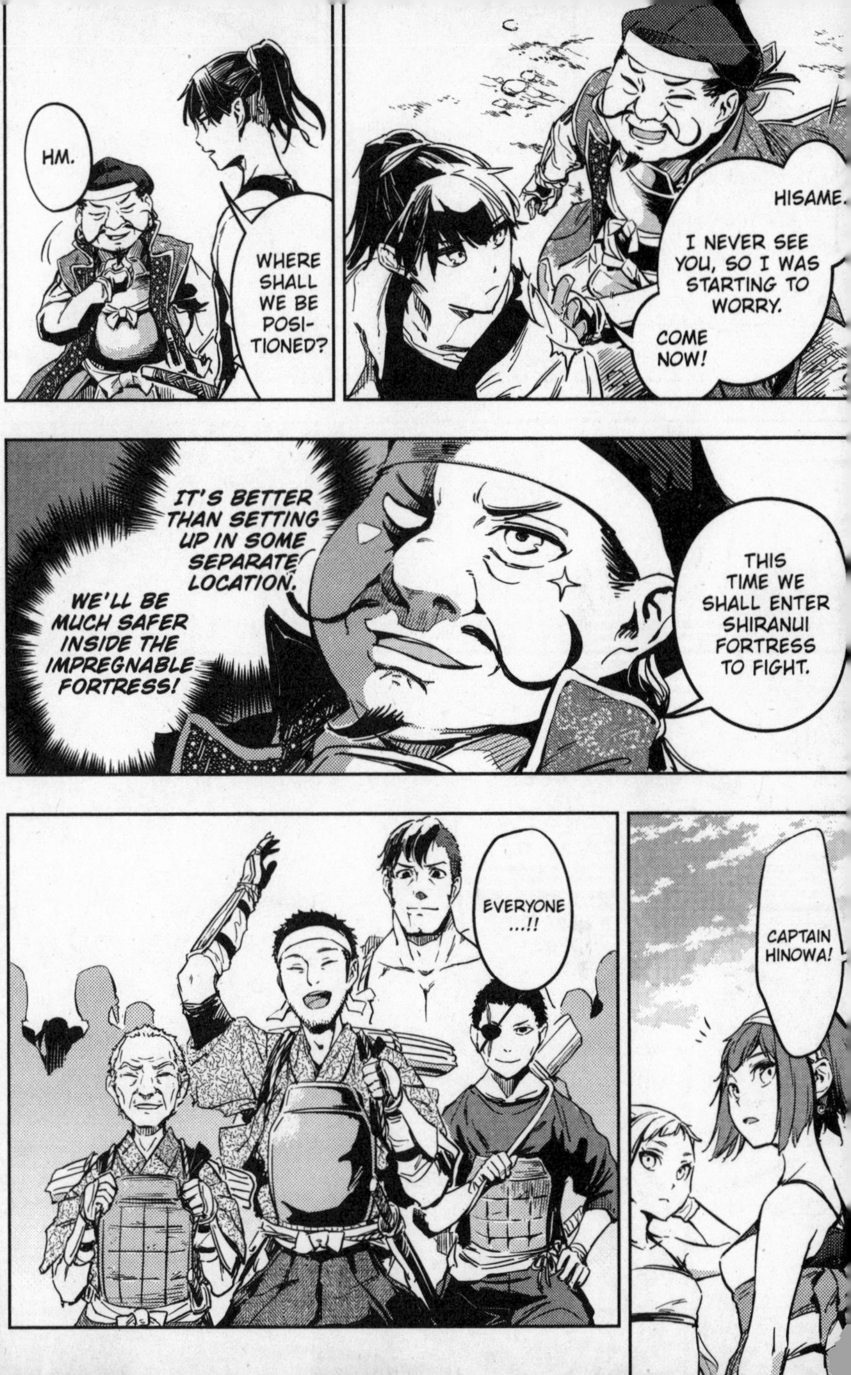
HISAME.
I NEVER SEE YOU, SO I WAS STARTING TO WORRY.
COME NOW!
WHERE SHALL WE BE POSI-TIONED?
HM.
THIS TIME WE SHALL ENTER SHIRANUI FORTRESS TO FIGHT.
IT'S BETTER THAN SETTING UP IN SOME SEPARATE LOCATION.
WE'LL BE MUCH SAFER INSIDE THE IMPREGNABLE FORTRESS!
CAPTAIN HINOWA!
EVERYONE ...!!

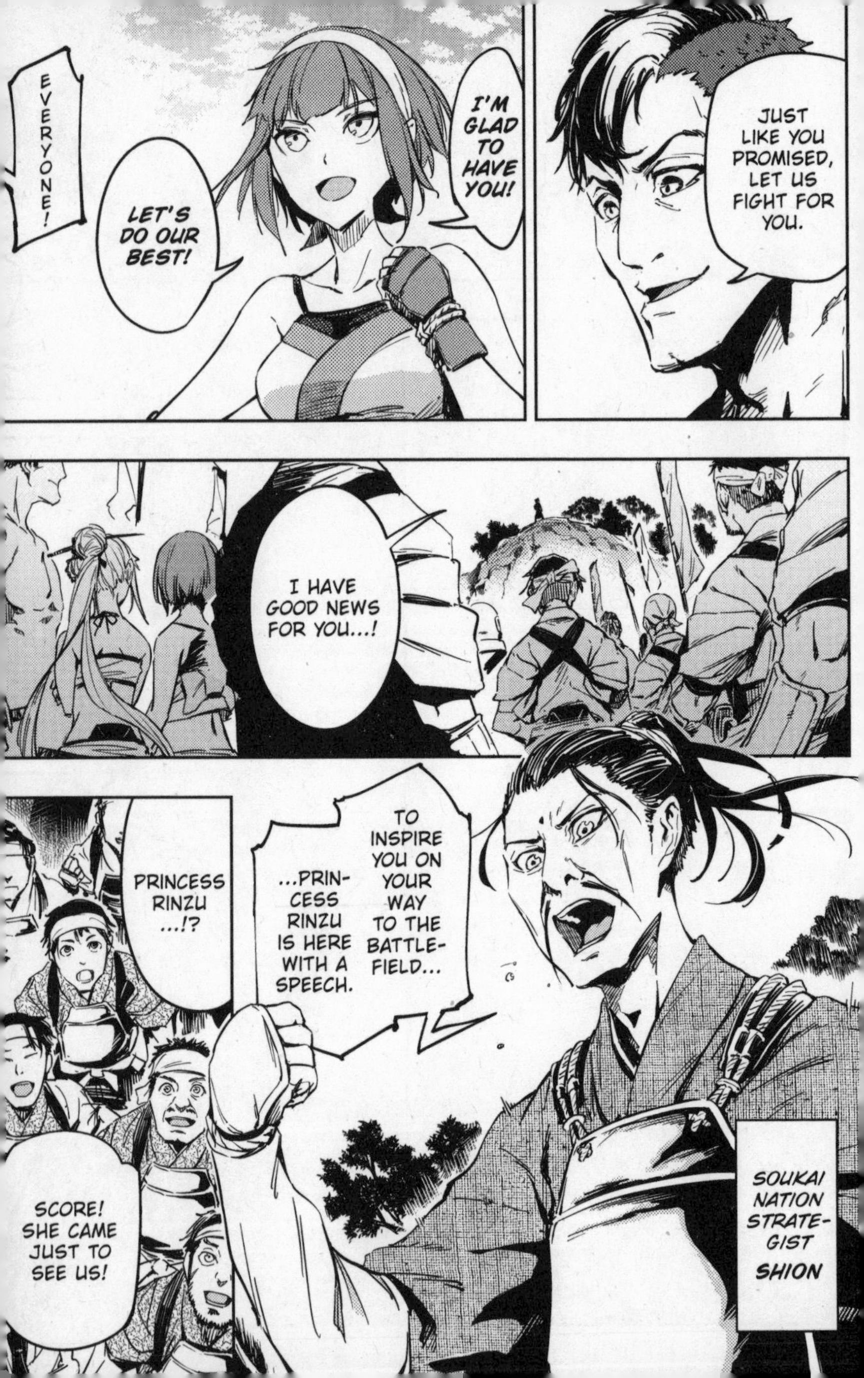
JUST LIKE YOU PROMISED, LET US FIGHT FOR YOU.
I'M GLAD TO HAVE YOU!
EVERYONE!
LET'S DO OUR BEST!
I HAVE GOOD NEWS FOR YOU...!
TO INSPIRE YOU ON YOUR WAY TO THE BATTLE-FIELD...
...PRIN-CESS RINZU IS HERE WITH A SPEECH.
PRINCESS RINZU ...!?
SOUKAI NATION STRATE-GIST SHION
SCORE! SHE CAME JUST TO SEE US!

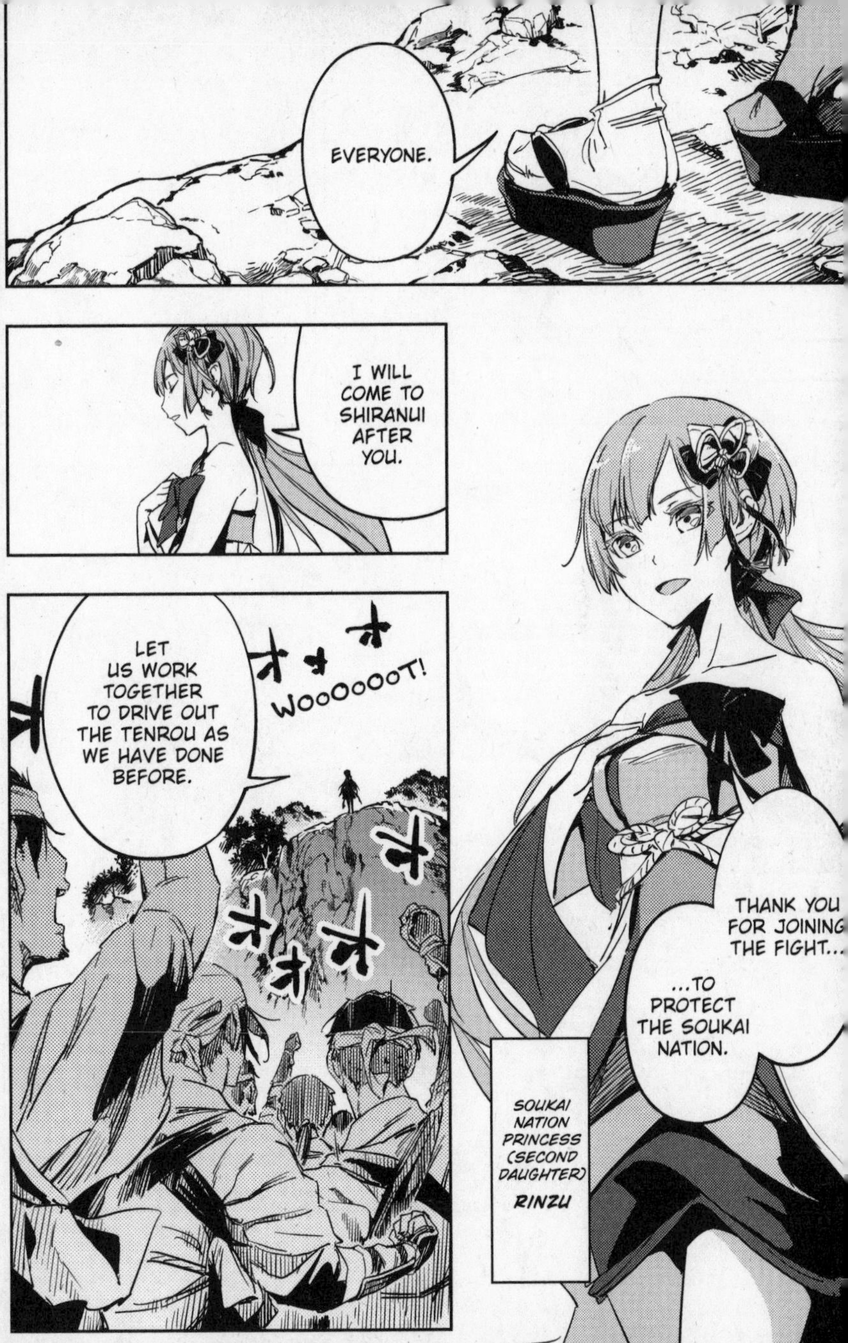
EVERYONE.
THANK YOU FOR JOINING THE FIGHT...
...TO PROTECT THE SOUKAI NATION.
SOUKAI NATION PRINCESS (SECOND DAUGHTER) RINZU
I WILL COME TO SHIRANUI AFTER YOU.
LET US WORK TOGETHER TO DRIVE OUT THE TENROU AS WE HAVE DONE BEFORE.
WOOOOOOT!

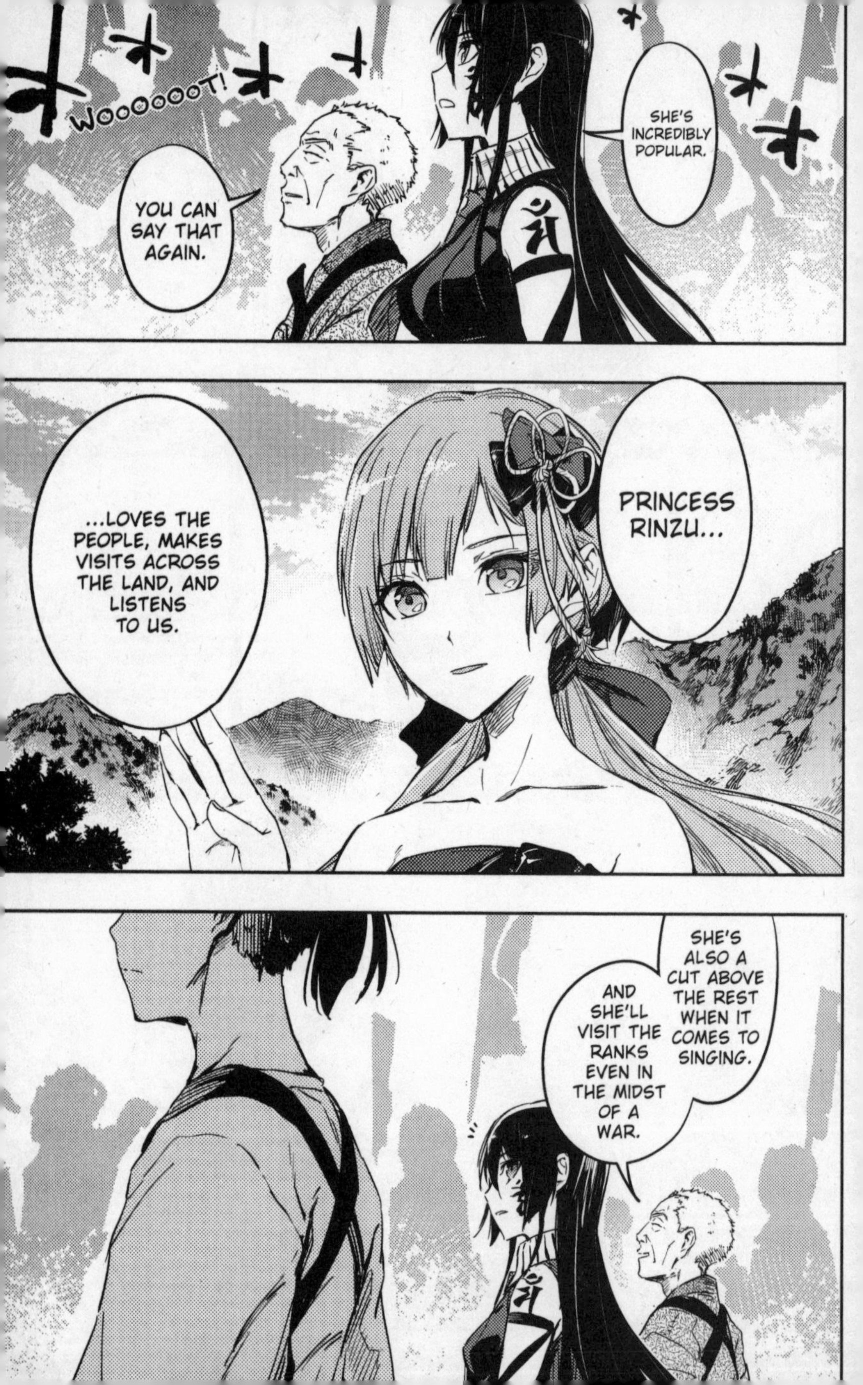
SHE'S INCREDIBLY POPULAR.
WOOOOOOT!
YOU CAN SAY THAT AGAIN.
PRINCESS RINZU...
...LOVES THE PEOPLE, MAKES VISITS ACROSS THE LAND, AND LISTENS TO US.
SHE'S ALSO A CUT ABOVE THE REST WHEN IT COMES TO SINGING.
AND SHE'LL VISIT THE RANKS EVEN IN THE MIDST OF A WAR.

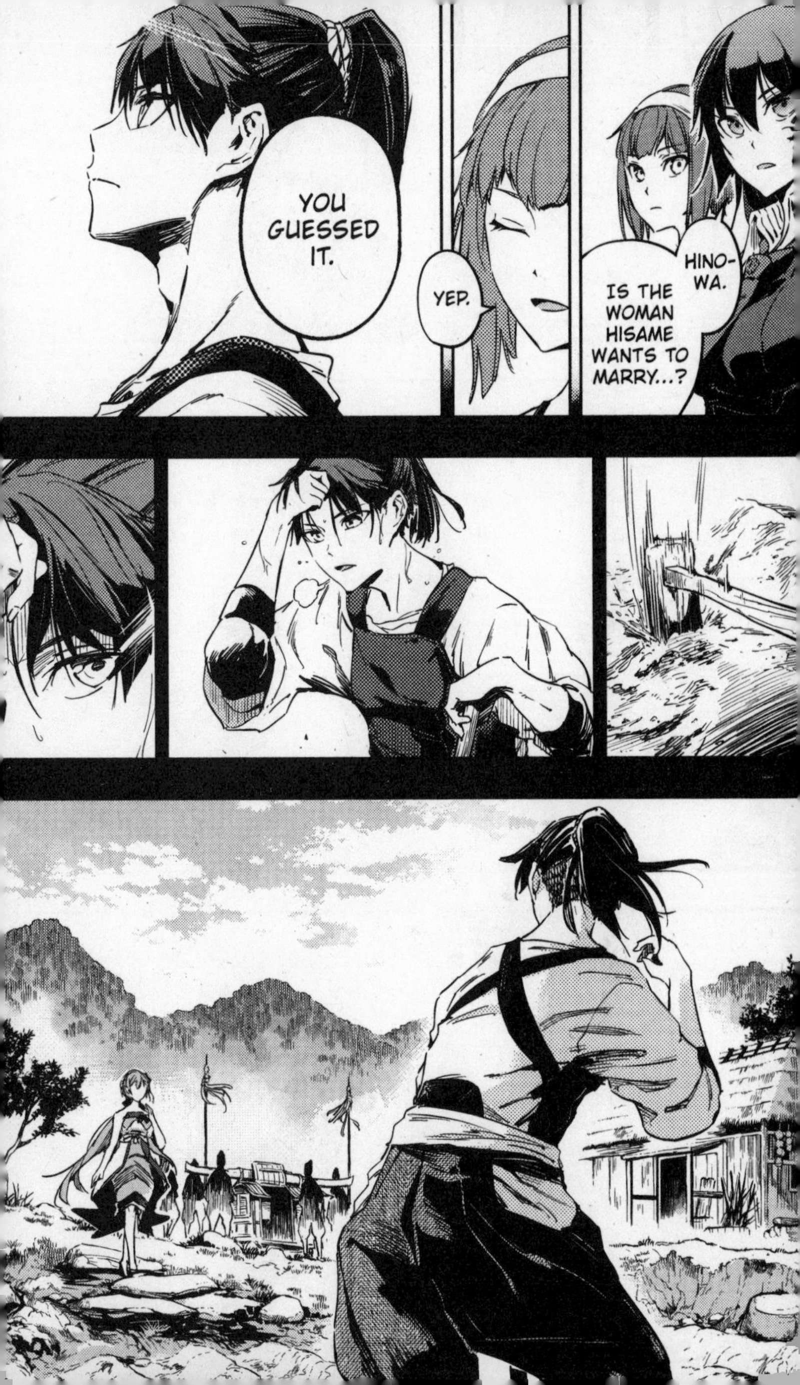
HINO-WA.
IS THE WOMAN HISAME WANTS TO MARRY...?
YEP.
YOU GUESSED IT.

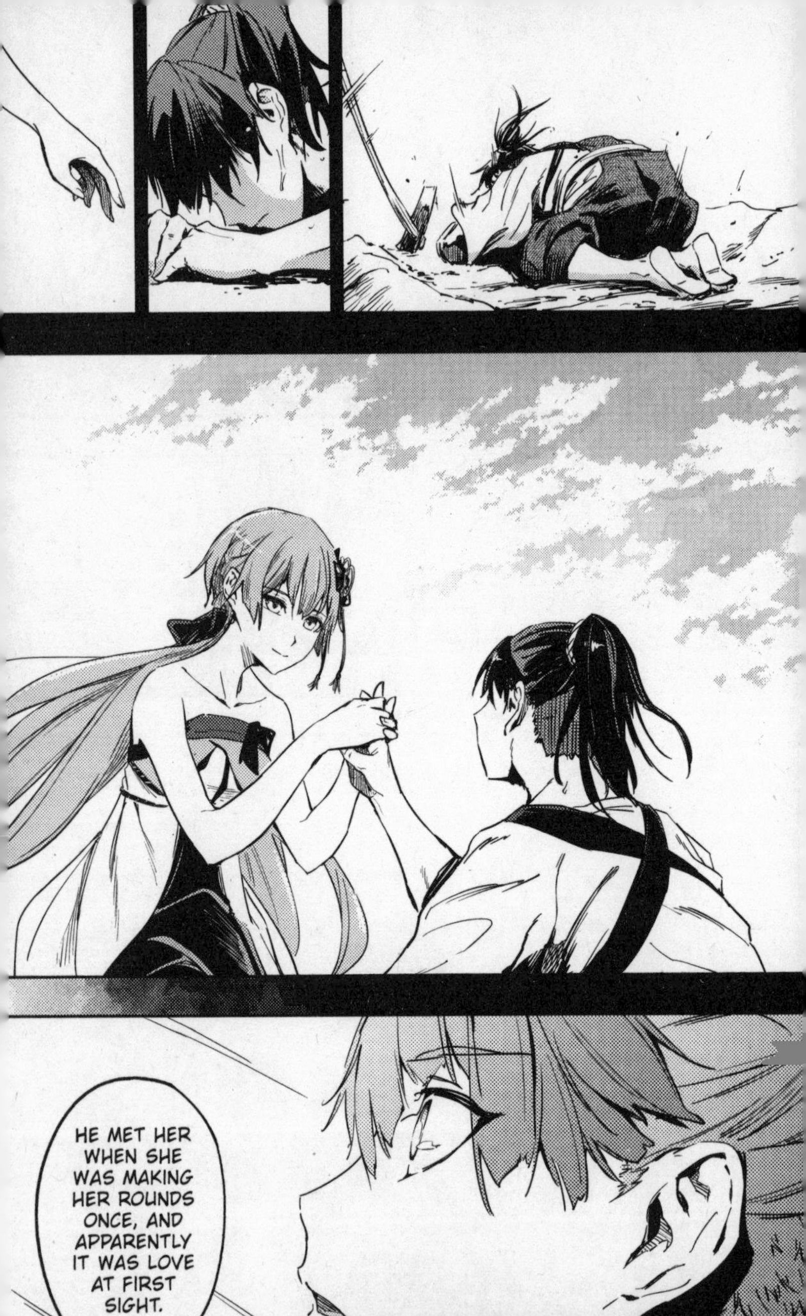
HE MET HER WHEN SHE WAS MAKING HER ROUNDS ONCE, AND APPARENTLY IT WAS LOVE AT FIRST SIGHT.

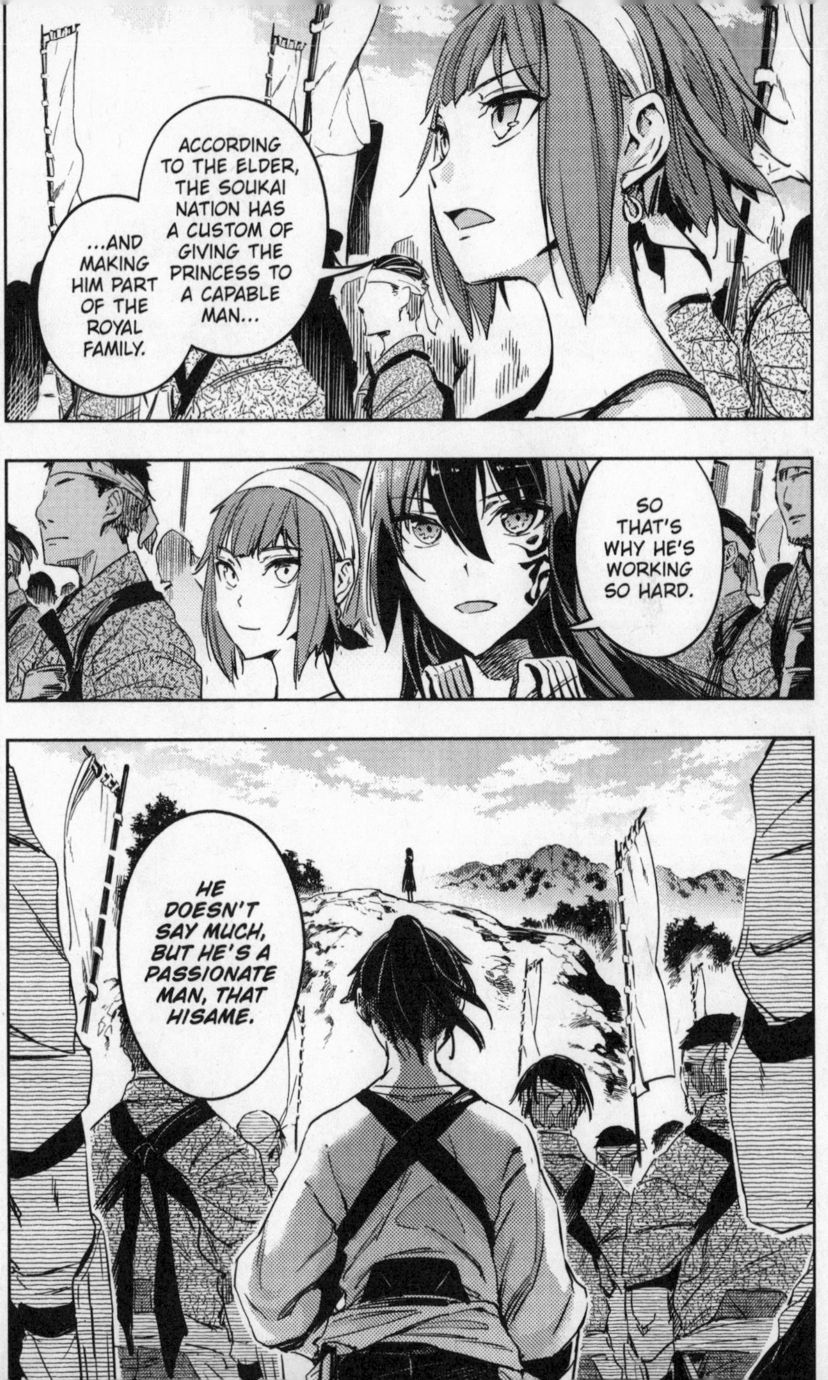
ACCORDING TO THE ELDER, THE SOUKAI NATION HAS A CUSTOM OF GIVING THE PRINCESS TO A CAPABLE MAN...
...AND MAKING HIM PART OF THE ROYAL FAMILY.
SO THAT'S WHY HE'S WORKING SO HARD.
HE DOESN'T SAY MUCH, BUT HE'S A PASSIONATE MAN, THAT HISAME.

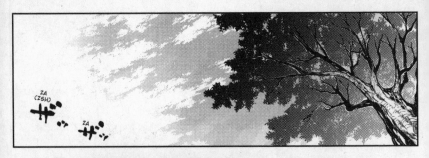

ZA
(ZSH)

ZA

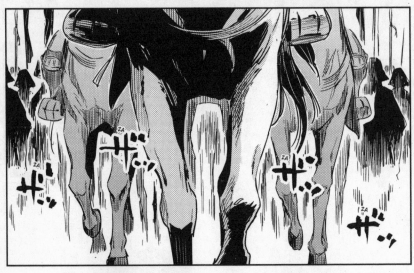

ZA

ZA

ZA

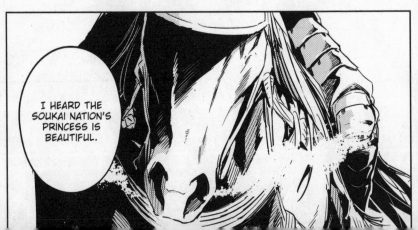

I HEARD THE
SOUKAI NATION'S
PRINCESS IS
BEAUTIFUL.

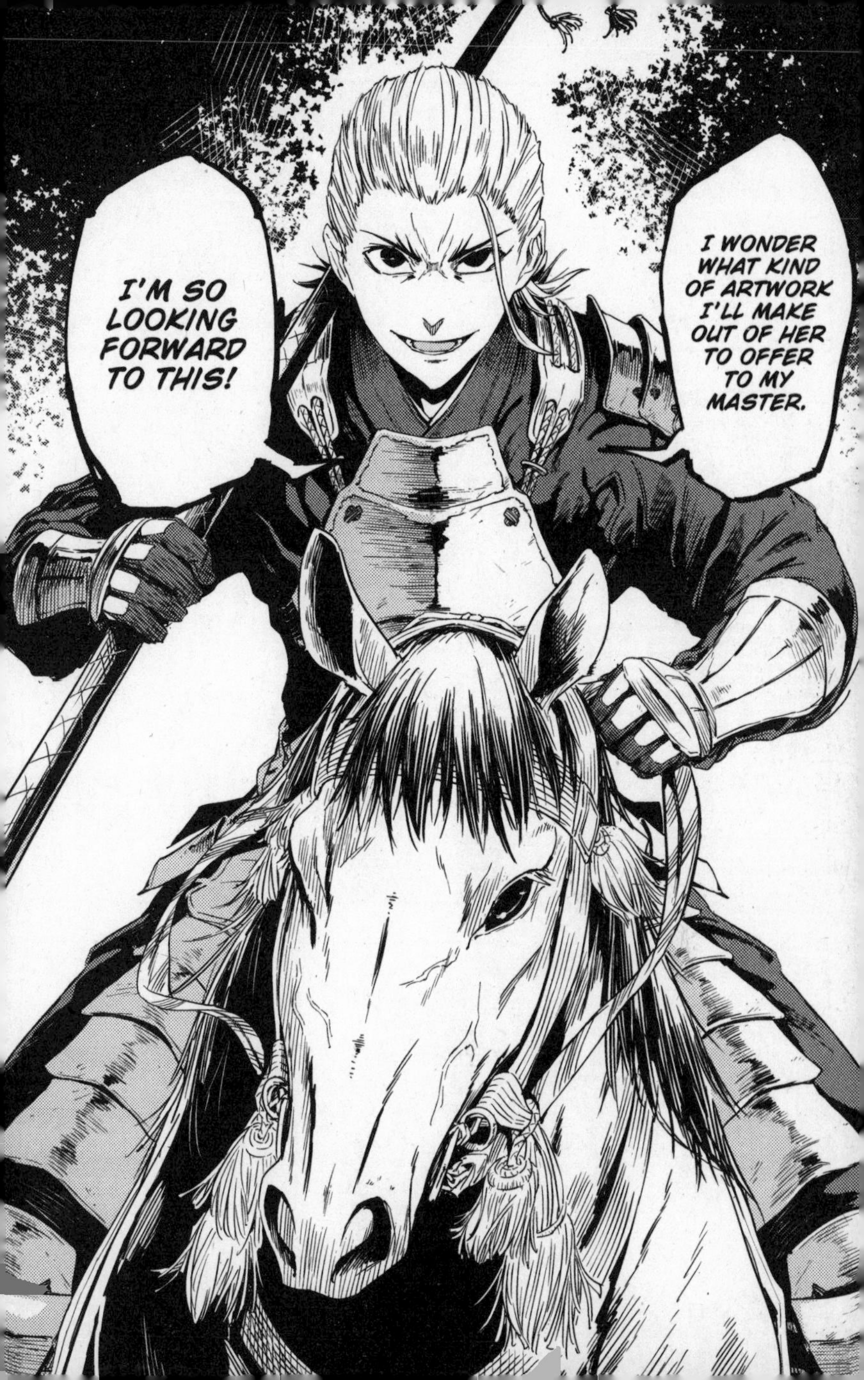
I WONDER WHAT KIND OF ARTWORK I'LL MAKE OUT OF HER TO OFFER TO MY MASTER.
I'M SO LOOKING FORWARD TO THIS!

CHAPTER 10 BATTLE AT SHIRANUI FORTRESS

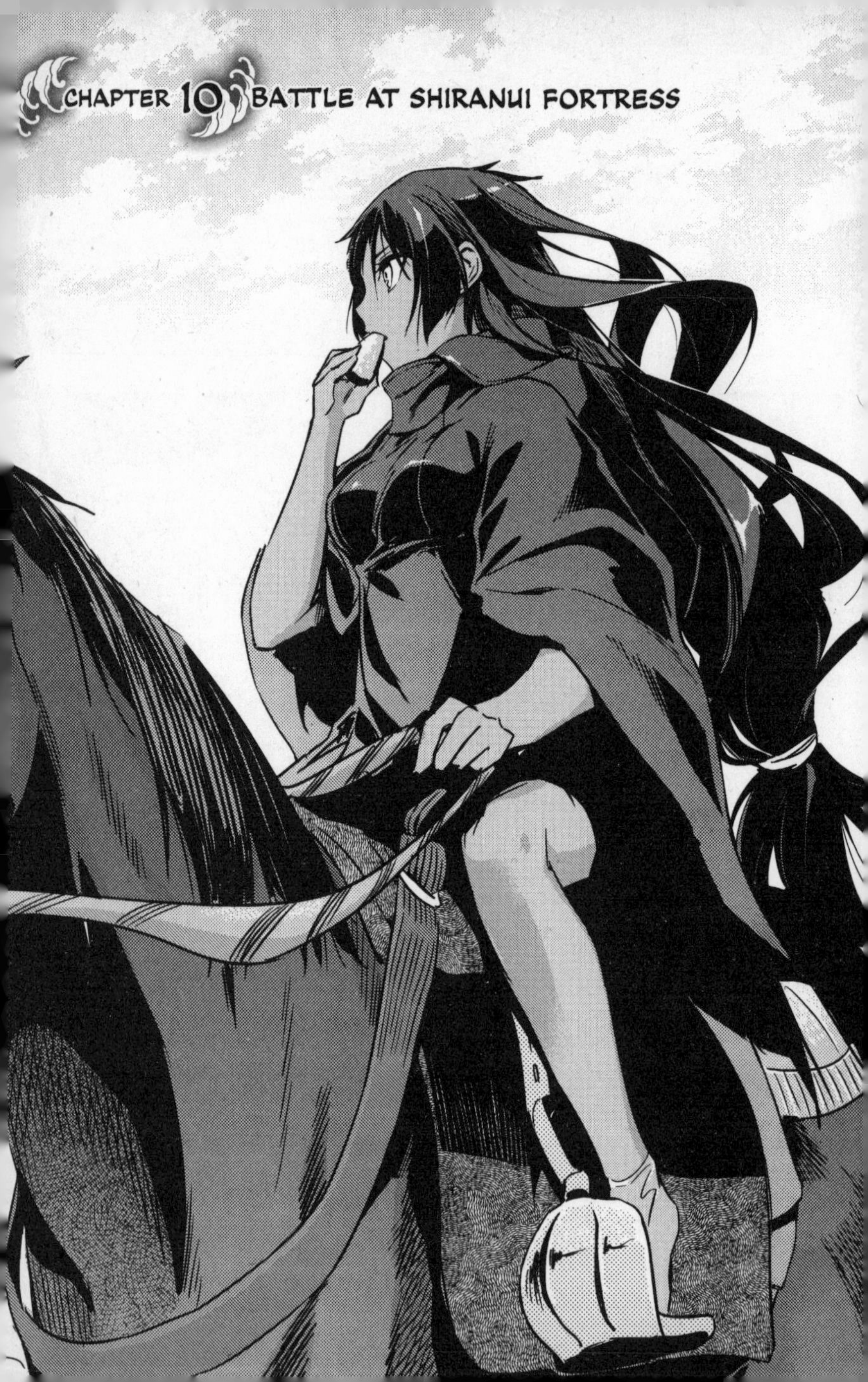

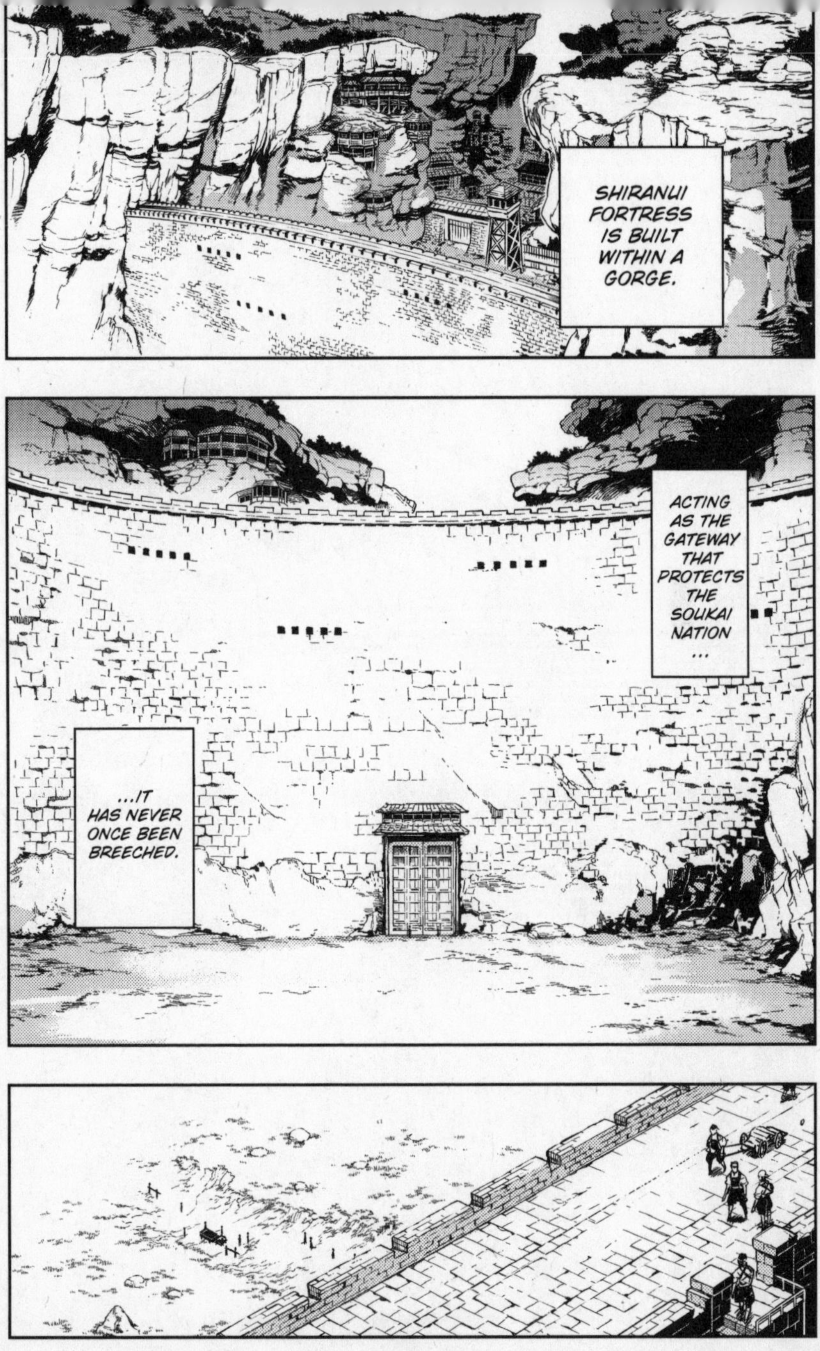

SHIRANUI FORTRESS IS BUILT WITHIN A GORGE.
ACTING AS THE GATEWAY THAT PROTECTS THE SOUKAI NATION...
...IT HAS NEVER ONCE BEEN BREECHED.

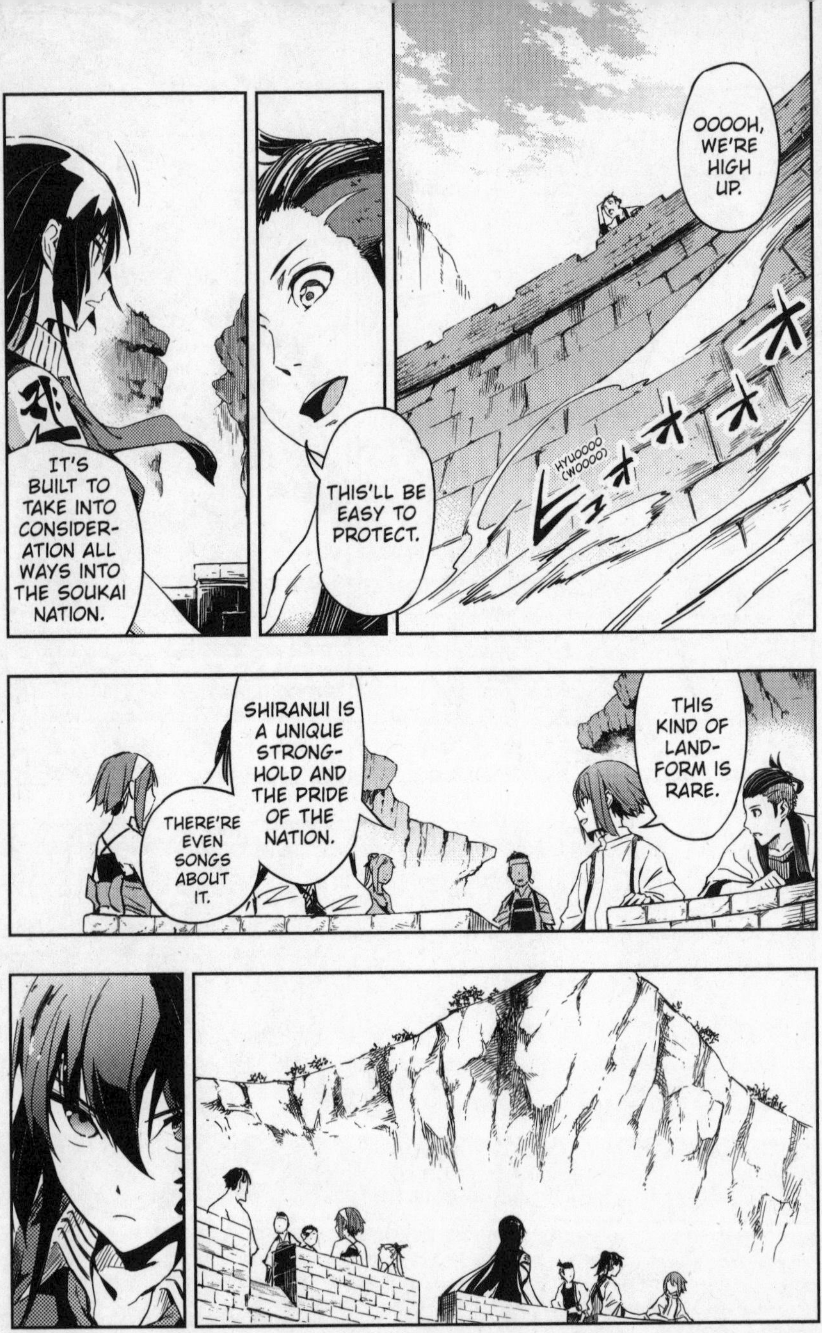
OOOOH, WE'RE HIGH UP.
HYUOOOO (WOOOO)
THIS'LL BE EASY TO PROTECT.
IT'S BUILT TO TAKE INTO CONSIDERATION ALL WAYS INTO THE SOUKAI NATION.
THIS KIND OF LANDFORM IS RARE.
SHIRANUI IS A UNIQUE STRONGHOLD AND THE PRIDE OF THE NATION.
THERE'RE EVEN SONGS ABOUT IT.

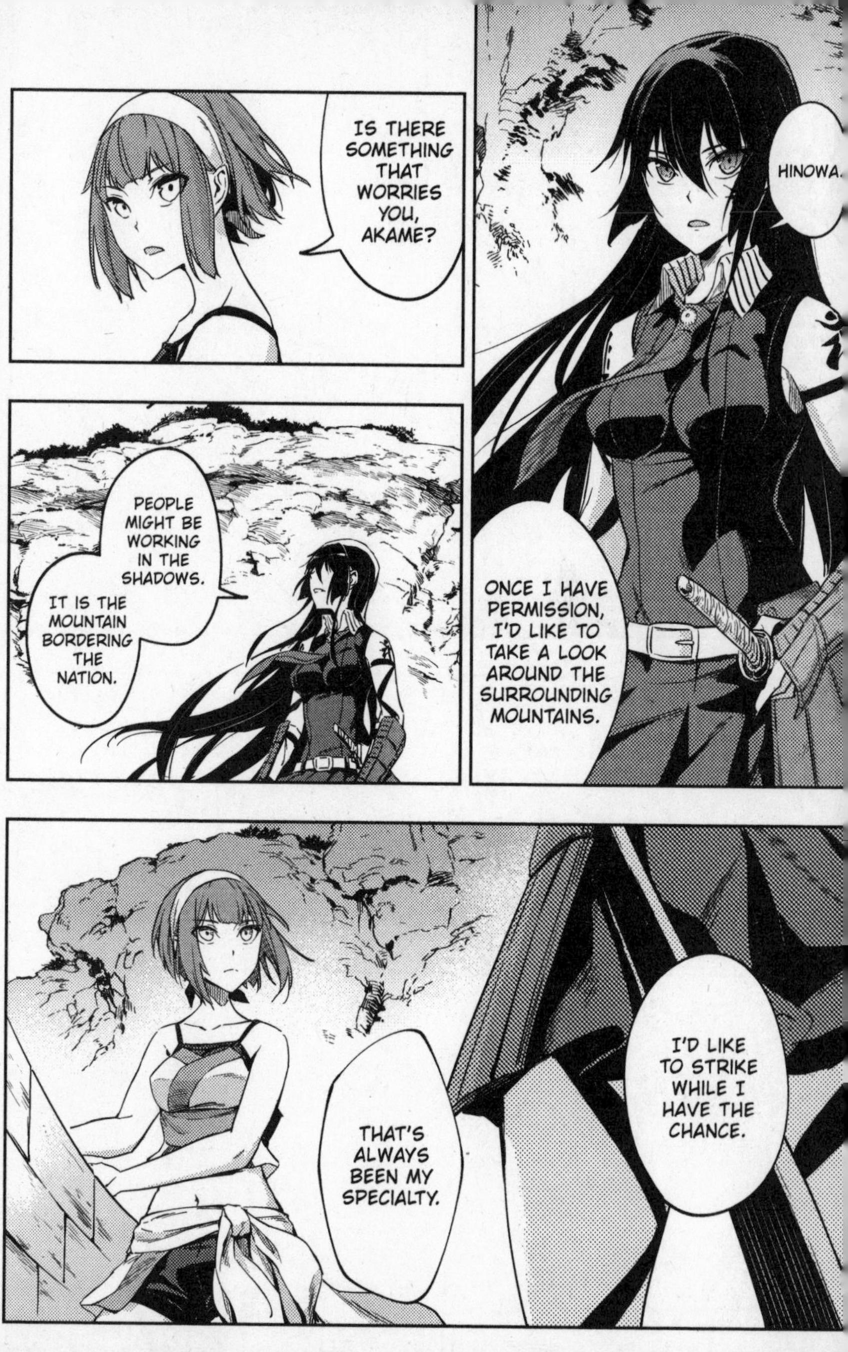
HINOWA.
ONCE I HAVE PERMISSION, I'D LIKE TO TAKE A LOOK AROUND THE SURROUNDING MOUNTAINS.
IS THERE SOMETHING THAT WORRIES YOU, AKAME?
PEOPLE MIGHT BE WORKING IN THE SHADOWS.
IT IS THE MOUNTAIN BORDERING THE NATION.
I'D LIKE TO STRIKE WHILE I HAVE THE CHANCE.
THAT'S ALWAYS BEEN MY SPECIALTY.

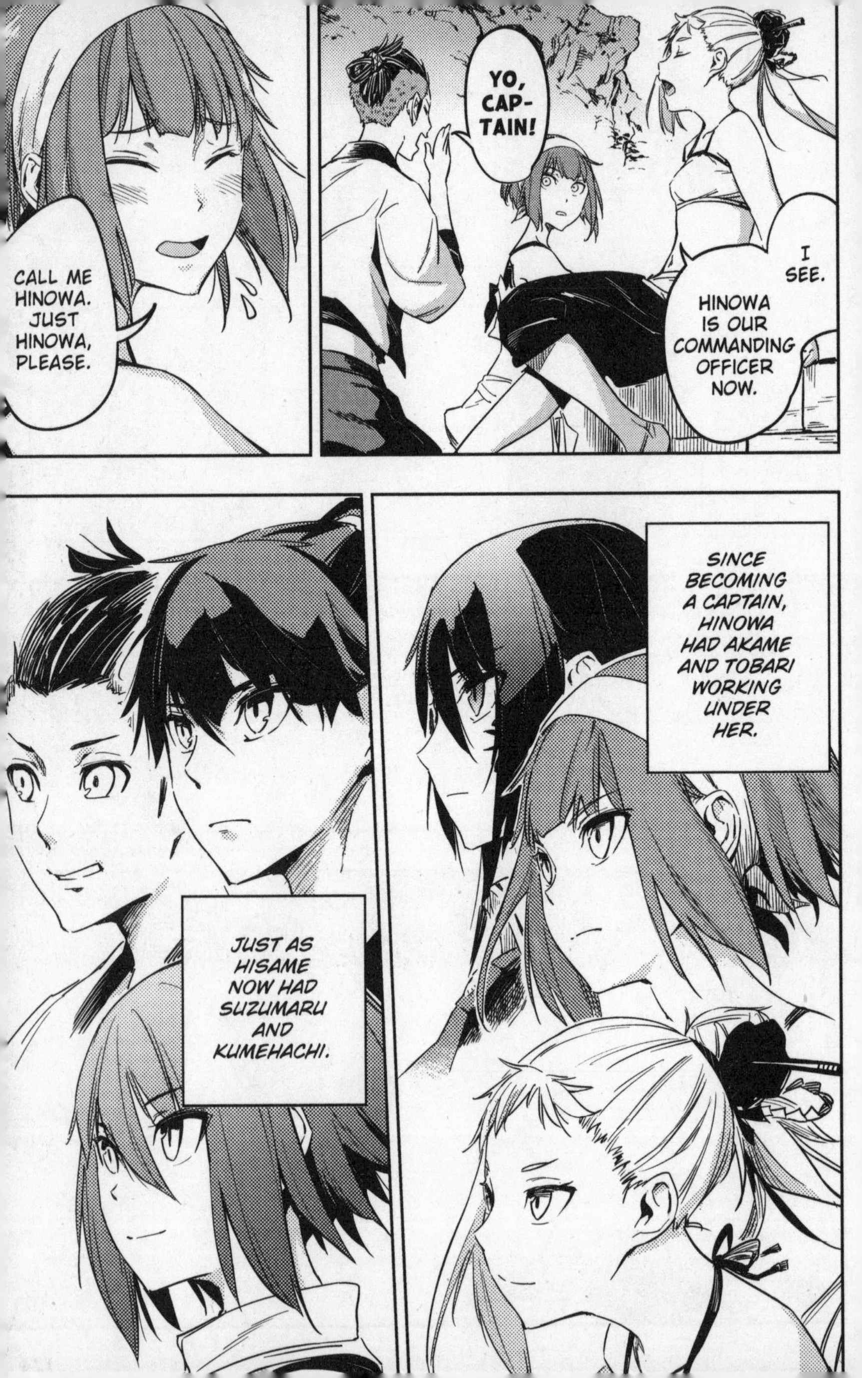
YO, CAP-TAIN!
I SEE.
HINOWA IS OUR COMMANDING OFFICER NOW.
CALL ME HINOWA. JUST HINOWA, PLEASE.
SINCE BECOMING A CAPTAIN, HINOWA HAD AKAME AND TOBARI WORKING UNDER HER.
JUST AS HISAME NOW HAD SUZUMARU AND KUMEHACHI.

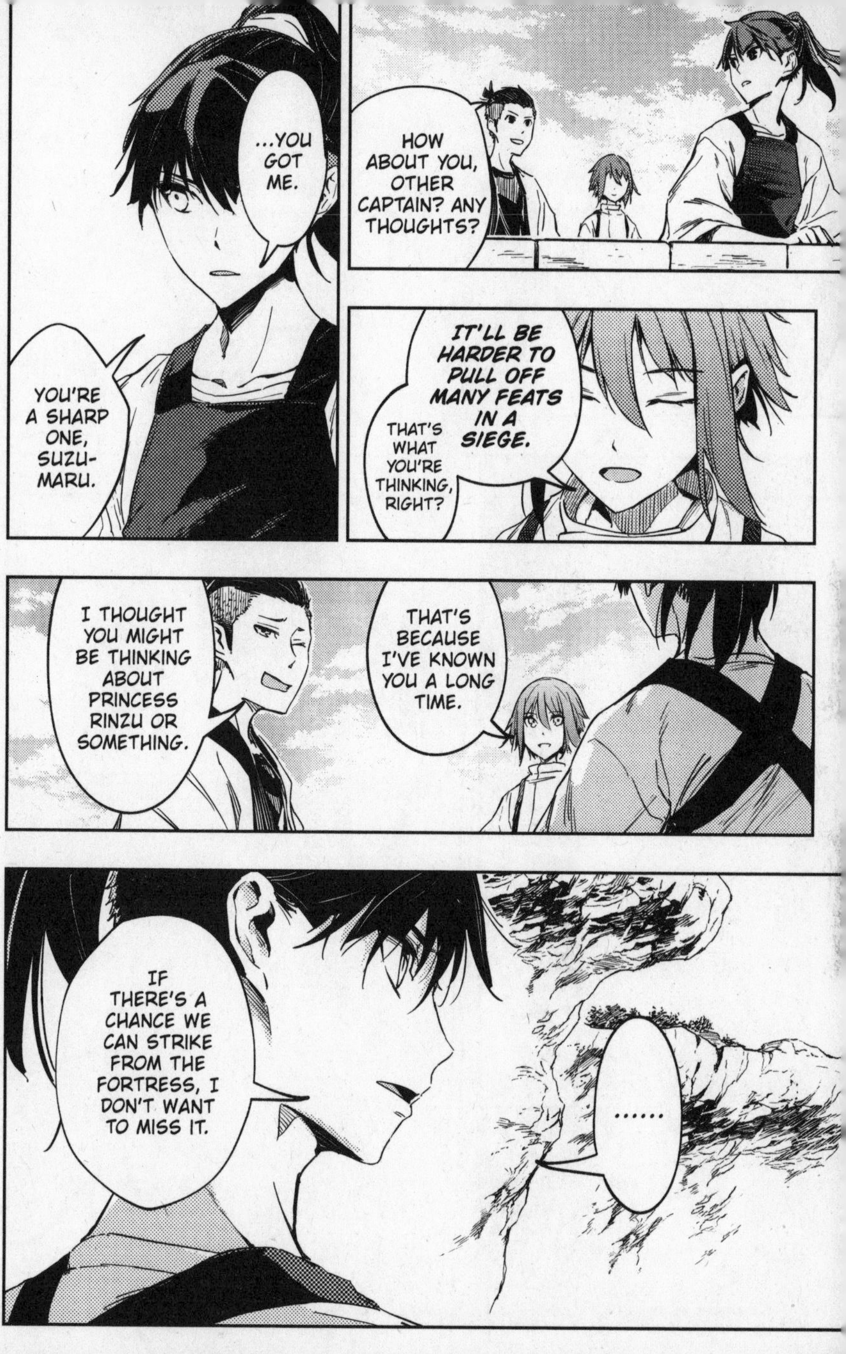
HOW ABOUT YOU, OTHER CAPTAIN? ANY THOUGHTS?
IT'LL BE HARDER TO PULL OFF MANY FEATS IN A SIEGE.
THAT'S WHAT YOU'RE THINKING, RIGHT?
...YOU GOT ME.
YOU'RE A SHARP ONE, SUZU-MARU.
THAT'S BECAUSE I'VE KNOWN YOU A LONG TIME.
I THOUGHT YOU MIGHT BE THINKING ABOUT PRINCESS RINZU OR SOMETHING.
......
IF THERE'S A CHANCE WE CAN STRIKE FROM THE FORTRESS, I DON'T WANT TO MISS IT.

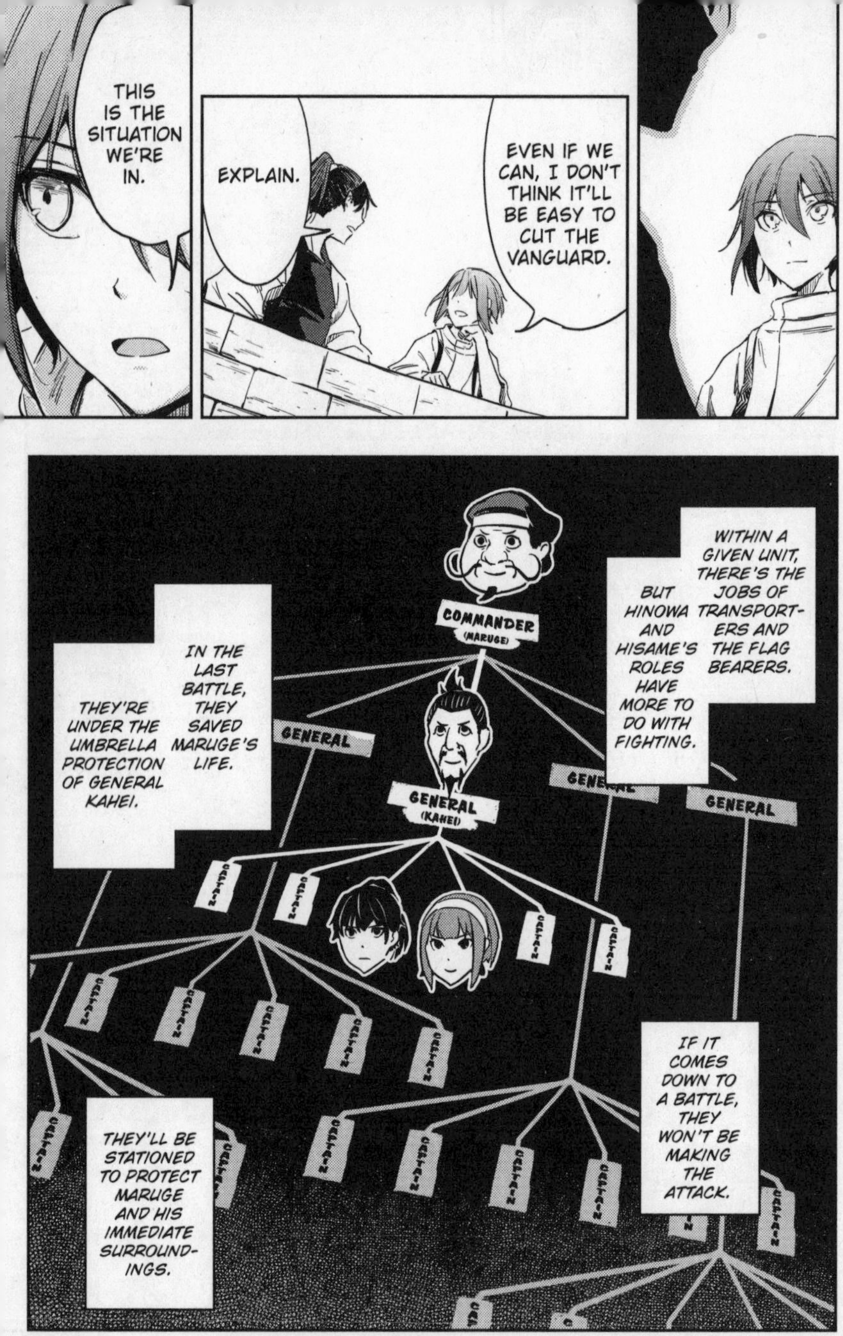
EVEN IF WE CAN, I DON'T THINK IT'LL BE EASY TO CUT THE VANGUARD.
EXPLAIN.
THIS IS THE SITUATION WE'RE IN.
WITHIN A GIVEN UNIT, THERE'S THE JOBS OF TRANSPORTERS AND THE FLAG BEARERS.
BUT HINOWA AND HISAME'S ROLES HAVE MORE TO DO WITH FIGHTING.
COMMANDER
(MARUGE)
IN THE LAST BATTLE, THEY SAVED MARUGE'S LIFE.
THEY'RE UNDER THE UMBRELLA PROTECTION OF GENERAL KAHEI.
GENERAL
GENERAL
(KAHEI)
GENERAL
GENERAL
CAPTAIN
IF IT COMES DOWN TO A BATTLE, THEY WON'T BE MAKING THE ATTACK.
THEY'LL BE STATIONED TO PROTECT MARUGE AND HIS IMMEDIATE SURROUNDINGS.

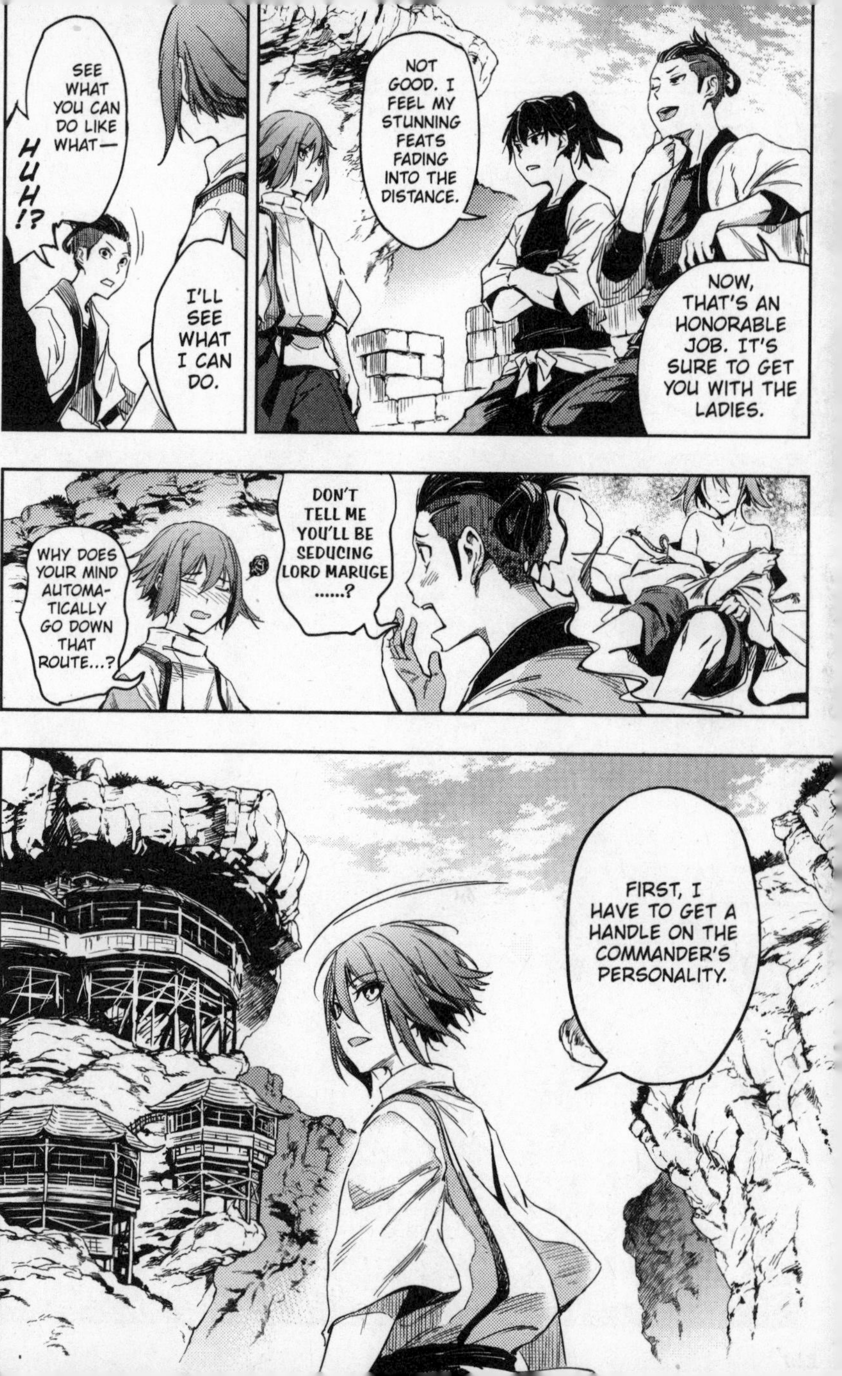
NOW, THAT'S AN HONORABLE JOB. IT'S SURE TO GET YOU WITH THE LADIES.
NOT GOOD. I FEEL MY STUNNING FEATS FADING INTO THE DISTANCE.
I'LL SEE WHAT I CAN DO.
SEE WHAT YOU CAN DO LIKE WHAT—
HUH!?
DON'T TELL ME YOU'LL BE SEDUCING LORD MARUGE ......?
WHY DOES YOUR MIND AUTOMATICALLY GO DOWN THAT ROUTE...?
FIRST, I HAVE TO GET A HANDLE ON THE COMMANDER'S PERSONALITY.

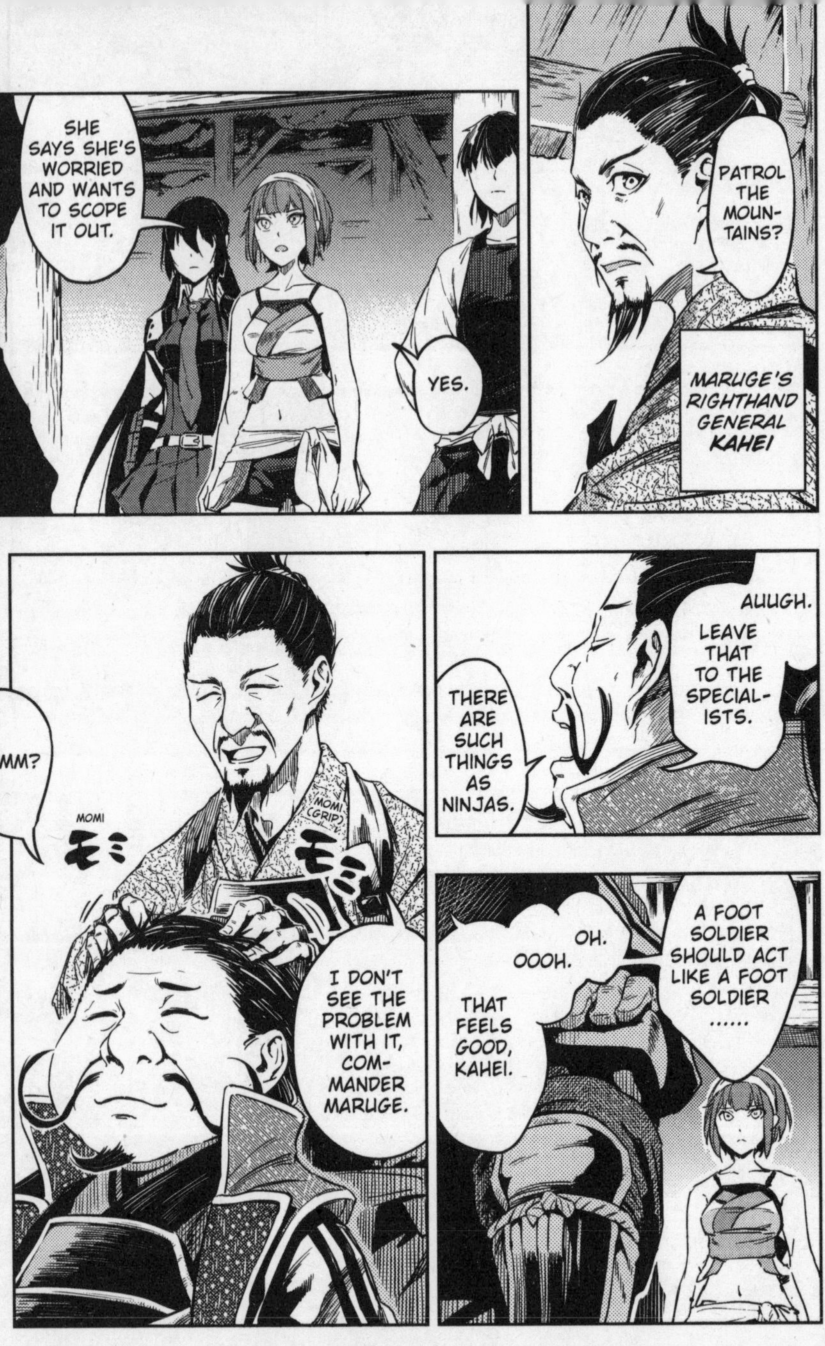
PATROL THE MOUNTAINS?
MARUGE'S RIGHTHAND GENERAL KAHEI
YES.
SHE SAYS SHE'S WORRIED AND WANTS TO SCOPE IT OUT.
AUUGH.
LEAVE THAT TO THE SPECIALISTS.
THERE ARE SUCH THINGS AS NINJAS.
A FOOT SOLDIER SHOULD ACT LIKE A FOOT SOLDIER ......
OH.
OOOH.
THAT FEELS GOOD, KAHEI.
MMM?
MOMI (GRIP)
MOMI
I DON'T SEE THE PROBLEM WITH IT, COM-MANDER MARUGE.

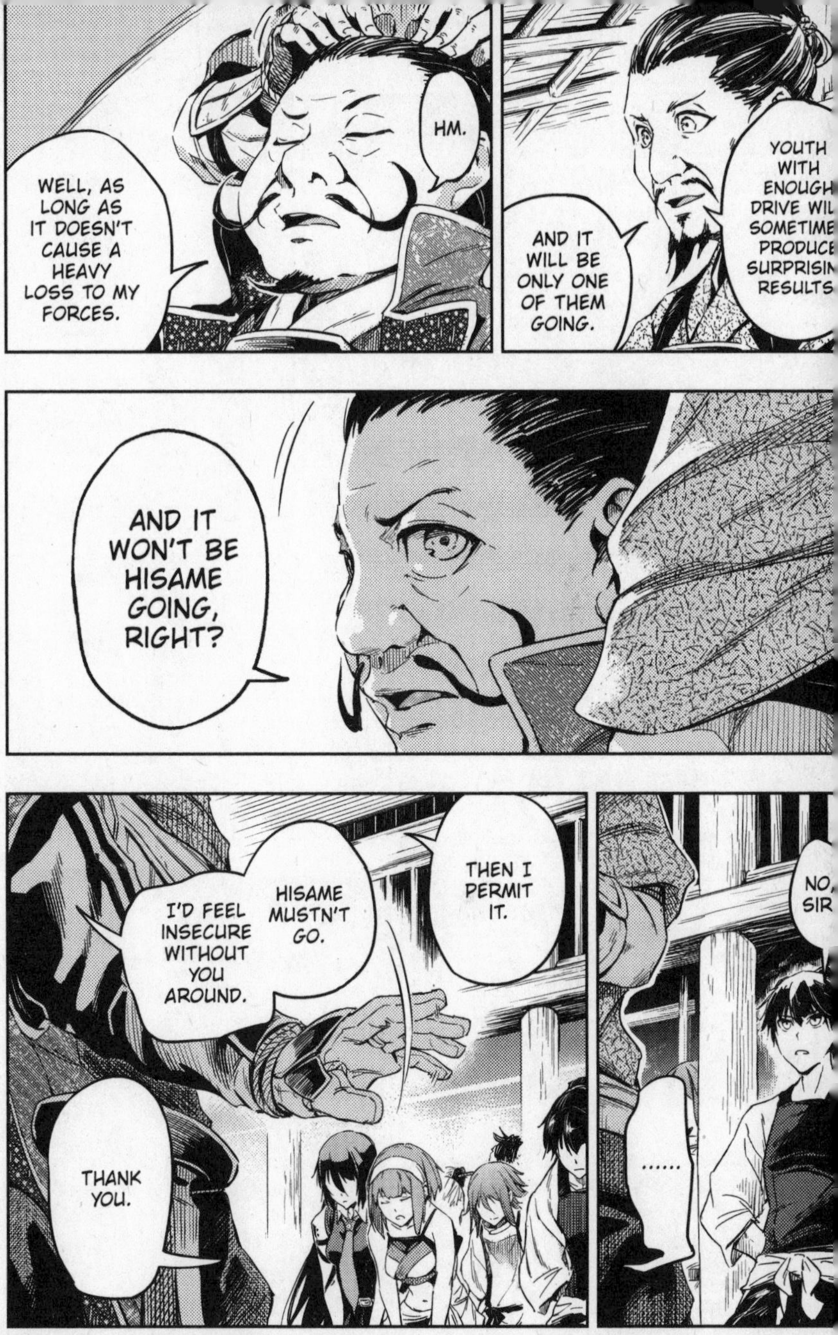
YOUTH WITH ENOUGH DRIVE WIL SOMETIME PRODUCE SURPRISIN RESULTS
AND IT WILL BE ONLY ONE OF THEM GOING.
HM.
WELL, AS LONG AS IT DOESN'T CAUSE A HEAVY LOSS TO MY FORCES.
AND IT WON'T BE HISAME GOING, RIGHT?
NO, SIR
......
THEN I PERMIT IT.
HISAME MUSTN'T GO.
I'D FEEL INSECURE WITHOUT YOU AROUND.
THANK YOU.

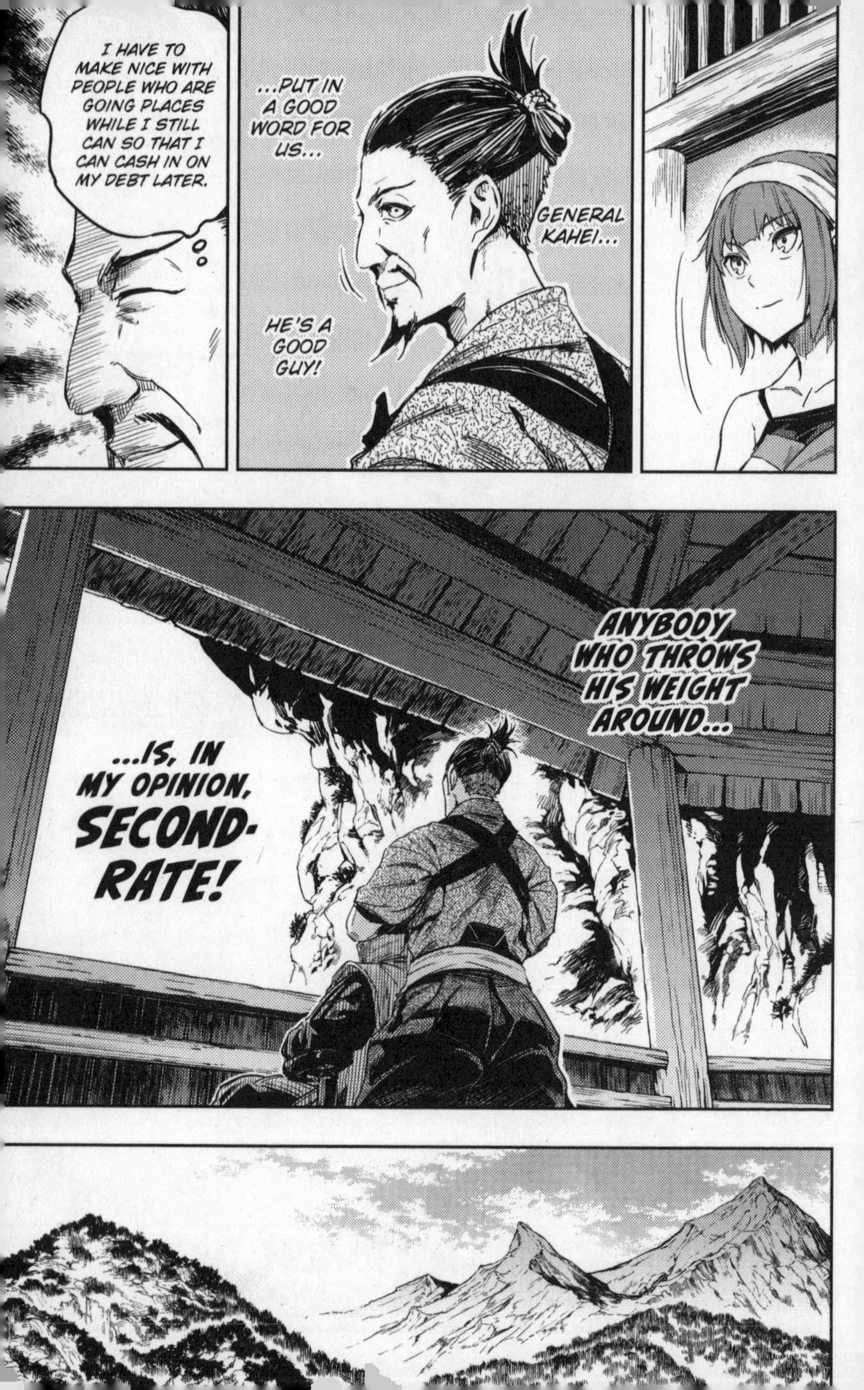
...PUT IN A GOOD WORD FOR US...
GENERAL KAHEI...
HE'S A GOOD GUY!
I HAVE TO MAKE NICE WITH PEOPLE WHO ARE GOING PLACES WHILE I STILL CAN SO THAT I CAN CASH IN ON MY DEBT LATER.
ANYBODY WHO THROWS HIS WEIGHT AROUND...
...IS, IN MY OPINION, SECOND-RATE!

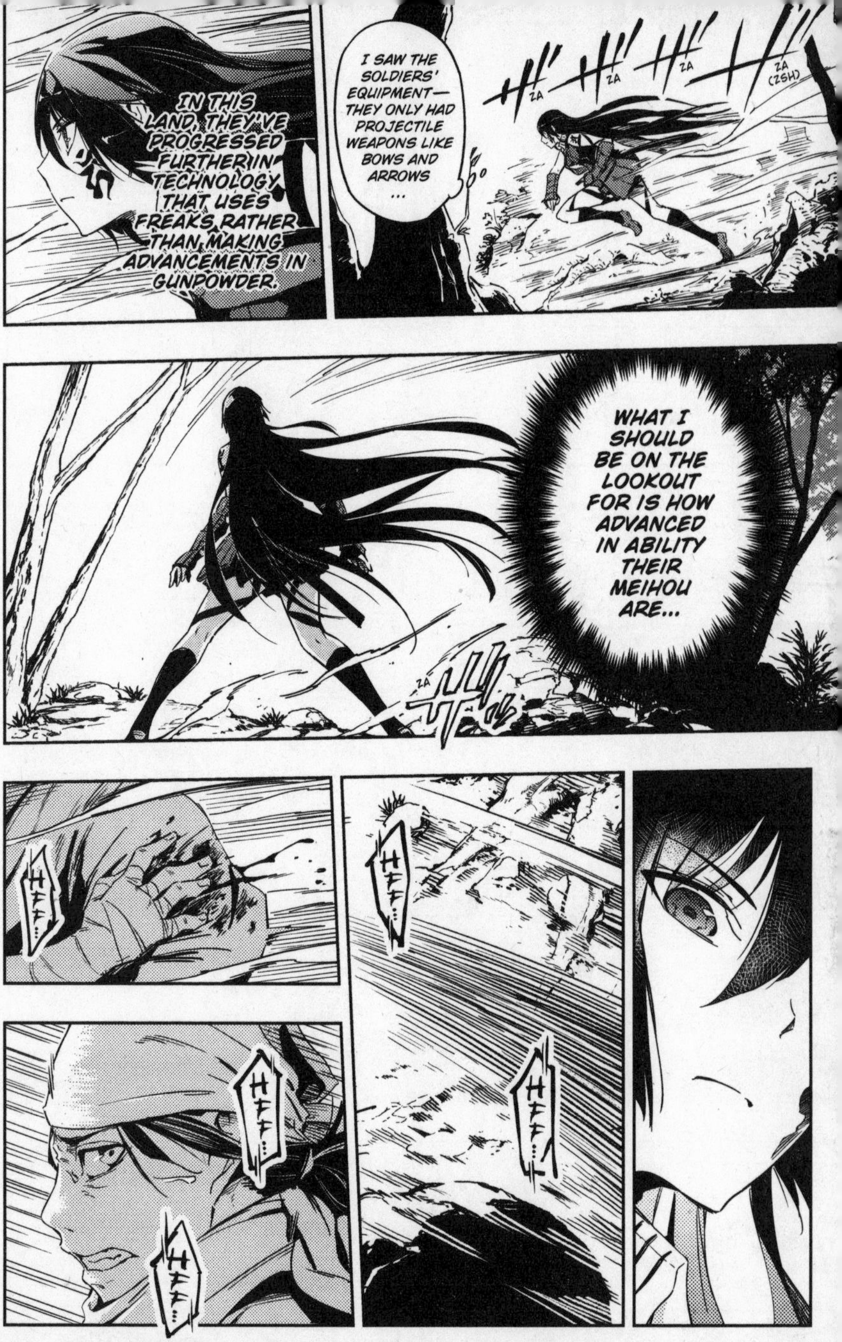
I SAW THE SOLDIERS' EQUIPMENT—THEY ONLY HAD PROJECTILE WEAPONS LIKE BOWS AND ARROWS ...
ZA ZA ZA ZA (ZSH)
IN THIS LAND, THEY'VE PROGRESSED FURTHER IN TECHNOLOGY THAT USES FREAKS RATHER THAN MAKING ADVANCEMENTS IN GUNPOWDER.
WHAT I SHOULD BE ON THE LOOKOUT FOR IS HOW ADVANCED IN ABILITY THEIR MEIHOU ARE...
ZA
HFF...
HFF...
HFF...
HFF...
HFF...

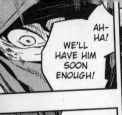

AH-HA! WE'LL HAVE HIM SOON ENOUGH!

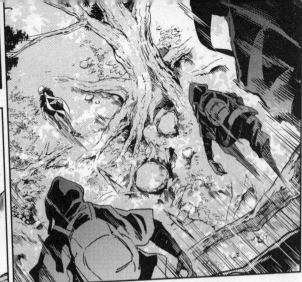

ONCE WE'VE CUT OFF HIS LIMBS AND HE CAN'T GET AWAY, WE'LL QUESTION HIM.

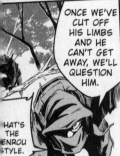

HAT'S THE ENROU STYLE.

ZA

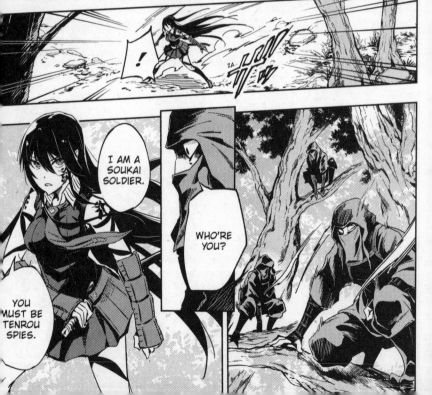

I AM A SOUKAI SOLDIER.

WHO'RE YOU?

YOU MUST BE TENROU SPIES.

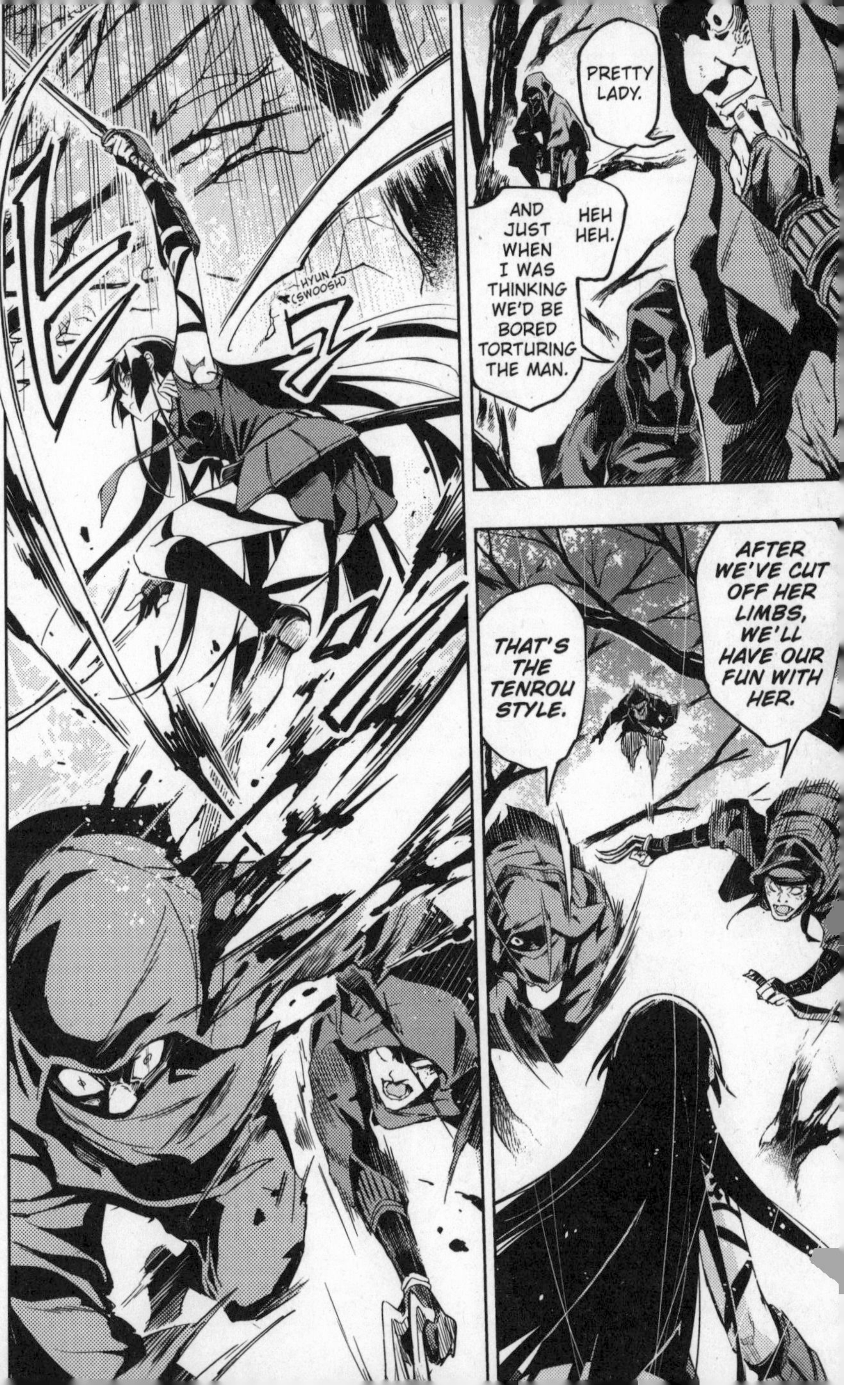
PRETTY LADY.
HEH HEH.
AND JUST WHEN I WAS THINKING WE'D BE BORED TORTURING THE MAN.
AFTER WE'VE CUT OFF HER LIMBS, WE'LL HAVE OUR FUN WITH HER.
THAT'S THE TENROU STYLE.
HYUN (SWOOSH)

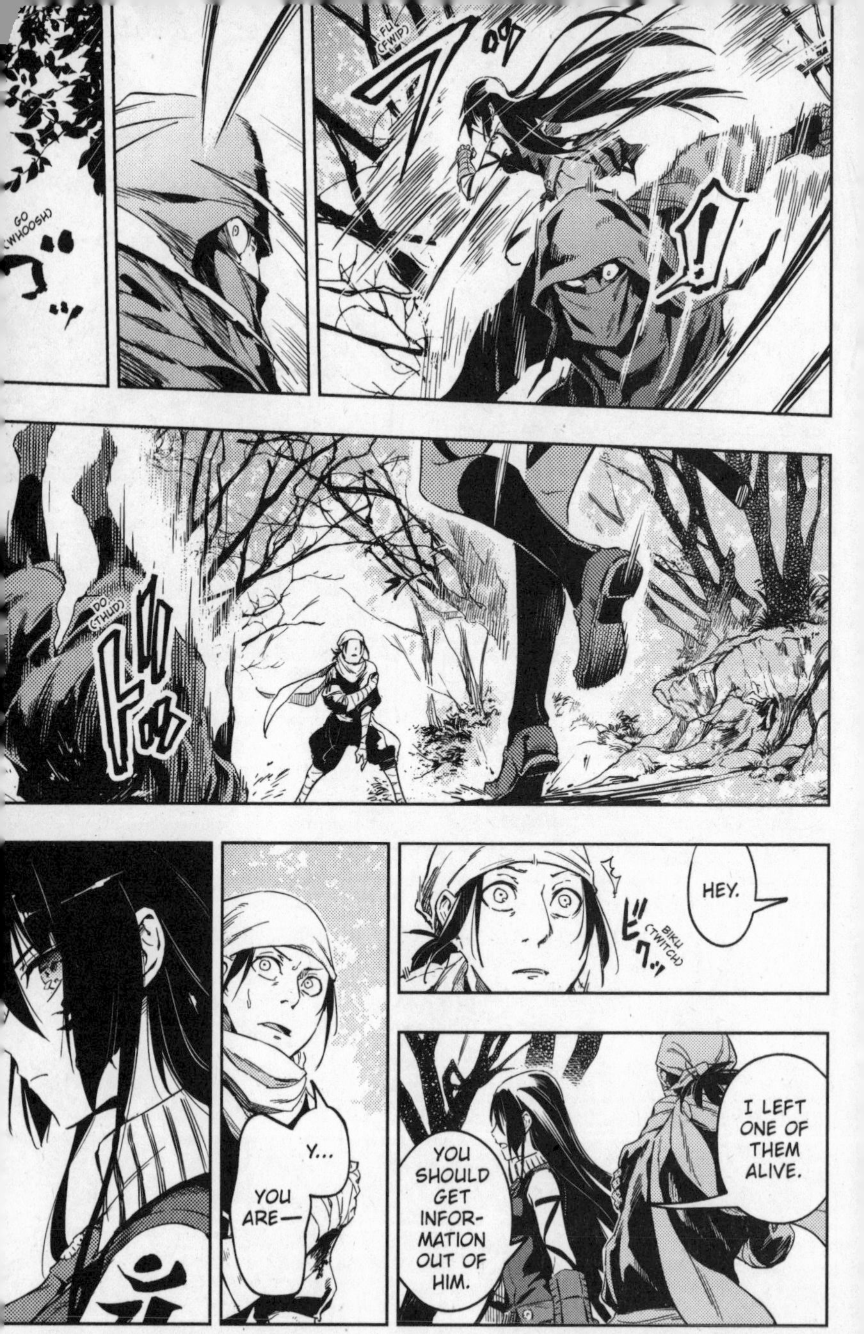
FU (FWIP)
!
GO (WHOOSH)
DO (THUD)
HEY.
BIKU (TWITCH)
I LEFT ONE OF THEM ALIVE.
YOU SHOULD GET INFORMATION OUT OF HIM.
Y... YOU ARE—

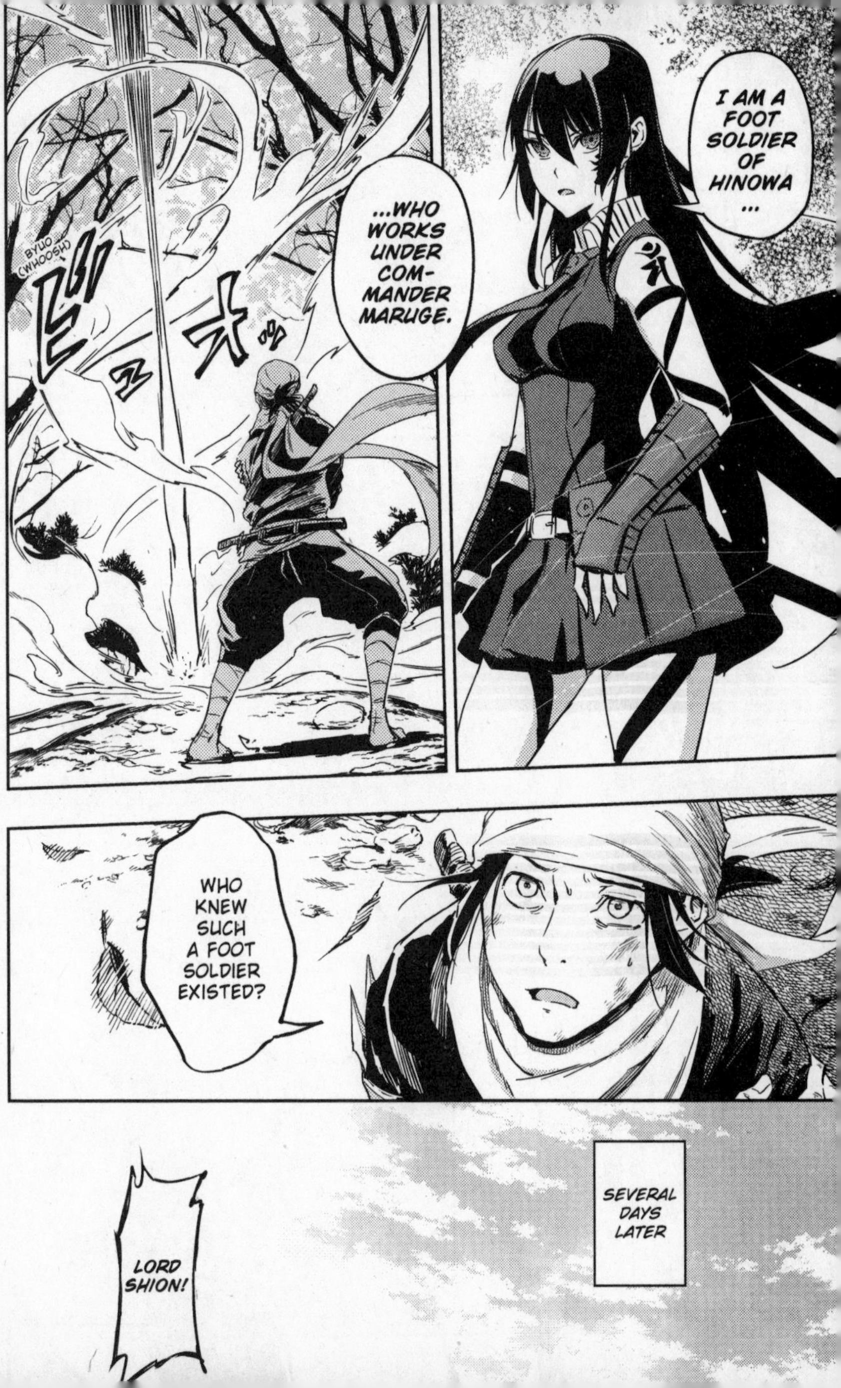
I AM A FOOT SOLDIER OF HINOWA...
...WHO WORKS UNDER COM-MANDER MARUGE.
BYUO (WHOOSH)
WHO KNEW SUCH A FOOT SOLDIER EXISTED?
SEVERAL DAYS LATER
LORD SHION!

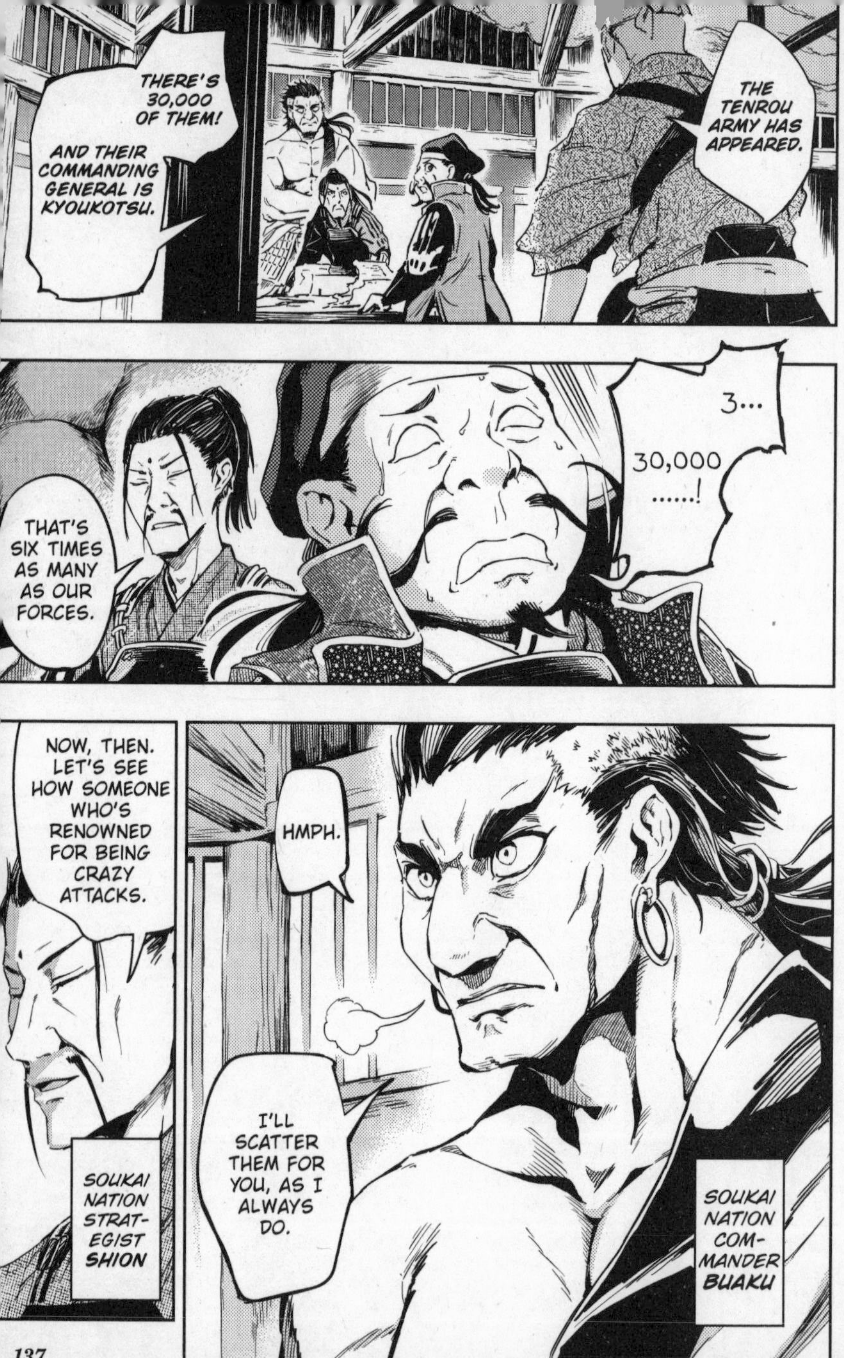
THE TENROU ARMY HAS APPEARED.
THERE'S 30,000 OF THEM!
AND THEIR COMMANDING GENERAL IS KYOUKOTSU.
3...
30,000 ......!
THAT'S SIX TIMES AS MANY AS OUR FORCES.
HMPH.
I'LL SCATTER THEM FOR YOU, AS I ALWAYS DO.
SOUKAI NATION COM-MANDER BUAKU
NOW, THEN. LET'S SEE HOW SOMEONE WHO'S RENOWNED FOR BEING CRAZY ATTACKS.
SOUKAI NATION STRAT-EGIST SHION

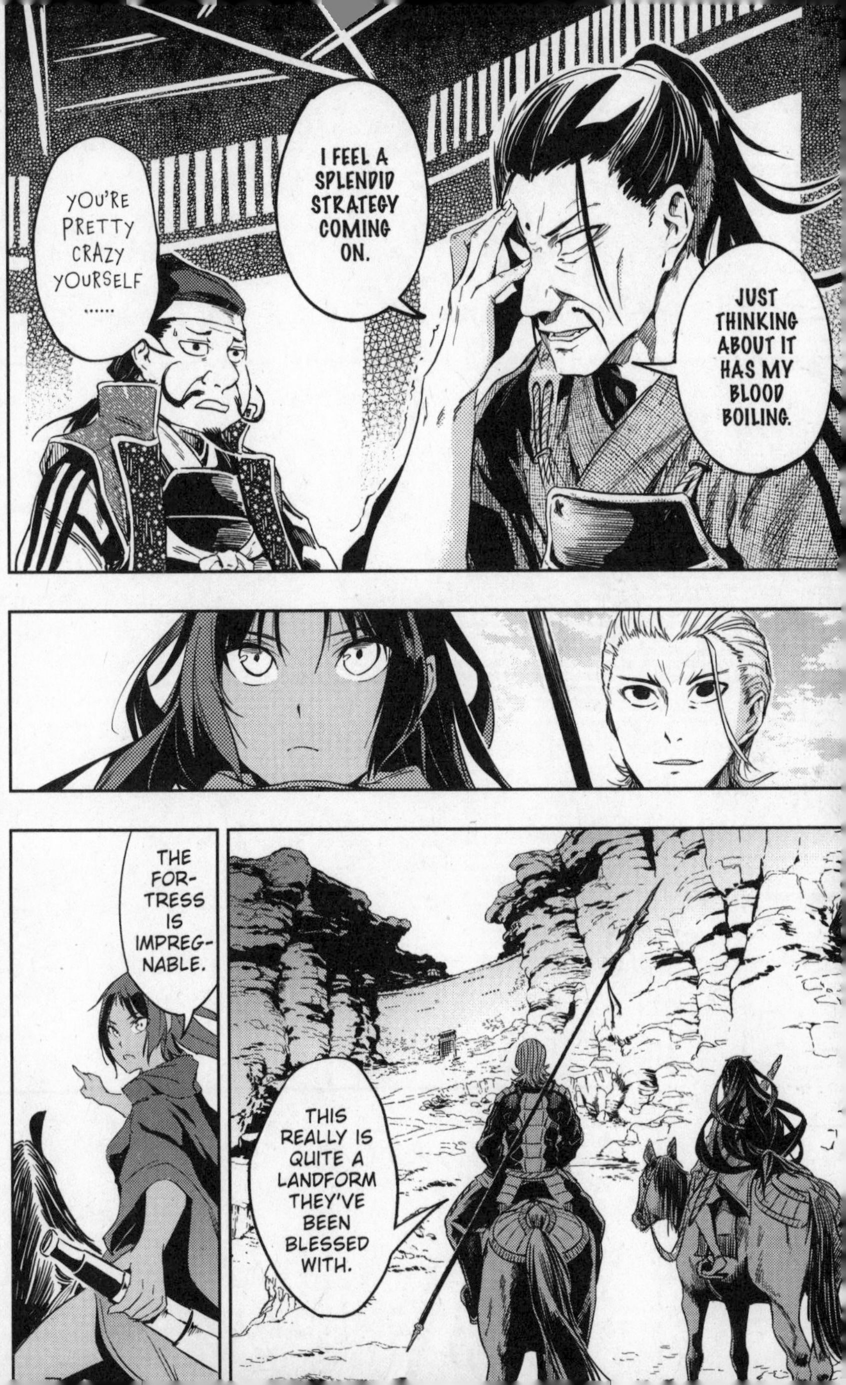
JUST THINKING ABOUT IT HAS MY BLOOD BOILING.
I FEEL A SPLENDID STRATEGY COMING ON.
YOU'RE PRETTY CRAZY YOURSELF ......
THIS REALLY IS QUITE A LANDFORM THEY'VE BEEN BLESSED WITH.
THE FOR-TRESS IS IMPREG-NABLE.

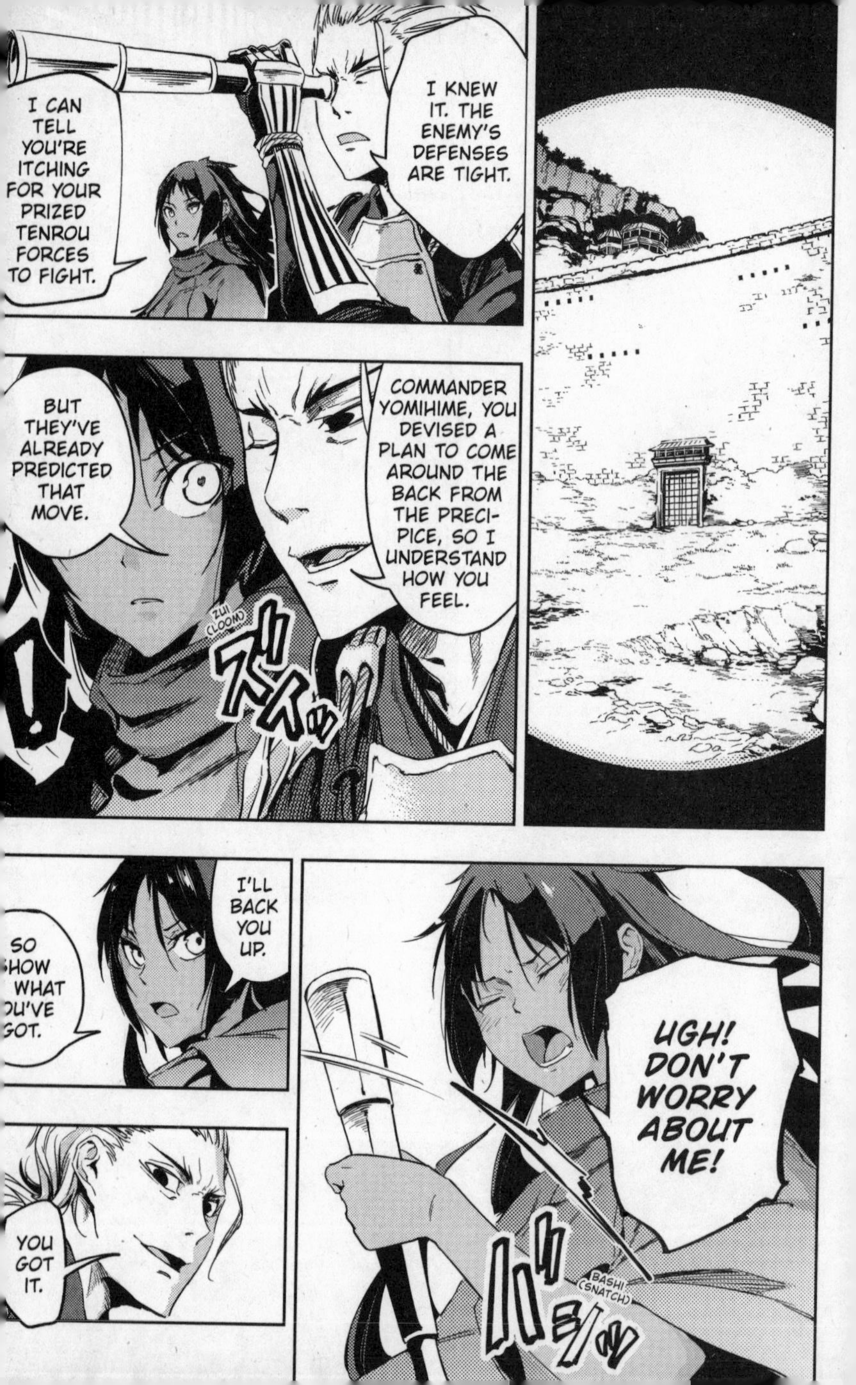
I KNEW IT. THE ENEMY'S DEFENSES ARE TIGHT.
I CAN TELL YOU'RE ITCHING FOR YOUR PRIZED TENROU FORCES TO FIGHT.
COMMANDER YOMIHIME, YOU DEVISED A PLAN TO COME AROUND THE BACK FROM THE PRECI-PICE, SO I UNDERSTAND HOW YOU FEEL.
BUT THEY'VE ALREADY PREDICTED THAT MOVE.
ZUI (LOOM)
UGH! DON'T WORRY ABOUT ME!
BASHI (SNATCH)
I'LL BACK YOU UP.
SO HOW WHAT OU'VE GOT.
YOU GOT IT.

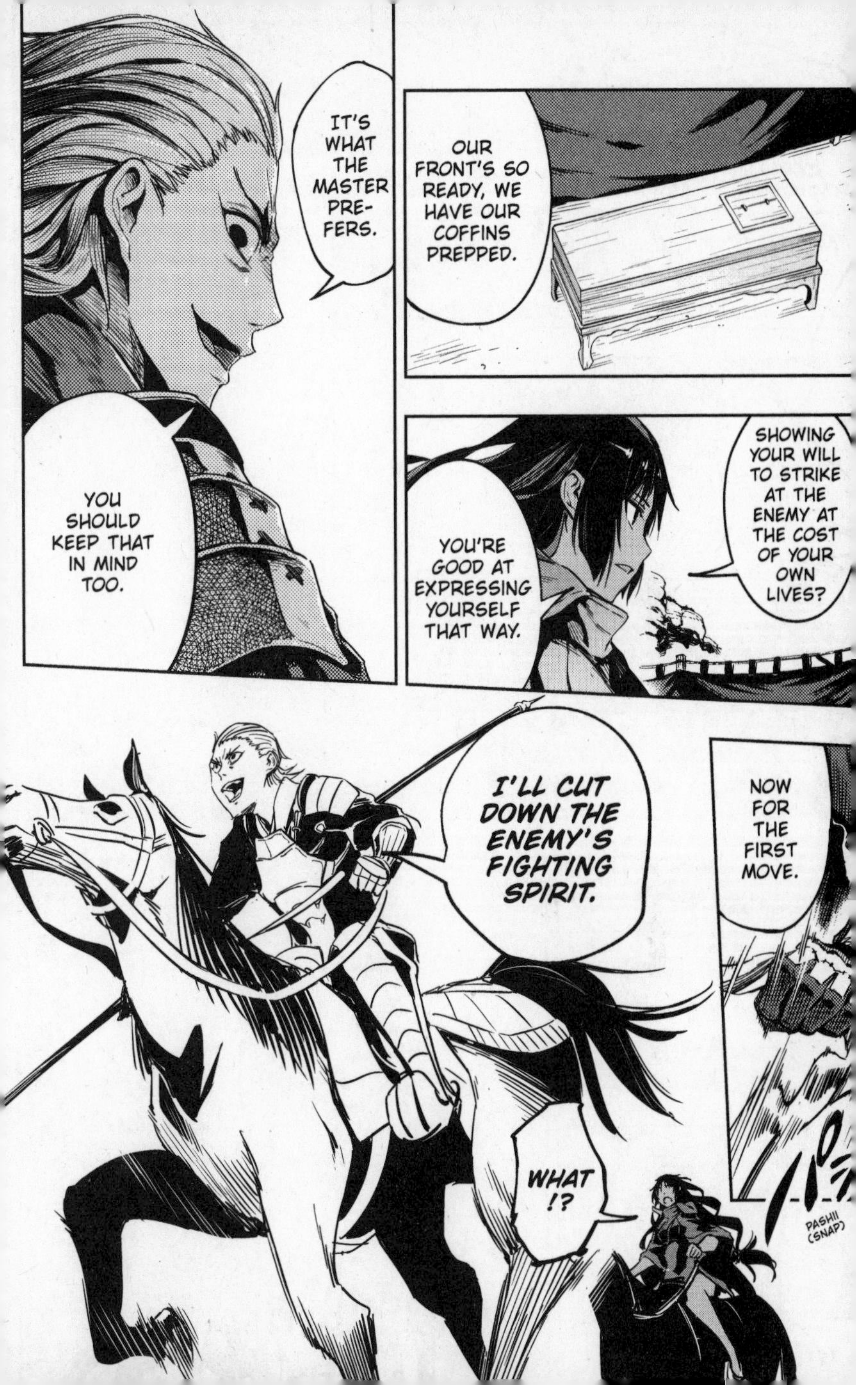
OUR FRONT'S SO READY, WE HAVE OUR COFFINS PREPPED.
SHOWING YOUR WILL TO STRIKE AT THE ENEMY AT THE COST OF YOUR OWN LIVES?
YOU'RE GOOD AT EXPRESSING YOURSELF THAT WAY.
IT'S WHAT THE MASTER PRE-FERS.
YOU SHOULD KEEP THAT IN MIND TOO.
NOW FOR THE FIRST MOVE.
PASHI! (SNAP)
I'LL CUT DOWN THE ENEMY'S FIGHTING SPIRIT.
WHAT!?

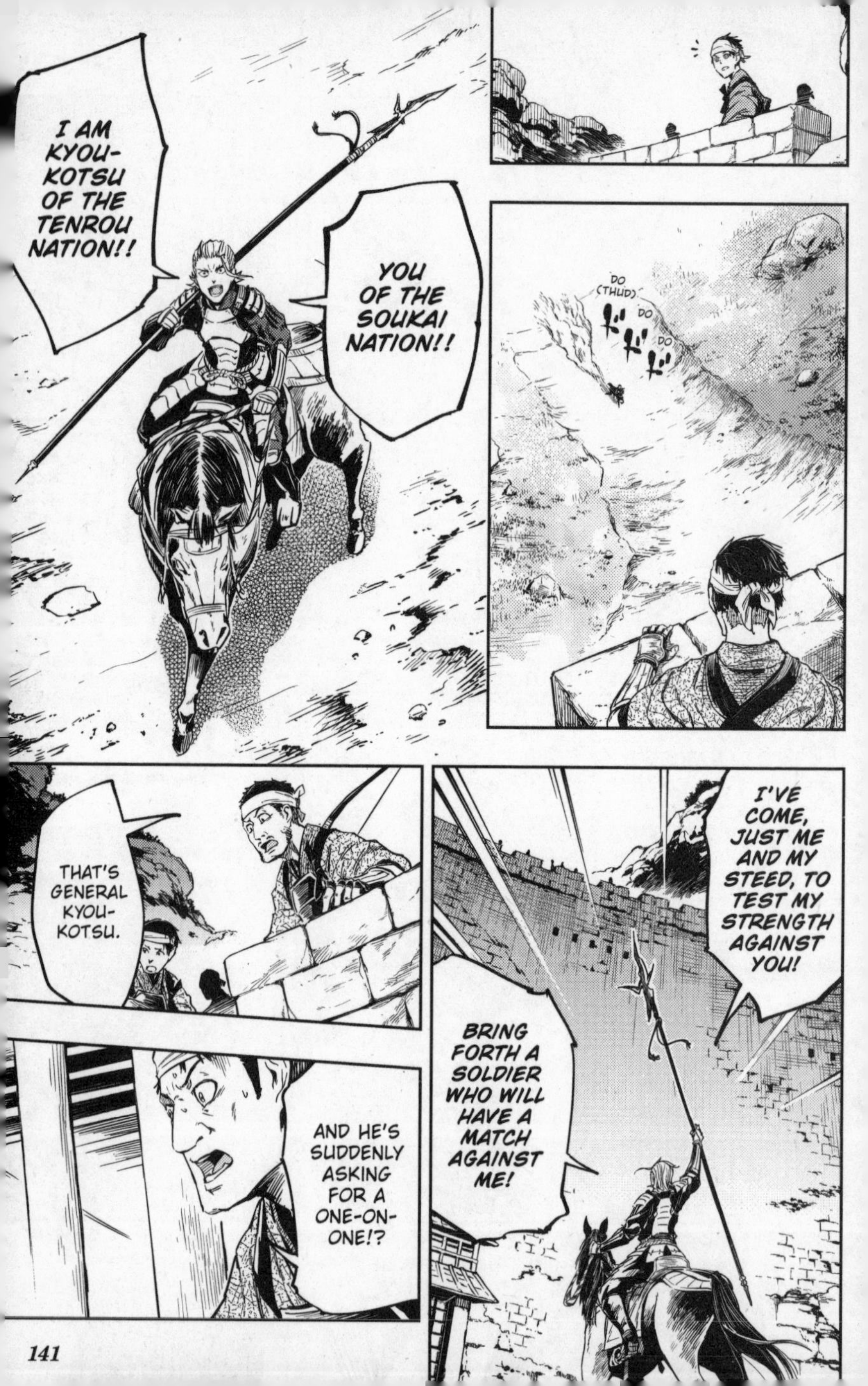
DO DO DO
(THUD)
I AM KYOU-KOTSU OF THE TENROU NATION!!
YOU OF THE SOUKAI NATION!!
I'VE COME, JUST ME AND MY STEED, TO TEST MY STRENGTH AGAINST YOU!
BRING FORTH A SOLDIER WHO WILL HAVE A MATCH AGAINST ME!
THAT'S GENERAL KYOU-KOTSU.
AND HE'S SUDDENLY ASKING FOR A ONE-ON-ONE!?

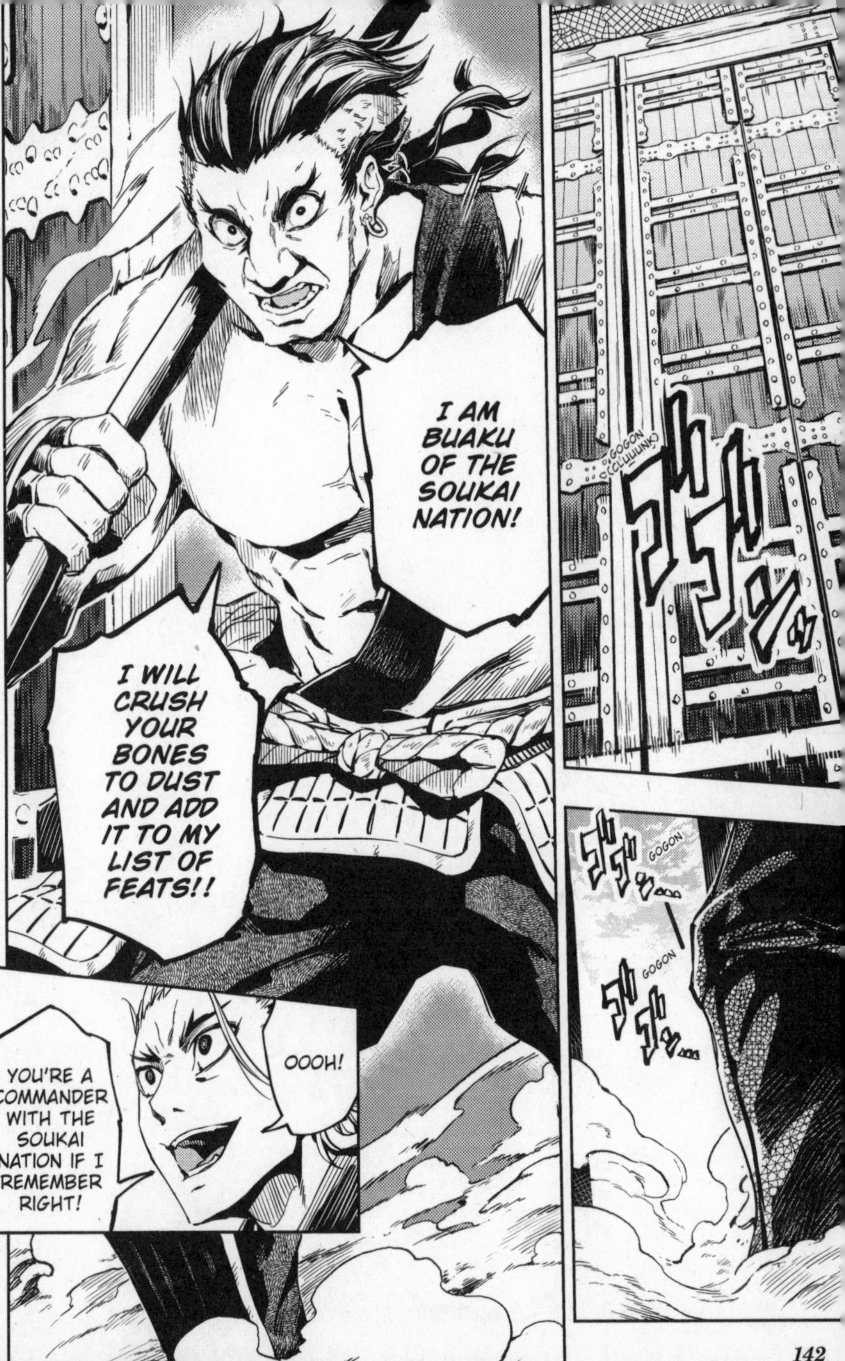
GOGON (CLUUUNK)
GOGON
GOGON
I AM BUAKU OF THE SOUKAI NATION!
I WILL CRUSH YOUR BONES TO DUST AND ADD IT TO MY LIST OF FEATS!!
OOOH!
YOU'RE A COMMANDER WITH THE SOUKAI NATION IF I REMEMBER RIGHT!

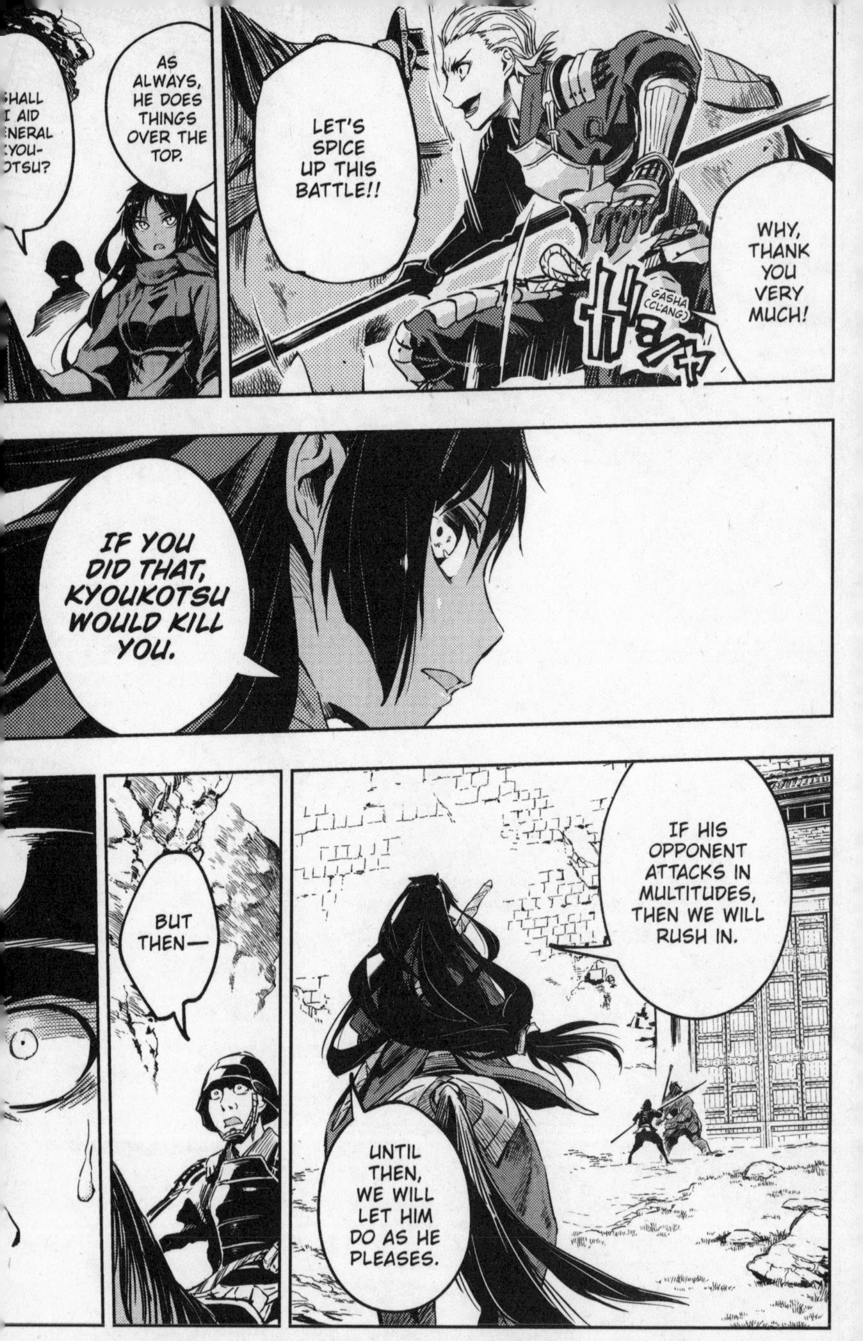
WHY, THANK YOU VERY MUCH!
GASHA (CLANG)
LET'S SPICE UP THIS BATTLE!!
AS ALWAYS, HE DOES THINGS OVER THE TOP.
SHALL I AID ENERAL KYOU- OTSU?
IF YOU DID THAT, KYOUKOTSU WOULD KILL YOU.
IF HIS OPPONENT ATTACKS IN MULTITUDES, THEN WE WILL RUSH IN.
UNTIL THEN, WE WILL LET HIM DO AS HE PLEASES.
BUT THEN—

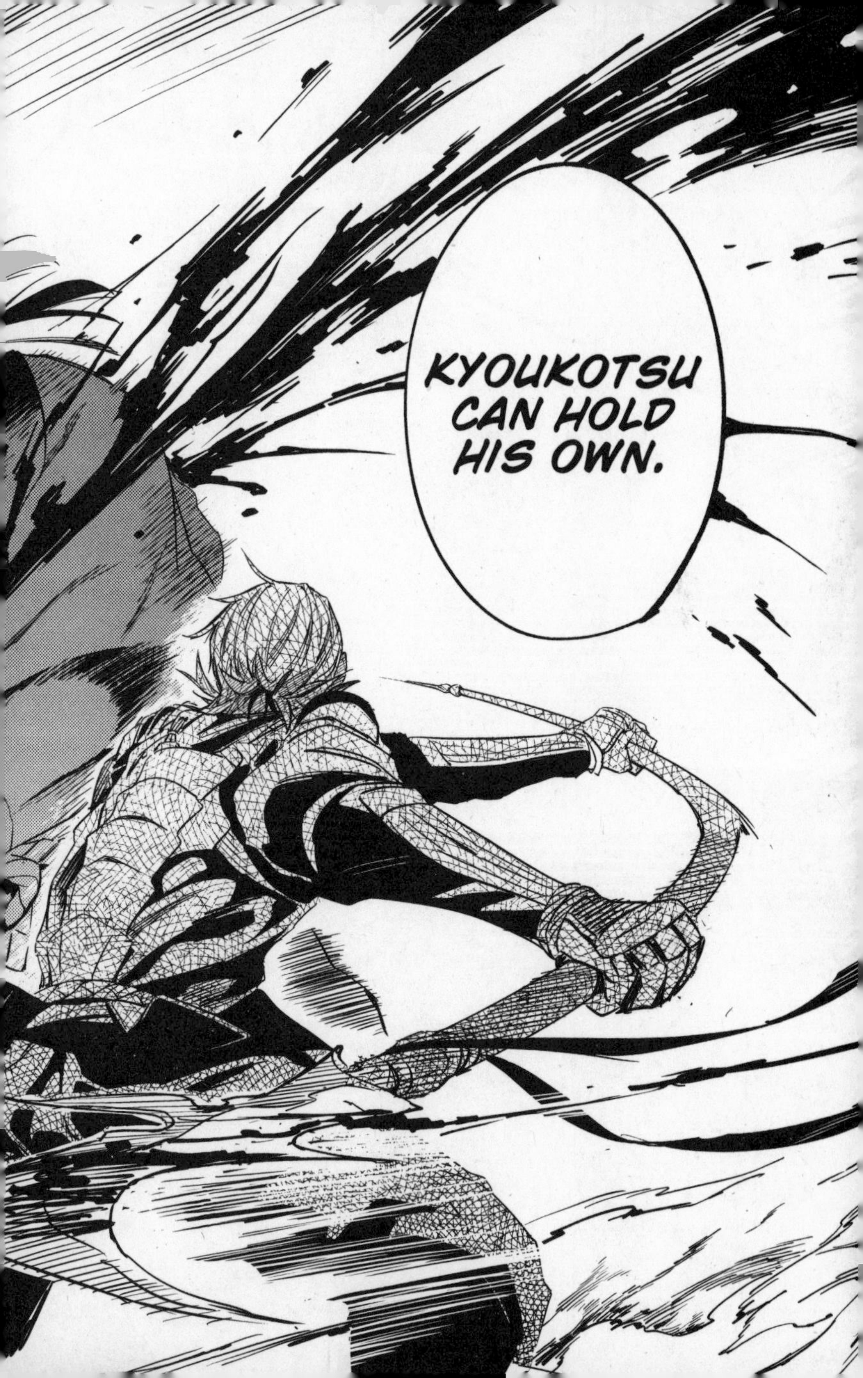
KYOUKOTSU CAN HOLD HIS OWN.

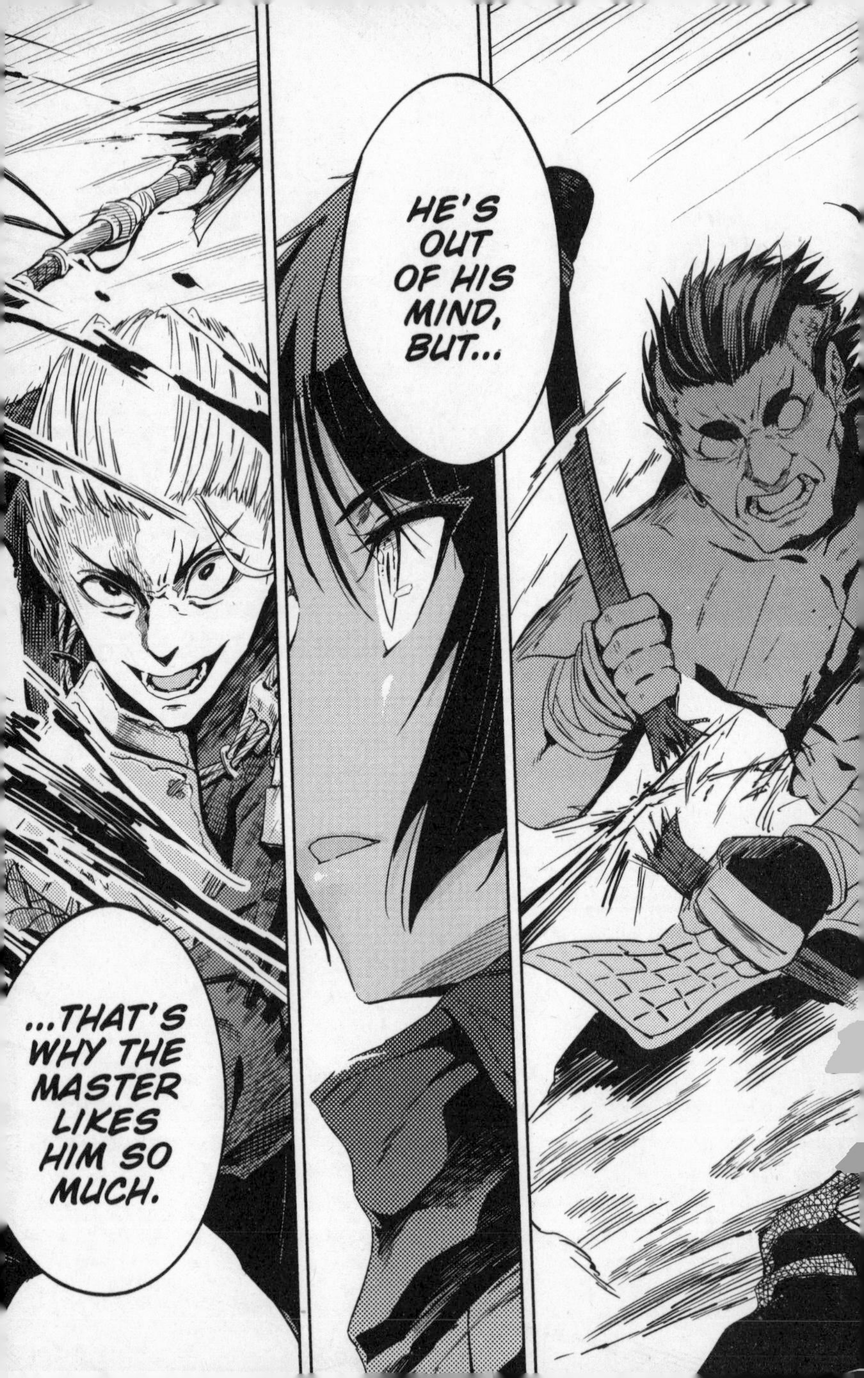
HE'S OUT OF HIS MIND, BUT...
...THAT'S WHY THE MASTER LIKES HIM SO MUCH.

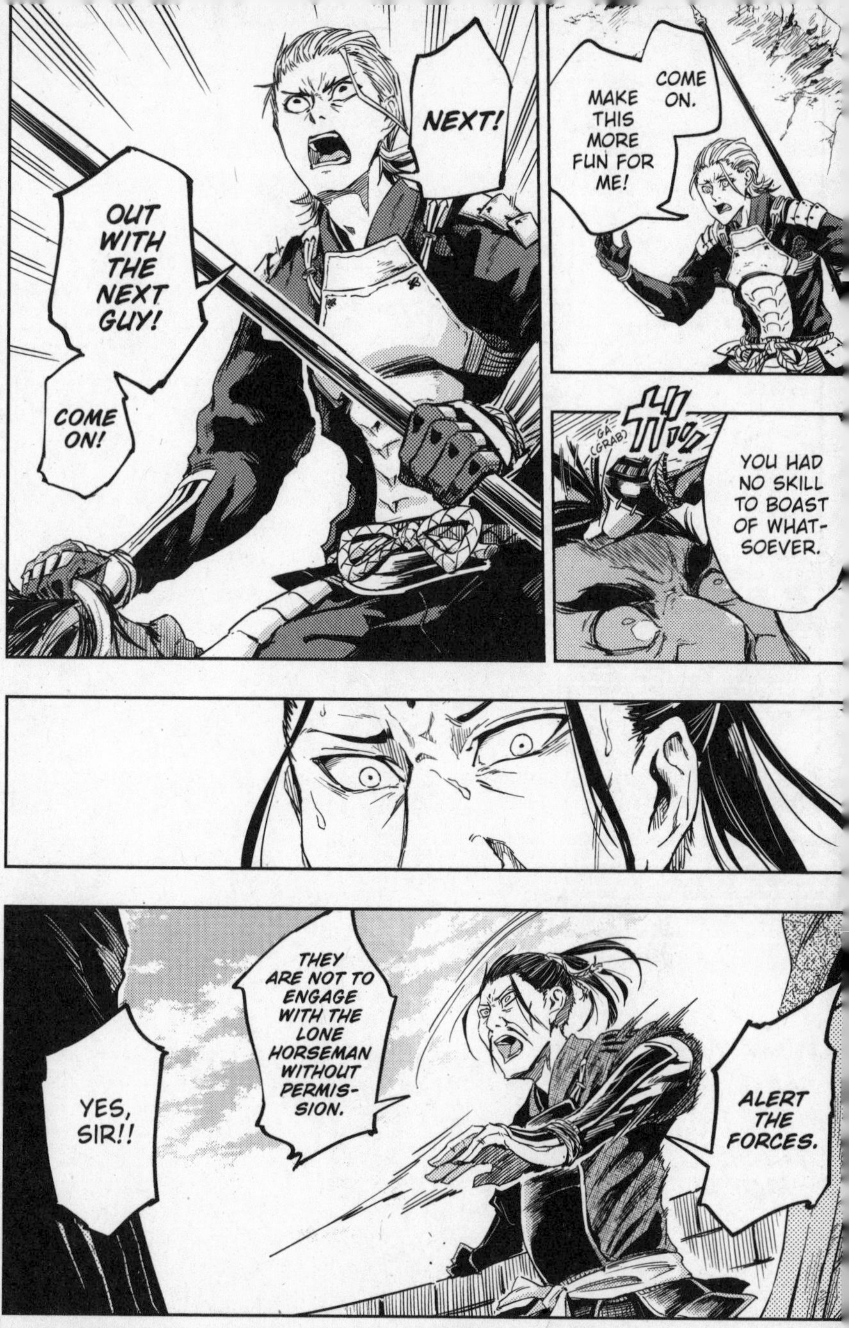
COME ON.
MAKE THIS MORE FUN FOR ME!
GA- (GRAB)
YOU HAD NO SKILL TO BOAST OF WHAT-SOEVER.
NEXT!
OUT WITH THE NEXT GUY!
COME ON!
ALERT THE FORCES.
THEY ARE NOT TO ENGAGE WITH THE LONE HORSEMAN WITHOUT PERMIS-SION.
YES, SIR!!

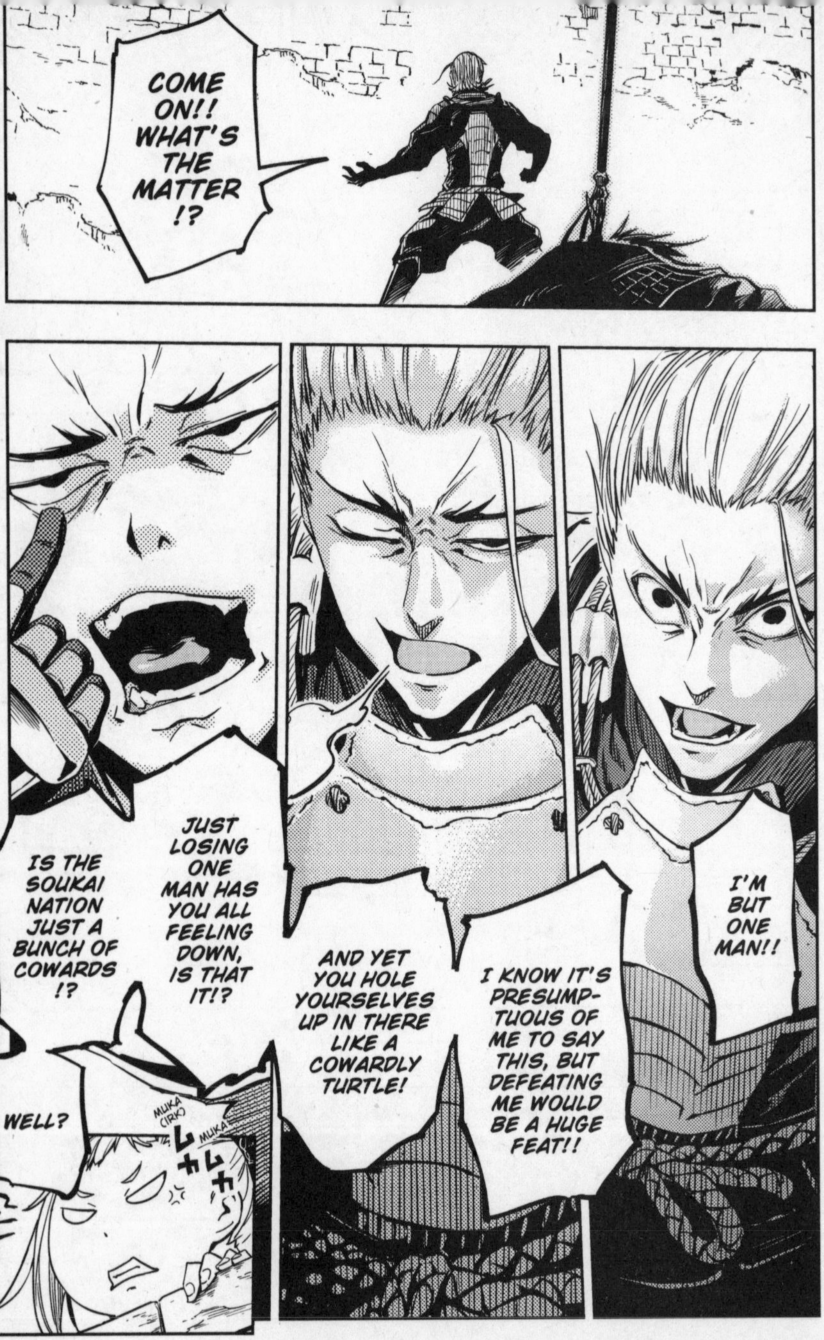
COME ON!! WHAT'S THE MATTER!?
I'M BUT ONE MAN!!
I KNOW IT'S PRESUMPTUOUS OF ME TO SAY THIS, BUT DEFEATING ME WOULD BE A HUGE FEAT!!
AND YET YOU HOLE YOURSELVES UP IN THERE LIKE A COWARDLY TURTLE!
JUST LOSING ONE MAN HAS YOU ALL FEELING DOWN, IS THAT IT!?
IS THE SOUKAI NATION JUST A BUNCH OF COWARDS!?
MUKA (IRK) MUKA
WELL?

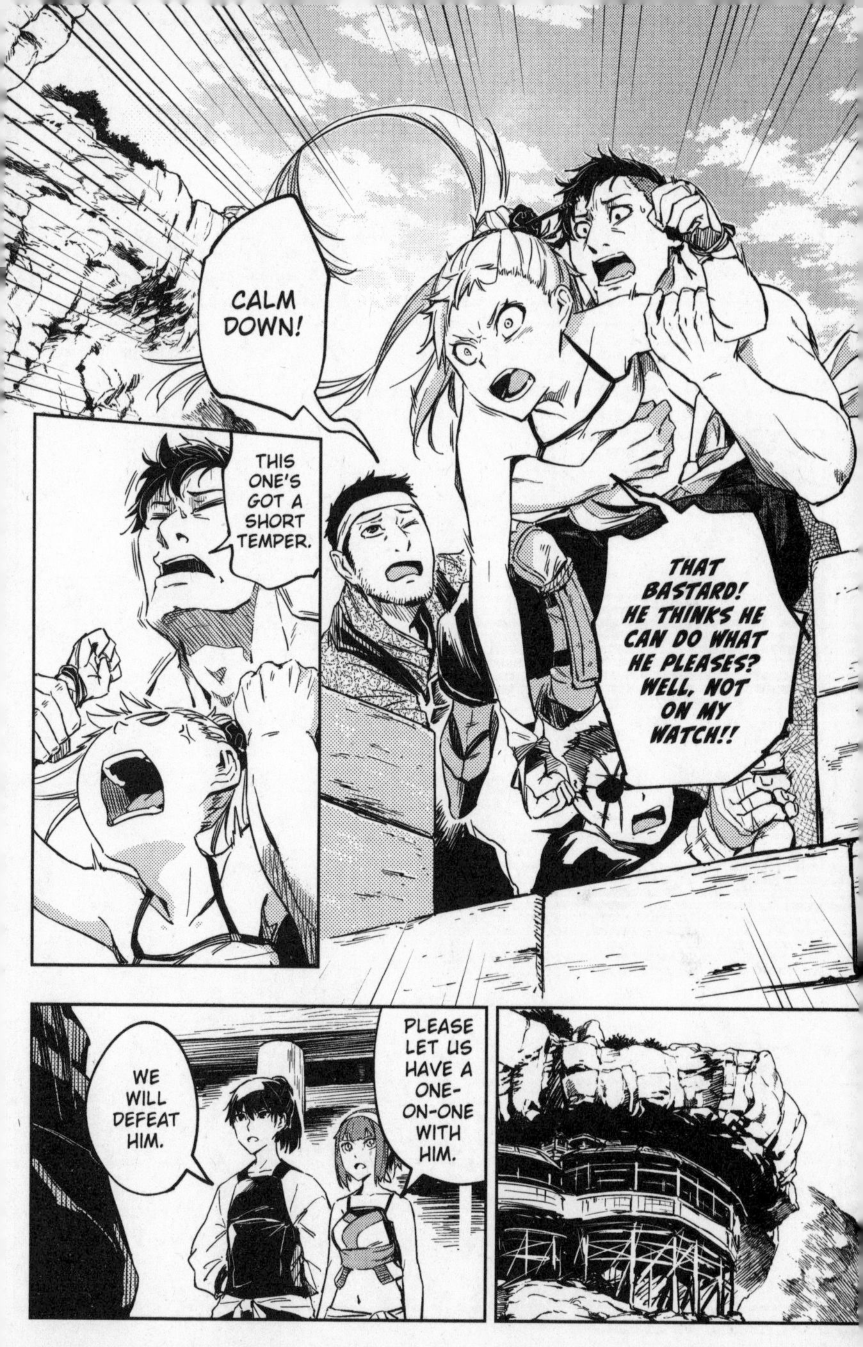
CALM DOWN!
THAT BASTARD! HE THINKS HE CAN DO WHAT HE PLEASES? WELL, NOT ON MY WATCH!!
THIS ONE'S GOT A SHORT TEMPER.
PLEASE LET US HAVE A ONE-ON-ONE WITH HIM.
WE WILL DEFEAT HIM.

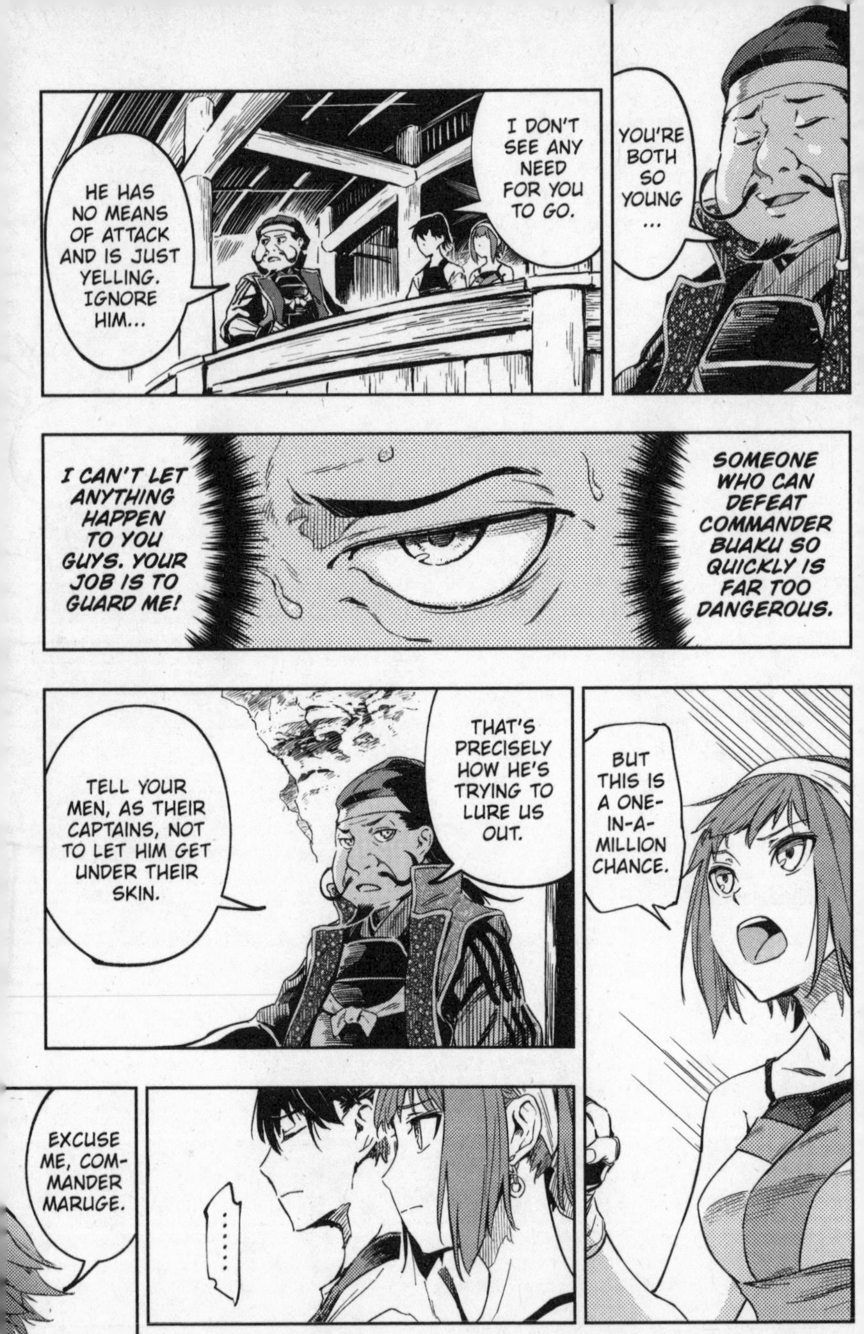
YOU'RE BOTH SO YOUNG ...
I DON'T SEE ANY NEED FOR YOU TO GO.
HE HAS NO MEANS OF ATTACK AND IS JUST YELLING. IGNORE HIM...
SOMEONE WHO CAN DEFEAT COMMANDER BUAKU SO QUICKLY IS FAR TOO DANGEROUS.
I CAN'T LET ANYTHING HAPPEN TO YOU GUYS. YOUR JOB IS TO GUARD ME!
BUT THIS IS A ONE-IN-A-MILLION CHANCE.
THAT'S PRECISELY HOW HE'S TRYING TO LURE US OUT.
TELL YOUR MEN, AS THEIR CAPTAINS, NOT TO LET HIM GET UNDER THEIR SKIN.
......
EXCUSE ME, COM-MANDER MARUGE.

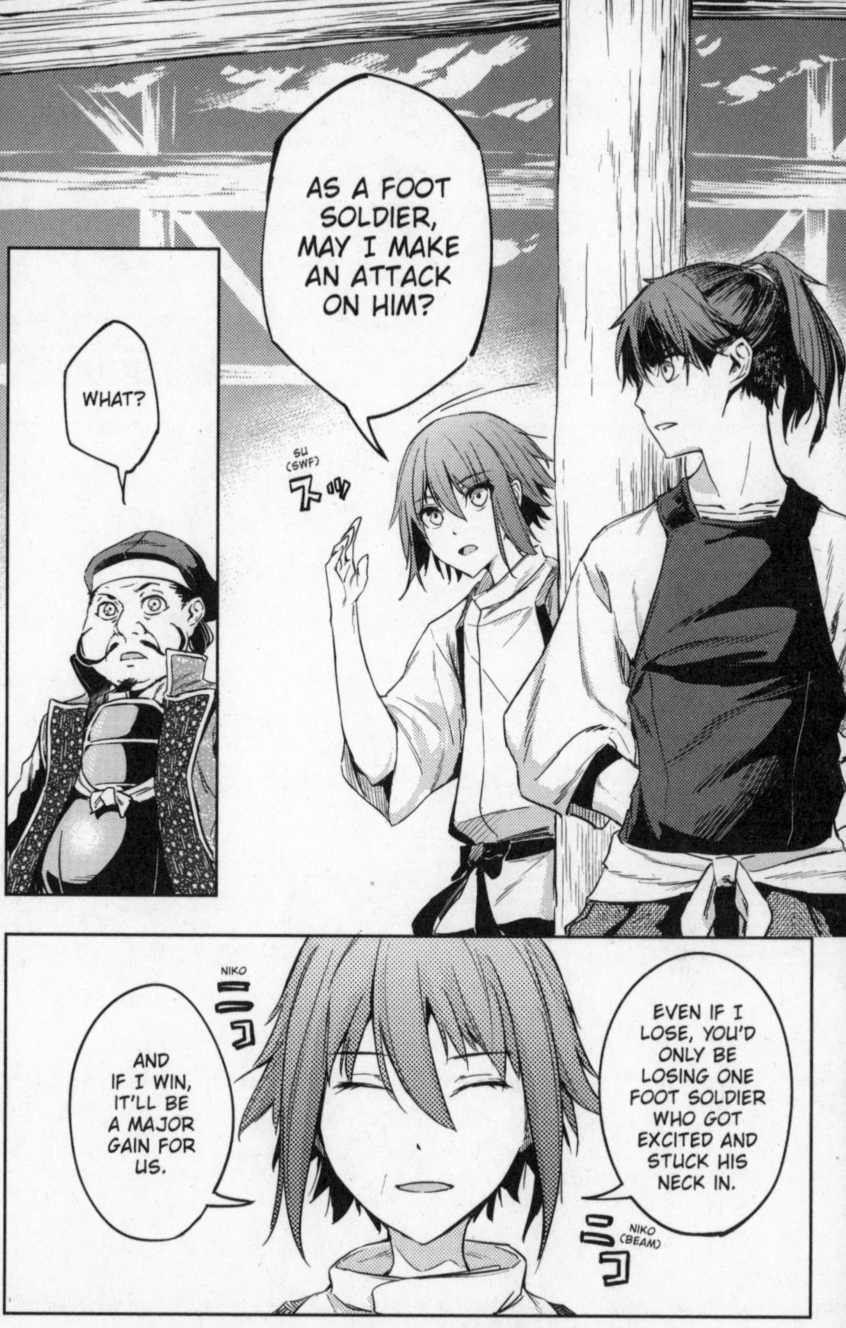
AS A FOOT SOLDIER, MAY I MAKE AN ATTACK ON HIM?
SU (SWF)
スッ
WHAT?
EVEN IF I LOSE, YOU'D ONLY BE LOSING ONE FOOT SOLDIER WHO GOT EXCITED AND STUCK HIS NECK IN.
NIKO (BEAM)
ニコ
AND IF I WIN, IT'LL BE A MAJOR GAIN FOR US.
NIKO
ニコ

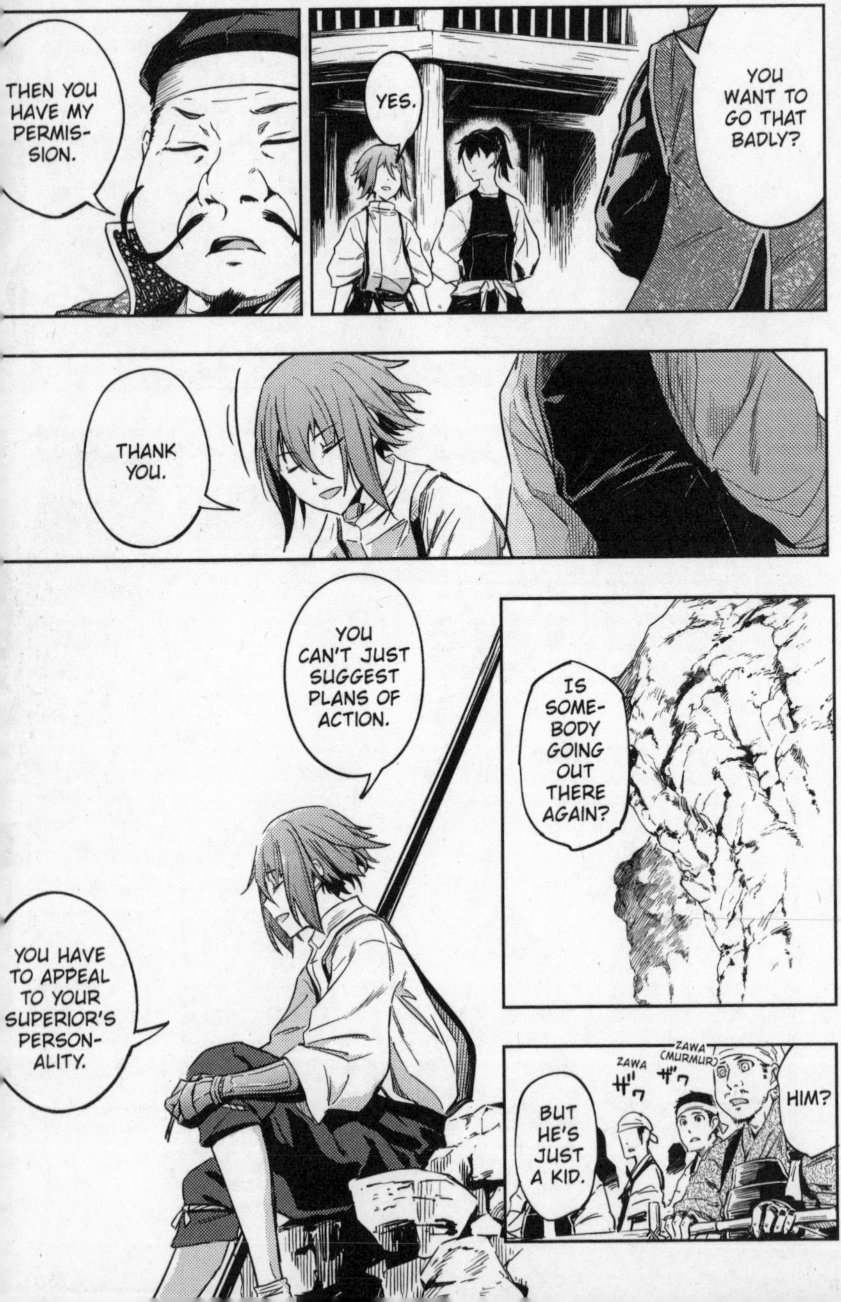
YOU WANT TO GO THAT BADLY?
YES.
THEN YOU HAVE MY PERMISSION.
THANK YOU.
IS SOMEBODY GOING OUT THERE AGAIN?
HIM?
ZAWA (MURMUR)
ZAWA
BUT HE'S JUST A KID.
YOU CAN'T JUST SUGGEST PLANS OF ACTION.
YOU HAVE TO APPEAL TO YOUR SUPERIOR'S PERSONALITY.

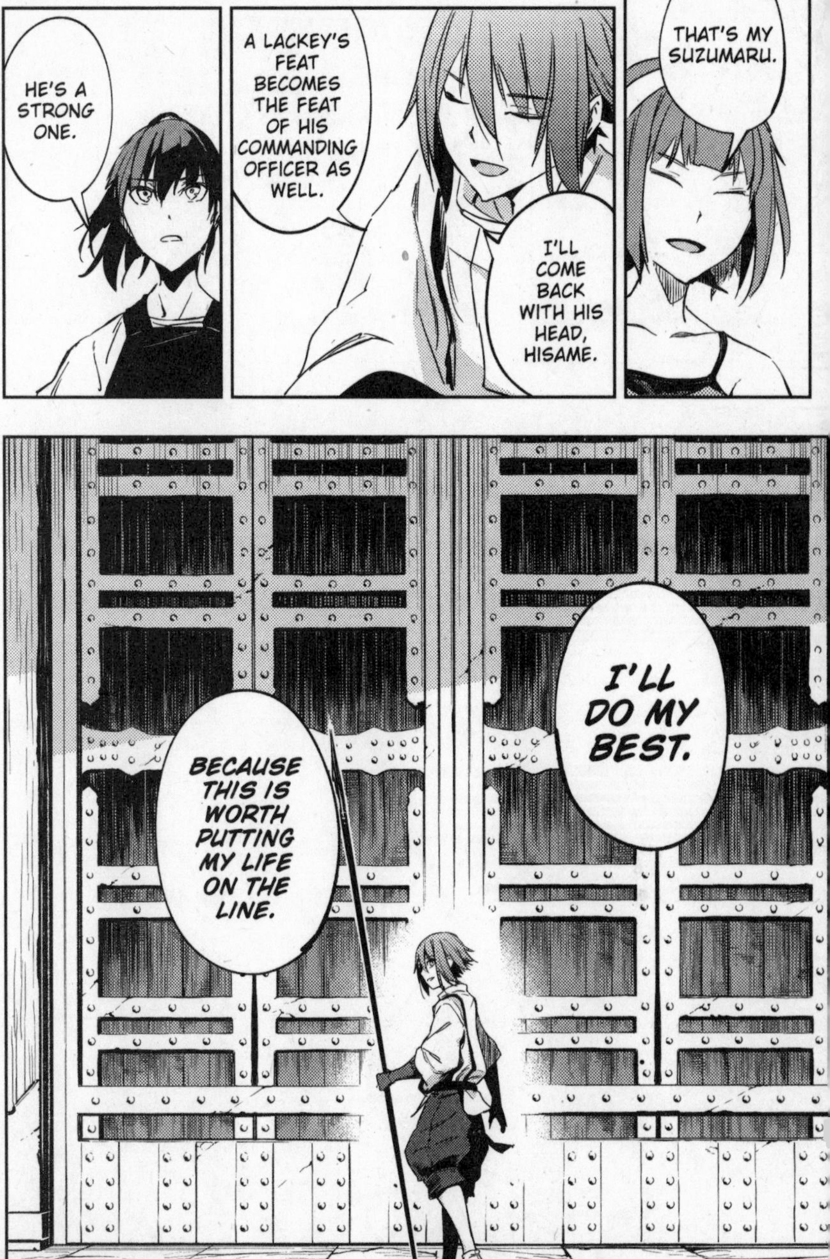
THAT'S MY SUZUMARU.
A LACKEY'S FEAT BECOMES THE FEAT OF HIS COMMANDING OFFICER AS WELL.
I'LL COME BACK WITH HIS HEAD, HISAME.
HE'S A STRONG ONE.
I'LL DO MY BEST.
BECAUSE THIS IS WORTH PUTTING MY LIFE ON THE LINE.

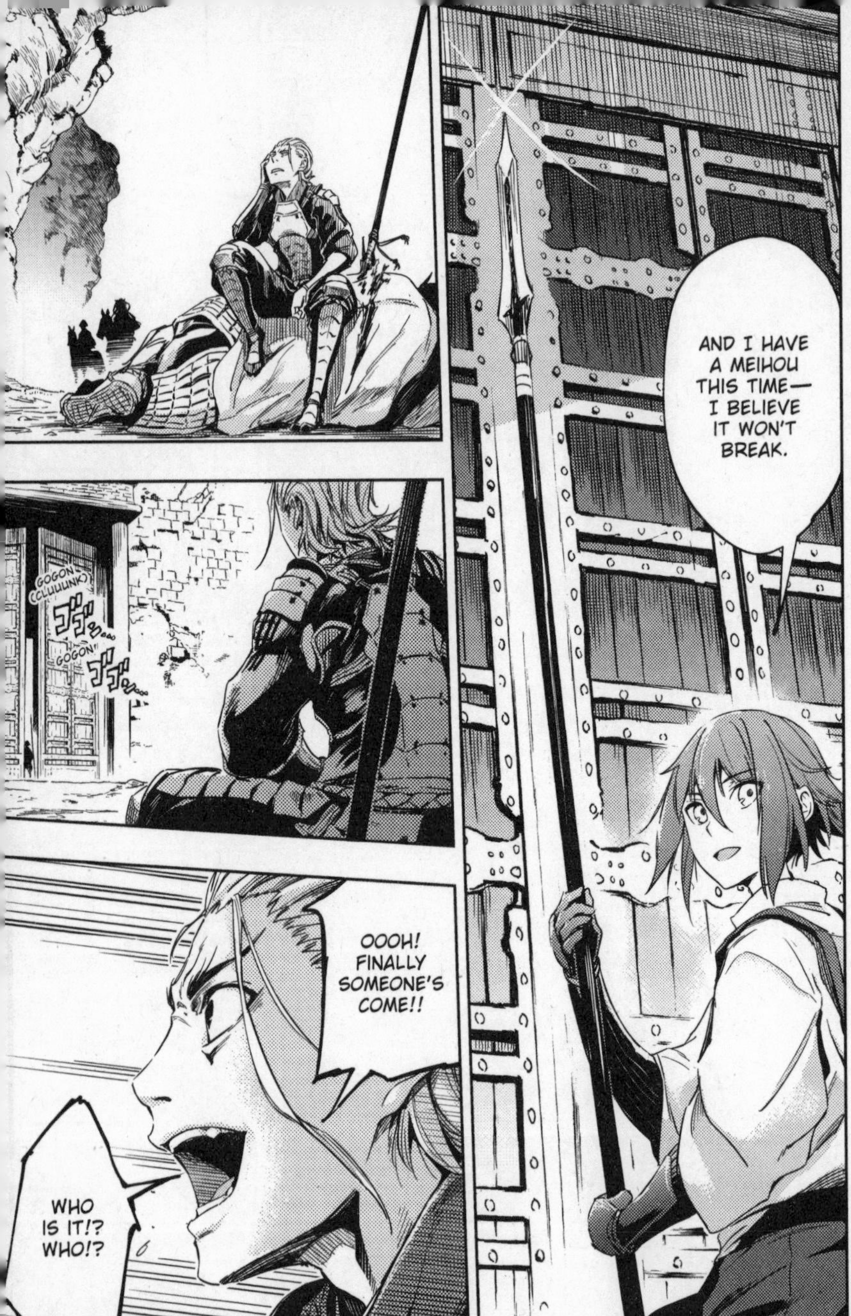
AND I HAVE A MEIHOU THIS TIME—I BELIEVE IT WON'T BREAK.
GOGON (CLUUUNK)
GOGON!!
OOOH! FINALLY SOMEONE'S COME!!
WHO IS IT!? WHO!?

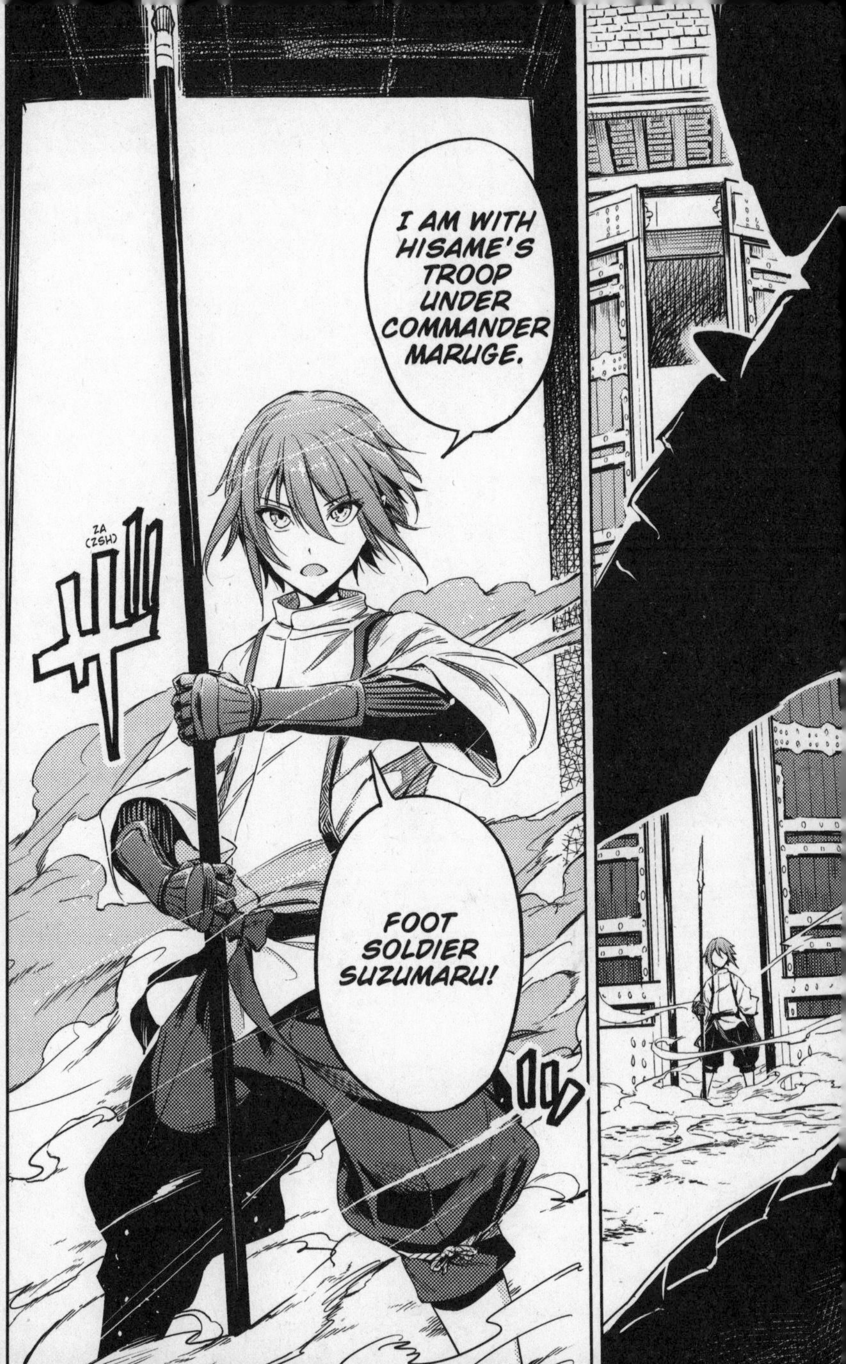
I AM WITH HISAME'S TROOP UNDER COMMANDER MARUGE.
ZA (ZSH)
FOOT SOLDIER SUZUMARU!

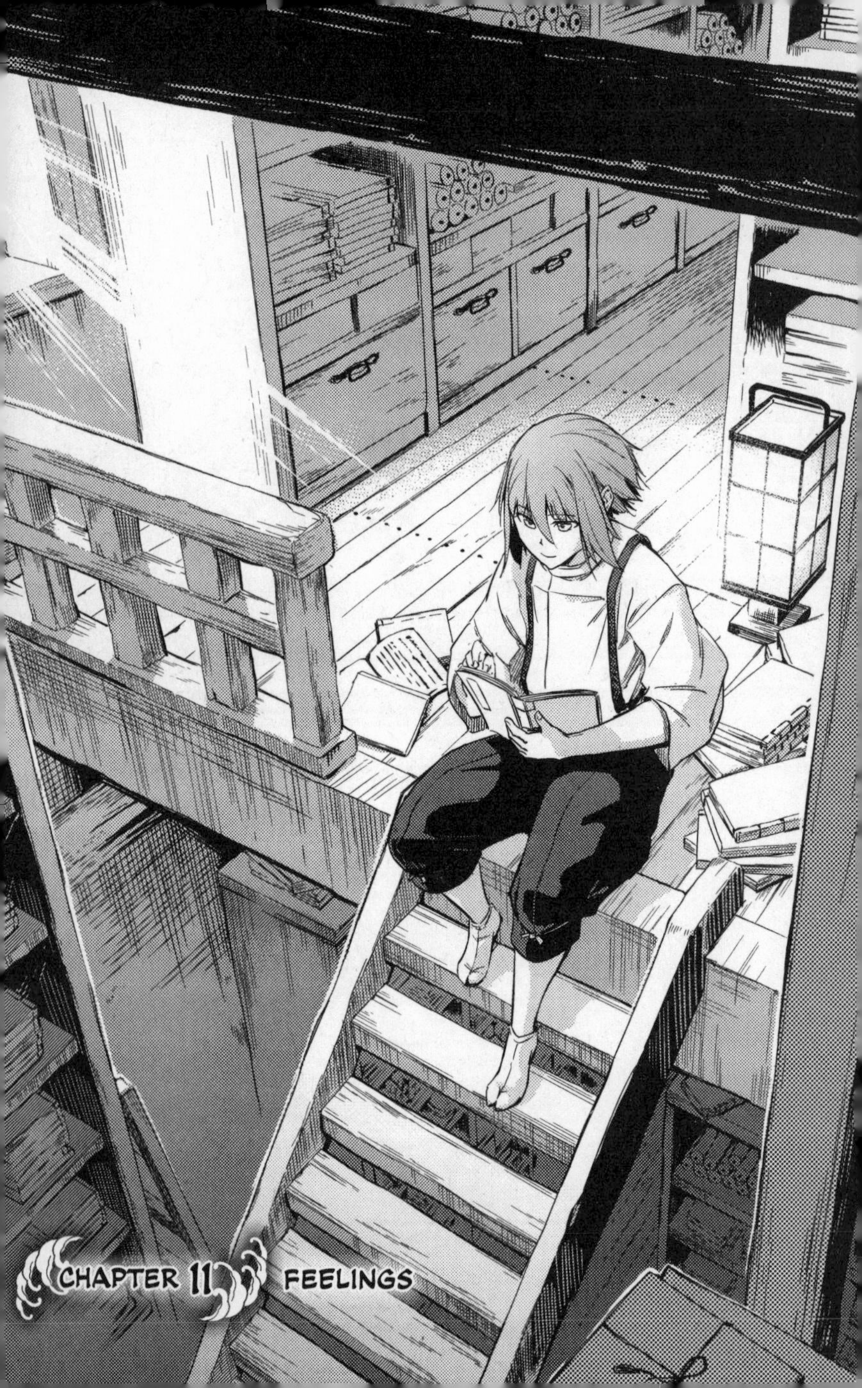
CHAPTER 11
FEELINGS

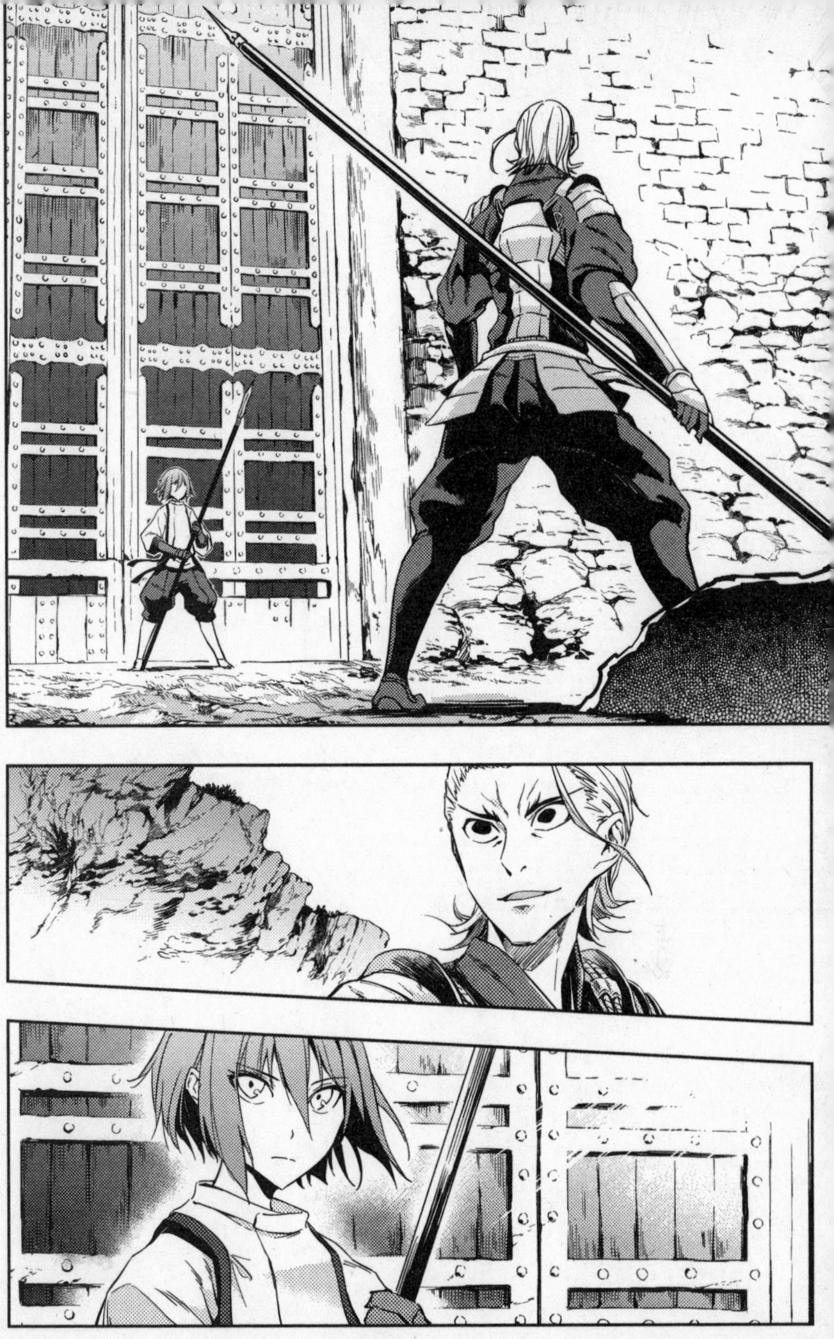

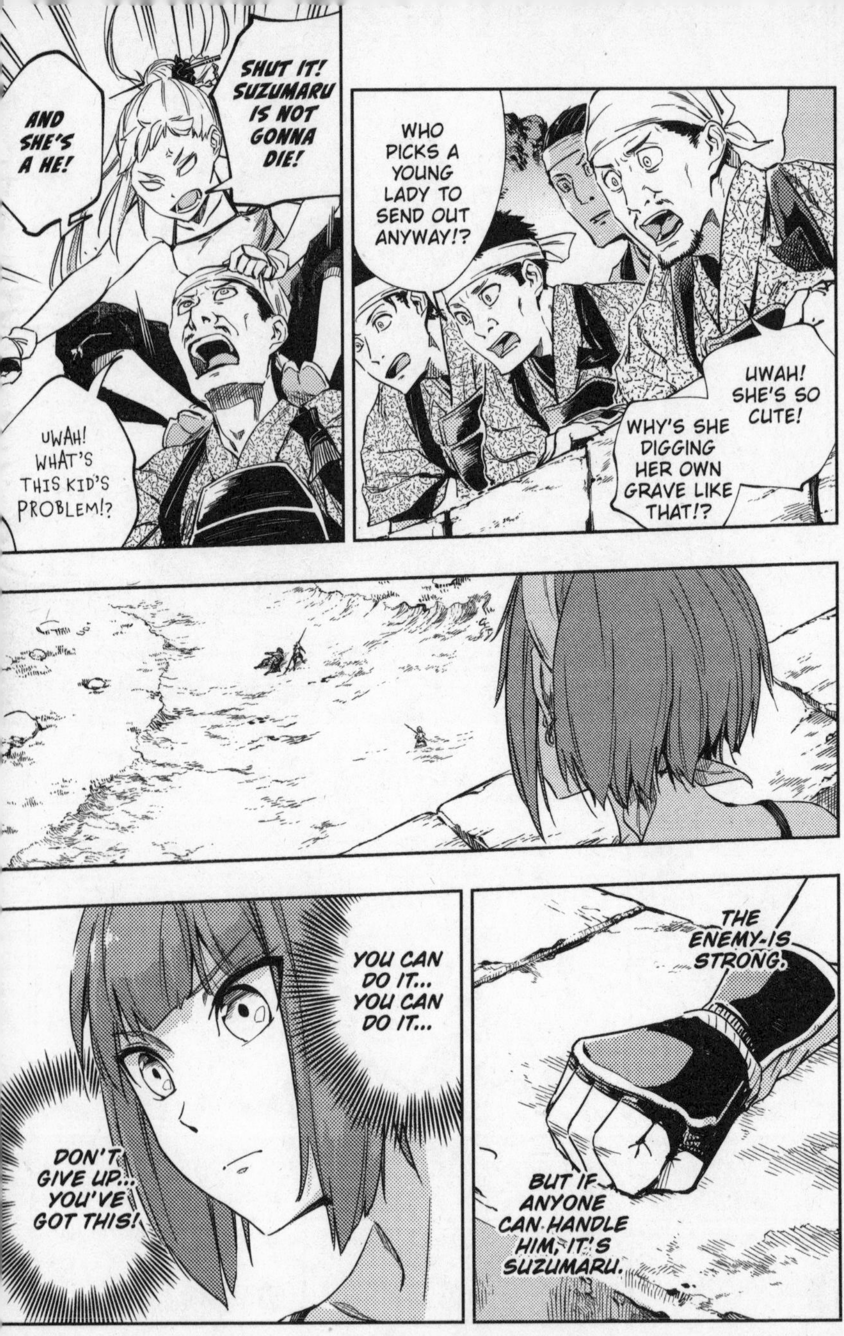
WHO PICKS A YOUNG LADY TO SEND OUT ANYWAY!?
UWAH! SHE'S SO CUTE!
WHY'S SHE DIGGING HER OWN GRAVE LIKE THAT!?
SHUT IT! SUZUMARU IS NOT GONNA DIE!
AND SHE'S A HE!
UWAH! WHAT'S THIS KID'S PROBLEM!?
THE ENEMY IS STRONG.
BUT IF ANYONE CAN HANDLE HIM, IT'S SUZUMARU.
YOU CAN DO IT... YOU CAN DO IT...
DON'T GIVE UP... YOU'VE GOT THIS!

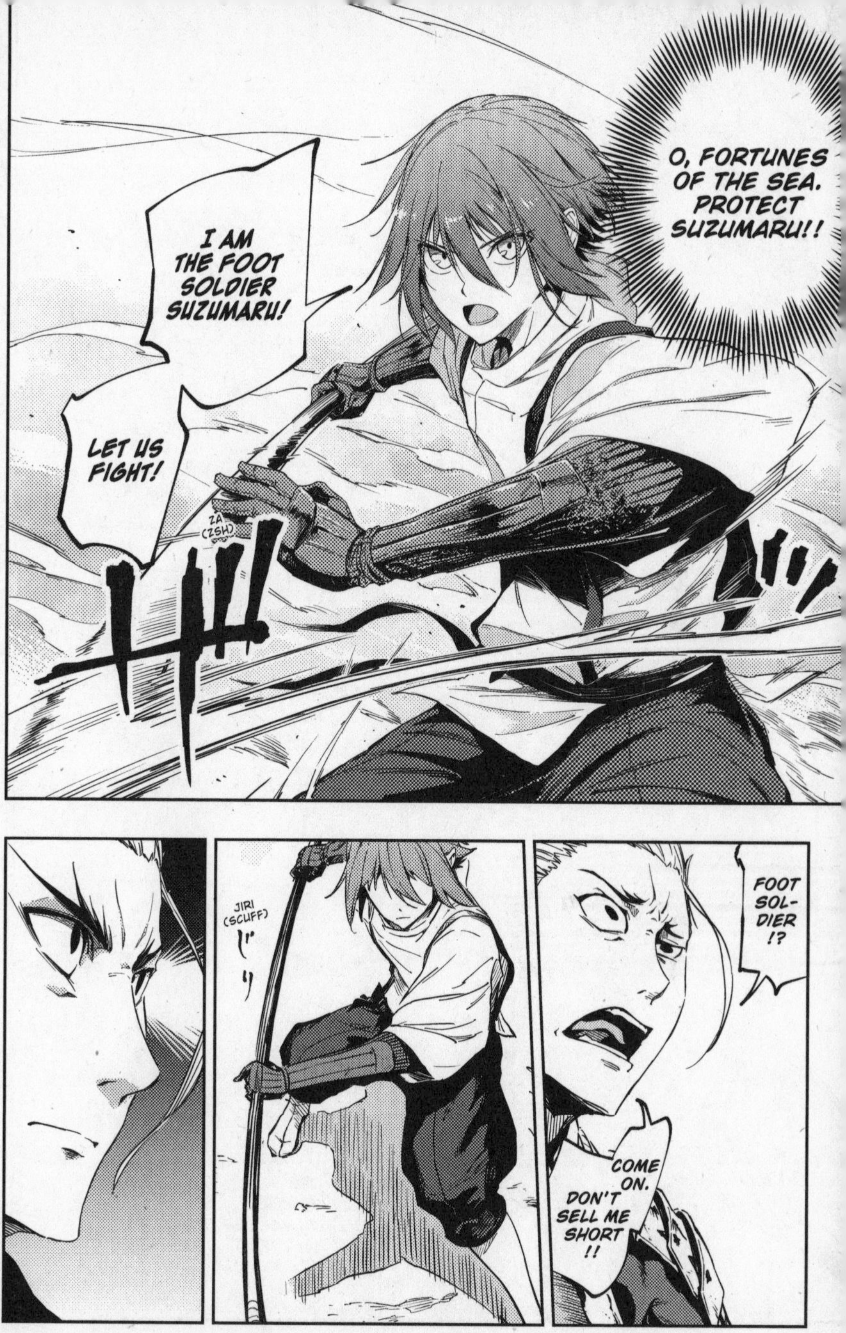
O, FORTUNES OF THE SEA. PROTECT SUZUMARU!!
I AM THE FOOT SOLDIER SUZUMARU!
LET US FIGHT!
ZA (ZSH)
FOOT SOL-DIER !?
COME ON. DON'T SELL ME SHORT !!
JIRI (SCUFF)

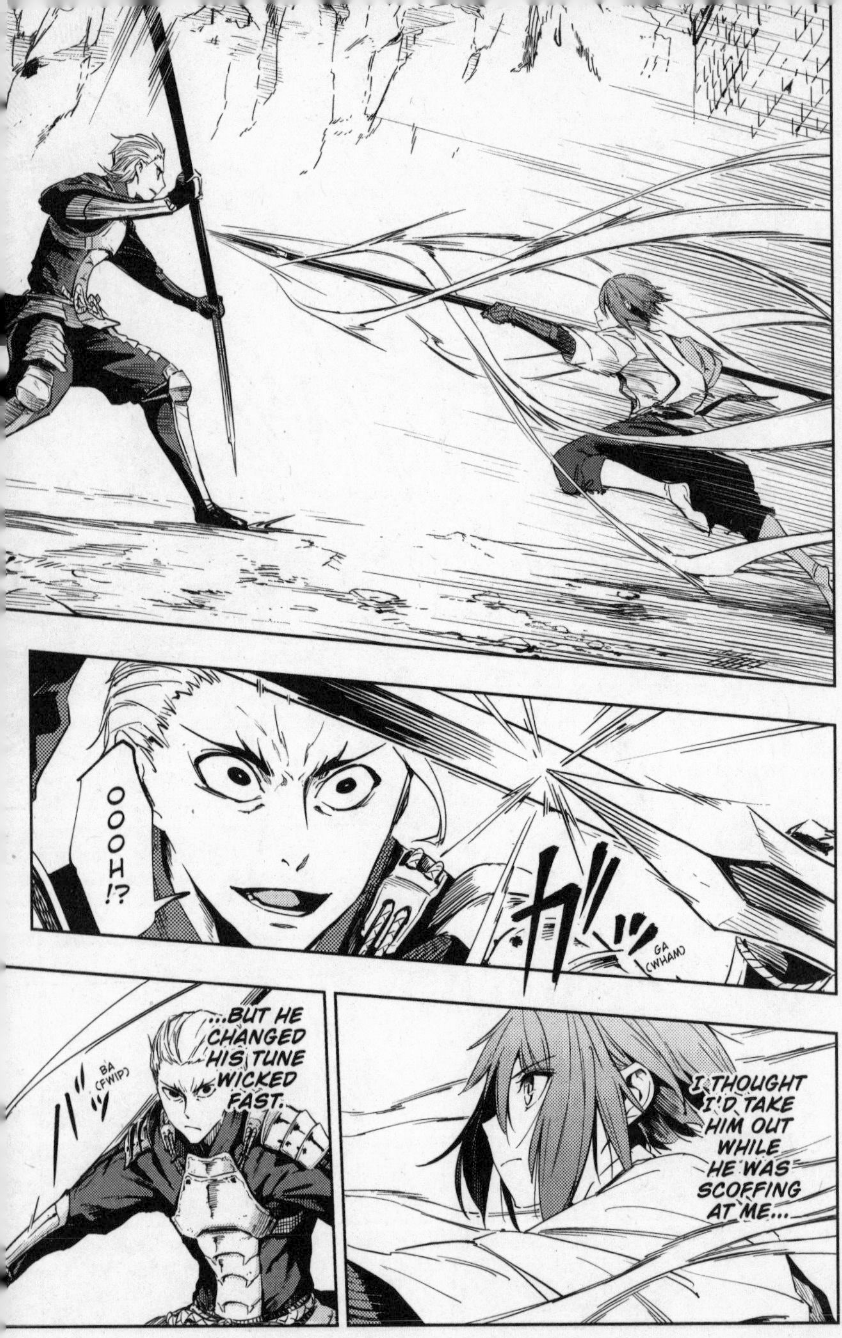
ガッ
GA (WHAM)
OOOOH!?
I THOUGHT I'D TAKE HIM OUT WHILE HE WAS SCOFFING AT ME...
...BUT HE CHANGED HIS TUNE WICKED FAST.
バッ
BA (FWIP)

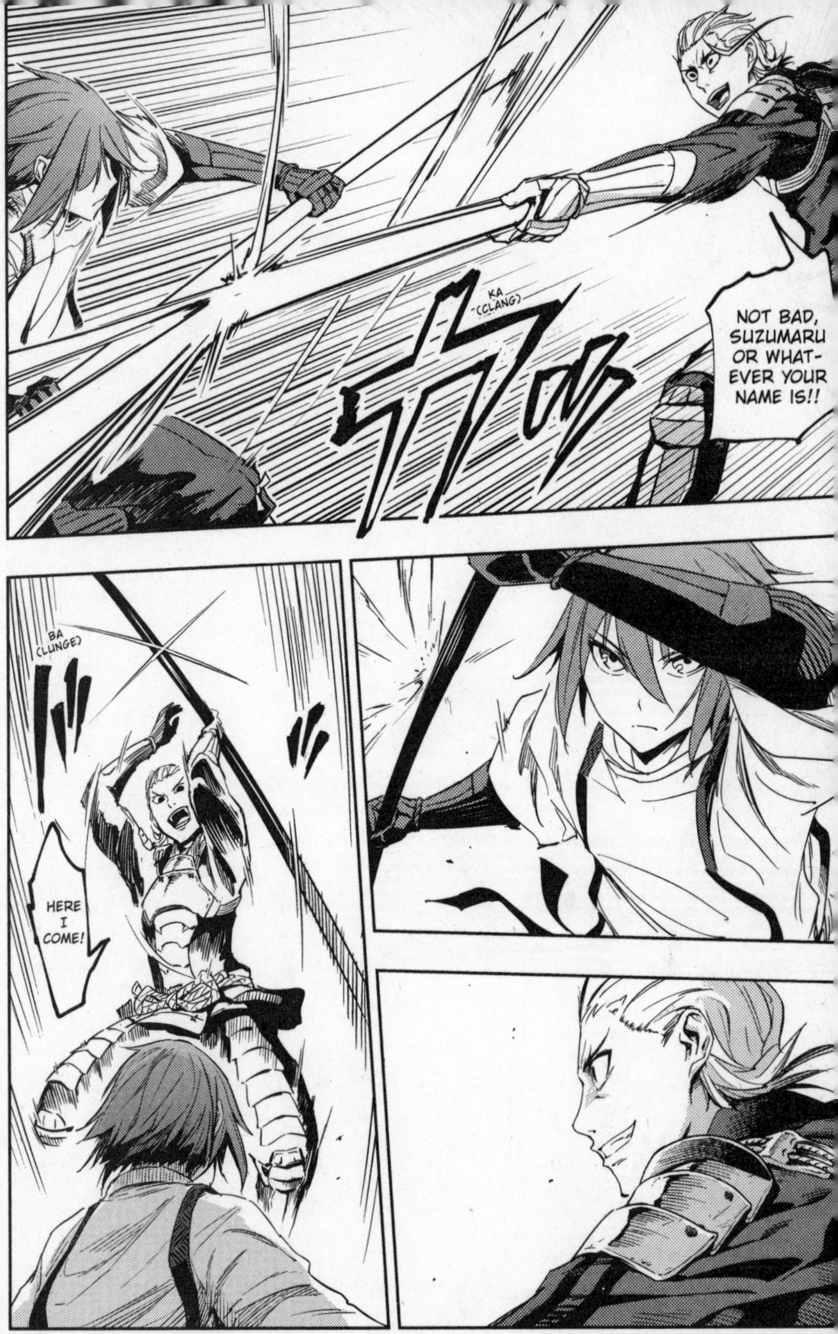
NOT BAD, SUZUMARU OR WHATEVER YOUR NAME IS!!
KA (CLANG)
BA (LUNGE)
HERE I COME!

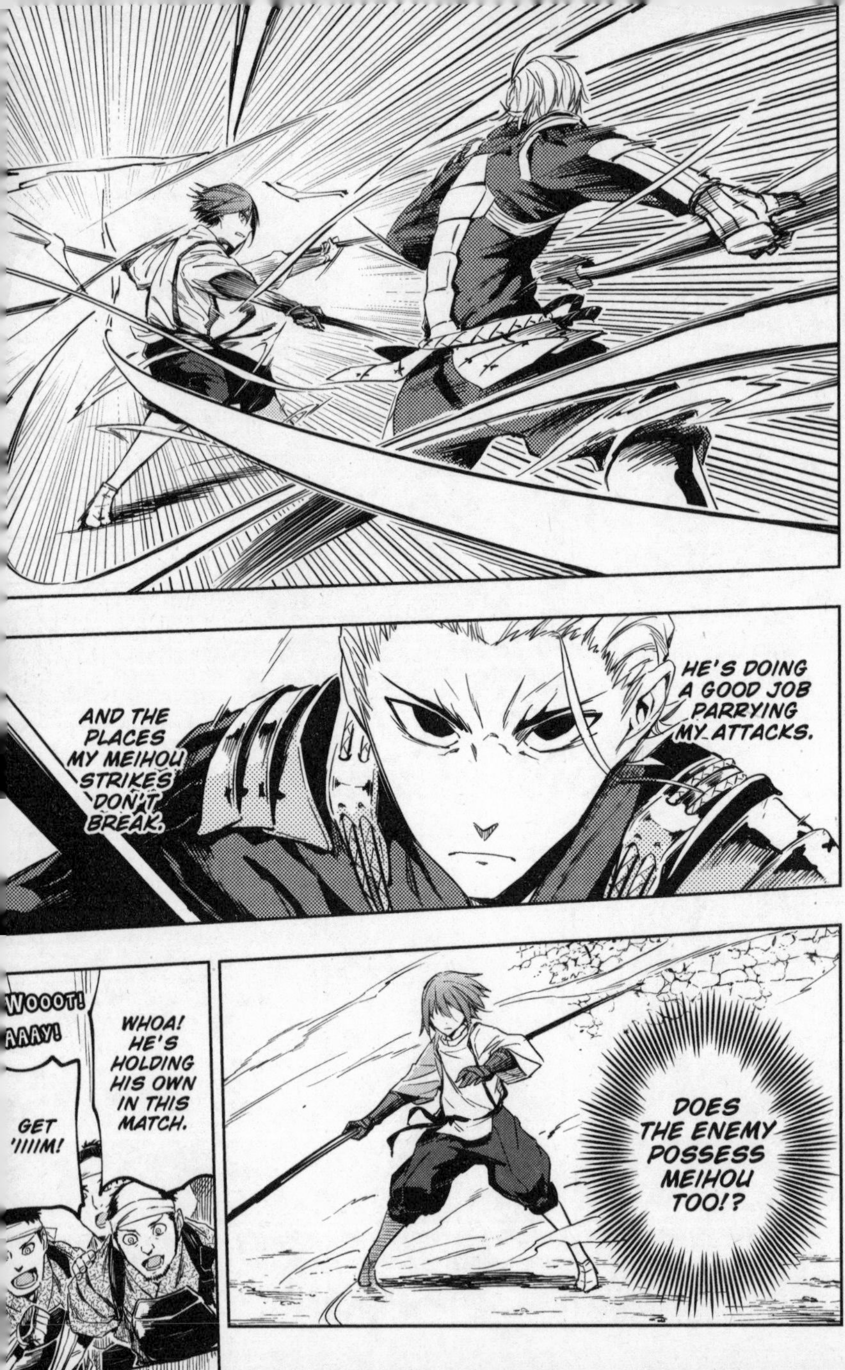
HE'S DOING A GOOD JOB PARRYING MY ATTACKS.
AND THE PLACES MY MEIHOU STRIKES DON'T BREAK.
DOES THE ENEMY POSSESS MEIHOU TOO!?
WOOOT!
WHOA! HE'S HOLDING HIS OWN IN THIS MATCH.
AAAY!
GET 'IIIIM!

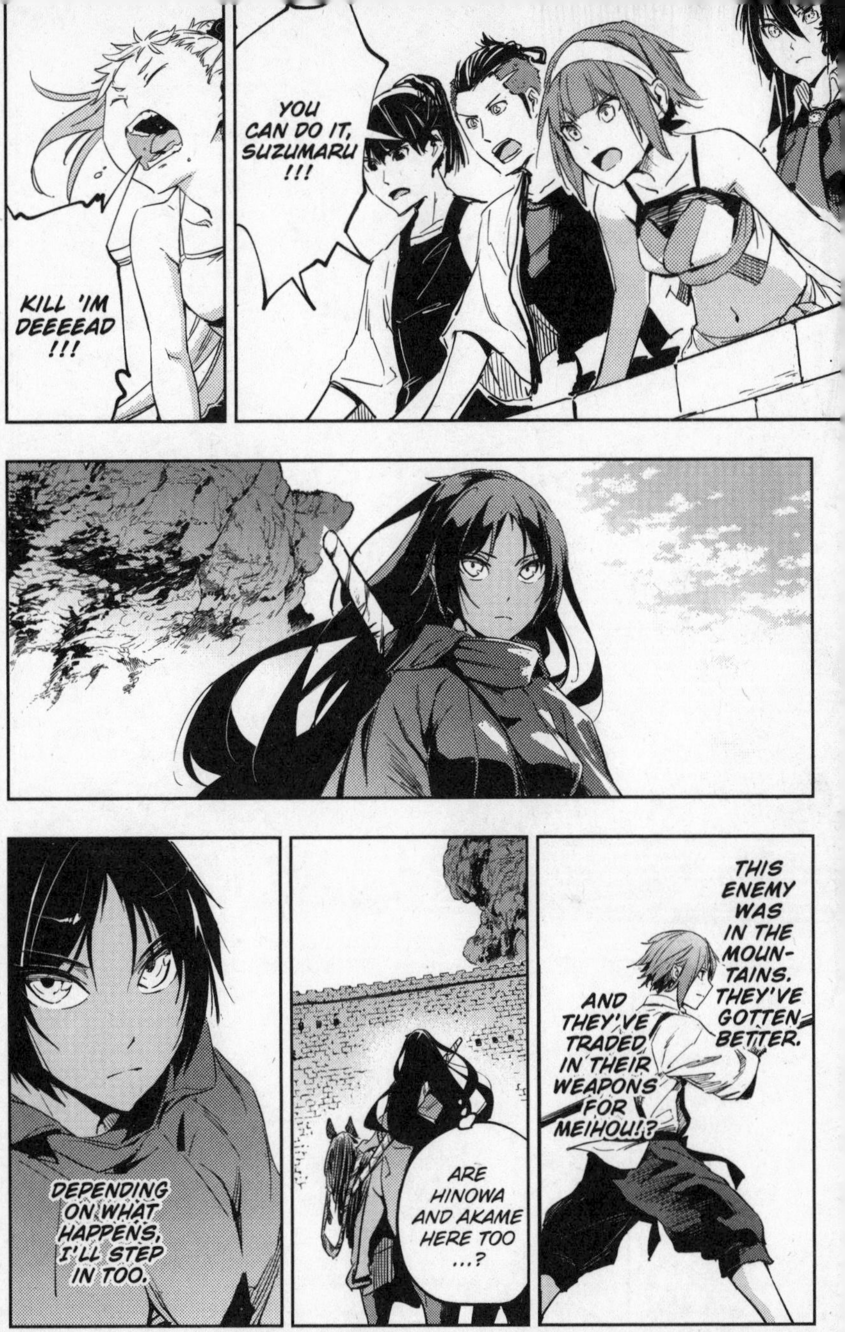
YOU CAN DO IT, SUZUMARU!!!
KILL 'IM DEEEEAD!!!
THIS ENEMY WAS IN THE MOUNTAINS. THEY'VE GOTTEN BETTER.
AND THEY'VE TRADED IN THEIR WEAPONS FOR MEIHOU!?
ARE HINOWA AND AKAME HERE TOO...?
DEPENDING ON WHAT HAPPENS, I'LL STEP IN TOO.

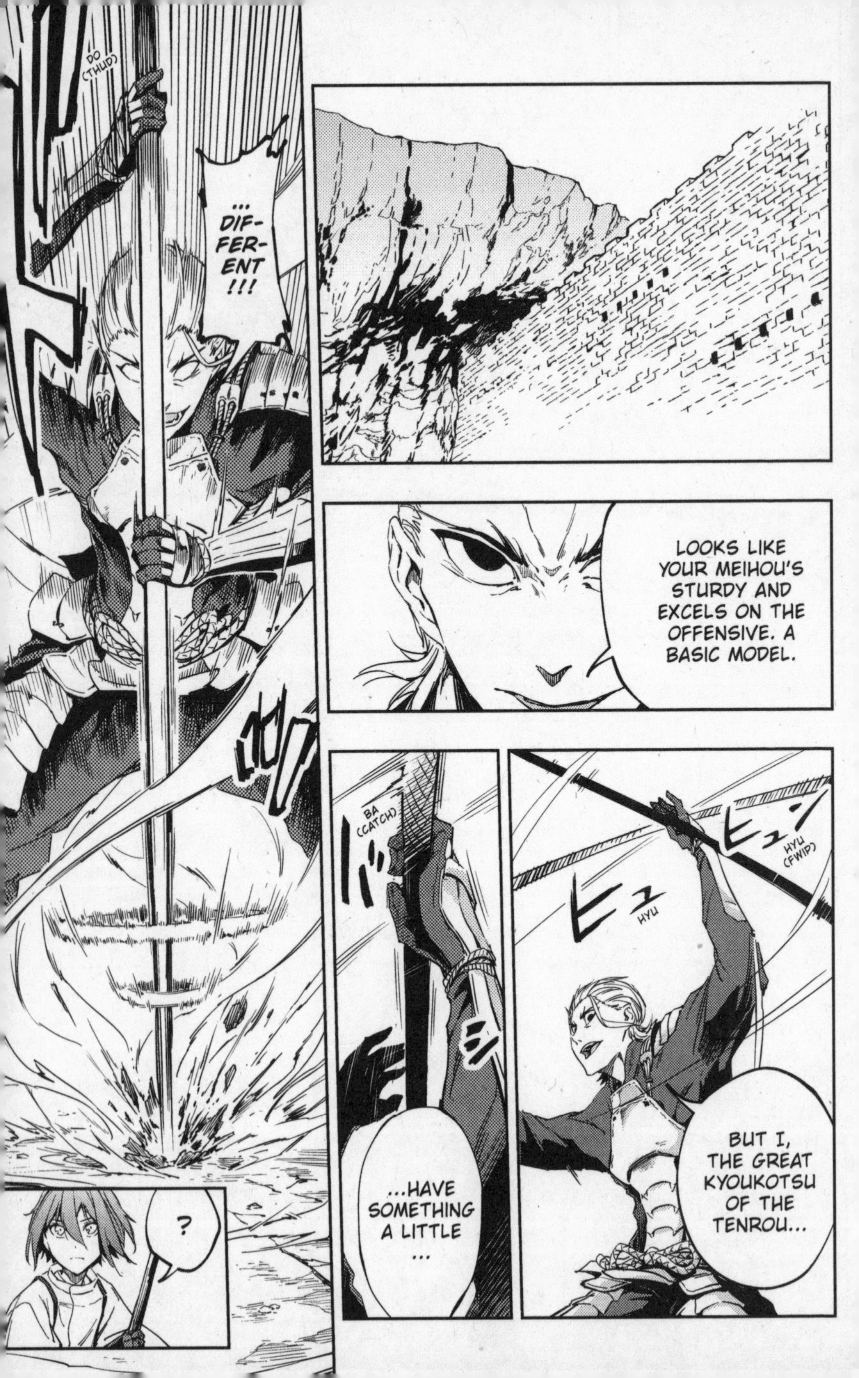
LOOKS LIKE YOUR MEIHOU'S STURDY AND EXCELS ON THE OFFENSIVE. A BASIC MODEL.
HYU (FWIP)
HYU
BUT I, THE GREAT KYOUKOTSU OF THE TENROU...
BA (CATCH)
...HAVE SOMETHING A LITTLE ...
DO (THUD)
... DIFF-ERENT !!!
?

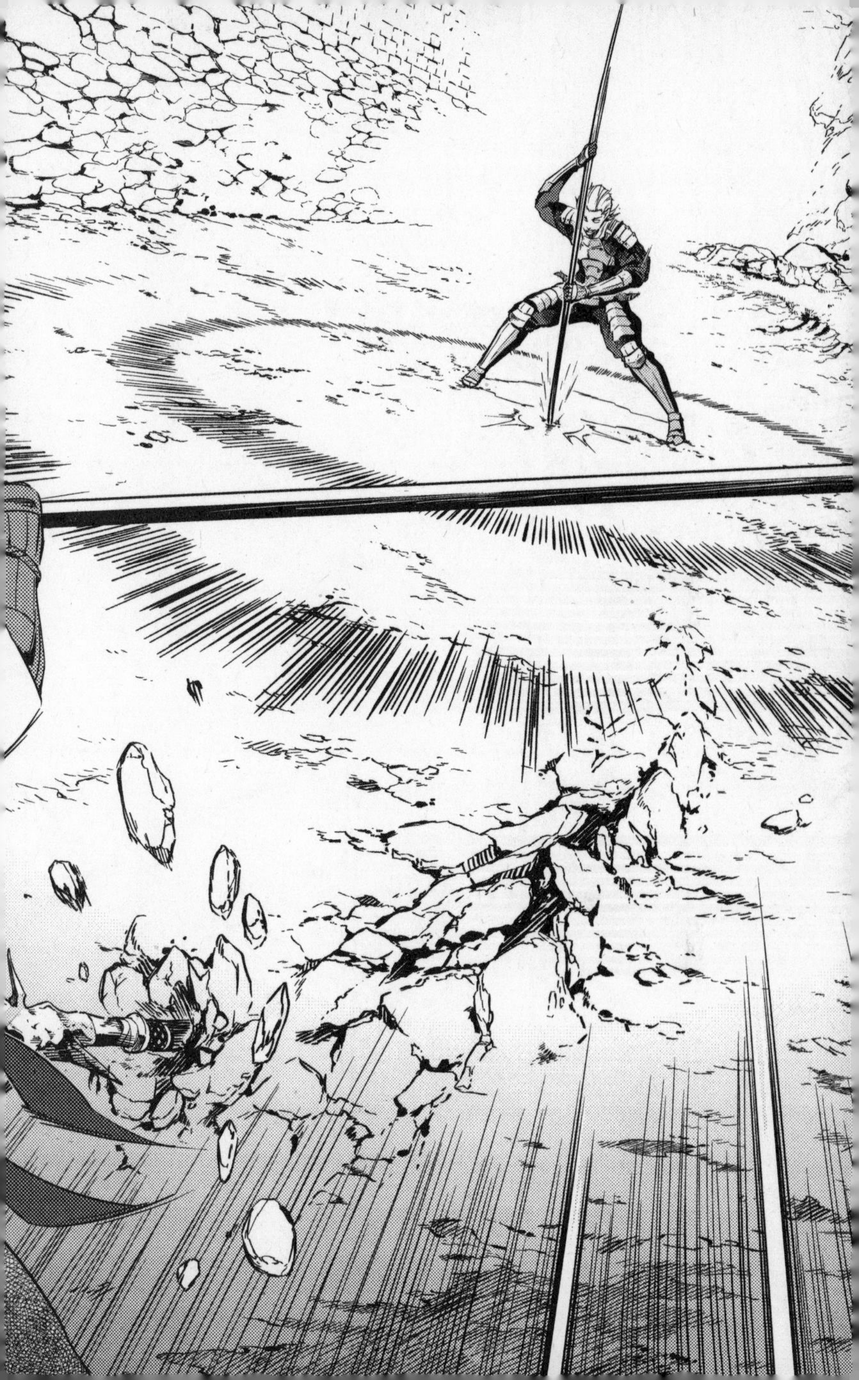

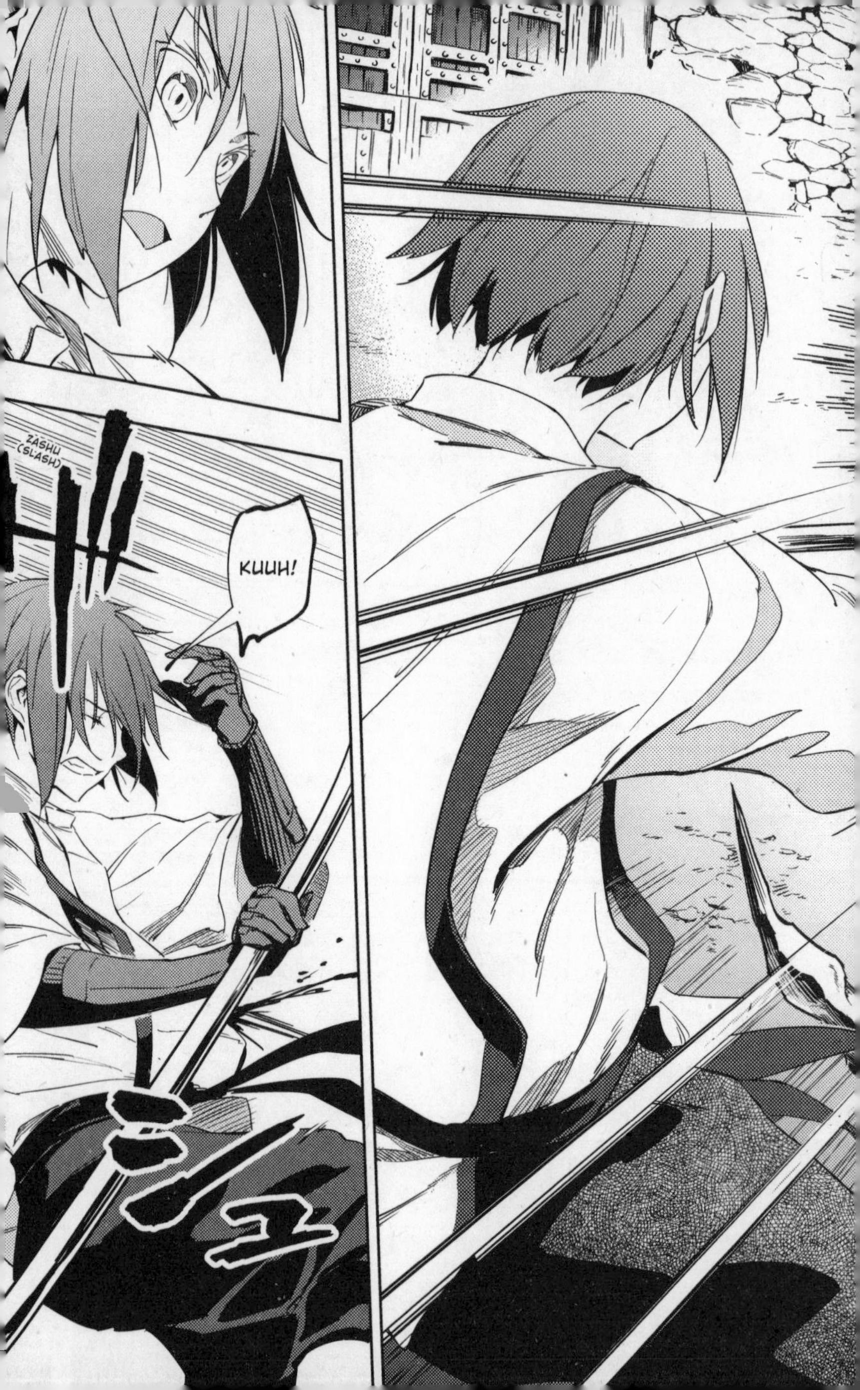
ZASHU (SLASH)
KUUH!

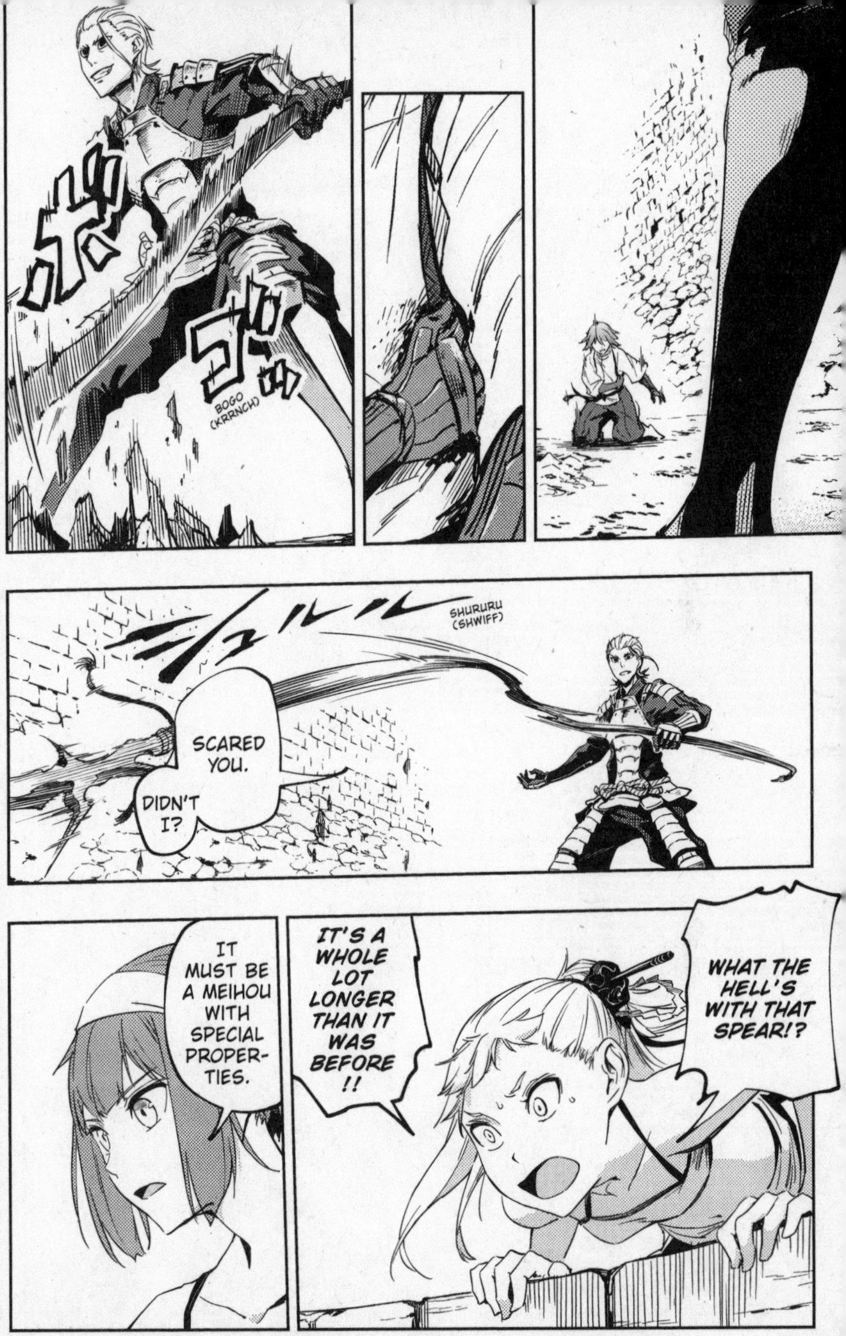
BOGO (KRRNCH)
SHURURU (SHWIFF)
SCARED YOU.
DIDN'T I?
WHAT THE HELL'S WITH THAT SPEAR!?
IT'S A WHOLE LOT LONGER THAN IT WAS BEFORE!!
IT MUST BE A MEIHOU WITH SPECIAL PROPERTIES.

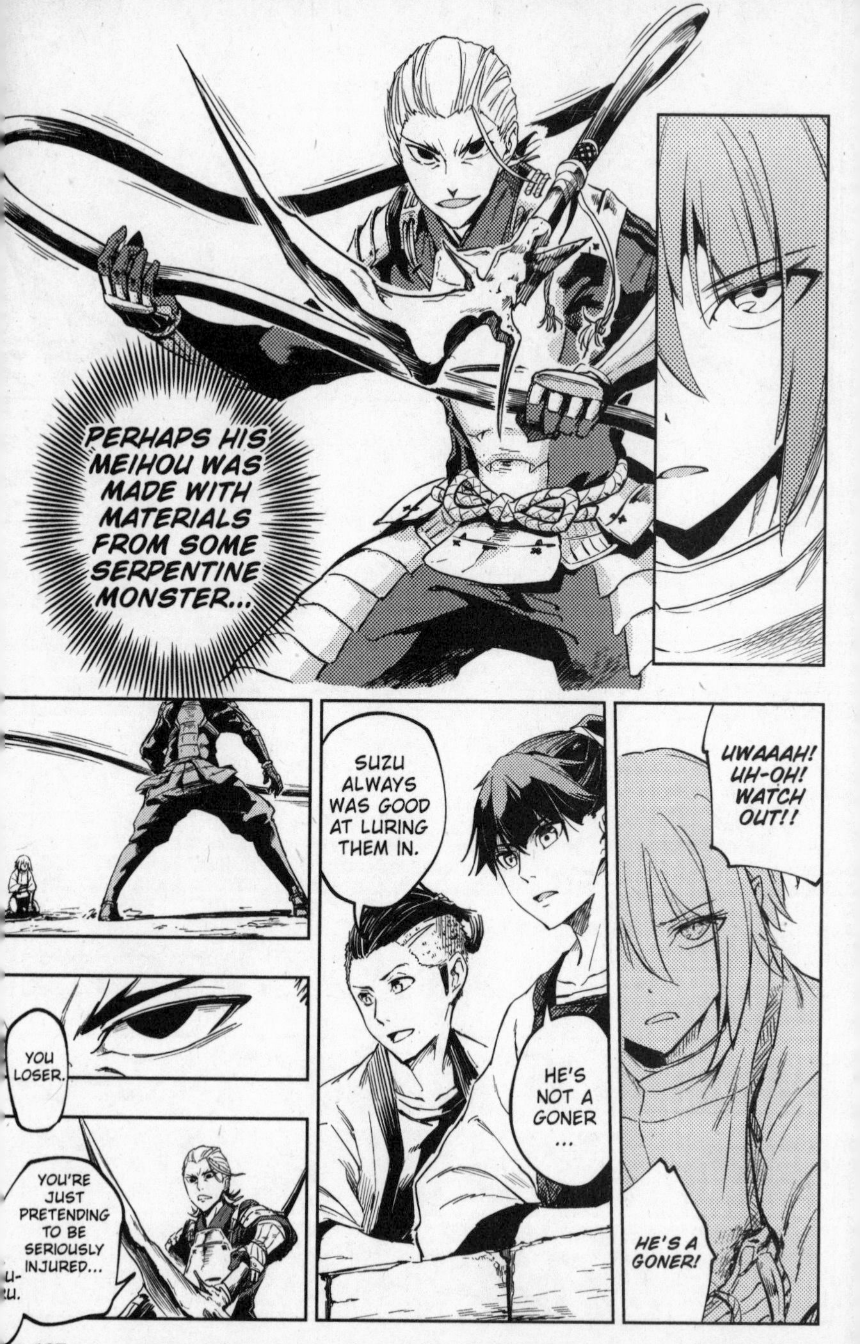
PERHAPS HIS MEIHOU WAS MADE WITH MATERIALS FROM SOME SERPENTINE MONSTER...
UWAAAH! UH-OH! WATCH OUT!!
HE'S A GONER!
SUZU ALWAYS WAS GOOD AT LURING THEM IN.
HE'S NOT A GONER ...
YOU LOSER.
YOU'RE JUST PRETENDING TO BE SERIOUSLY INJURED...

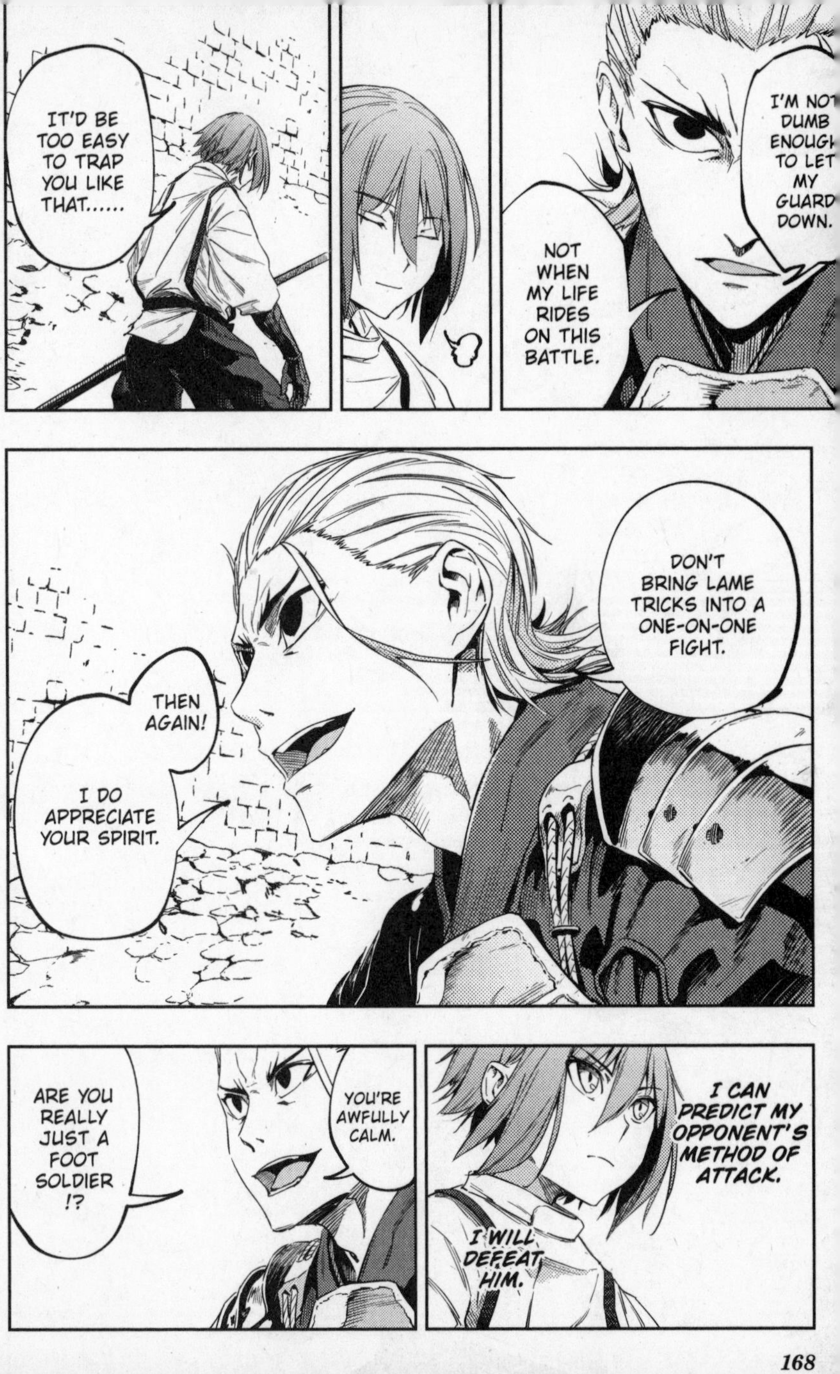
I'M NOT DUMB ENOUGH TO LET MY GUARD DOWN.
NOT WHEN MY LIFE RIDES ON THIS BATTLE.
IT'D BE TOO EASY TO TRAP YOU LIKE THAT......
DON'T BRING LAME TRICKS INTO A ONE-ON-ONE FIGHT.
THEN AGAIN!
I DO APPRECIATE YOUR SPIRIT.
I CAN PREDICT MY OPPONENT'S METHOD OF ATTACK.
I WILL DEFEAT HIM.
YOU'RE AWFULLY CALM.
ARE YOU REALLY JUST A FOOT SOLDIER!?

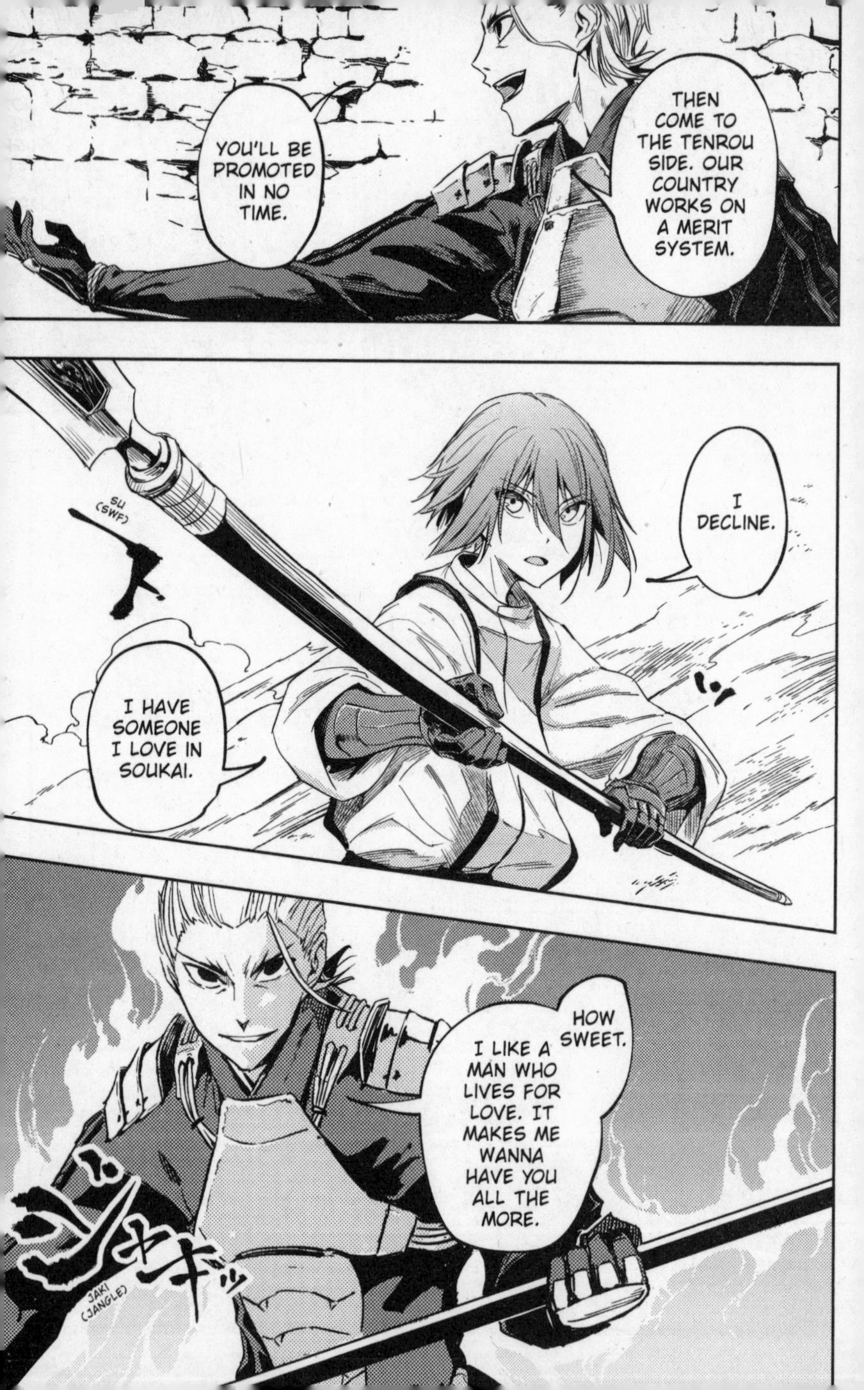
THEN COME TO THE TENROU SIDE. OUR COUNTRY WORKS ON A MERIT SYSTEM.
YOU'LL BE PROMOTED IN NO TIME.
I DECLINE.
SU (SWF)
I HAVE SOMEONE I LOVE IN SOUKAI.
HOW SWEET.
I LIKE A MAN WHO LIVES FOR LOVE. IT MAKES ME WANNA HAVE YOU ALL THE MORE.
JAKI (JANGLE)

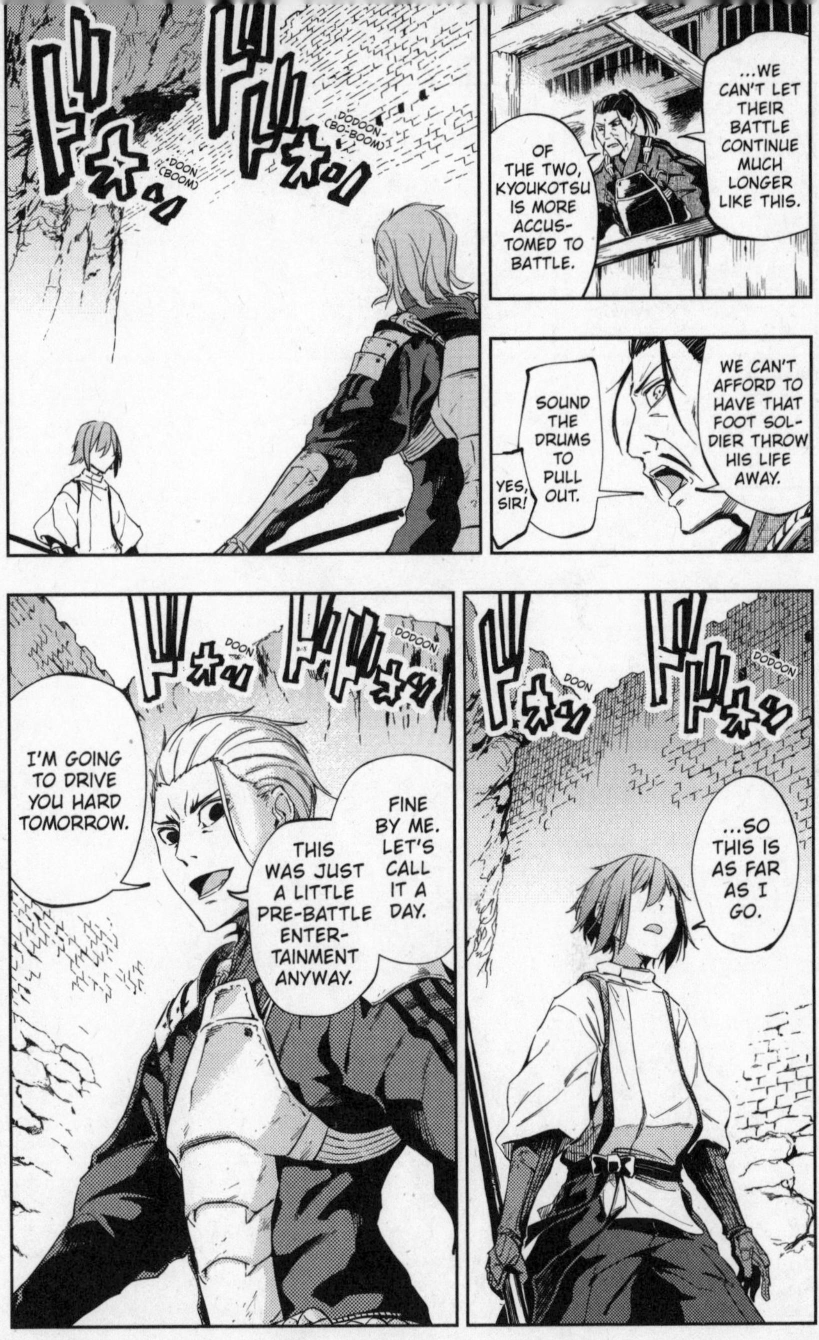
...WE CAN'T LET THEIR BATTLE CONTINUE MUCH LONGER LIKE THIS.
OF THE TWO, KYOUKOTSU IS MORE ACCUS-TOMED TO BATTLE.
WE CAN'T AFFORD TO HAVE THAT FOOT SOL-DIER THROW HIS LIFE AWAY.
SOUND THE DRUMS TO PULL OUT.
YES, SIR!
DODOON (BO-BOOM)
DOON (BOOM)
DODOON
DOON
...SO THIS IS AS FAR AS I GO.
DODOON
DOON
FINE BY ME. LET'S CALL IT A DAY.
THIS WAS JUST A LITTLE PRE-BATTLE ENTER-TAINMENT ANYWAY.
I'M GOING TO DRIVE YOU HARD TOMORROW.

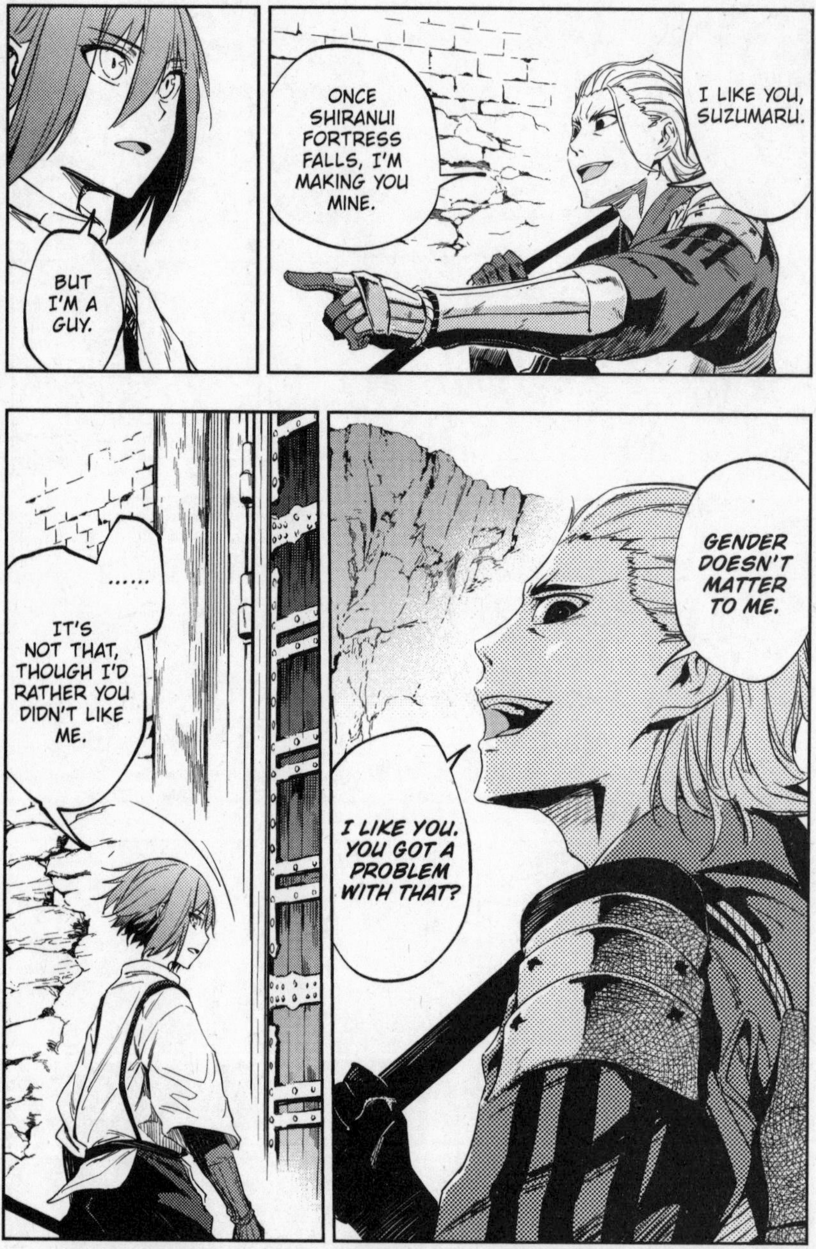
I LIKE YOU, SUZUMARU.
ONCE SHIRANUI FORTRESS FALLS, I'M MAKING YOU MINE.
BUT I'M A GUY.
GENDER DOESN'T MATTER TO ME.
I LIKE YOU. YOU GOT A PROBLEM WITH THAT?
......
IT'S NOT THAT, THOUGH I'D RATHER YOU DIDN'T LIKE ME.

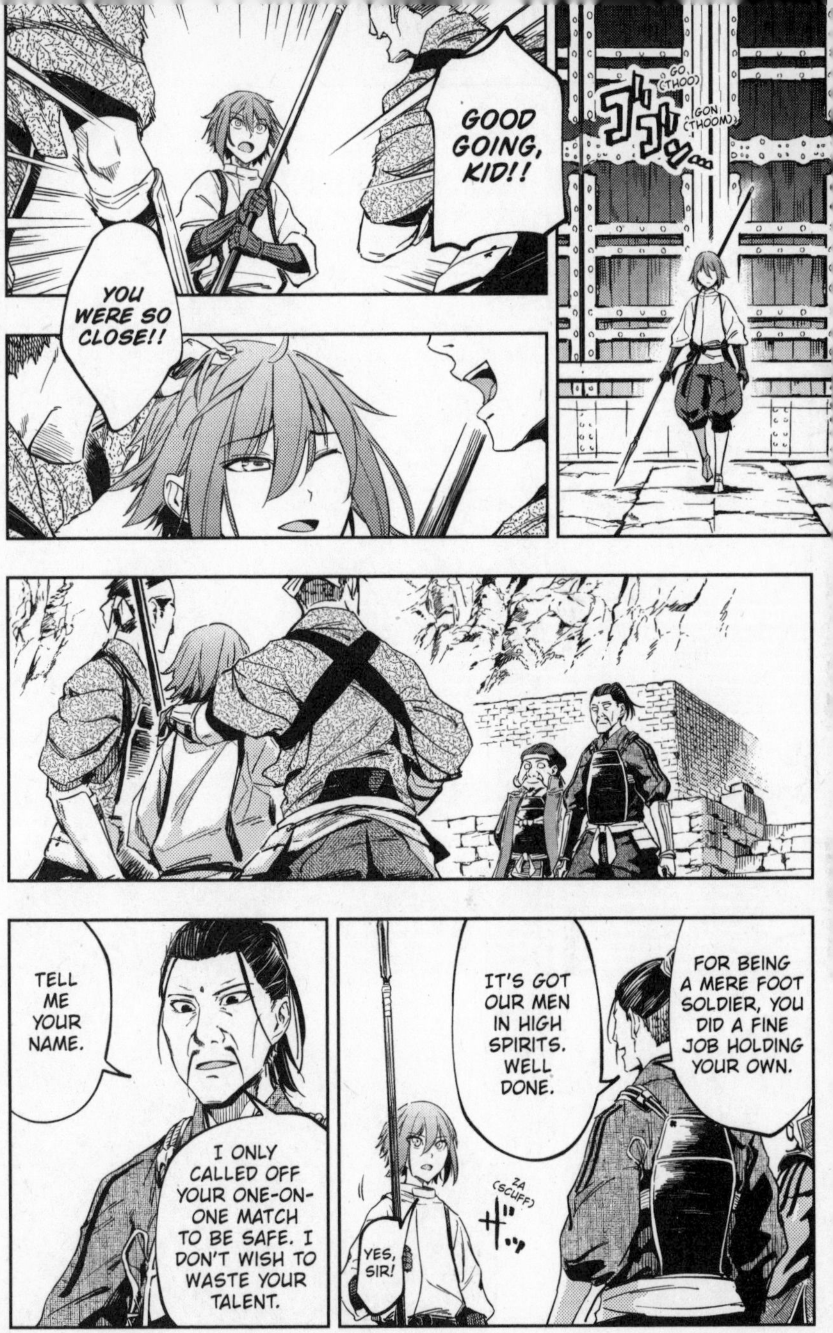
GO (THOO)
GON (THOOM)
GOOD GOING, KID!!
YOU WERE SO CLOSE!!
FOR BEING A MERE FOOT SOLDIER, YOU DID A FINE JOB HOLDING YOUR OWN.
IT'S GOT OUR MEN IN HIGH SPIRITS. WELL DONE.
ZA (SCUFF)
YES, SIR!
I ONLY CALLED OFF YOUR ONE-ON-ONE MATCH TO BE SAFE. I DON'T WISH TO WASTE YOUR TALENT.
TELL ME YOUR NAME.

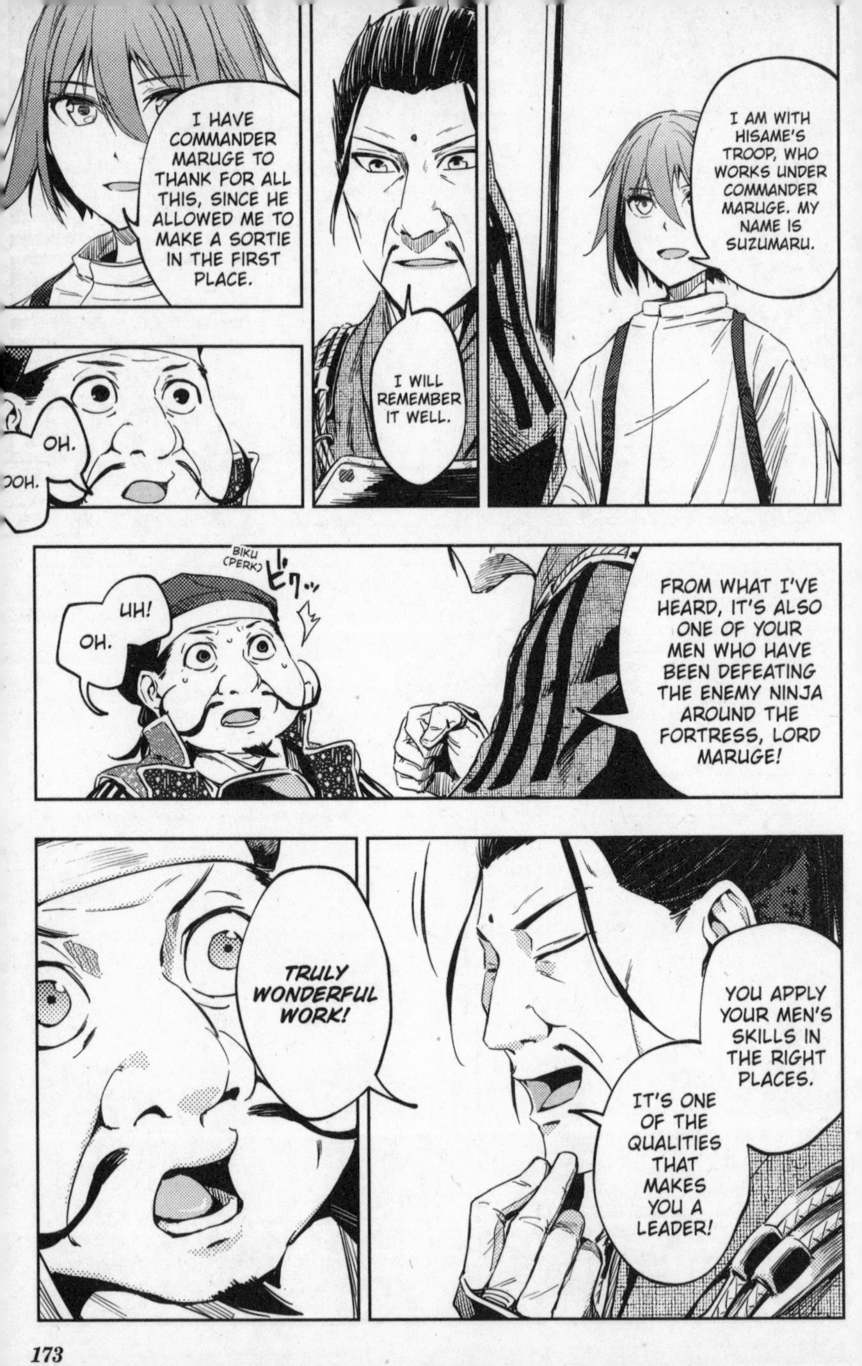

I AM WITH HISAME'S TROOP, WHO WORKS UNDER COMMANDER MARUGE. MY NAME IS SUZUMARU.
I WILL REMEMBER IT WELL.
I HAVE COMMANDER MARUGE TO THANK FOR ALL THIS, SINCE HE ALLOWED ME TO MAKE A SORTIE IN THE FIRST PLACE.
OH.
OOH.
FROM WHAT I'VE HEARD, IT'S ALSO ONE OF YOUR MEN WHO HAVE BEEN DEFEATING THE ENEMY NINJA AROUND THE FORTRESS, LORD MARUGE!
BIKU (PERK)
UH!
OH.
YOU APPLY YOUR MEN'S SKILLS IN THE RIGHT PLACES.
IT'S ONE OF THE QUALITIES THAT MAKES YOU A LEADER!
TRULY WONDERFUL WORK!

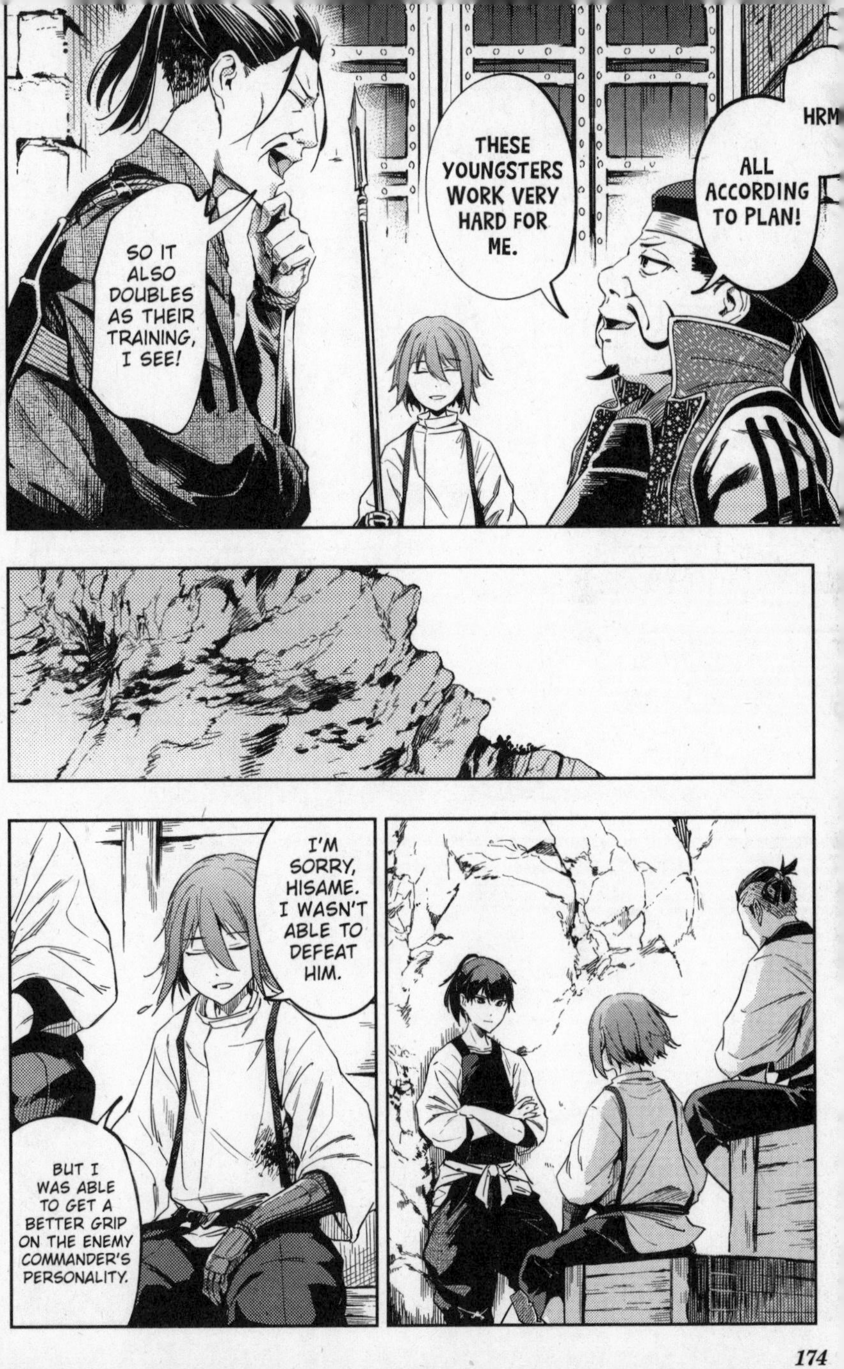
HRM
ALL ACCORDING TO PLAN!
THESE YOUNGSTERS WORK VERY HARD FOR ME.
SO IT ALSO DOUBLES AS THEIR TRAINING, I SEE!
I'M SORRY, HISAME. I WASN'T ABLE TO DEFEAT HIM.
BUT I WAS ABLE TO GET A BETTER GRIP ON THE ENEMY COMMANDER'S PERSONALITY.

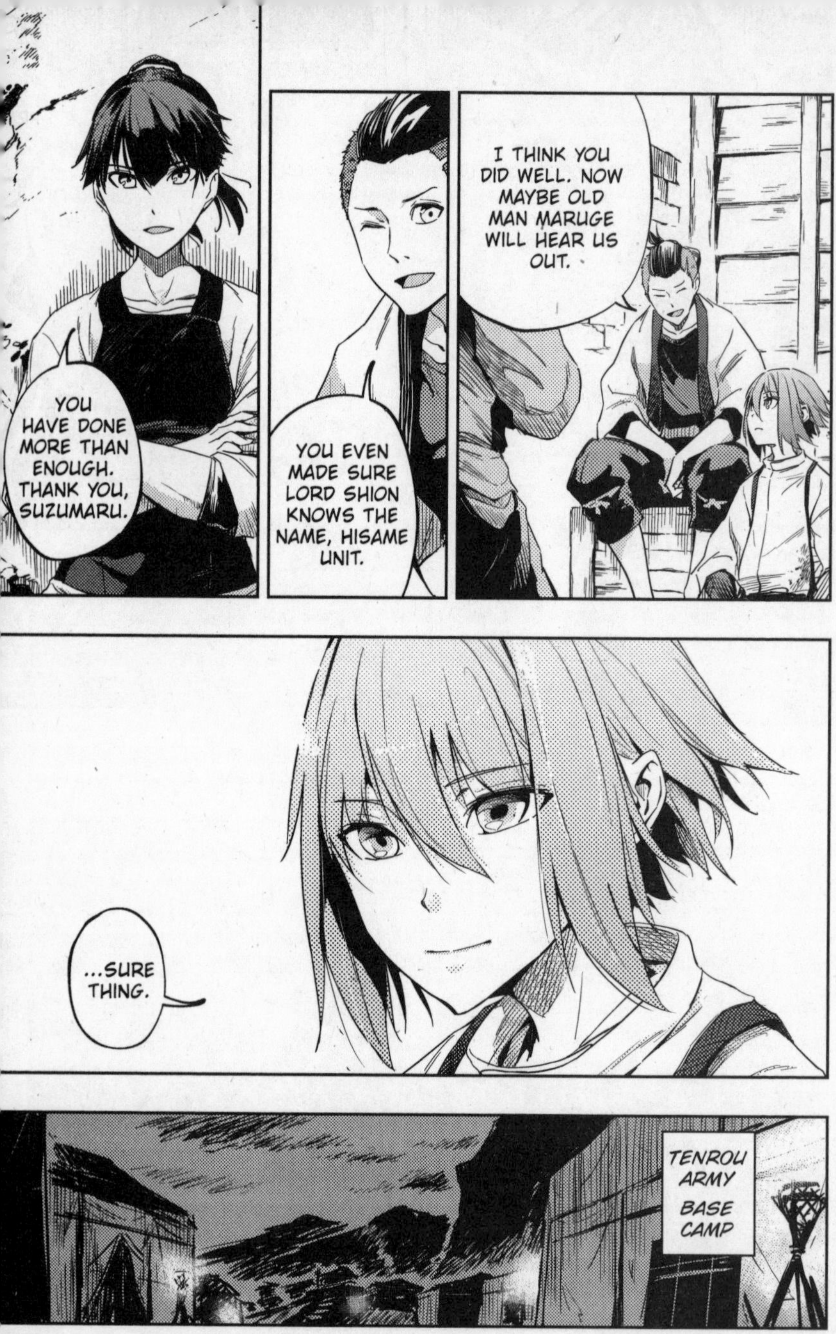
I THINK YOU DID WELL. NOW MAYBE OLD MAN MARUGE WILL HEAR US OUT.
YOU EVEN MADE SURE LORD SHION KNOWS THE NAME, HISAME UNIT.
YOU HAVE DONE MORE THAN ENOUGH. THANK YOU, SUZUMARU.
...SURE THING.
TENROU ARMY BASE CAMP

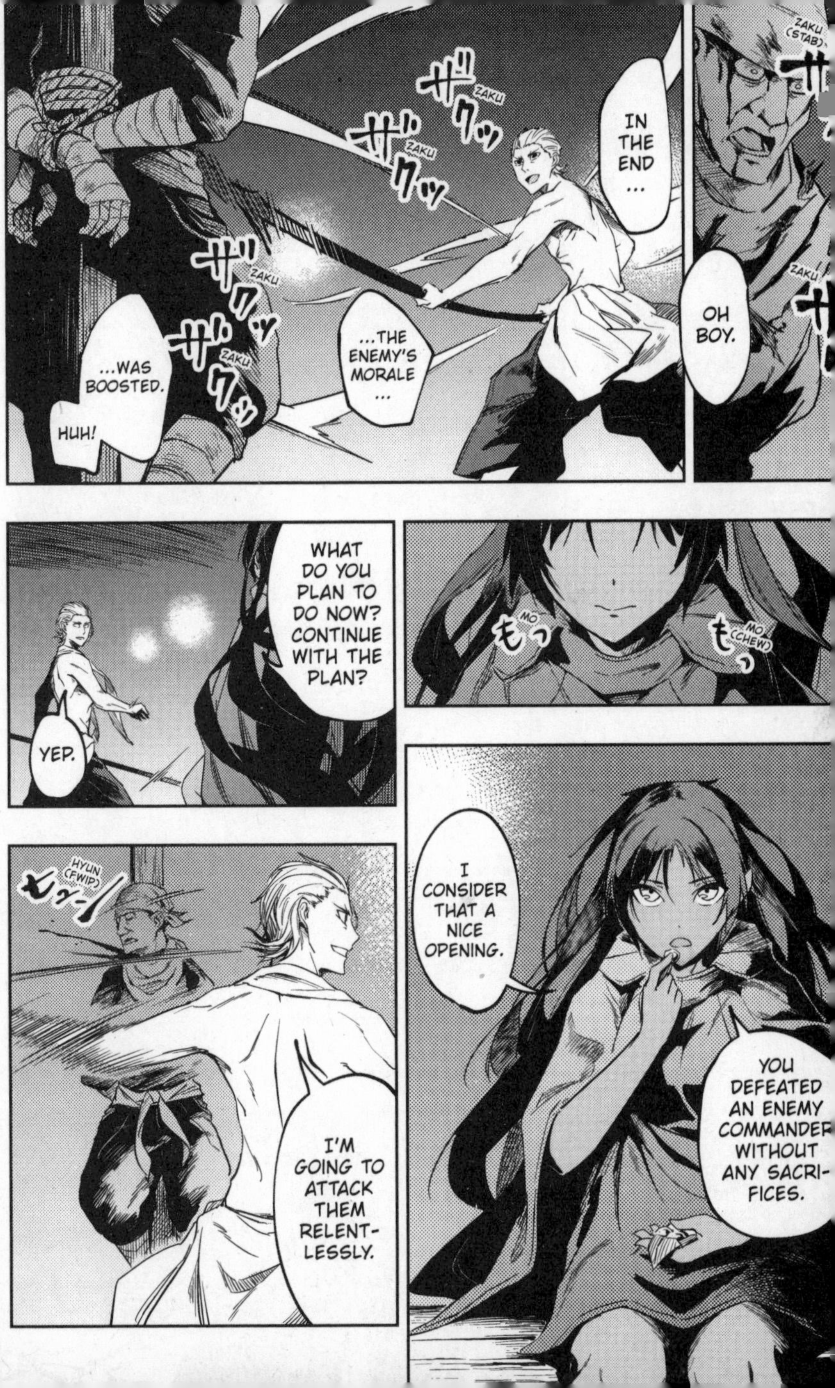
ZAKU (STAB)
ZAKU
OH BOY.
ZAKU
ZAKU
IN THE END ...
ZAKU
ZAKU
...THE ENEMY'S MORALE ...
...WAS BOOSTED.
HUH!
MO
MO (CHEW)
WHAT DO YOU PLAN TO DO NOW? CONTINUE WITH THE PLAN?
YEP.
I CONSIDER THAT A NICE OPENING.
YOU DEFEATED AN ENEMY COMMANDER WITHOUT ANY SACRI-FICES.
HYUN (FWIP)
I'M GOING TO ATTACK THEM RELENT-LESSLY.

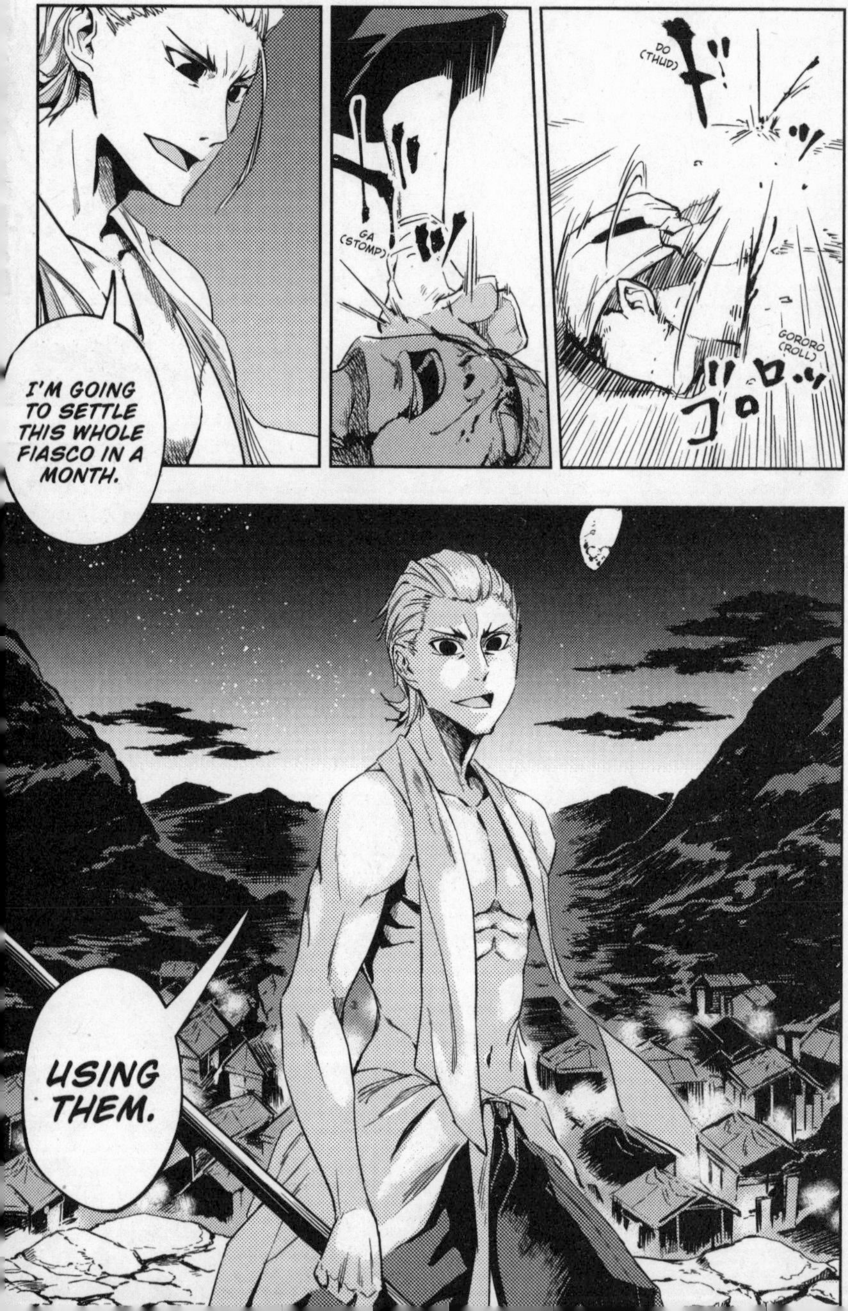
DO (THUD)
GA (STOMP)
GORORO (ROLL)
I'M GOING TO SETTLE THIS WHOLE FIASCO IN A MONTH.
USING THEM.

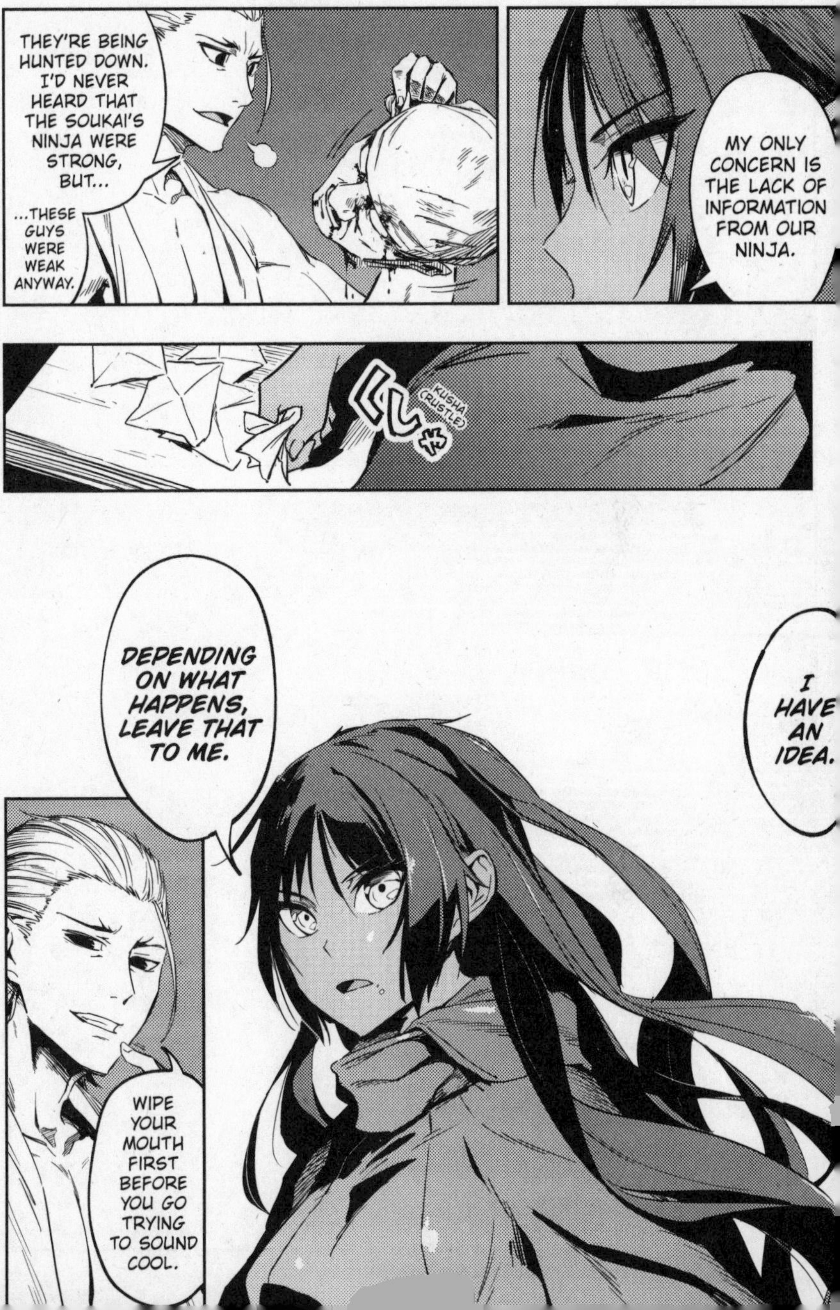
MY ONLY CONCERN IS THE LACK OF INFORMATION FROM OUR NINJA.
THEY'RE BEING HUNTED DOWN. I'D NEVER HEARD THAT THE SOUKAI'S NINJA WERE STRONG, BUT...
...THESE GUYS WERE WEAK ANYWAY.
くしゃ
KUSHA (RUSTLE)
I HAVE AN IDEA.
DEPENDING ON WHAT HAPPENS, LEAVE THAT TO ME.
WIPE YOUR MOUTH FIRST BEFORE YOU GO TRYING TO SOUND COOL.

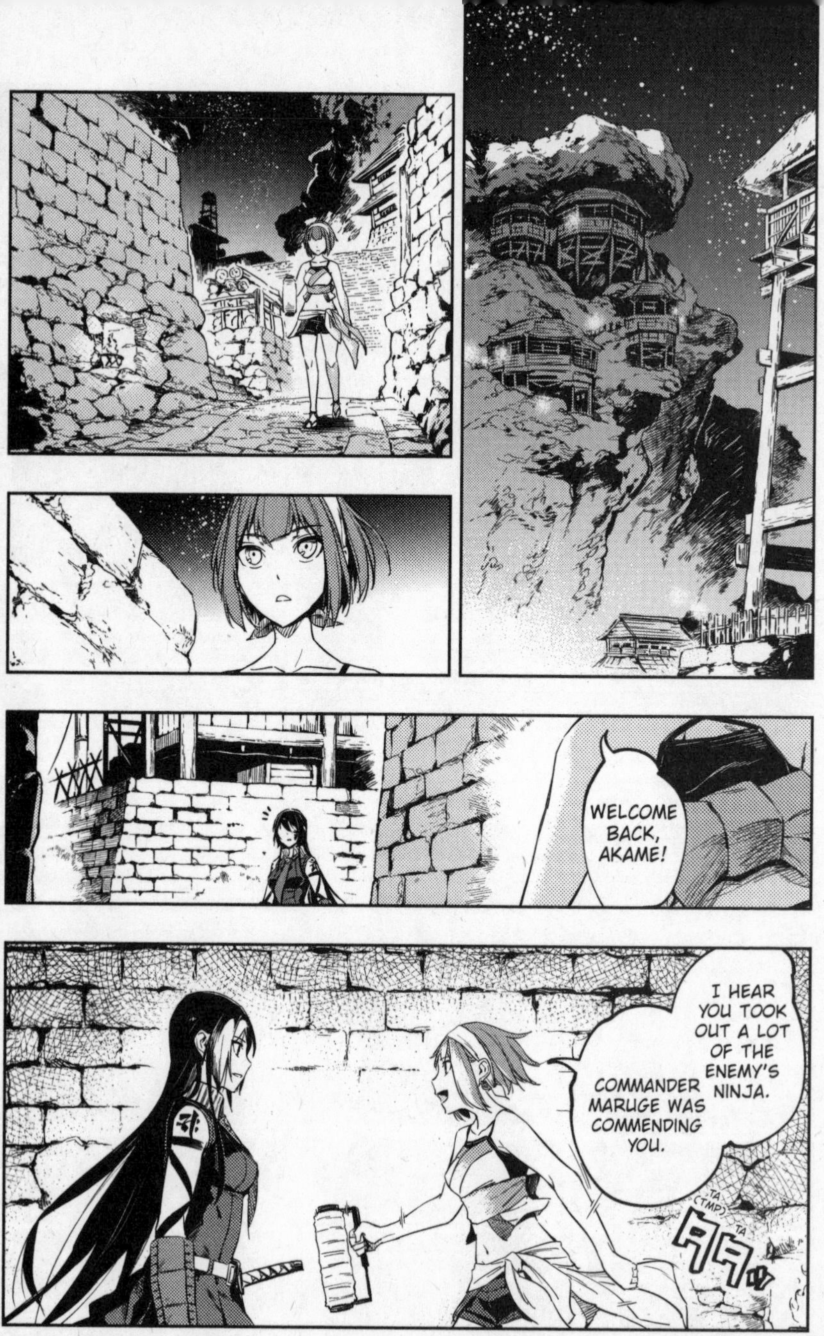
WELCOME BACK, AKAME!
I HEAR YOU TOOK OUT A LOT OF THE ENEMY'S NINJA.
COMMANDER MARUGE WAS COMMENDING YOU.
TA (TMP) TA

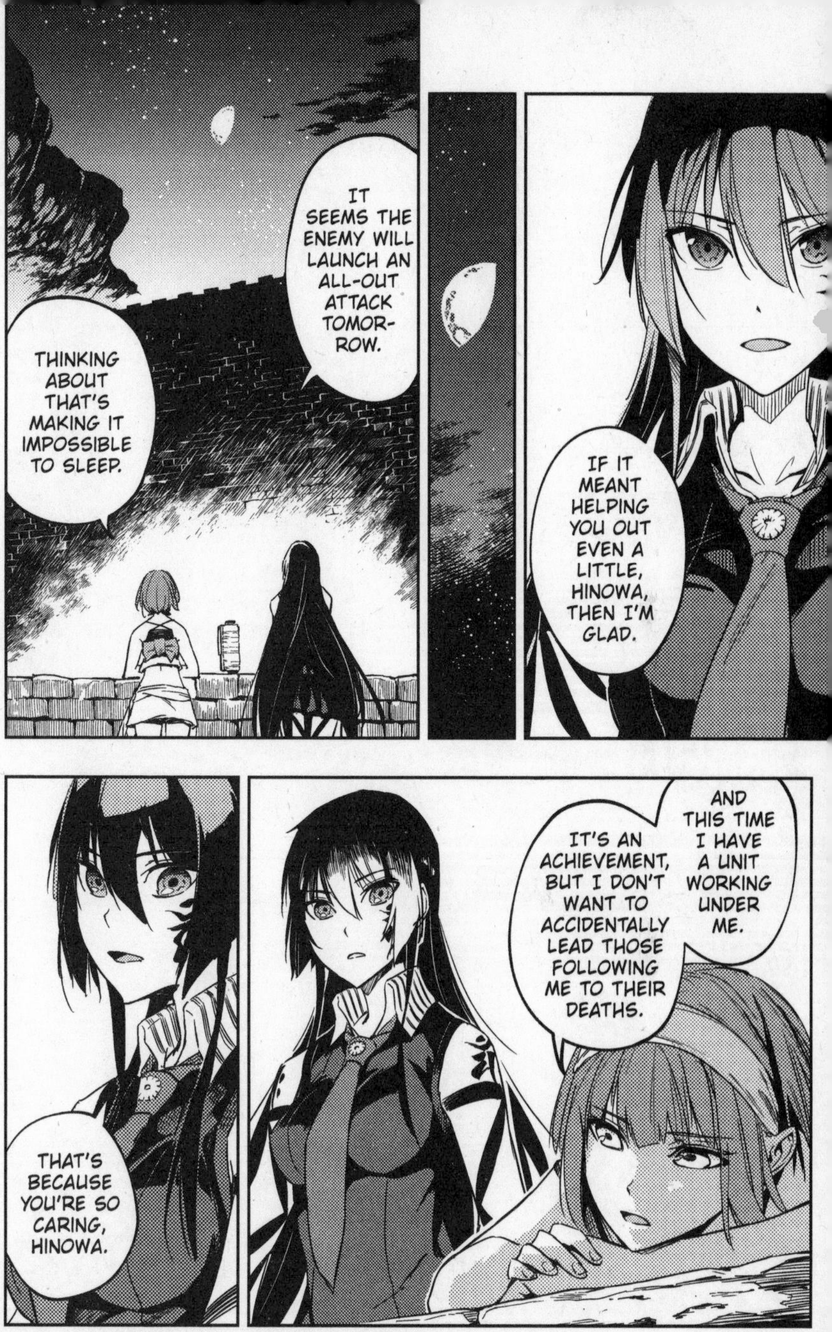
IF IT MEANT HELPING YOU OUT EVEN A LITTLE, HINOWA, THEN I'M GLAD.
IT SEEMS THE ENEMY WILL LAUNCH AN ALL-OUT ATTACK TOMORROW.
THINKING ABOUT THAT'S MAKING IT IMPOSSIBLE TO SLEEP.
AND THIS TIME I HAVE A UNIT WORKING UNDER ME.
IT'S AN ACHIEVEMENT, BUT I DON'T WANT TO ACCIDENTALLY LEAD THOSE FOLLOWING ME TO THEIR DEATHS.
THAT'S BECAUSE YOU'RE SO CARING, HINOWA.

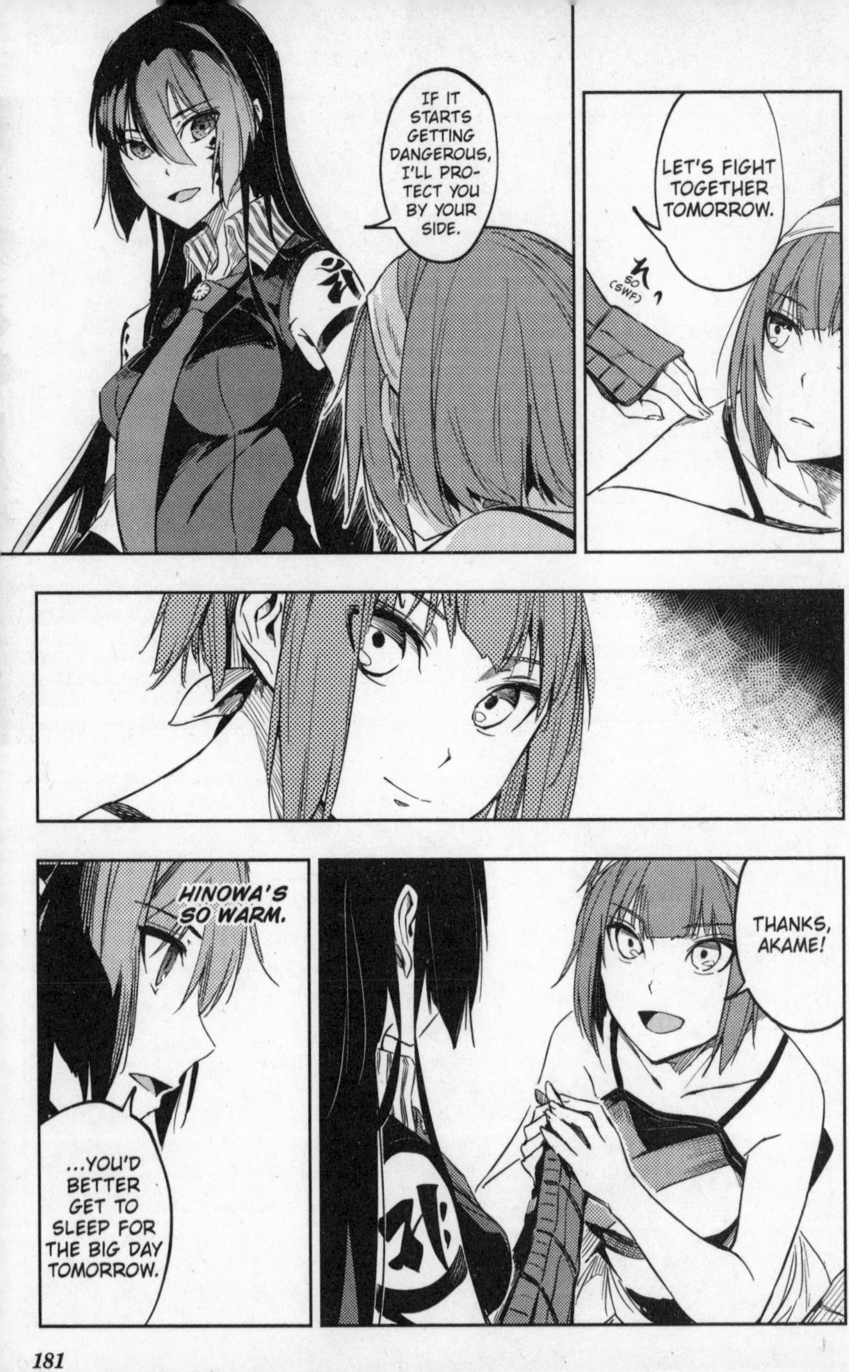
LET'S FIGHT TOGETHER TOMORROW.
SO (SWF)
IF IT STARTS GETTING DANGEROUS, I'LL PROTECT YOU BY YOUR SIDE.
THANKS, AKAME!
HINOWA'S SO WARM.
...YOU'D BETTER GET TO SLEEP FOR THE BIG DAY TOMORROW.

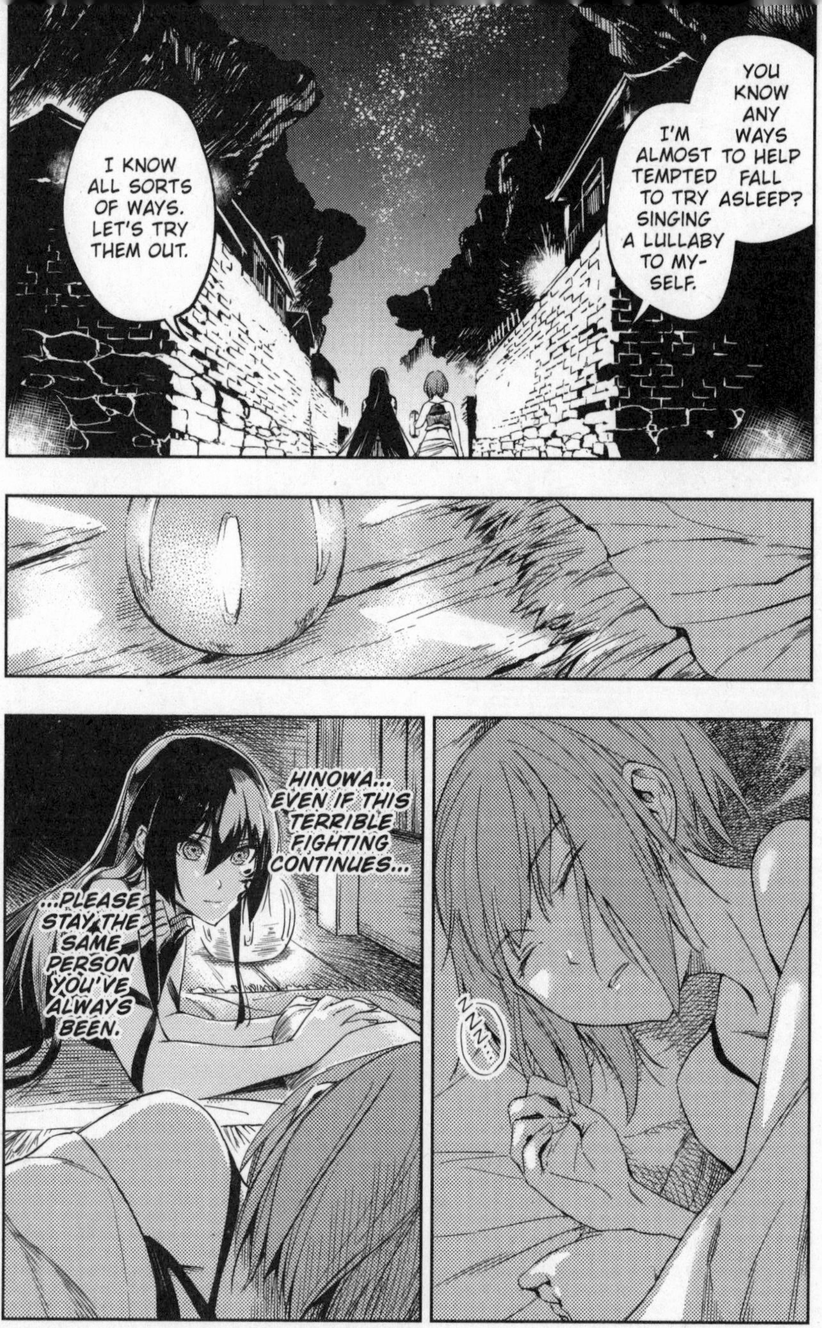
YOU KNOW ANY WAYS TO HELP FALL ASLEEP?
I'M ALMOST TEMPTED TO TRY SINGING A LULLABY TO MY-SELF.
I KNOW ALL SORTS OF WAYS. LET'S TRY THEM OUT.
ZNN...
HINOWA... EVEN IF THIS TERRIBLE FIGHTING CONTINUES...
...PLEASE STAY THE SAME PERSON YOU'VE ALWAYS BEEN.

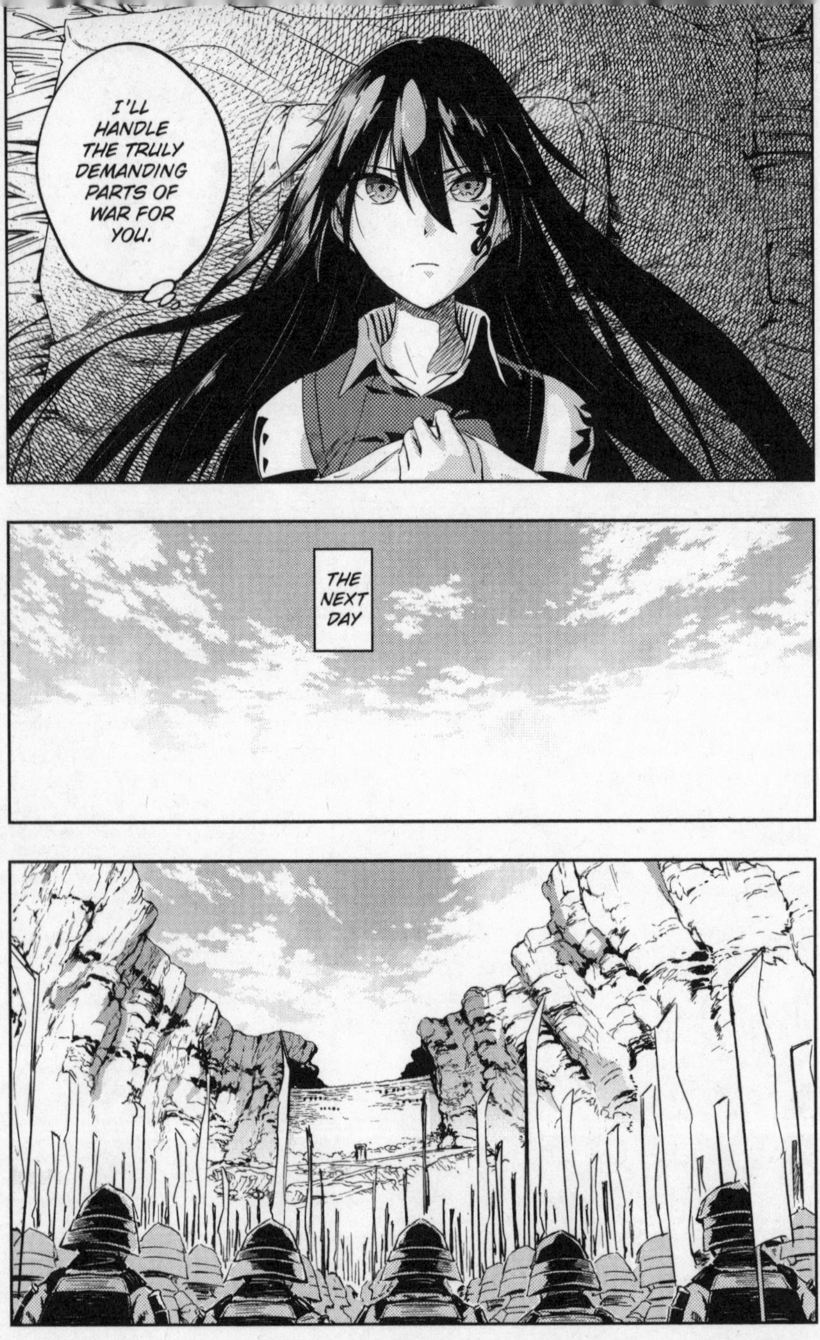
I'LL HANDLE THE TRULY DEMANDING PARTS OF WAR FOR YOU.
THE NEXT DAY

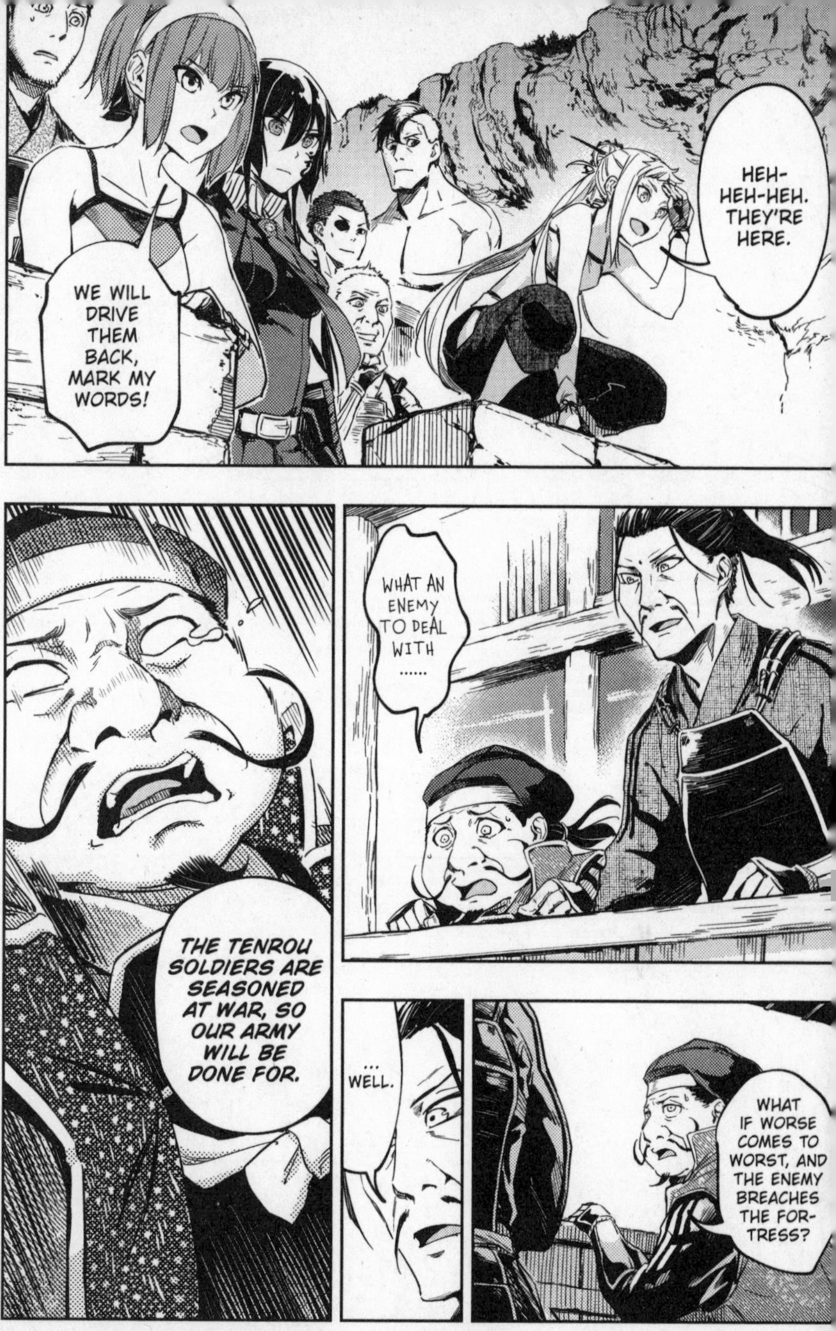
HEH-HEH-HEH. THEY'RE HERE.
WE WILL DRIVE THEM BACK, MARK MY WORDS!
WHAT AN ENEMY TO DEAL WITH ......
WHAT IF WORSE COMES TO WORST, AND THE ENEMY BREACHES THE FOR-TRESS?
... WELL.
THE TENROU SOLDIERS ARE SEASONED AT WAR, SO OUR ARMY WILL BE DONE FOR.

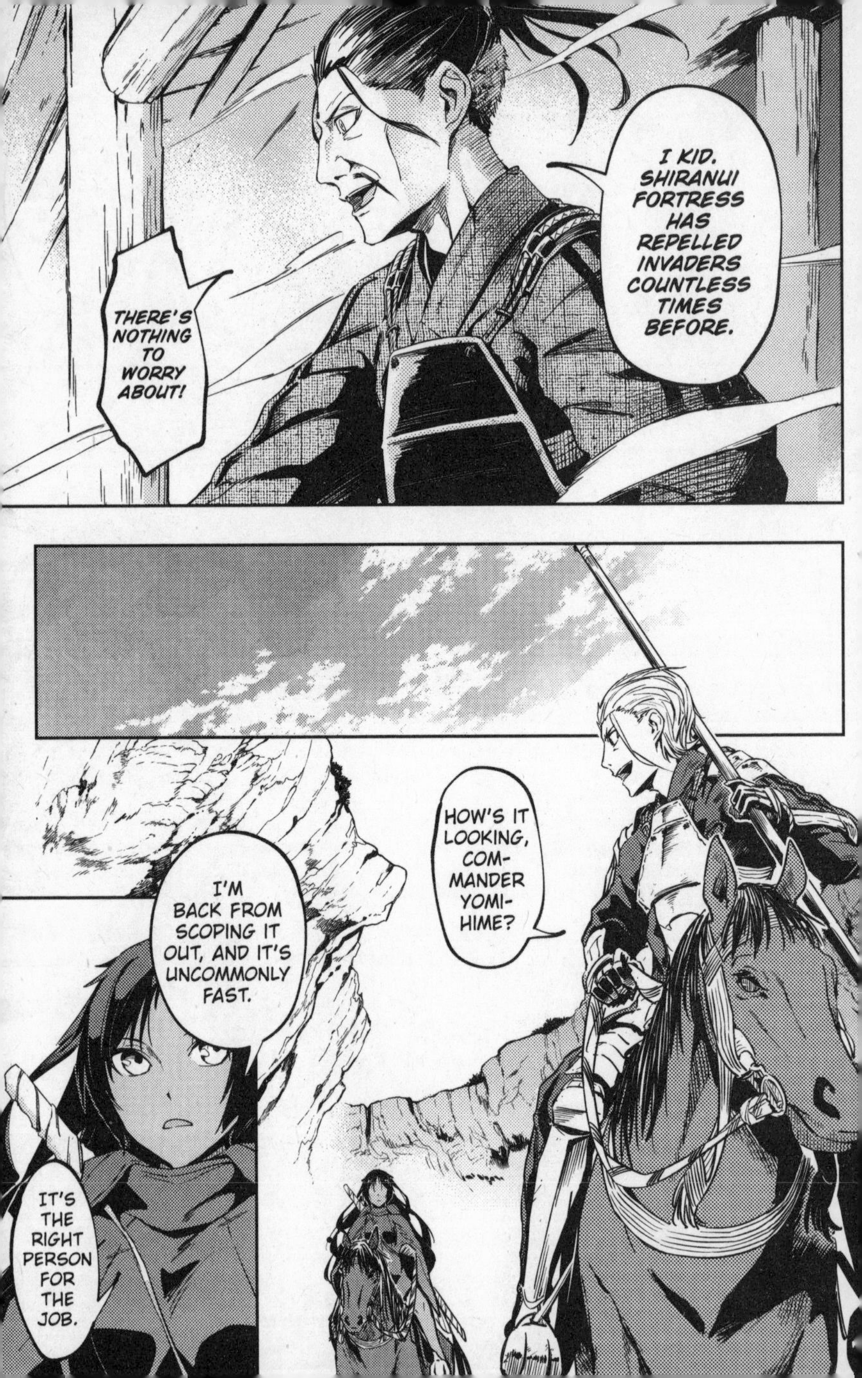
I KID. SHIRANUI FORTRESS HAS REPELLED INVADERS COUNTLESS TIMES BEFORE.
THERE'S NOTHING TO WORRY ABOUT!
HOW'S IT LOOKING, COM-MANDER YOMI-HIME?
I'M BACK FROM SCOPING IT OUT, AND IT'S UNCOMMONLY FAST.
IT'S THE RIGHT PERSON FOR THE JOB.

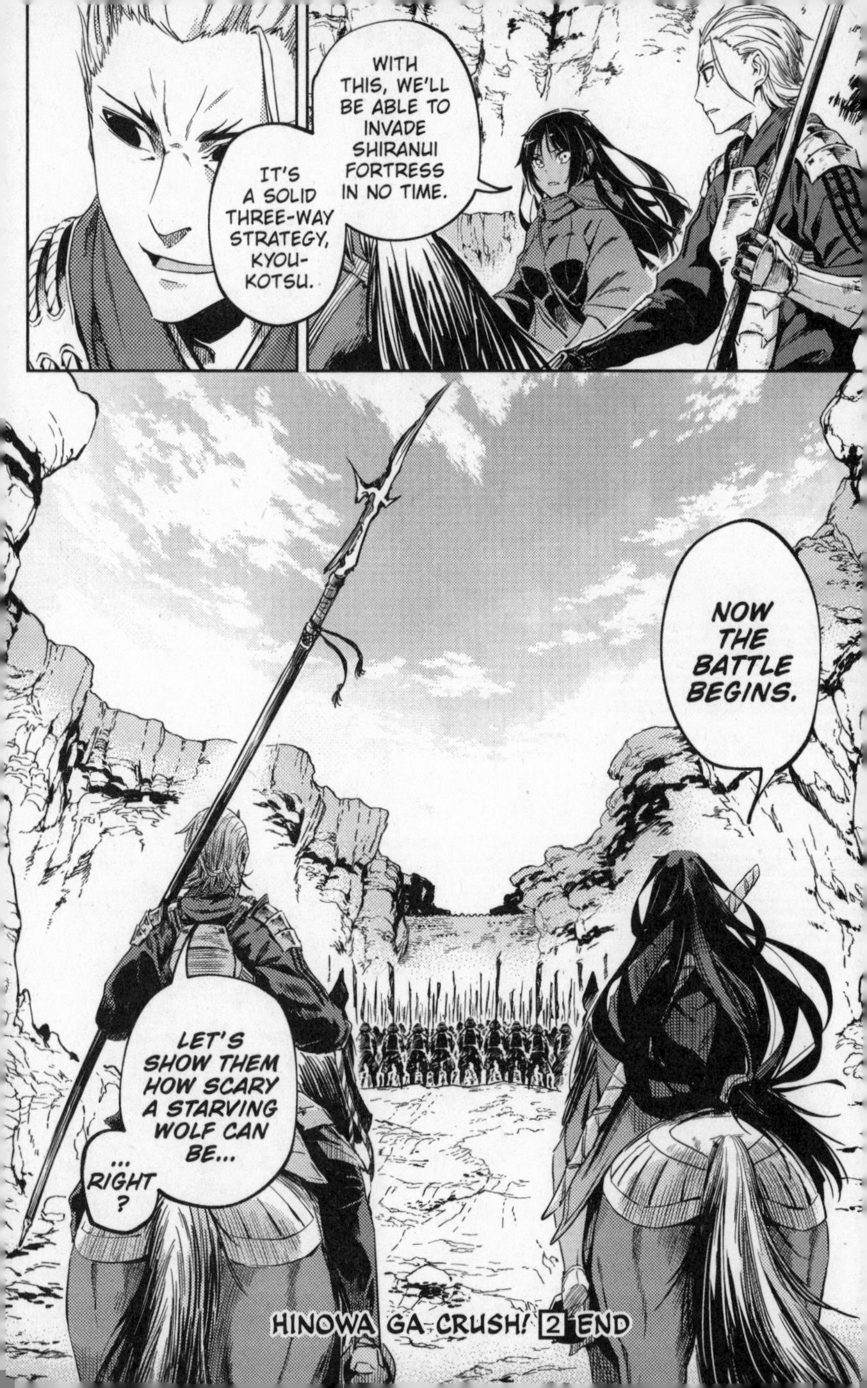
WITH THIS, WE'LL BE ABLE TO INVADE SHIRANUI FORTRESS IN NO TIME.
IT'S A SOLID THREE-WAY STRATEGY, KYOU-KOTSU.
NOW THE BATTLE BEGINS.
LET'S SHOW THEM HOW SCARY A STARVING WOLF CAN BE...
...RIGHT?
HINOWA GA CRUSH! 2 END

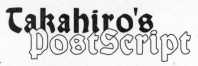Takahiro's PostScript

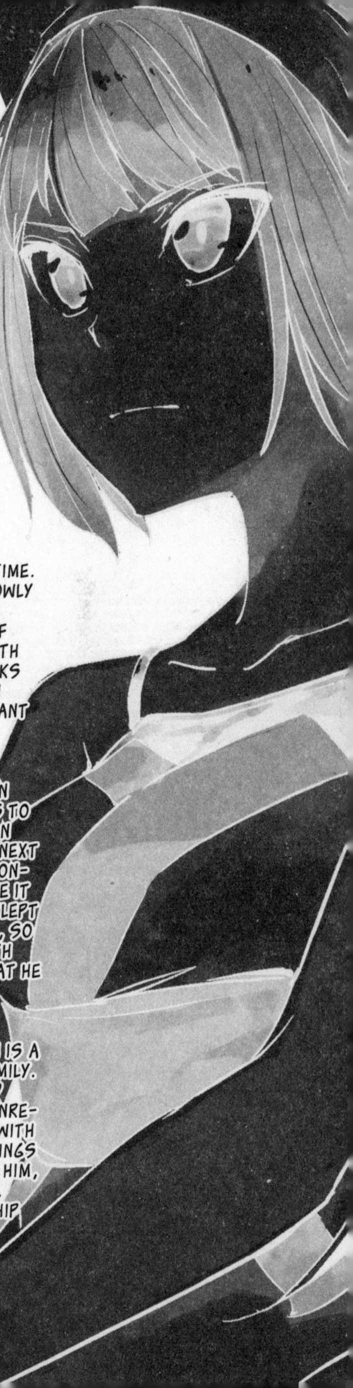

HELLO, EVERYONE. THIS IS THE AUTHOR, TAKAHIRO. I'D LIKE TO TAKE THIS OPPORTUNITY TO DESCRIBE SOME OF THE CHARACTERS WHO I DIDN'T HAVE ROOM TO PORTRAY IN THE CHARACTER DIRECTORIES.

★MARUGE

HE'S FIFTY-TWO YEARS OLD AND TENDS TO SOUND LIKE A DAMSEL IN DISTRESS. HE IS THE THIRD ELDEST SON OF A FAMILY THAT HAS FALLEN TO RUIN, AND WHAT HE HAD TO SAY ABOUT HIS CIRCUMSTANCES IN VOLUME 1 IS ALL TRUE. HE'S TREATED CRUELLY AT HOME.

★KAHEI

MARUGE'S AIDE WHO HAS BEEN WITH HIM FOR A LONG TIME. WITH HIS MASTERY OF THE ART OF FLATTERY, HE'S SLOWLY BUT SURELY RISEN UP IN RANK. HE WON'T THINK TWICE ABOUT RESORTING TO BRIBERY. AS THEY SAY, BIRDS OF A FEATHER FLOCK TOGETHER, AND HE SYMPATHIZES WITH MARUGE'S STRUGGLE TO SURVIVE, HENCE WHY HE STICKS BY HIM. HE'S A BACHELOR BECAUSE AFTER SEEING HOW POORLY MARUGE'S FAMILY TREATS HIM, HE DOESN'T WANT TO END UP IN THE SAME SITUATION.

★SHION

THE SOKAI NATION'S STRATEGIST. HE'S NOT STRONG IN COMBAT BUT HAS GOTTEN WHERE HE IS IN LIFE THANKS TO HIS SMARTS. HE EXCELS AT READING THE SITUATION ON THE BATTLEFIELD AND CAN EASILY GUESS A PERSON'S NEXT COURSE OF ACTION. HIS FRAGILE HEALTH MAKES HIM CONCERNED ABOUT HOW LONG HE'LL LIVE, BUT HE HAS MADE IT THIS FAR. WHEN HE WAS YOUNG, HE LIKED GIRLS AND SLEPT AROUND, BUT SHALLOW FLINGS COULDN'T SATISFY HIM, SO HE FINDS MORE PLEASURE IN HAVING INTERCOURSE WITH SEA CREATURES. IT'S WHEN HE FEELS TRULY ALIVE THAT HE GETS STRUCK WITH HIS INGENIOUS STRATEGIES.

★KISARU

SUZUMARU'S OLDER HALF-BROTHER. SINCE SUZUMARU IS A BASTARD CHILD, HE IS THE LEGITIMATE SON IN THE FAMILY. HIS OWN FATHER IS RECOGNIZED AS AN ACCOMPLISHED MERCHANT, BUT HE'S ALWAYS BURDENED WITH SUCH UNREALISTIC EXPECTATIONS FROM HIM THAT IT'S LEFT HIM WITH A SKEWED WAY OF SEEING THINGS. HE HAS MIXED FEELINGS WHEN IT COMES TO SUZUMARU. HE'S SARCASTIC WITH HIM, BUT HE'S ALSO BASICALLY LIKE THAT WITH EVERYBODY. IT'S CLEAR TO SEE HE HAS AN UNHEALTHY RELATIONSHIP WITH HIS FATHER.

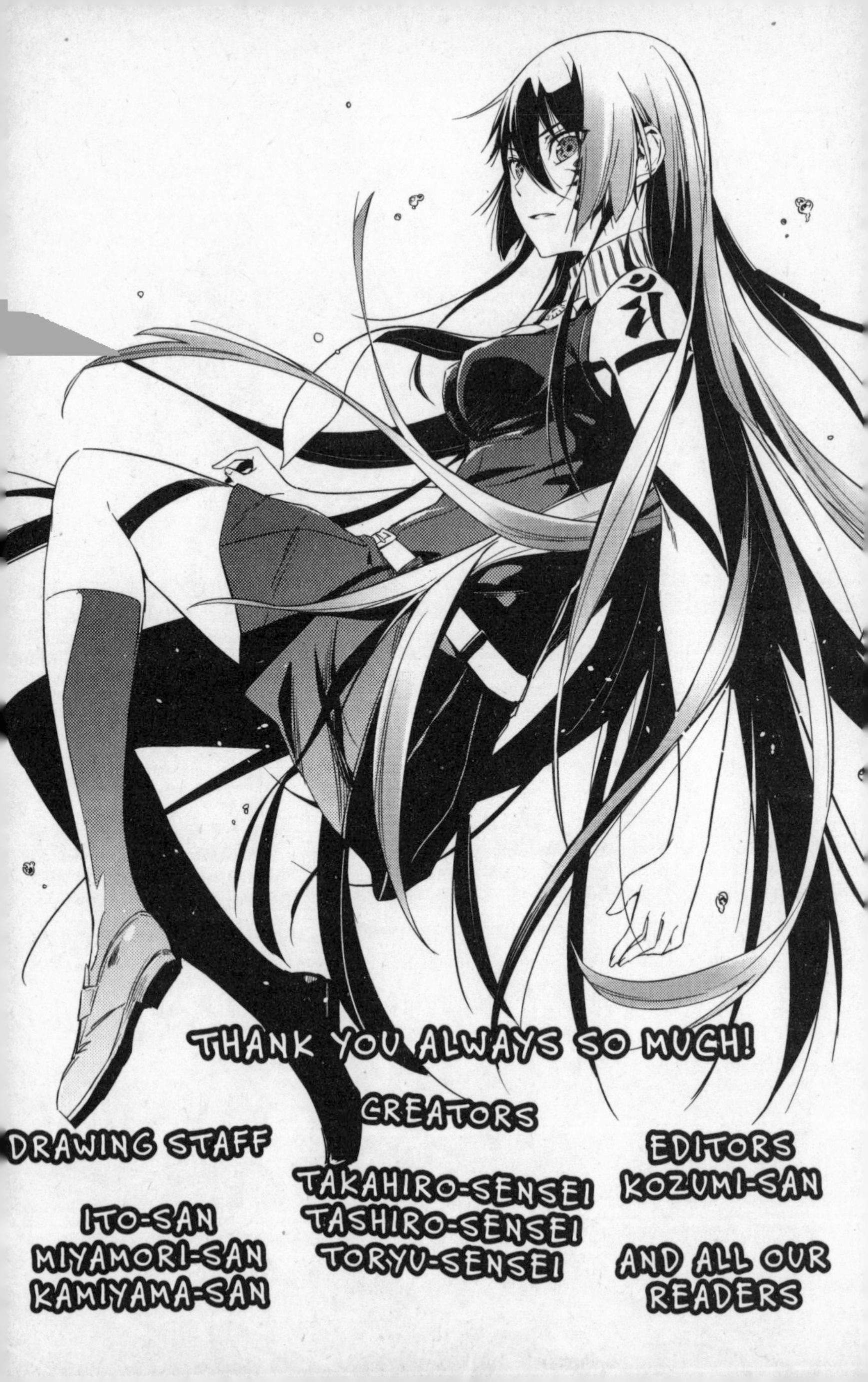
THANK YOU ALWAYS SO MUCH!
CREATORS
TAKAHIRO-SENSEI
TASHIRO-SENSEI
TORYU-SENSEI
DRAWING STAFF
ITO-SAN
MIYAMORI-SAN
KAMIYAMA-SAN
EDITORS
KOZUMI-SAN
AND ALL OUR READERS

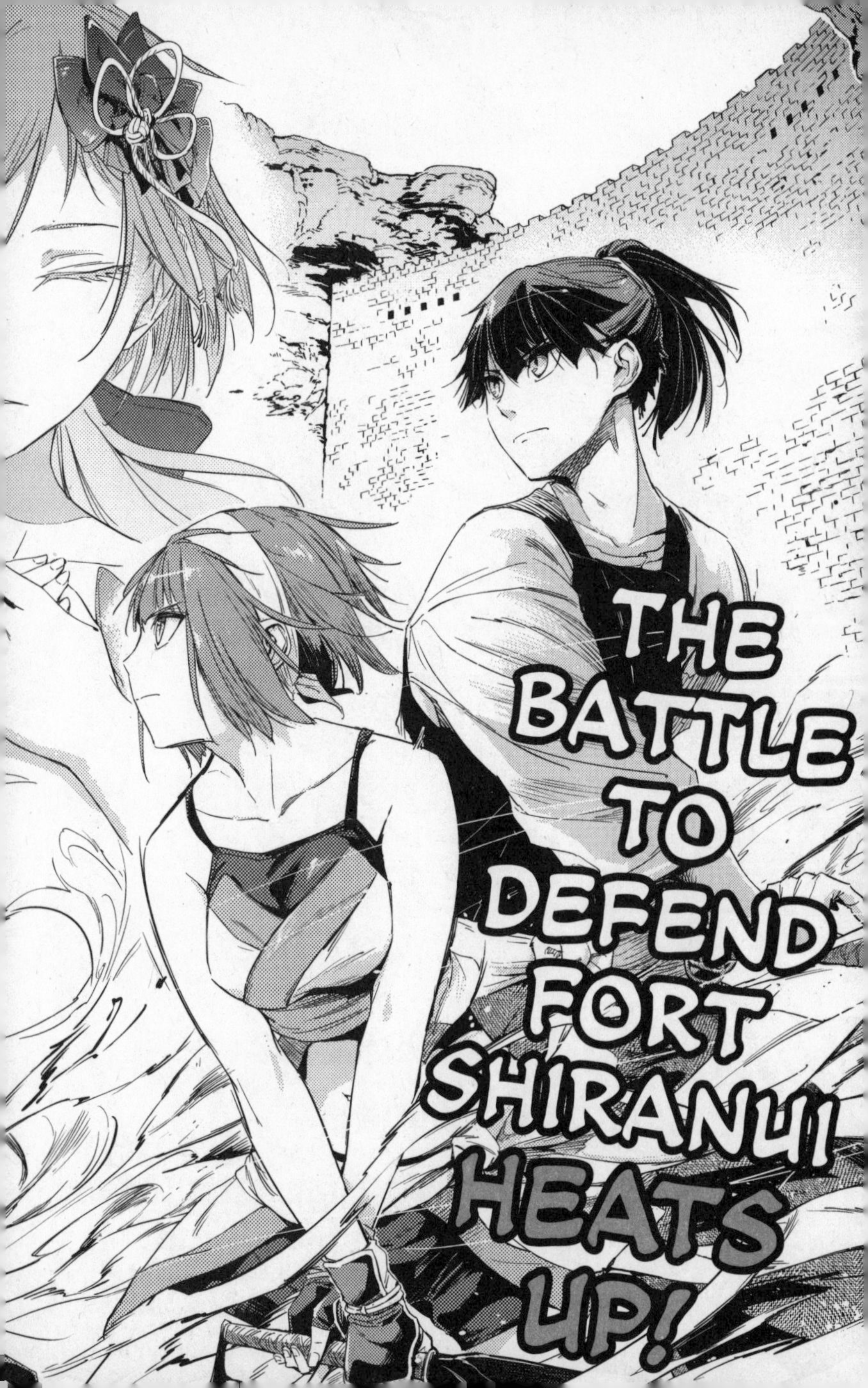
THE BATTLE TO DEFEND FORT SHIRANUI
HEATS UP!

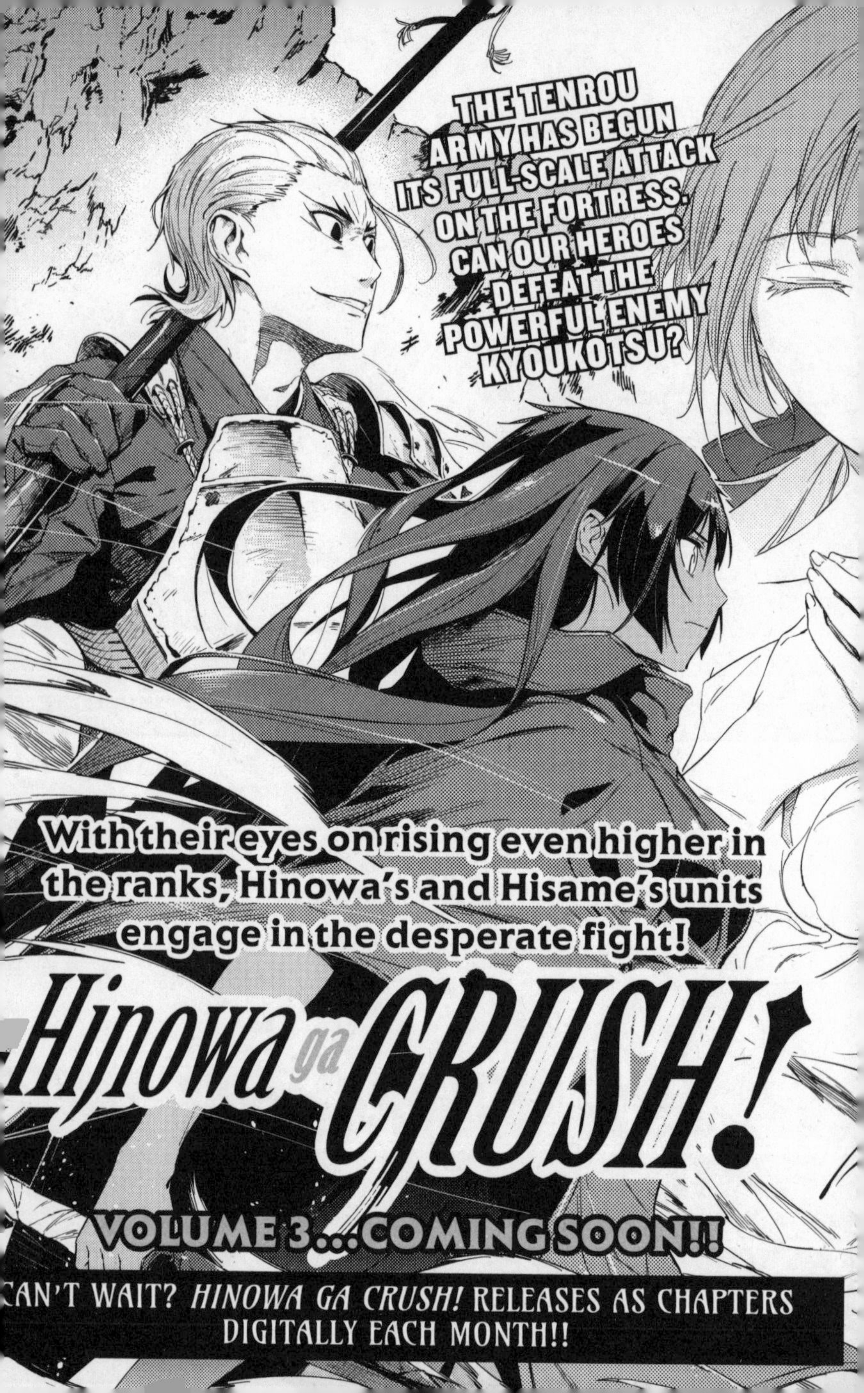
THE TENROU ARMY HAS BEGUN ITS FULL-SCALE ATTACK ON THE FORTRESS. CAN OUR HEROES DEFEAT THE POWERFUL ENEMY KYOUKOTSU?
With their eyes on rising even higher in the ranks, Hinowa's and Hisame's units engage in the desperate fight!
Hinowa ga CRUSH!
VOLUME 3...COMING SOON!!
CAN'T WAIT? HINOWA GA CRUSH! RELEASES AS CHAPTERS DIGITALLY EACH MONTH!!

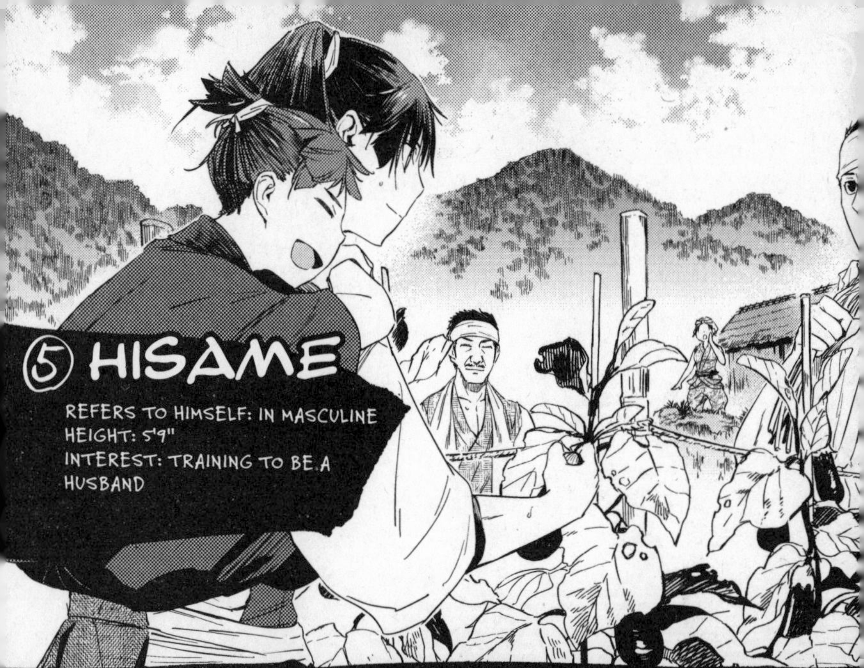
⑤ HISAME
REFERS TO HIMSELF: IN MASCULINE
HEIGHT: 5'9"
INTEREST: TRAINING TO BE A HUSBAND

CHARACTER DIRECTORY

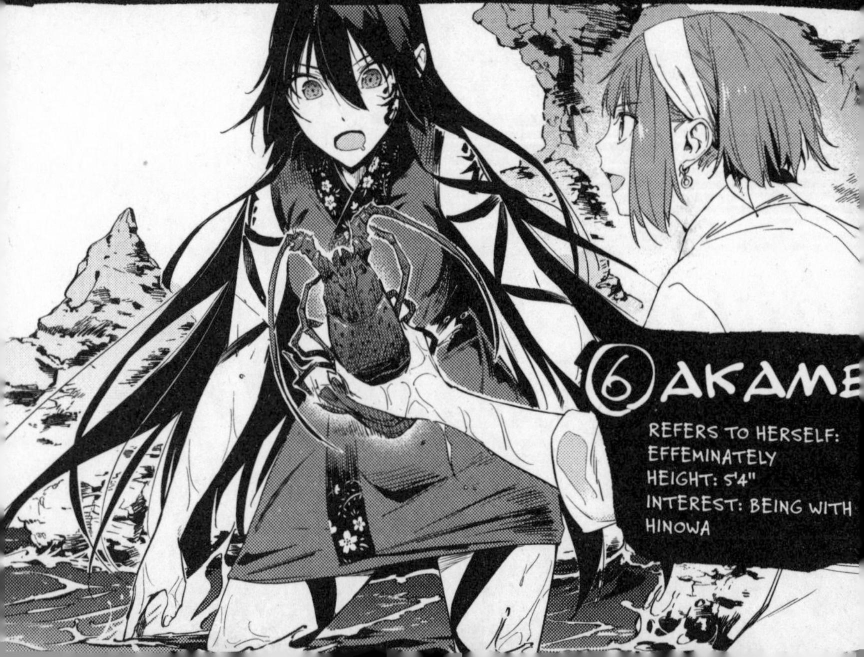
⑥ AKAME
REFERS TO HERSELF: EFFEMINATELY
HEIGHT: 5'4"
INTEREST: BEING WITH HINOWA

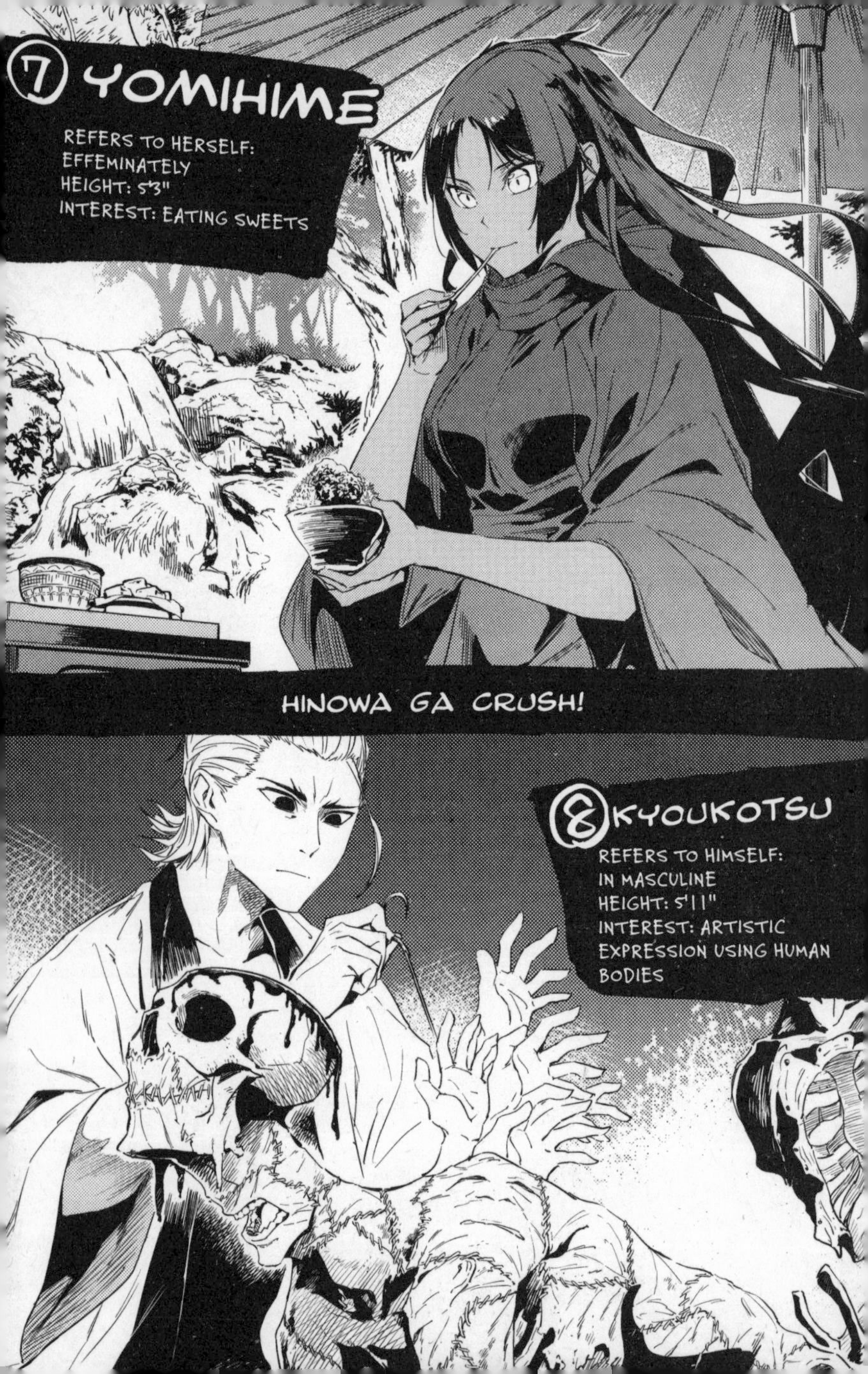

⑦ YOMIHIME
REFERS TO HERSELF: EFFEMINATELY
HEIGHT: 5'3"
INTEREST: EATING SWEETS
HINOWA GA CRUSH!
⑧ KYOUKOTSU
REFERS TO HIMSELF: IN MASCULINE
HEIGHT: 5'11"
INTEREST: ARTISTIC EXPRESSION USING HUMAN BODIES

Translation Notes

Page 70
An *umibouzu* is a powerful mythical creature of the sea. *Isonade* are a kind of mythical shark, and *dorotabou* are the ghosts of old men who worked in the rice fields.

Hjnowa ga CRUSH!

Hinowa ga Ch...

STORY: TAKAHIRO **ART: strelka**

Translation: Christine Dashiell

Lettering: Rochelle Gancio & Rachel J. Pierce

HINOWA GA YUKU! Volume 2 © 2018 Takahiro, strelka / SQUARE ENIX CO., LTD. First published in Japan in 2018 by SQUARE ENIX CO., LTD. English translation rights arranged with SQUARE ENIX CO., LTD. and Yen Press, LLC through Tuttle-Mori Agency, Inc., Tokyo.

English translation © 2019 by SQUARE ENIX CO., LTD.

Yen Press
1290 Avenue of the Americas
New York, NY 10104

Visit us at yenpress.com
facebook.com/yenpress
twitter.com/yenpress
yenpress.tumblr.com
instagram.com/yenpress

First Yen Press Edition: May 2019
The chapters in this volume were originally published as ebooks by Yen Press.

Yen Press is an imprint of Yen Press, LLC.
The Yen Press name and logo are trademarks of Yen Press, LLC.

The publisher is not responsible for websites (or their content) that are not owned by the

Library of Cor

ISBNs: 978-1-
        978-1-

10 9 8 7 6 5 4

WOR

Printed in the United States of America